Critical Issues in Ecotourism: Understanding a complex tourism phenomenon

James Higham (Ed)

ELSEVIER

AMSTERDAM • BOSTON • HEIDELBERG • LONDON •
NEW YORK • OXFORD • PARIS • SAN DIEGO •
SAN FRANCISCO • SINGAPORE • SYDNEY • TOKYO
Butterworth-Heinemann is an imprint of Elsevier

Butterworth-Heinemann is an imprint of Elsevier
Linacre House, Jordan Hill, Oxford OX2 8DP, UK
30 Corporate Drive, Suite 400, Burlington, MA 01803, USA

First edition 2007

British Library Cataloguing in Publication Data
A catalogue record for this book is available from the British Library

Library of Congress Control Number:
A catalogue record for this book is available from the Library of Congress

ISBN-10: 0-7506-6878-4
ISBN-13: 978-0-7506-6878-1

For information on all publications visit our web site at
http://books.elsevier.com

Typeset by Charon Tec Ltd (A Macmillan Company), Chennai, India
www.charontec.com

Printed and bound in Great Britain

Working together to grow libraries in developing countries

www.elsevier.com | www.bookaid.org | www.sabre.org

ELSEVIER   BOOK AID International   Sabre Foundation

Critical Issues in Ecotourism: Understanding a complex tourism phenomenon

This book is dedicated to
Polly and Charles Higham

Contents

List of Tables

List of Figures

Acknowledgements

As is commonly the case, this book is the product of combined efforts. Francesca Ford (Elsevier Butterworth Heinemann) has greatly facilitated the publication process from start to finish. She has provided the personal interface with a supportive publisher. Prof. David Fennell (Editor, *Journal of Ecotourism*) and Anna Roderick (Production Editor, *Multilingual Matters*) made possible the use of Erlet Cater's chapter in this book.

I am very grateful for the professionalism of the authors who contributed their original work to this book: Susanne Becken, Peter Björk, Anna Carr, Erlet Cater, Janet Cochrane, Megan Epler Wood, David Fennell, Xavier Font, Stefan Gössling, C. Michael Hall, Michael Lück, David Lusseau, Sanjay K. Nepal, Cesar Moran-Cahusac, Agnes M. Nowaczek, Matthias Schellhorn, Regina Scheyvens, Eric Shelton, Trevor Sofield, Pamela Wight and Heather Zeppel. Their works collectively address a huge diversity of challenging issues that must be critically considered by stakeholders who might otherwise continue a widespread tradition of blind adherence to promises associated with ecotourism development.

My academic work serving the field of ecotourism has been inspired by a number of writing and research collaborators. They include Michael Hall, Anna Carr, Eric Shelton, Wiebke Finkler, Tara Rowe, David Purdie, Angela Dickey, Stephane Gale, Stuart Dymond (University of Otago), Michael Lück (Auckland University of Technology), David Lusseau (Dalhousie University), Lars Bejder (Murdoch University), Ghazali Musa (University of Malaysia), Kay Booth, Stephen Espiner (Lincoln University), Harry Maher, and Christopher Robertson (Department of Conservation). I have also benefited greatly from professional contact with, and the subsequent support of, a number of scholars in the international academic community particularly David Fennell (Brock University), Ross Dowling

(Edith Cowan University), Tom Hinch (University of Alberta), Dick Butler (Strathclyde), Simon Milne (Auckland University of Technology) and Bernard Lane.

I have enjoyed the support of Alan MacGregor (Dean, School of Business), Michael Hall (Head of Department, Department of Tourism) and my colleagues at the Department of Tourism, University of Otago who include Michael Hall, Hazel Tucker, Anna Carr, David Duval, Richard Mitchell, Brent Lovelock, Jan Mosedale, Caroline Orchiston, Teresa Leopold, Donna Keen, Andrea Valentine, Eric Shelton, Monica Graham and Diana Evans. The research assistance provided by Sarah Fredric (University of Otago) during the preparation of this book is also deserving of special mention.

I am extremely fortunate to enjoy the strong support of family and friends, and most particularly I am indebted to my immediate family. I owe a heartfelt thanks to Linda Buxton for the huge support that she had given to my career, particularly during times that I have been away from home, and of course Alexandra, Katie and George.

List of Contributors

Susanne Becken is a Principal Research Officer at Lincoln University. Her areas of expertise are tourist travel patterns, transport, energy use and greenhouse gas emissions, and tourism and climate change. She has recently edited a special issue of the *Journal of Sustainable Tourism on Transport* and is currently writing a book on Tourism and Climate Change.

Peter Björk PhD is an Acting Professor of Marketing at Swedish School of Economics and Business Administration (HANKEN), Finland. His main research interests are tourism marketing, focusing in particular on e-services, sustainable tourism and ecotourism. He is an Associate Editor of *Scandinavian Journal of Hospitality and Tourism*.

Anna Carr is a Senior Lecturer at the Department of Tourism, University of Otago. Prior to academia she worked for the Department of Conservation for 9 years and was co-owner of two adventure tourism businesses. Her research interests include ecotourism and adventure tourism operations, natural area and wilderness management; recreation and visitor interpretation/education.

Erlet Cater is a Senior Lecturer in Tourism and Development in the Department of Geography, University of Reading. She is on the Environment and Society Forum of the Royal Geographical Society with The Institute of British Geographers and the Advisory Board of Coral Cay Conservation. She judged the British Airways Tourism for Tomorrow Awards several times and is on the Editorial Boards of *Tourism Geographies, Journal of Ecotourism* and *Tourism in Marine Environments*. Amongst her publications, she is Co-editor of *Ecotourism: A Sustainable Option?*

published by John Wiley and co-author, with Carl Cater, of the forthcoming book for *CABI, Marine Ecotourism: Between the Devil and the Deep Blue Sea*.

Janet Cochrane worked in Indonesia for several years as an English teacher and for an environmental NGO, and then in London as a producer with the BBC World Service. She subsequently pursued a varied career of writing about Indonesia, tour leading to remote areas of South-East Asia, and nature tourism consultancy in even more remote areas for agencies such as WWF and The Nature Conservancy. She is currently Senior Research Fellow in Tourism at Leeds Metropolitan University, UK, with research interests which include the contribution of tourism to the management of protected areas.

Megan Epler Wood is the Principal of EplerWood International, a US-based consultancy firm which has worked in Asia, Africa and Latin America on the development of ecotourism and sustainable tourism as a tool to alleviate poverty and conserve natural resources. Epler Wood was the Founder of The International Ecotourism Society (TIES) in 1990 and was its President for 12 years. She was the Principal Lecturer on Ecotourism at The George Washington University from 1995 to 2000, and has spoken at Duke, Stanford, Wellesley, Columbia Business School and Harvard University on sustainable tourism development.

David A. Fennell (Department of Tourism and Environment, Brock University in Canada) teaches and researches mainly in the areas of ecotourism and tourism ethics. He has published widely in these areas, including sole authored books on *Ecotourism Programme Planning, a General Text on Ecotourism* (3rd edition forthcoming), *Tourism Ethics*, and a forthcoming title on *Codes of Ethics in Tourism* (he has edited two other books). Fennell is the Founding Editor-in-Chief of the *Journal of Ecotourism*, and is an active member on editorial boards of many academic journals.

Xavier Font is Principal Lecturer in Tourism Management at Leeds Metropolitan University. In the last 5 years he has undertaken research and consultancy in sustainable tourism for UNEP, UNCTAD, WTO, EC, WWF, Ford Foundation and the Travel Foundation. He has a Degree in Tourism Management from the University of Girona (Spain), Masters in Tourism Marketing from Surrey (UK) and PhD in sustainable tourism certification from Leeds Metropolitan University (UK). Formerly he lectured at Buckinghamshire Chilterns University College and was Project Officer for an EU project on forest tourism. His research focuses on marketing of sustainable tourism, including standard setting and certification, and supply chain management. He has co-authored and co-edited four books and published in a variety of academic journals including recent papers in *Annals of Tourism Research, Tourism Management,* and *Corporate Social Responsibility and Environmental Management.*

Stefan Gössling is an Associate Professor at the Department of Service Management, Lund University. His main field of interest is sustainable tourism, with a focus on global environmental change, transports and carbon offsets. He has published three edited books including *Tourism and Development in Tropical Islands, Tourism and Global Environmental Change* (with C.M. Hall) and *Ecotourism in Scandinavia* (with J. Hultman).

C. Michael Hall is currently Professor of Marketing in the College of Business and Economics, University of Canterbury, Christchurch, New Zealand and Docent, Department of Geography, University of Oulu, Finland. He was formerly at the University of Otago, New Zealand. Co-editor of *Current Issues in Tourism* he has published widely on tourism and temporary mobility, regional development and environmental history. Current research includes social marketing perspectives on tourism, place marketing, gastronomy, tourism and international business, and global environmental change.

James Higham holds the position of Professor at the Department of Tourism (University of Otago, New Zealand). His research interests focus on tourism and environmental change. His research has examined tourist interactions with wildlife in an attempt to situate tourism impacts within the wider field of wildlife dynamics, and understand effective approaches to managing tourist engagements with wildlife populations based on an understanding of spatial ecology. His work in this field has also examined the relationship between tourism and climate change. He serves on the editorial boards of *Journal of Sustainable Tourism, Journal of Ecotourism* (both Channel View), *Tourism in Marine Environments* (Cognizant Corp.) and *Journal of Sport and Tourism* (Francis and Taylor).

Michael Lück having taught in Germany, New Zealand, Scotland and Canada, currently holds the position of Associate Professor at the School of Hospitality and Tourism of AUT University (Auckland, New Zealand). His research interests focus on marine tourism, ecotourism, wildlife tourism, education and interpretation, sustainable tourism and teaching technologies. Michael has published in various international journals and co-edited two books on ecotourism. Most recently, he co-edited the book *Nautical Tourism: Concepts and Issues* (Cognizant Communication Corp., in press), and is the overall editor for the *Encyclopedia of Tourism and Recreation in Marine Environments* (CABI, exp. 2007). Michael serves on the Editorial Board of the *Journal of Ecotourism* and is Editor-in-Chief of *Tourism in Marine Environments*. He is Chair of the Organizing Committee for the *5th International Coastal and Marine Tourism Congress*, to be held in Auckland in 2007.

David Lusseau is currently Killam Postdoctoral Fellow at Dalhousie University, Canada working on the dynamics of social interactions in cetaceans. He previously held postdoctoral fellowships at the University of Aberdeen in Scotland working on the socioecology and conservation of bottlenose dolphins. David obtained his PhD from the University of Otago, Dunedin, New Zealand studying the impacts of boat interactions on bottlenose dolphins in Fiordland. He provides advice on whale-watching issues to a number of international and national governing bodies.

Cesar Moran-Cahusac is currently a Director of Conservation of the Amazon Conservation Association. He holds a Masters degree in Environmental Management from the Yale School of Forestry where he studied the gaps between conservation and ecotourism. He has worked in a vast array of conservation projects. At the Agrarian University of Lima – La Molina where he studied animal sciences, he developed a "hands-on" environmental educational programme based on organic gardening for school children in Lima. Later on, he worked for a period of 7 years as the Project Coordinator for the Machu Picchu Program, a debt for nature swap between the countries of Finland and Peru which supported this park in environmental issues. His main research interests include ecotourism, conservation, green design and GIS-based mapping.

Sanjay K. Nepal has a PhD in Geography and a Masters Degree in Rural and Regional Planning. His research interests are in tourism impacts, indigenous peoples and protected area conservation. He is currently Assistant Professor at the Department of Recreation, Park and Tourism Sciences at Texas A&M University, College Station, Texas, USA.

Agnes M. Nowaczek is a PhD candidate at the Department of Recreation and Leisure Studies, Faculty of Applied Health

Sciences, at the University of Waterloo, Ontario. Her research interests include ecotourism ethics, measurement of various psychographic constructs (i.e. scale development), conceptualization and deconstruction of ecotourism and ecotourists in cross-cultural contexts, spirituality and wilderness, effectiveness of codes of ethics, ecotourism development in Eastern Europe and less developed countries, urban outdoor recreation, management of protected areas, green infrastructure and ecological sustainability.

Matthias Schellhorn is an independent consultant based at Lincoln University/New Zealand, where he teaches as a contract lecturer in the fields of tourism and development studies. In consultancy, he focuses mainly on pro-poor and community-based tourism projects in Asia. Recent assignments include a tourism plan for a conservation area in Nepal, a wildlife tourism feasibility study in Cambodia (both for WWF) and the ADB-funded Mekong Tourism Development Project.

Regina Scheyvens is Associate Professor of Development Studies at Massey University. She authored *Tourism for Development: Empowering Communities* (2002) and has published a number of scholarly articles on ecotourism, backpacker tourism, community development, and tourism in small island states. Her current research involves a critical examination of pro-poor tourism.

Eric J. Shelton teaches in the Tourism Department, University of Otago, where he works to situate nature-based tourism within environmental philosophy, focusing on impacts of tourism, ecotourism theory and practice, and nature-based product development. Eric's PhD research explores how tourists to remote places experience self and identity through narratives constructed from personal philosophies of nature.

Trevor Sofield is Foundation Professor of Tourism, University of Tasmania. He has been undertaking tourism research in China since 1993, has made more than 20 research visits in the past decade, and has more than 30 publications on China to his name. He has been involved with the Chinese authorities in formulating ecotourism and cultural tourism policies in a number of Provinces in China including Anhui, Hubei, Hunan, Sichuan, Sha'anxi, Xinjiang, Yunnan and the Tibet Autonomous Region. He is currently Team Leader for the Mekong Tourism Development Project based in Phnom Penh. Cambodia, which also covers Guangxi and Yunnan Provinces of China, Laos, Myanmar, Thailand and Vietnam. Dr Sofield serves on the editorial boards of Annals of Tourism Research, Journal of Sustainable Tourism, and Journal of Ecotourism, among others. He is the author of Empowerment and Sustainable Tourism Development (Pergamon, 2003) and Editor-in-Chief and Co-author of the seven series of publications by UNCTAD on community based tourism and poverty alleviation which includes volumes on cultural and ecotourism (ITC, Geneva, 2005).

Pamela Wight is President of Pam Wight & Associates, an international consultancy focusing on sustainable tourism planning and development, adapting leading-edge theory to the range of political, sociocultural and environmental contexts of real-world development situations. Clients include national governments, UN-WTO, UNEP, ITC, UNDP/GEF, IFC and international conservation NGOs. She is an internationally recognized author and workshop leader in sustainable tourism, and was asked to give the 2002 Ambassador Lane Lecture on Sustainable Tourism at the University of Hawaii.

Heather Zeppel is a Senior Lecturer in the Tourism Program, School of Business at James Cook University in Cairns, North Queensland, Australia. She lectures on Tourism and the Environment, Australian Ecotourism and Wildlife Tourism Management, Tourism Issues in Developing Countries, and Tourism Analysis. Heather's research interests include Indigenous tourism, ecotourism, wildlife tourism and environmental best practice. She is the author of *Indigenous Ecotourism: Sustainable Development and Management* (CABI, 2006).

Sarah Li PhD is an expert on tourism development in China, having undertaken more than 20 tourism research projects and consultancies in a wide range of provinces over the past 15 years. Her focus has been on tourism planning and destination management, China's tourism development and its global impact, and ecotourism and sustainable development. In the past year she has been involved with conceptualisation and design of interpretation centres in two of China's foremost natural world heritage sites, Jiuzhaigou National Nature Reserve and Wolong National Nature Reserve, the latter the most significant remaining habitat of the giant panda in China. She has lectured at the Hong Kong Polytechnic University and the University of Tasmania and is currently an Adjunct Lecturer at Murdoch University, Western Australia, while she pursues her research interests in China and the Greater Mekong Sub-region, based in Phnom Penh, Cambodia.

CHAPTER 1

Ecotourism: competing and conflicting schools of thought

James Higham

Varacious wolf in lamb's clothing, the sensitive traveller is the real perpetrator of the global spread of tourism and in this capacity must take responsibility for some of tourism's adverse impact.

(Wheeller, 1992, p. 105)

Few issues in the academic study of travel and tourism are as contentious, drawing divided and polarised lines of debate, as the concept of ecotourism. Since the term entered the vernacular in the 1960s (Hetzer, 1965), it has been widely espoused as a benign form of tourism that offers great potential for interests in economic development and conservation to walk hand in hand (Ceballos-Lascurain, 1987, 1991a, b). In the mid-1960s Hetzer (1965) referred to a form of tourism '... *based principally upon natural and archaeological resources such as caves, fossil sites (and) archaeological sites'*. By the 1980s, following the rise of global environmental issues in the late 1960s and 1970s (McCormick, 1989), the term 'ecotourism' had become firmly established. In 1987 Ceballos-Lascurain coined one of the first of many definitions of ecotourism stating that '*we may define ecological tourism or ecotourism as that tourism that involves travelling to relatively undisturbed or uncontaminated natural areas with the specific object of studying, admiring and enjoying the scenery and its wild plants and animals'* (Ceballos-Lascurain, 1987, p. 13). He also made reference to '*any existing cultural manifestations (both past and present) found in these areas'* as an essential part of the ecotourism resource (Ceballos-Lascurain, 1987, p. 14).

However, within a short period of time discourses emerged that have drawn attention to the complexities of ecotourism development (Butler, 1990; Wheeller, 1991, 1992, 1993, 1994, 1995; Hall, 1994). In addressing 'tourism's troubled times' in the early 1990s, Wheeller (1991) has been steadfast in arguing the case that the so-called 'responsible' forms of tourism, including ecotourism, are not the answer. Instead he viewed alternative forms of tourism as an elaborate ruse and effective marketing tool for building further demand for tourism at a time of growing concern for the impacts of popular mass tourism. 'By clothing itself in a green mantle, the industry is being provided with a shield with which it can both deflect valid criticism and improve its own image while, in reality, continuing its familiar short tourism commercial march' (Wheeller, 1991, p. 96). Recent decades have therefore seen the emergence and entrenchment of two competing arguments addressing the merits of ecotourism (Butler, 1990; Wheeller, 1993, 1994), and the potential and pitfalls of ecotourism development (Boo, 1990; Bramwell and Lane, 1993; Wheeller, 1995).

On the surface ecotourism is a passive and appealing form of tourism (Dowling, 1999, 2000). Compelling arguments have been put forward to the effect that ecotourism contributes to the protection of natural environments, conservation of endangered species, the creation of employment and the empowerment of communities. Examples exist that demonstrate that such claims may be true. This is what Butler (1990) refers to as the 'pious hope' of ecotourism. The work of Dowling and Field (1999) on guiding and interpretation initiatives, and Dowling and Sharp (1996) on conservation-tourism partnerships (both in Western Australia), for example, have been influential in seeking ways to achieve sustainable ecotourism development in a regional context.

It has been widely stated that ecotourism offers the potential for economic transition, regional development, community empowerment and the creation of employment opportunities for peripheral areas (Hall and Boyd, 2003) and indigenous communities (Butler and Hinch, 1996). Advocates for ecotourism also point to the argument that ecotourism businesses may be well placed to make active contributions to conservation through, for example, the communication of conservation messages to the general public (Beaumont, 1998, 2001). Orams (1997) strongly advocates the potential role for well-developed education programmes to contribute to this end. Weiler and Ham (2001) provide detailed insights into the multiple roles of tour guides and the critical interpretation roles that they serve which, if successful, may have enduring consequences for the environmental values and conservation interests of visitors.

The work of Higham and Carr (2003a) addresses the potential for ecotourism businesses in New Zealand to achieve positive outcomes in two different dimensions. In the social dimension of ecotourism they found that ecotourism businesses were able to deliver high-quality visitor experiences and effective visitor interpretation programmes, contributing to conservation advocacy and raising visitor awareness of both global and national/regional environmental issues. Within the ecological dimension they found that ecotourism businesses were actively and successfully providing low-impact visitor experiences while contributing to conservation goals through such initiatives as predator eradication and revegetation programmes. A number of ecotourism businesses were actively contributing to science and research programmes through the collection of observational data and monitoring wildlife populations. Some were committed to ecological restoration through the reintroduction of regionally extinct species into protected areas (Higham and Carr, 2003a). These were seen as defining criteria of ecotourism by many visitors.

Yet the extent to which ecotourism delivers on the high aspirations associated with this form of tourism development is open to heated debate. Critics argue that lacking is the empirical research that is needed to provide evidence that words and realities actually coincide. Thus Butler (1990) raises the notion of the 'Trojan horse' of alternative forms of tourism. The intriguing insights provided by Hinch (1998, 2001) into the realities and complexities of indigenous-based ecotourism in Canada give a clear example of the 'Trojan horse' in an ecotourism context. So too do Hall's studies of ecotourism as new forms of ecological imperialism and Western domination (Hall, 1994).

One of the most common criticisms of ecotourism has been the sheer breadth of definitions that have been proposed to delineate the phenomenon (Fennell, 1998, 1999, 2001). The development of definitions is accurately described by Fennell (2001, p. 403) as 'one of the most habitual practices in the subfield of ecotourism'. The weight of academic energy paid to the definition of ecotourism is disproportionate to the general lack of consensus arising from such concerted scholarly effort. This is a situation that hinders the effective and sustainable development of ecotourism due to the uncertain policy, planning and development foundations that underpin the sector (Higham and Carr, 2003b).

Two contrasting approaches to defining ecotourism highlight the ineffective policy and planning contexts associated with a poorly understood phenomenon. Ballantine and Eagles (1994) evaluated Canadian tourists visiting Kenya against a definition consisting of three criteria: a social motive (educational component), the desire to visit 'wilderness/undisturbed areas' and a temporal component relating to the proportion of total time in Kenya spent on safari. Given the breadth of these criteria it is no surprise that 84% of all Canadian visitors to Kenya who were surveyed by Ballantine and Eagles (1994) were defined as ecotourists. Orams (1995) takes this scenario to its logical extreme stating that by definitions such as this, all tourism can be called 'ecotourism'.

Butler (1992), by contrast, presented a paper to the *IVth World Congress on National Parks and Protected Areas* with a more rigorous and detailed checklist for ecotourists (Table 1.1). The checklist highlights the opposite pole of the definitional scale. These criteria cover most aspects of the numerous definitions found throughout the literature. While most would applaud Butler's (1992) defining criteria, in many developing world contexts these criteria may be viewed as too purist in terms of the practical realities of ecotourism development. The logical extension of this definition, again as articulated by Orams (1995), is to assume that ecotourism is impossible. Under such an approach no tourism development can possibly fulfil the lofty aspirations of the most purist definitions. Thus the search for an operational definition remains an illusive goal (Blamey, 1997).

Table 1.1 Principles and characteristics of ecotourism

1. It must be consistent with a positive environmental ethic, fostering preferred behaviour.
2. It does not denigrate the resource. There is no erosion of resource integrity.
3. It concentrates on intrinsic rather than extrinsic values.
4. It is biocentric rather than homocentric in philosophy, in that an ecotourist accepts nature largely on its terms, rather than significantly transforming the environment for personal convenience.
5. Ecotourism must benefit the resource. The environment must experience a net benefit from the activity, although there are often spin-offs of social, economic, political or scientific benefits.
6. It is first-hand experience with the natural environment.
7. There is, in ecotourism, an expectation of gratification measured in appreciation and education, not in thrill-seeking or physical achievement. These latter elements are consistent with adventure tourism, the other division of natural environment (wildland) tourism.
8. There are high cognitive (informational) and effective (emotional) dimensions to the experience, requiring a high level of preparation from both leaders and participants.

Source: After Butler (1992), in Acott *et al.* (1998).

Ecotourism provides an intriguing and hitherto unresolved definitional conundrum. Numerous attempts of varied degrees of merit have been made to define ecotourism (e.g. Ceballos-Lascurain, 1987; Ashton, 1991; Buckley, 1994; Ecotourism Association of Australia, 1996; Weaver, 2001). Yet from the plethora of articles contributing to the literature on ecotourism emerges little consensus. Indeed, Fennell (2001, p. 403) states that *'the reasons for such a proliferation of definitions is unknown'*. However, despite suggestions that scholars need to move beyond the definition stalemate, the need to clearly define the phenomenon remains a live issue. The reasons why it remains important to define ecotourism are important to consider (Table 1.2).

The absence of a clear statement of definition hinders the sustainable development of ecotourism by diluting and compromising the coordinated and collective interests and activities of public/private, government/non-government groups and organisations, and visitors. The term *ecotourism* has been applied widely (Wight, 1993), to the point that it has to some degree become

Table 1.2 The policy, planning and development context, and the need for workable definitions of ecotourism

1. *Identity*: The search for a dividing line between ecotourism and nature tourism is critical to recognising excellence in the ecotourism sector (e.g. through industry awards).
2. *Research*: The definition of ecotourism allows the accurate expression of supply and demand. This is important for defining ecotourism operations and researching/profiling visitors.
3. *Planning and development*: A conceptual basis from which planning and development can proceed is critical to the ecotourism sector.
4. *Product development*: A clear identity based on definition affords advantages in terms of focused data, reporting and information dissemination. This may assist in product development and fostering links to the demand side of tourism through marketing and promotional avenues.
5. *Awareness*: Public awareness of issues affecting the ecotourism sector may be enhanced with a more rigorous understanding of ecotourism experiences and activities.
6. *Government support*: Government support, measuring change, understanding the opportunities that ecotourism development may offer regional or peripheral economies and advocacy are facilitated through accurate definition.
7. *Sustainability*: Industry development, certification, product development and impact management. These aspects of ecotourism relate closely to industry reputation, particularly in light of the emerging cynicism associated with issues of 'egotourism', 'ecoterrorism' and 'ecosell' (Wight, 1993).
8. *Policy*: The development of appropriate policy by relevant administrative and government agencies must be guided by definition.
9. *International comparability*: A common understanding of the definition of ecotourism may enhance international comparison and communication.
10. *International reputation*: The development of national and international standards may be achieved, notwithstanding the differences that will invariably exist between ecotourism operations in different environmental, social, cultural economic and political contexts.

Source: Higham and Carr (2003b).

meaningless (Chirgwin and Hughes, 1997). This situation is undesirable and counterproductive to the development of ecotourism. It disadvantages both operators who may be unsure of the values, motivations and expectations of visitors, and tourists who may be unsure of the product offered by 'eco' operators and the qualities of experience that they seek to provide (Higham *et al.*, 2001).

It has been argued by Pearce (1994), Blamey (1997) and Bjork (2000) that developing a single definition of ecotourism is an exercise in futility. However Bjork (2000) acknowledges that defining ecotourism is necessary to provide a conceptual basis from which planning and development can proceed. *'Only by having a strict theoretical definition (an ideal situation) is it possible to go on and adjust the dimensions in accordance with the unique characteristics of a specific tourism area'* (2000, p. 190). Bjork (2000) accurately states that ecotourism takes place in many varied contexts and, as such, the existence of exceptions to any definition of ecotourism is inevitable. It is, therefore, necessary to adopt definitions that reflect national and regional tourism contexts. Facilitating this process requires consensus on definition parameters that can be applied with different weighting in these differing contexts.

From this scenario, and in support of Wheeller's (1991) assessment of alternative tourism, some have questioned the very term 'ecotourist' based on empirical research findings (Higham and Carr, 2002). The term 'ecotourist' has effectively been defined either so narrowly or so broadly as to render it meaningless. Higham and Carr (2002) argue that while visitors to natural areas in New Zealand may be considered 'ecotourists' this effectively implies that all visitors are ecotourists simply because of the very nature of the experiences of most who visit New Zealand (Tourism New Zealand, 2006). Such a blunt approach to defining any phenomenon is counterproductive. Blamey and Braithwaite (1997) provide similar findings. They performed a social values segmentation of the potential Australian ecotourism market finding that the majority do not have the 'green' social values that one might associate with tourists who in the guise of ecotourism seek the experiences of nature. Who, then, are ecotourists, and how precisely are they to be defined?

The contradictions and constraints that are embodied in many definitions of ecotourism confirm its general inoperability. These contradictions may be overviewed with emphasis placed on the economic and environmental dimensions of ecotourism. Notwithstanding the rhetoric of sustainable tourism development, economic viability is the bottom line of sustainable tourism operations. Ecotourism operations face challenging and perplexing barriers to commercial viability. By definition they should be small scale (Butler, 1990; Thomlinson and Getz, 1996; Ryan *et al.*, 2000), resolute in limiting business growth (Butler, 1990) and, by implication, blinkered to economic theory relating to economies of scale. The recommendation that visitors are managed by maintaining an appropriate ratio of guides to visitors also brings with it economic challenges relating to pricing and commercial viability.

A range of environmental challenges also exist under current definitions of ecotourism. Not the least of these relates to the fact that ecotourism operations should take place in unmodified (Ceballos-Lascurain, 1987; Valentine, 1993), natural (Valentine, 1993; Boyd *et al.*, 1995; Orams, 1995; Blamey, 1997; Fennell, 1998; Swarbrooke and Horner, 1999) or pristine (Ceballos-Lascurain, 1987) areas. With this emerges a raft of challenges that hitherto have not been adequately addressed. These challenges relate to the management of visitor activities in environments that are fragile, finite and valued primarily for conservation. This operational environment is difficult to reconcile with the further definitional requirement that ecotourism visitor operations and activities should be low in impact (Wight, 1993; Orams, 1995; Lindberg and McKercher, 1997; Acott *et al.*, 1998; Honey 1999).

Furthermore, ecotourism operations, according to definition, should take place in natural areas removed from the accoutrements of civilised life (Boyd *et al.*, 1995). If this is so then as a consequence ecotourism operations are either removed from, or required to develop, the infrastructures that Cooper *et al.* (1998) identify to be critical to tourism; those relating to transportation, accommodation, services and activities. The viability of ecotourism operations clearly hinges on two fundamental requirements: (1) A resource base that demonstrates some degree of naturalness and (2) The infrastructure that is fundamental to commercial tourism operations. Herein lies a contradiction in terms because one cannot comfortably exist in the company of the other, yet both are required to facilitate viable ecotourism experiences. While 'degrees of naturalness' is not the same as a total absence of anthropogenic change, it still exists in relation to tourism and service infrastructure only in relative degress.

The complexities of the interface between the social sciences of tourism and the natural sciences of environmental management are highlighted by Duffus and Dearden (1990). Their conceptual framework demonstrates both the dynamics of ecotourism as a social phenomenon and the dynamics of ecotourism environments as ecological phenomena. In terms of the former, they employ an expert–novice (specialist–generalist) continuum to highlight that tourist types evolve over time. Thus, in the absence of very deliberate visitor management interventions, it is inevitable that purist or expert visitors will be sequentially displaced by novices as any given ecotourism site develops over time. Simultaneously the same sequence will bring new forces of change to bear upon ecotourism environments.

Duffus and Dearden (1990) apply the limits of acceptable change (LAC) visitor management approach in their conceptual framework to highlight the environmental dynamics brought about by ecotourism. But how best should these dynamics be managed? Many of the arguably most significant environmental impacts associated with ecotourism are brought about by the exploratory visits of Duffus and Dearden's (1990) 'experts'. These tourists may unwittingly be vectors for the translocation of insect pests, biological micro-organisms and disease pathogens. Island ecosystems are particularly vulnerable to biological introductions (deliberate or otherwise) due to the high endemism associated with island ecologies. The introduction of disease pathogens from peri-Antarctic islands to Antarctic penguin populations was, for example, an issue of lengthy discussion at the 2002 International Association of Antarctic Tourism Operators (IAATO) meeting in Cambridge (United Kingdom). So too, of course, does this apply to the more numerous 'novices' who typically follow in the footsteps of the initial 'expert' visitors. However, such troublesome impacts often become secondary to the more immediate and pressing impact issues associated with site development, transport impacts and the more 'blatant' impacts that commonly occur when tourists are brought in increasing numbers into contact with wild animal populations (Gordon *et al.*, 1992; Constantine, 1999; Bejder, 2005).

The venues for ecotourism development, including fragile ecologies, wildlife populations and coral reefs are as a rule fragile and high in conservation value. These venues are subject to the interests of those with tourism development ambitions, as well as local and central governments seeking to promote employment creation, not to mention the insatiable appetites of tourists seeking the experiences of nature. Tourist demand is difficult to forecast, and often runs far ahead of the development of effective legislation and management responsiveness. Thus management is inevitably reactive and retrospective. Sheer weight of demand, and the pace with which demand may develop, contributes to policy paralysis as management agencies are often unable to react effectively to increasing tourist demand, or the findings of empirical research.

Many of these issues were brought to a head in 2002 which was celebrated by the United Nations as the International Year of Ecotourism (IYE) (and the International Year of Mountains). During that year the United Nations Environment Programme (UNEP) and the World Tourism Organisation (WTO) were mandated by the United Nations (Resolution 53/200) to organise a range of events, the most notable of which was the World Ecotourism Summit (WES) (Quebec, Canada) (Hillel, 2002). In his address at the launch of IYE 2002 at the UN Headquarters, WTO, Secretary-General Francesco Frangialli stated that 'ecotourism is far from being a fringe activity. It should not be regarded as a passing fad or a gimmick, or even as a secondary market niche, but rather as one of the trump cards of this industry of the future. And for a simple reason: it is crucial to the problem of developing a balanced, sustainable and responsible tourism sector' (Frangialli, 2002). Deputy Secretary-General Louise Fréchette stated the 'urgent need to alert public opinion to the many effects of tourism on our natural and cultural heritage, and to promote responsible tourism'. Her statement, however, also largely centred on the potential rewards of ecotourism in terms of addressing issues of ecological conservation, social inequality and empowerment.

These comments are essentially endorsed by Hounsell (2002) who highlights the resurgence in traditional ways of life and the emergence of economic opportunities for indigenous communities that have come to grips with the social problems they have had to face. Hounsell, Chair of Aboriginal Tourism (Canada), noted in 2002 the existence of 1,500 aboriginal businesses in Canada, most of them both small and nature-based. Hounsell (2002) claims that 'Ecotourism is a natural fit for Aboriginals. Of course, it also has the potential to commercialise, to disturb sacred sites, to disrupt close-knit communities, but those are things we have to control. The elders and others have to determine which part of their culture they should reveal to tourists and which they won't. Visitors have to understand that there are cultural limits they have to respect. With aboriginal population increasing, tourism may be a means of meeting the challenge of providing employment for the population' (Hounsell, 2002, n.p.).

By the end of 2002 the UNEP reported that a range of successful outcomes had been achieved (UNEP and WTO, 2002a). They included:

1. *Ecotourism policy*: During the IYE 2002 over 50 countries had developed special policies and strategies focused on ecotourism at the national level. The WES was attended by more than 1,100 delegates from 133 countries (45 ministerial level officials). It stressed the participation of host communities and mandated the educational value of leisure experiences.
2. *Ecotourism and sustainable development*: If managed in a sustainable manner, ecotourism helps conserve biodiversity, alleviates poverty in rural areas, and can provide benefits to local and indigenous communities situated near, or in, officially protected areas.
3. *Ecotourism as a global economic driver*: The main challenge for the future is to apply the principles of ecotourism/sustainable tourism to all forms of tourism development.

Other key outcomes were identified by UNEP and WTO (2002a). These included a global network of specialists and practitioners, with strengthened regional presence which was developed and made 'operational through the consultative process of the IYE 2002, managed by UNEP, the WTO, The International Ecotourism Society (TIES) and several other partners' (UNEP and WTO, 2002, n.p.). From the WES in Quebec the main outcome was the *Quebec Declaration on Ecotourism* (UNEP and WTO, 2002b) which represented the culmination of multistakeholder dialogue involving over 5,000 experts globally, and a set of UN-level recommendations for the development of ecotourism activities in the context of sustainable development (UNEP and WTO, 2002). A positive view, albeit from a very different standpoint, was expressed by Patricia Barnett (2002) (Director of *Tourism Concern*) who noted that *'Tourism Concern* is pleased that campaigning organisations in destination countries have pressurised the IYE to recognise that even ecotourism can have serious negative impacts on local people and environments and needs careful consideration' (www.tourismconcern.org.uk, 2002).

However, despite the rhetoric, IYE 2002 also stimulated considerable debate on the contentious issues associated with ecotourism. Critics have argued that IYE invited widespread government and investor sponsored development programmes that may have been ill-conceived, ill-advised and poorly planned (Cater, 2006). On its website the Third World Network (TWN) presented a letter that 'vigorously questions claims that ecotourism rectifies the economic inequalities, social injustices and ecological problems associated with conventional tourism' (Pleumarom, 2002, n.p.). Rather, it warned, such developments have 'opened opportunities for a whole range of investors to gain access to remote rural, forest, coastal and marine areas', and 'more encroachments, illegal logging, mining and plundering of biological resources …' (Pleumarom, 2005, n.p.). Similarly TWN (2002, n.p.) reported in a letter to the United Nations that in Thailand an 'upsurge of ecotourism demand had resulted in a construction frenzy in rural and natural areas to provide accommodation and infrastructure for visitors'.

Widespread concerns centred on the possibility that IYE 2002 may have had a largely unintended outcome of prompting wholesale ecotourism development initiatives in the absence of sufficient planning and policy development. These issues were raised by a number of NGOs which in 2002 voiced concerns about the IYE. *Tourism Concern*, for example, highlighted concern surrounding a sudden growth in demand for ecotourism experiences, which was not deemed to be in the best interests of local and indigenous communities. *Tourism Concern* pointed out that '… the problems of unsustainable tourism development cannot be solved by promoting "ecotourism", which is a small, niche market and also, by its nature, necessitates developing tourism in fragile, sensitive areas. This could be fraught with difficulties if demand for ecotourism increases significantly' (Barnett, 2002, n.p.).

Hsu (2002) then reports a classic case in point. In a direct response to the United Nation's 2002 IYE declaration this initiative was mirrored nationally when 2002 was declared the year of ecotourism in Taiwan. Ambitious development goals, and a government investment of NT$30 million, were put in place in order to focus attention on large scale ecotourism development. Hsu (2002) notes that the principle aim was to 'build up Taiwan as an ecotourism island in the hope that the world's ecotourists will flock here to see the island's rich and diversified ecological resources'.

In order to achieve these outcomes, various plans were put in place. These generally focused on such things as 'building up ecotourism environments, including the establishment of ecotourism service facilities, selection of ecotourism spots, eco-tourism guidance, and to elaborate an evaluation or accreditation of ecotour programmes' (Hsu, 2002), as well as the implementation of a comprehensive and regular series of ecotourism promotions, particularly targeting the *China Post* with features on Taiwan's whales and dolphins, among other things (Hsu, 2002). This, one can surely assume, was not the intention of the United Nations declaration.

In response to these criticisms, TIES declared IYE 2002, and particularly the WES held in Québec, Canada, in May 2002, a success. At the end of 2002 it was noted that IYE had presented '... an opportunity to critically assess the status of eco-tourism, while urging as open and participatory a process as possible, including the voices of the poor, indigenous, and local communities' (Wight, 2002, n.p.). However, it is apparent that critical issues in ecotourism remain largely unresolved.

Two current examples illustrate this view. First, while much stock has been placed on self-regulation of ecotourism, with the efforts of the IAATO being upheld as an exemplar of self-regulation, a groundswell of doubt and concern surrounding self-regulation has developed in recent years. These concerns are borne out by Font's research on accreditation and certification (Font and Buckley, 2001; Font and Tribe, 2001). His work confirms that certification is best suited to countries where the infrastructures and financial resources required to support tourism are well established (Font, 2005). Such cases, in places where ecotourism development is advocated, and where eco-tourism development was widely endorsed in 2002, are generally the exception rather than the rule.

Second, the research of marine biologists demonstrates that impacts of biological significance associated with tourist interactions with marine mammals are generally ignored or dispelled by tour operators and government agencies due to the conviction that short- and medium-term impacts are either undetected or of undue concern (Bejder *et al.*, 1999; Lusseau and Higham, 2004; Bejder, 2005; Bejder *et al.*, 2006). Ananthaswamy (2004) notes that tourist interactions with wildlife populations may have adverse impacts that are difficult to identify. Immediate effects include changes in heart rate, physiology, stress hormone levels and social behaviour, and the long-term consequences of these impacts are likely to be biologically significant. The same findings are derived from the work of Ellenberg *et al.* (2006) in their study of Humboldt penguins. These findings have resulted in a call from biologists for the collection of 'pre-tourism data' to provide benchmarks of animal behaviour. Furthermore wildlife-based tourism needs to be developed under the precautionary principle (Fennell and Ebert, 2004) at least until rigorous scientific insights into the impacts of tourist on wildlife populations have been established. In order to achieve such insights it is necessary to collect data from both tourism and control sites to allow comparative analyses to be performed. Only then will sufficiently rigorous insights into visitor impacts be achieved to guide effective management practice (Higham and Bejder, personal communication).

Clearly, regardless of whether it was intended or not, the United National declaration of 2002 as IYE stimulated large-scale ecotourism development initiatives that were generally not undertaken in association with any principles of precaution. These issues clearly bear out widespread concerns that IYE 2002 would cause more damage than good. They would indicate that the United National declaration of 2002 as the IYE was premature. The chorus of dissenting voices that were raised in response to IYE 2002 leaves little doubt about it (Cater, 2006). It is a statement of the obvious, one may argue, that much scholarly work remains to be done, and many issues remain outstanding in terms of an adequate understanding of ecotourism phenomena.

This book sets out with two principal aims. The first is to raise a range of critical issues associated with ecotourism, and draw the attention of the reader to the importance of considering these issues, among others. If, in doing so, it stimulates further research into critical issues associated with ecotourism, then this aim will have been fulfilled. The second is to provide the reader with insights into these critical issues, and the challenges that they pose. This book is organised into two parts. The first introduces and addresses generic issues in ecotourism that apply universally. These include inescapable issues that are associated with ecotourism such as, for example, global environmental change (Gössling, Chapter 4), energy use and global climate change (Becken and Schellhorn, Chapter 5), biosecurity (Hall, Chapter 6), ethics (Nowaczek, Moran-Cahusac and Fennell, Chapter 8), poverty alleviation (Epler Wood, Chapter 9) and gender issues (Scheyvens, Chapter 10).

The second part of this book examines more specific issues that relate to the policy, planning and management settings for ecotourism in different regional and national contexts. Thus the chapters presented in the second part of this book address such issues as understanding the spatial ecology of marine mammals as a critical step towards managing tourist interactions with cetaceans (Higham and Lusseau, Chapter 13), the complexities of wildlife habitation (Shelton and Higham, Chapter 14), biodiversity conservation in Asia (Cochrane, Chapter 15), the indistinct boundaries between ecotourism and cultural tourism in China (Sofield, Chapter 18) and the critical issues faced by ecotourism business operators in New Zealand (Carr, Chapter 20).

The chapters that follow address a raft of issues that are both provocative and perplexing. They challenge the reader to critically consider the merits of ecotourism as it exists in different social, cultural, political, economic and environmental contexts. It is hoped that having considered the chapters that comprise this book the reader will be well placed to draw their own informed conclusions on ecotourism development as it exists in different national and regional contexts, and the critical issues that accompanies it, many of which remain unsatisfactorily resolved.

This chapter highlights two contrasting and largely conflicting schools of thought. One sees ecotourism as a relatively benign avenue of economic development; one that justifies the protection or restoration of natural environments, while also affording opportunities for economic development, employment creation and the empowerment or indigenous peoples and communities (Weaver, 2001). The other sees ecotourism as a means of perpetuating dominant Western interests in economic development (Hall, 1994; Wheeller, 1994; Cater, 2006) and a form of tourism that brings serious impacts, some subtle and others not so subtle, to bear where they are least needed. Those who conform with this school of thought also question the theory of trickle-down economics and the potential for ecotourism to empower local communities (Wheeller, 1991). At present these scenarios remain difficult to reconcile. Ultimately it will be left to the reader to decide which school of thought should prevail.

References

Acott, T.G., La Trobe, H.L. and Howard, S.H. (1998). An evaluation of deep ecotourism and shallow ecotourism. *Journal of Sustainable Tourism* 6(3): 238–253.

Ananthaswamy, A. (2004). Beware the ecotourist. *New Scientist* 181(2437): 6–7.

Ashton, R.E. (1991). *Fundamentals of Ecotourism: A Workbook for Nonprofit Travel Programmes*. Water and Air Research Inc, Gainesville, FL.

Ballantine, J.L. and Eagles, P.F.J. (1994). Defining Canadian ecotourists. *Journal of Sustainable Tourism* 2(4): 210–214.

Barnett, P. (2002). *Why Tourism Concern is Cautious About the International Year of Ecotourism*. Tourism Concern press statement. www.tourismconcern.org.uk (accessed 19 January 2006).

Beaumont, N. (1998). The conservation benefits of ecotourism: Does it produce pro-environmental attitudes or are ecotourists already converted to the cause? Paper presented at *the 1998 Australian Tourism and Hospitality Research Conference*, University of Western Sydney, Australia.

Beaumont, N. (2001). Ecotourism and the conservation ethic: recruiting the uninitiated or preaching to the converted? *Journal of Sustainable Tourism* 9(4): 317–341.

Bejder, L. (2005). *Linking Short and Long Term Effects of Nature-Based Tourism on Cetaceans*, PhD Thesis, Dalhousie University, Canada.

Bejder, L., Dawson, S.M. and Harraway, J.A. (1999). Responses by Hector's dolphins to boats and swimmers in Porpoise Bay, New Zealand. *Marine Mammal Science* 15(3): 738–750.

Bejder, L., Samuels, A., Whitehead, H., Gales, N., Mann, J., Connor, R., Heithaus, M., Watson-Capps, J., Flaherty, C. and Kruetzen, M. (2006). Decline in relative abundance of bottlenose dolphins (*Tursiops* sp.) exposed to long-term disturbance. *Conservation Biology* DOI: 10.1111/j.1523-1739.2006.00540.x

Bjork, D.P. (2000). Ecotourism from a conceptual perspective: an extended definition of a unique tourism form. *International Journal of Tourism Research* 2(3): 189–202.

Blamey, R. and Braithwaite, V. (1997). A social values segmentation of the potential ecotourism market. *Journal of Sustainable Tourism* 5(1): 29–45.

Blamey, R.K. (1997). Ecotourism: the search for an operational definition. *Journal of Sustainable Tourism* 5(2): 109–130.

Boo, E. (1990). *Ecotourism: The Potentials and Pitfalls*, Vol. 1. World Wildlife Fund, Washington, DC.

Boyd, S.W., Butler, R.W., Haider, W. and Perera, A. (1995). Identifying areas for ecotourism in Northern Ontario: application of a geographical information systems methodology. *Journal of Applied Recreation Research* 19(1): 41–66.

Bramwell, B. and Lane, B. (1993). Interpretation and sustainable tourism: the potential and the pitfalls. *Journal of Sustainable Tourism* 1(2): 71–80.

Buckley, R. (1994) A framework for ecotourism. *Annals of Tourism Research* 21(3): 661–665.

Butler, R.W. (1990). Alternative tourism: pious hope or Trojan horse? *Journal of Travel Research* 28(3): 40–45.

Butler, R.W. (1992). Ecotourism: its changing face and evolving philosophy. Paper presented to the *IV World Congress on National Parks and Protected Areas*, Caracas, Venezuela.

Butler, R.W. and Hinch, T.D. (eds) (1996). *Tourism and Indigenous Peoples*. International Thomson Business Press, Boston, MA.

Cater, E. (2006). Ecotourism as a western construct. *Journal of Ecotourism* 5(1&2): 23–39.

Ceballos-Lascurain, H. (1987). The future of 'ecotourism'. *Mexico Journal* 13–14.

Ceballos-Lascurain, H. (1991a). Tourism, ecotourism and protected areas. *Parks* 2(3): 31–35.

Ceballos-Lascurain, H. (1991b). Tourism, ecotourism and protected areas. In Kusler, J.A. (compiler), *Ecotourism and Resource Conservation: A Collection of Papers*, Vol. 1. Omnipress, Madison, WI. pp 24–30.

Chirgwin, S. and Hughes, K. (1997). Ecotourism: the participants' perceptions. *Journal of Tourism Studies* 8(2): 2–7.

Constantine, R. (1999). *Effects of Tourism on Marine Mammals in New Zealand*. Report No. 60, Department of Conservation, Wellington.

Cooper, C., Fletcher, J., Gilbert, D., Shepherd, S. and Wanhill, S. (1998). *Tourism: Principles and Practice* (2nd edn). Addison Wesley Longman Ltd, Harlow.

Dowling, R.K. (1999). Harnessing the benefits of regional ecotourism development: lessons from Western Australia. In Weir, B., McArthur, S. and Crabtree, A. (eds), *Developing Ecotourism into the Millennium. Proceedings of the Ecotourism Association of Australia National Conference 1998*, Margaret River, Western Australia. Ecotourism Association of Australia, Brisbane, pp. 31–35.

Dowling, R.K. (2000). Conference report: developing ecotourism into the millennium. *International Journal of Tourism Research* 2: 203–208.

Dowling, R.K. and Field, G. (1999). Guiding initiatives in Western Australia. In: Weir, B., McArthur, S. and Crabtree, A. (eds), *Developing Ecotourism into the Millennium. Proceedings of the Ecotourism Association of Australia National Conference 1998*,

Margaret River, Western Australia. Ecotourism Association of Australia, Brisbane, pp. 54–57.

Dowling, R.K. and Sharp, J. (1996). Conservation-tourism partnerships in Western Australia. *Tourism Recreation Research* 22(1): 55–60.

Duffus, D.A. and Dearden, P. (1990). Non-consumptive wildlife-oriented recreation: a conceptual framework. *Biological Conservation* 53: 213–231.

Ellenberg, U., Mattern, T., Seddon, P. and Jorquera, G.L. (2006). Physiological and reproductive consequences of human disturbance in Humboldt penguins: the need for species-specific visitor management. *Biological Conservation* 133: 95–106.

Fennell, D.A. (1998). Ecotourism in Canada. *Annals of Tourism Research* 25(1): 231–234.

Fennell, D.A. (1999). *Ecotourism: An Introduction*. Routledge, New York.

Fennell, D.A. (2001). A content analysis of ecotourism definitions. *Current Issues in Tourism* 4(5): 403–421.

Fennell, D.A. and Ebert, K. (2004). Tourism and the precautionary principle. *Journal of Sustainable Tourism* 12(6): 461–479.

Font, X. (2005). Critical review of certification and accreditation in sustainable tourism governance. http://www.ecotourism.org/onlineLib/Uploaded/Cert_accreditation_sustainable_tourism_governance.pdf (accessed 2 March 2006).

Font, X. and Buckley, R. (eds) (2001). *Tourism Ecolabelling: Certification and Promotion of Sustainable Management*. CABI Publishing Ltd, Wallingford, Oxon, UK.

Font, X. and Tribe, J. (2001). Promoting green tourism: the future of environmental awards. *International Journal of Tourism Research* 3: 9–21.

Frangialli, F. (2002). *International Year of Ecotourism Launched at Headquarters Event*. United National Information Service, 29 January 2002.

Gordon, J., Leaper, R., Hartley, F.G. and Chappell, O. (1992). *Effects of Whale Watching Vessels on the Surface and Underwater Acoustic Behaviour of Sperm Whales off Kaikoura, New Zealand*. Science and Research Series No. 52, Department of Conservation, Wellington, New Zealand.

Hall, C.M. (1994). Ecotourism in Australia, New Zealand and the South Pacific: appropriate tourism or a new form of ecological imperialism? In Cater, E. and Lowman, G.L. (eds), *Ecotourism: A Sustainable Option?* John Wiley & Sons, Chichester, UK, pp. 137–158.

Hall, C.M. and Boyd, S. (2003). *Ecotourism in Peripheral Areas*. Channel View Publications, Clevedon, UK.

Hetzer, D. (1965). Environment, tourism, culture. *Links* 1: n.p.

Higham, J.E.S. and Carr, A. (2002). Profiling visitors to ecotourism operations. *Annals of Tourism Research* 29(4): 1168–1171.

Higham, J.E.S. and Carr, A. (2003a). Wildlife tourism and the protection of rare and endangered endemic species in New Zealand: an analysis of visitor experiences. *Human Dimensions of Wildlife* 8(1): 25–36.

Higham, J.E.S. and Carr, A. (2003b). Defining ecotourism in New Zealand: differentiating between the defining parameters within a national/regional context. *Journal of Ecotourism* 2(1): 17–32.

Higham, J.E.S., Carr, A.M. and Gale, S. (2001). Profiling visitors to New Zealand ecotourism operations. He tauhokohoko ngā whakaaturanga a ngā manuhiri ki rawa whenua o Aotearoa. Research Paper Number 10. Department of Tourism, University of Otago.

Hillel, O. (2002). *International Year of Ecotourism (IYE) 2002*. UNEP, Division of Technology, Industry and Economics, Paris, France.

Hinch, T. (1998). Ecotourists and indigenous hosts: diverging views on their relationship with nature. *Current Issues in Tourism* 1(1): 120–124.

Hinch, T. (2001). Indigenous territories. In Weaver, D. (ed.), *The Encyclopaedia of Ecotourism*. CABI Publishing, Wallingford, UK, pp. 345–357.

Honey, M. (1999). *Ecotourism and Sustainable Development: Who Owns Paradise?* Island Press, Washington, DC.

Hounsell, D. (2002). *Indigenous People Speak Out at Ecotourism Summit*. http://www.peopleandplant.net (accessed 3 February 2006).

Hsu, D. (2002). 2002 declared year of ecotourism in Taiwan. *China Post* (24 May), p. 17.

Lindberg, K. and McKercher B. (1997). Ecotourism: a critical overview. *Pacific Tourism Review* 1: 65–79.

Lusseau, D. and Higham, J.E.S. (2004). Managing the impacts of dolphin-based tourism through the definition of critical habitats: the case of bottlenose dolphins (*Tursiops* spp.) in doubtful sound, New Zealand. *Tourism Management* 25(5): 657–667.

McCormick, J. (1989). *The Global Environmental Movement*. Belhaven Press, London, UK.

Orams, M.B. (1995). Towards a more desirable form of ecotourism. *Tourism Management* 16(1): 3–8.

Orams, M.B. (1997). The effectiveness of environmental education: can we turn tourists into 'greenies'? *Progress in Tourism and Hospitality Research* 3: 295–306.

Pearce, D.G. (1994). Alternative tourism: concepts, classifications and questions. In Smith, V. and Eadington, W. (eds),

Tourism Alternatives. Potential and Problems in the Development of Tourism. John Wiley & Sons, Chichester, UK, pp. 15–30.

Pleumarom, A. (2002). *Do We Need the International Year of Ecotourism?* Third World Network. www.twnside.org.sg/tour.htm (accessed 17 February 2006).

Ryan, C., Hughes, K. and Chirgwin, S. (2000). The gaze, spectacle and ecotourism. *Annals of Tourism Research* 27(1): 148–163.

Swarbrooke, J. and Horner, S. (1999). *Consumer Behaviour in Tourism.* Butterworth-Heinemann, Oxford.

Thomlinson, E. and Getz, D. (1996). The question of scale in ecotourism: case study of two small ecotour operators in the Mundo Maya region of Central America. *Journal of Sustainable Tourism* 4(4): 183–200.

Tourism New Zealand (2006). *International Visitor Motivations.* Wellington, New Zealand.

TWN (Third World Network) (2002). *Letter from the Rethinking Tourism Project (RTP).* http://www2.planeta.com/mader/ecotravel/resources/rtp/rtp.html (accessed 25 January 2006).

UNEP and WTO (2002a). *The World Ecotourism Summit Final Report.* UNEP and WTO, Paris.

UNEP and WTO (2002b). *The Quebec Declaration on Ecotourism.* UNEP and WTO, Quebec.

Valentine, P.S. (1993). Ecotourism and nature conservation: a definition with some recent developments in Micronesia. *Tourism Management* 14(2): 107–115.

Weaver, D. (ed.) (2001). *The Encyclopaedia of Ecotourism.* CABI Publishing, Wallingford, UK.

Weiler, B. and Ham, S. (2001). Tour guides and interpretation. In Weaver, D. (ed.), *The Encyclopaedia of Ecotourism.* CABI Publishing, Wallingford, UK, pp. 549–564.

Wheeller, B. (1991). Tourism's troubled times: responsible tourism is not the answer. *Tourism Management* 12(2): 91–96.

Wheeller, B. (1992). Is progressive tourism appropriate? *Tourism Management* 13(1): 104–105.

Wheeller, B. (1993). Sustaining the ego. *Journal of Sustainable Tourism* 3(1): 29–44.

Wheeller, B. (1994). Ecotourism: a ruse by any other name. In Cooper, C. and Lockwood, A. (eds), *Progress in Tourism, Recreation and Hospitality Management*, Vol. 7. Belhaven Press, London, UK, pp. 3–11.

Wheeller, B. (1995). Egotourism, sustainable tourism and the environment – a symbiotic, symbolic or shambolic relationship? In Seaton, A.V. (ed.), *Tourism the State of the Art.* John Wiley & Sons, Brisbane, pp. 647–654.

Wight, P. (1993). Ecotourism: ethics or eco-sell? *Journal of Travel Research* 31(3): 3–9.

Part One

Generic Issues in Ecotourism

CHAPTER 2

Definition Paradoxes: From concept to definition

Peter Björk

Introduction

Ecotourism is often positioned as an alternative to mass tourism, a sustainable nature- and culture-based tourism (Weaver, 2001; Fennell, 2003). Ecotourism as a concept has been praised but has also been flouted at, and compared to related tourism forms. Tourism, the generic concept, defined as *'activities of persons traveling to and staying in places outside their usual environment for not more than one consecutive year for leisure, business and other purposes not related to the exercise of an activity remunerated from within the place visited'* (WTO, 2001, p. 1) has been specified by different types of prefixes (terms). Descriptive (adventure, nature) as well as value-based terms (ethical, sustainable) have been used in the literature to define different types of tourism products. One such term used is 'eco' as in ecotourism. This combination has generated a lot of discussion, and disparate views on what ecotourism stands for have been presented. The term 'eco-' in ecotourism has generally been linked to the ecological concept in allusion to ecologically sustainable. However, the sustainability dimension of ecotourism promises more than just preserving the biodiversity of an area. The 'eco' term in ecotourism does also have an economic development dimension, a dimension of special interest for the private sector.

The ideal balance of preserving and developing at the same time is described in most ecotourism definitions. This paradox is not a unique one for ecotourism, but can be found in related concepts, as for example sustainability and sustainable tourism development, on which ecotourism is built. Existing ecotourism definitions have been criticized because of their vagueness or for being too lofty. The abstract concepts used in most ecotourism definitions have been considered hard to operationalize (Blamey, 1997). Despite this critique, presented ecotourism definitions may not be completely wrong. Sirakaya *et al.* (1999) used a supply-side approach and analyzed 282 US-based ecotour operators, who confirmed the relevance of existing ecotourism definitions.

The ecotourism concept, which was introduced in the 1960s, discussed by ecologists in the 1970s, accepted by tourism researchers in the 1980s and considered as the fastest-growing segment of the tourism industry in the 1990s, has been considered theoretically sound but hard to implement (see Weaver, 2001 and Fennell, 2002, 2003 for a historical discussion). Experts and practitioners have during the last 10 years tried to develop and present ecotourism as a viable alternative to mass tourism: as a small-scale, locally owned and sustainable tourism form. The year 2002 was celebrated as 'the International Year of Ecotourism' by the United Nations, an event that was questioned by some NGOs (e.g. Third World Network (TWN), www.twnside. org.sg) due to fear of an accelerated exploitation of virgin natural areas by insensible travelers (supported by suspicious tour operators).

Ecotourism development in practice has been plagued with problems. Non-realization of promised benefits, none or weak development and an absence of management, have been attributed to a lack of coordination between the stakeholders involved in ecotourism. Another reason for existing implementation problems could be the concept itself and how it has been operationalized. Ecotourism has been considered more an ideal than a reality (Cater, 1995). The many competing definitions of ecotourism do not ease the situation by providing a homogeneous picture of what ecotourism stands for. The major challenge of ecotourism today is not to present another 'better' definition, but how to translate the meaning of ecotourism into relevant and usable principles (guidelines) and criteria. This is, without doubt, a difficult task given that different ecotourism areas, regions and destinations around the globe are unique in most respects. Even the many diverging stakeholder perspectives that have to be coordinated is an issue that has to be solved.

This chapter discusses in the first section some of the most often used ecotourism definitions. A chronological approach is used and two development paths of ecotourism definitions are presented. Content analysis of existing definitions has been used to unfold the complexity of the concept. The basic principles of ecotourism are then addressed. Some of these basic principles are shared with related tourism forms, but there are also distinguishing criteria. Ecotourism is compared to similar tourism forms in section three. Comprehensive ecotourism definitions are very restrictive. There have been attempts to introduce different types of 'light' or 'weak' ecotourism in contrast. This kind of a continuum approach is presented in section four. To add another prefix to the ecotourism concepts does not simplify the theoretical discussions because the concept is still included. Ecotourism belongs to a family of related concepts. The founding principles of ecotourism can be identified in concepts such as sustainability and sustainable development, two concepts that are presented. The paradox between development and preservation is discussed in section five. This section discusses how preservation and development are dimensions found in all outcome variables. Discussions about the ecotourism concept must be more distinct in the future. Theoretical ambitions must be separated from implementation-oriented case studies. The final section discusses how the ecotourism concept will probably develop at these two levels.

The development of ecotourism definitions

The historical origin of the ecotourism concept can be traced back to the 1960s when ecologists and environmentalists became concerned over the inappropriate use of natural resources. The preservation of biodiversity was threatened in favor of economic interest and the exploitation of natural resources. The Mexican ecologist Hetzer introduced the term 'ecotourism' and identified four normative principles (pillars) in 1965. According to Hetzer ecotourism should have (1) minimum environmental impact, (2) minimum impact on – and maximum respect for – host cultures, (3) maximum economic benefits to the host country's grassroots, and (4) maximum recreational satisfaction to participating tourists.

These principles, which can be found in most subsequent definitions, define a system of stakeholders and outcomes. Ecotourism should have minimum effects on the environment (preserve) and culture (respect), and maximize the economic development of the host population and the satisfaction level of the visitors. These first ecotourism principles have well served the discussion on ecotourism during the last 40 years although new dimensions have been added. The complexity of ecotourism has especially been recognized. The number of stakeholders (different interests) involved in ecotourism has been extended and an educational, learning dimension has been added (Weaver, 2001). An analysis of the evolution of the ecotourism concept reveals (1) how different dimensions in different ecotourism definitions are stressed and (2) how today two main types of ecotourism definitions exist.

The fine line between preservation and development was partly lost in the first ecotourism definition of Ceballos-Lascurain (1987, p. 14) *'traveling to relatively undisturbed or uncontaminated natural areas with the specific objective of studying, admiring, and enjoying the scenery and its wild plants and animals, as well as any existing cultural manifestation (both past and present) found in these areas'*. The main focus of this definition was on the behavior of the travelers and the characteristics of the area visited. The preservation dimension was not explicitly included. This definition was revised in 1993 by Ceballos-Lascurain (and appears in the book 'Tourism, Ecotourism and Protected Areas' published in 1996). He added the preservation dimension, and the seminal thought of Hetzer (1965) was again identified, that is to maximize the outcome for some while minimizing the effects on culture and nature.

'Ecotourism is environmentally responsible travel and visitation to relatively undisturbed natural areas, in order to enjoy and appreciate nature (and any accompanying cultural features – both past and present) that promotes conservation, has low negative visitor impact, and provides beneficially active socio-economic involvement of local populations'.

(Ceballos-Lascurain, 1996)

All ecotourism definitions were from the very beginning replete with elusive concepts, such as, responsible, conservation, protection, and sustainable. Ecotourism was for example defined by WWF (1995) as the following: *'ecotourism is responsible traveling contributing to the protection of natural areas and the well-being of the local population'* (Sæþórsdóttir et al., 1998, p. 32). These general and vague ecotourism definitions have been criticized because they leave too much room for interpretation. Different stakeholders have different interests in ecotourism, and too selfish attitudes may jeopardize the whole ecotourism system and disregard the balanced approach that should underpin ecotourism. Fennell (2001) compared ecotourism definitions from different time periods and his results show that the preservation dimension is better represented in more recent definitions (those presented during 1994–1996 and 1997–1999).

There are two categories of ecotourism definitions found in the literature today. The first category consists of multidimensional comprehensive definitions, as for example the one offered by Ziffer (1989, p. 6):

'a form of tourism inspired primarily by the natural history of an area, including its indigenous cultures. The ecotourist visits relatively undeveloped areas in the spirit of appreciation, participation and sensitivity. The ecotourist practices a non-consumptive use of wildlife and natural resources and contributes to the visited area through labor or financial means aimed at directly benefiting the conservation of the site and the economic well-being of the local residents. The visit should strengthen the ecotourist's appreciation and dedication to conservation issues in general, and to the specific needs of the locale. Ecotourism also implies a management approach by the host country or region which commits itself to establishing and maintaining the sites with the participation of local residents, marketing them appropriately, enforcing regulations, and using the proceeds of the enterprise to fund the area's land management as well as community development'.

The second category of definitions is shorter (one or two sentences long), and extended by appending lists of principles and/or criteria. TIES (The International Ecotourism Society) for example

defines ecotourism as *'responsible travel to natural areas that con-serves the environment and improves the well-being of local people'*, and adds the following principles:
Ecotourism:

- Minimizes impact.
- Builds environmental and cultural awareness and respect.
- Provides positive experiences for both visitors and hosts.
- Provides direct financial benefits for conservation.
- Provides financial benefits and empowerment for local people.
- Raises sensitivity to the host country's political, environmental, and social climate.
- Supports international human rights and labor agreements.

Another general definition is found in The Quebec Declaration on Ecotourism (2002) (presented at The World Ecotourism Summit), where ecotourism 'embraces the principles of sustainable tourism concerning the economic, social and environmental impacts of tourism. It also embraces the following principles which distin-guish it from the wider concept of sustainable tourism:

- Contributes actively to the conservation of natural and cul-tural heritage.
- Includes local and indigenous communities in its planning, development and operation, contributing to their well-being.
- Interprets the natural and cultural heritage of the destination to visitor.
- Lends itself better to independent travelers, as well as to organized tours for small size groups'.

The number of principles can be very large, as for example in the above-mentioned list. There are 49 recommendations sorted into six categories in this document.

The first draft of a National Ecotourism Strategy for Australia presented in 1993 was built on a non-restricted ecotourism def-inition, *'Ecotourism is nature-based tourism that includes an educa-tional component and is managed to be sustainable'* (p. 15) and has four principles:

- Natural area component: the natural value of an area is in focus.
- Ecological sustainability: the carrying capacity of an area should not be exceeded or the biodiversity altered significantly.

- Education and interpretation: educational opportunities should be given to tourists and an appropriated level of environmental and cultural interpretation must be provided.
- Local and regional benefits: the benefits should be equitably distributed.

These principles were initially identified in ecotourism definitions presented by Ceballos-Lascurain (1991), Figgis (1993), Young (1992), and Valentine (1991)

One of the first Nordic ecotourism initiatives (started in 1994) used the ecotourism definition of WWF *'ecotourism is responsible traveling contributing to the protection of natural areas and the well-being of location populations'* and the appending 10 commands (Sæþórsdóttir *et al.*, 1998, p. 32), which are:

- Ecological and social sustainability shall be all-important (Group size).
- All travel companies should delegate responsibility for the environment to a particular employee and develop an environmental plan (Plan).
- Environmental responsibility also applies to subcontractors at the travel destination (Subcontractor agreements).
- Select environmentally adapted hotel sites (Accommodation).
- Genuinely knowledgeable guides are crucial (Guides).
- Support the local economy (Economy).
- Encourage a respectful attitude among travelers (visitors).
- Don't buy their lives (purchase/shopping).
- Ecotourism requires that travelers are well informed (education).
- Ecotourism shall contribute to the protection of the natural surroundings and local development (Protect and develop).

The Code of Conduct presented by WWF has been updated and today consists of the following list:

- The integration of tourism development and environmental conservation.
- Support the preservation and conservation of wilderness and biodiversity.
- Use natural resources in a sustainable way.
- Minimize consumption, waste, and pollution.
- Respect local cultures.
- Respect historic sites.

- Local communities should benefit from tourism.
- Choose tours with trained and professional staff.
- Make your trip an opportunity to learn about the area.
- Comply with regulations and follow safety rules (www. wwf.com).

Factors that have substantially influenced the development of ecotourism definitions are the global expansion of this tourism form and the recognition that tourism is a complex system consisting of a multitude of interests. Ecotourism was initially used in a Third World setting but is today a global phenomenon (Che, 2006) and the initially presented frameworks of actors involved in ecotourism (Björk, 1997) have been extended (see e.g. Planeta. com,www.planeta.com/ecotravel/tour/players. html). These circumstances, in combination with the fact that ecotourism is still discussed and used by both researchers and practitioners, have raised the standards for comprehensive definitions. No tourism area is alike, and to find a globally useful comprehensive definition is demonstrably difficult, especially if it also to be put in practice. Most of the 'homegrown' ecotourism definitions (e.g. Edwards *et al.* (1998)) analyzed were far less comprehensive than the appending policy documents. Their results indicate that (a) general definitions need specifying criteria and (b) it is not enough just to analyze the definitions in use (in an area) in order to understand how the ecotourism concept is interpreted and used, but the appending policy documents do also have to be included.

The content of ecotourism definitions

The many diverse ecotourism definitions presented in the literature have not only had a constructive effect, but also created a lot of uncertainty and confusion. One way to chisel out the founding principles of ecotourism has been to undertake content analysis of existing definitions and in so doing try to understand the concept. This has been practiced by Björk (1997) and Edwards *et al.* (1998) who used a set of questions and by means of the answers described ecotourism. Björk (2000) identified four core dimensions of ecotourism. These are the characteristics of the area visited, the behavior of the tourists, the object in focus and the outcome. The analysis Edwards *et al.* (1998, p. 3) carried out on the 'homegrown' ecotourism definitions of governmental tourism agencies in the Americas use resulted in a definitions-based conceptual model which consists of seven elements, that is questions policy-makers need to ask when developing ecotourism. The elements are:

WHO	needs to be involved in ecotourism policy development?
WHICH	are the principles we want to guide our development of ecotourism?
WHY	will individuals and organizations want to be involved in ecotourism?
WHERE	do we want ecotourism to take place?
WHAT	kind of activities should make up ecotourism?
HOW	should we deliver ecotourism, if at all?
SO WHAT	are the intended outcomes we want from eco-tourism and to whom or what should they accrue?

These questions were presented as essential to ask when developing ecotourism and the answers will ultimately define how ecotourism is developed. These questions, which are value-free, are most useful in combination with development directions dictated by comprehensive ecotourism definitions.

Fennell (2003), Diamantis (1999), and Sirakaya *et al.* (1999) used a more descriptive approach to identify the basic principles of ecotourism (Table 2.1).

The basic principles presented in Table 2.1 describe ecotourism as responsible, low-impact, small-scale, ethical, nature- and culture-based, educational and conservationist.

Björk (1997), Sirakaya *et al.* (1999), Weaver (2001), and Fennell (2003) compared a set of previously presented ecotourism definitions and out of a content analysis presented their own interpretation.

Ecotourism is 'an activity where the authorities, the tourism industry, tourists and local people cooperate to make it possible for tourists to travel to genuine areas in order to admire, study, and enjoy the nature and culture in a way that does not exploit the resources, but contributes to sustainable development'.

(Björk, 1997, p. 305)

'Ecotourism is a form of tourism that fosters learning experiences and appreciation of the natural environment, or some component thereof, within its associated cultural context. It has the appearance (in concert with best practice) of being environmentally and social-culturally sustainable, preferably in a way that enhances the natural and cultural resources base of the destination and promotes the viability of the operation'.

Weaver (2001, p. 15)

Table 2.1 Ecotourism dimensions/components/themes

Fennell (2003)	Diamantis (1999)	Sirakaya *et al.* (1999)
Interest in nature	Natural-based component (protected and non-protected natural areas)	Environmentally friendly tourism
Contribution to conservation	Sustainable management component (nature-centered approach)	Responsible travel
Reliance on parks and protected areas	Educational/interpretation component (educational programs)	Educational travel
Benefit local people/ long-term benefits		Low-impact travel
Education and study		Recreational and romantic trips to natural sites
Low-impact/ non-consumptive		Contribution to local welfare
Ethics/responsibility		Ecocultural travel
Management		Sustainable/ non-consumptive tourism
Sustainable		Responsible business approach to travel
Enjoyment/appreciation		Community involvement
Culture		Tourist involvement in preservation
Adventure		Buzzword
Small scale		Contribution to conservation

'Ecotourism is a sustainable form of natural resource-based tourism that focuses on experiencing and learning about nature, and which is ethically managed to be low-impact, non-consumptive, and locally oriented (control, benefits, and scale). It typically occurs in natural areas, and should contribute to the conservation or preservation of such areas'.

(Fennell, 2003, p. 25)

'Ecotourism is a new form of non-consumptive, educational, and romantic tourism to relatively undisturbed and undervisited areas of immense natural beauty, and cultural and historical importance for the purposes of understanding and appreciating the natural and socio-cultural history of the host destination'.

(Sirakaya et al., 1999, p. 171)

These comprehensive definitions can be modified and used as a base for country-specific definitions. Three examples are presented, the ecotourism definition of Kenya, Laos, and Australia.

Ecotourism in Kenya

Ecotourism is nature and culture-based tourism gically sustainable and supports the well-be...g or local communities. It appeals to visitors who want contact with nature, local communities and indigenous cultures. Ecotourism targets travelers with special interests who are looking for unique and authentic experiences. It takes into account the impacts of the visitor industry upon the environmental, social, cultural and economic fabrics of the local community and strives to conduct its activities in harmony with nature. Communities are therefore a key component of ecotourism (www.esok.org/?q=node/view/32).

Ecotourism in Laos

Tourism activity in rural and protected areas minimizes negative impacts and is directed toward the conservation of natural and cultural resources, rural socio-economic development and visitor understanding of, and appreciation for, the places they are visiting in Laos. (Laos National Tourism Administration, National Ecotourism Strategy and Action Plan, 2005–2010.)

Ecotourism in Australia

Ecotourism is ecologically sustainable tourism with a primary focus on experiencing natural areas that fosters environmental and cultural understanding, appreciation and conservation (www.ecotourism.org.au/) (NEAP).

The dimensions, components and themes identified in existing ecotourism definitions portray the map of ecotourism well. The basic principles of ecotourism described in ecotourism definitions are most often magnitude-free, that is the outcome of ecotourism is described in very general terms. Ecotourism, for example, should be managed 'to be low-impact' (Fennell, 2003). The question is how low is 'low'? To identify and define the maximum and minimum levels on the different ecotourism dimensions seems to be a much more demanding task than extending the definitions with another dimension. Indicators and recommendations for ecotourism can also be found in all those ecotourism labeling programs and award systems that are in use around the world (see e.g. Font and Buckley, 2001). Ecotourism labeling systems consist of benchmark criteria which have to be passed in order to be awarded. The aim of this chapter is not to discuss these criteria, but it is sufficient to say here that they have to be based on an understanding of what ecotourism stands for.

Ecotourism and related tourism forms

Ecotourism has been compared to many related tourism forms. Such an approach is justified because some of the basic principles of ecotourism are indeed shared with other tourism forms. However, ecotourism also has very unique, distinguishing dimensions. Ecotourism is related to nature, culture, farm, wildlife, and adventure tourism, and can be described as a sub-category of nature and culture tourism, a tourism form that can be practiced on farms or in wildlife, and consists of an adventurous nature. Different tourism forms are most often defined out of one dimension only. The descriptive terms nature, culture, farm, and wildlife tell us about the context of the tourism (where) and adventure about the performance (how to) (Table 2.2).

Ecotourism definitions, in comparison, are multidimensional. The outcome dimensions included in existing ecotourism definitions distinguish ecotourism from related tourism forms. Ecotourists travel to naturally beautiful areas as do nature tourists, but their visit should result in local benefits – environmentally, culturally as well as economically. The physical

Table 2.2 Different forms of tourism

Tourism form	Definition
Nature tourism	Travel to participate in outdoor activities utilizing the natural resources of an area (Ingram and Durst, 1987)
Culture tourism	Travel to areas where culture can be studied or participated in
Farm tourism	Travel to participate on a working farm (Busby and Rendle, 2000)
Wildlife tourism	Travel to areas where wildlife can be watched (Shackley, 1996)
Adventure tourism	Travel that involve risk, danger and adrenalin; a tourism that may require physical stamina (Kane and Zink, 2004)

environment is very much involved in ecotourism 'acting as the central focus of the product offering' (Peattie and Moutinho, 2000) as well as the well-being of the host population. The positive and negative local effects of ecotourism have been discussed in the literature. The outcome of ecotourism has also been discussed on a more general level, how ecotourism can be linked to the concepts of sustainability and sustainable development.

Ecotourism is a sub-category of sustainable tourism and thereby contributes to sustainable development and sustainability. Sustainability is an umbrella term that describes a situation when all human activities are practiced so that the society and its members are able to meet their needs and wants, while preserving environmental and socio-cultural systems indefinitely. Sustainable development was introduced in one of the seminal environmental documents of the 20th century, The Brundland Report (*Our Common Future*), and defined as 'to meet the needs and aspirations of the present without compromising the ability to meet those of the future'. This definition was later on used in the Agenda 21 program (*The United Nations Conference on Environment and Development 'UNCED'*, Earth Summit, 1992). A program that has been followed up in two special conferences *'Rio + 5'* and on the Earth Summit 2002, *'Rio + 10'*.

The Agenda 21 has been criticized for inhibiting a sustainable development by putting environment and development functions in separate categories, and uniting development and trade (not trade and environment). This separation of two central dimensions in sustainable development has filtered down to many of the existing sustainable tourism development programs and can today be picked up as a paradox even in ecotourism.

Sustainable tourism is in this chapter discussed as a final phase of a sustainable tourism development, when pre-defined principles and criteria, derived from the sustainability and sustainable development concepts, are fulfilled (Table 2.3).

It appears natural to incorporate ecotourism as a part of the sustainable tourism concept, but other tourism forms can also be defined as sustainable tourism. The criteria are the outcome of the practiced tourism. The alternative tourism concept has been used to embrace all those tourism forms that are more sustainable than mass tourism. This approach is very categorical: sustainable tourism on one side and mass tourism on the other. A central point here is that ecotourism is not an antithesis of mass tourism but a complementary part of the industry. The size of the tourist groups or the number of tourists visiting an

Table 2.3 Sustainable tourism and sustainable tourism development (selected definitions)

Sustainable tourism development (STD)	Sustainable tourism (ST)
Sustainable tourism development 'meets the needs of present tourists and host regions while protecting and enhancing opportunity for the future. It is envisaged as leading to management of all resources in such a way that economic, social, and esthetic needs can be fulfilled while maintaining cultural, integrity, essential ecological processes, biological diversity, and life support systems' (Agenda 21 for the travel & Tourism Industry – Towards Environmentally Sustainable Development, 1995, p. 30)	Sustainable tourism 'is conveniently defined as all types of tourism (conventional or alternative forms) that are compatible with or contribute to sustainable development' (Liu, 2003, p. 461)
Sustainable tourism development 'meets the goals of the present without compromising the ability of future generations to meet their own needs' (World Commission on Environment and Development, 1987, p. 43)	'all forms of tourism development, management and activity, which maintain the environmental, social and economic integrity and well-being of natural, built and cultural resources in perpetuity' (Heukemes, 1993, p. 5)
Sustainable tourism development 'will be: • Comprehensive: including social, cultural, environmental, economic, political implications • Iterative/Dynamic: readily responding to environmental and policy changes • Integrative: functioning within wider approaches to community development • Community oriented: all stakeholders needs addressed through community involvement • Renewable: incorporating principles which take into account the needs of future generations • Goal oriented: a portfolio of realistic targets results in equitable distribution of' benefits (Simpson, 2001, p. 7)	The definition implies that all concerned (owners of the industry, employees, tourists, hosts) benefit, resources are not over-consumed, that natural and human environments are protected, and that tourism is integrated with other activities (Eber, 1992, p. 2)
The success of STD is to analyze, plan and coordinate the following environments; the natural physical environment, the man-made physical environment and the living cultural environment (Misra, 1993)	Sustainable tourism 'shall be based on criteria of sustainability, which means that it must be ecologically bearable in the long term, as well as economically viable, and ethically and socially equitable for local communities' (Marin, 1995, p. 12)

area is not explicitly an issue in the presented ecotourism definitions (see e.g. Björk, 1997; Weaver, 2001; Fennell, 2003).

Ecotourism and practice, restrictive and shallow definitions

Ecotourism planners and managers need programs and guidelines for ecotourism development (see Best Practice Tour, 2000; Catalogue of exemplary Practices and Adventure Travel and Ecotourism, 1999). Recommendations for practice are most often extracted out of the ecotourism definitions in use. The operationalization aspects of ecotourism definitions have been debated. Restricted definitions with many and exact characteristics provide good support for the developers in those cases (areas) where the pre-requisites can be fulfilled, that is the definition is usable. Unfortunately, there are few such cases and the usefulness of restrictive ecotourism definitions may suffer because of their limited usability (only usable in a small number of situations). In response one can claim that ecotourism in a worldwide tourism perspective still is and should be kept as a niche market.

Shallow definitions are built on vague concepts and the appending criteria are very selective or do not have absolute minimum thresholds that have to be passed. These definitions are easier to apply and include more degrees of freedom when used in practice. The downside of these benefits is that their guiding power in an ecotourism management process is weak. Ecotourism development supported by development plans includes missions, visions, and strategies to be followed. A lack of guiding principles may result in anarchistic development that may disturb the balance between preservation and development.

There are four different approaches to sustainable development based on different types of sustainability, according to Hunter (1997). This trade-off approach to reasoning has also been applied to ecotourism. Diamantis and Westlake (2001, p. 34) presented four categories of trade-off definitions of ecotourism (from very weak to very strong) based on an evaluation of three dimensions (tourism area, educational dimension and level of sustainability) (Table 2.4).

Most of the presented definitions in this chapter belong to the 'strong' or 'very strong' categories as presented by Diamantis and Westlake (2001). There are also some other attempts to frame ecotourism as a continuum. Orams (1995) used a four-category framework. The opposing poles were 'All tourism is ecotourism' and 'Ecotourism impossible', and the two middle categories, to which existing ecotourism definitions belong, were 'passive ecotourism' and 'active ecotourism'. The level of human responsibility and

Table 2.4 Trade-off definitions of ecotourism

Different types of ecotourism	Tourism area	Educational dimension	Sustainable dimension
Very weak	Protected/ non-protected	Not present	Not present
Weak	Protected/ non-protected	Interpretation and training programs	Economic and/or socio-economic elements
Strong	Protected/ non-protected	Interpretation and training programs	Equal emphasis on economic and socio-cultural elements
Very strong	Protected/ non-protected	Interpretation and training programs	Emphasis on socio-cultural elements rather than on economic elements

Source: Diamantis and Westlake (2001, p. 34), modified layout.

outcomes were set as evaluation dimensions. The first definition of Ceballos-Lascurain (1987) describes a passive ecotourism. An example of an active ecotourism definition is the one presented by Ziffer (1989). Active ecotourism contributes to the protection of resources and the improvement of the natural environment. A passive ecotourism, on the other hand, seeks to minimize damage to the natural environment (Orams, 1995). Weaver (1999) used the continuum of Orams (1995) and 'opted for a liberal ecotourism model' an ecotourism that is sustainable in intention and that can take place in natural as well as in modified landscapes.

Another approach to ecotourism has been introduced by researchers who believe ecotourism can be classified along a deep and shallow axis. Acott, *et al.* (1998) present a classification framework which ranges from deep ecotourism to shallow ecotourism and mass tourism. Deep ecotourism is built on a strong sustainability position and all qualities are equally important. Nature in shallow ecotourism is 'valued according to its usefulness to humans' (Acott *et al.*, 1998, p. 244), and a decline of environmental quality can be accepted as long as other forms of capital can be increased. All steps in favor of a sustainable development must be considered but ecotourism, as defined today, does not accept a tourism that allows a degradation of any resources (capital) in the long run. All attempts to debilitate the criteria of ecotourism must be critically analyzed.

Change of perspective from development vs. preservation to a preservation and development

The concepts *development* and *preservation* are by connotation paradoxical. 'Action of preserving' and 'action of developing' are two opposing poles on a one-dimensional scale. A multidimensional approach on the other hand can be used to transform this relationship, and the new platform interlinks preservation and development.

Ecotourism has as an industry three goals according to Hvenegaard and Dearden (1998). The *natural and cultural* resources ecotourism is reliant on must be preserved; ecotourism must provide for *public access*, and *ecotourism firms* must be given a chance to survive. These three goals can be extended by a social dimension linked to the host community (Weaver, 2001; Fennell, 2003). Goals and interests can be combined. There are according to Cater (1995) at least four categories of interest involved in ecotourism. *Ecotourists* travel to experience unspoiled areas and for educational purposes (Saleh and Karwacki, 1996). *Organizations* involved in ecotourism use this tourism form for community development. The interest of the *host population* is based on the positive impacts ecotourism has on their social well-being, and the fourth category of interest is that of *nature and culture*. Björk (2000) added a fifth category of interests, that of the *tourism business*. Ecotourism management requires careful coordination of this multitude of interests and goals, and one dimension stressed in successful ecotourism development projects is the cooperation between different types of actors (governments, organizations, NGOs, tourists, tourism firms, residents, etc.) (Long, 1993; Weinberg *et al.*, 2002).

To frame the paradox of ecotourism as a conflict between ecological preservation and economic development is too simple. It is more a simultaneous discussion about ecological and economic preservation and development. The positive and negative impacts of ecotourism development have been identified in the literature (Boo, 1993) and categorized into four groups (Herbig and O'Hara, 1997). These are cultural, social (usually combined to socio-cultural effects), economic, and environmental impacts. The fine line between a positive and a negative impact is dependent on how the development and preservation is balanced. Too much or too little development, or too much or too little preservation will hamper a fruitful development. A fine-tuned impact framework is needed; a model that accepts that all impact variables are analyzed according to both the preservation and development perspectives (Table 2.5).

Table 2.5 The positive impacts of the preservation and development of ecotourism

Impact dimensions	Preservation implies	Development implies
Ecological	Conservation and improvement of biosystems	New natural parks and zones
		Access to new areas
Economic	To uphold traditional handicraft	New tourism firms
	Mitigation of seasonality effects	Influx of money
Cultural	Conservation of heritage sites and cultures	Restoration of cultural monuments, renewed pride in culture
	Maintenance of value-systems	New museums
Social	Preservation of social structures	Improvement of infrastructures and social well-being
	Maintenance of local control	

This discussion claims that ecotourism development is not just about finding a balance between the preservation of nature- and cultural-resources found in an area and a development of the economic and social dimensions. All outcome dimensions presented in Table 2.5 must be analyzed according to the preservation as well as development perspectives simultaneously.

Conclusion

Inappropriate ecotourism development degrades habitats and landscape, depletes natural resources, disturbs the economic system and generates waste and pollution. Ecotourism, managed and supported by all stakeholders, can take place in the absence of these elements of negative change. Ecotourism is one form of tourism among other forms of nature- and culture-based tourism. Ecotourism is not mass tourism, and can therefore not be the (only) solution to sustainable tourism development. Ecotourism is per definition sustainable, but this niche business is just a marginal phenomenon in a more general discussion on sustainability. Those who advocate for the development of ecotourism should pause to consider the possibility that sustainable mass tourism may have more positive environmental effects on a global level than ecotourism (see Becken and Schellhorn, this volume).

Our knowledge of ecotourism as a concept wi[ll]
by adding value-added prefixes, such as strong, we[ak],
or extreme ecotourism, or by specifying the area by [...]
Arctic, rural, or maritime ecotourism. All these kinds of specifications still include the ecotourism concept, and the terms added
just show that ecotourism can be developed for many different
types of areas. Lofty ecotourism definitions have been criticized
because they describe an ideal situation not a reality. Fennell
(2003) identifies two ways to solve this dilemma. One way is to
loosen up the criteria and modify the definitions to be more for-
giving. The second way is to consider existing restricted definitions as descriptions of a unique tourism form, found only in
selected areas on the globe. One argument for preserving these
comprehensive definitions is operational. All stakeholders in
ecotourism are not always equally well represented (with equal
negotiation power) in development projects, which could result
in the unequal distribution of benefits or neglect of interests of
some party. Even the goals to aim at may be unclear if the objectives are not well defined and on a level that satisfies all stakeholders. To just talk about a balance between ecological and
economical interests is not enough; the minimum level must also
be defined. This chapter is not in favor of a continuum approach
of ecotourism definitions, hard ecotourism on one side and soft
ecotourism on the other (Weaver, 2001). Passive ecotourists
making short stop-overs in natural areas do not amount to the
intention of a 'nature-centered approach' and/or the 'educa-
tional/interpretation component' (Diamantis, 1999). Edwards
et al. (1998, p. 49) conclude after having analyzed 42 different
definitions: 'we are not convinced that a universal definition is
ideal, since this would imply a definition that is mandated from
outside of a government agency, organization, or community'.
This argument is plausible considering the relevance of stakeholder support in general and government support in particular. Whale watching in Norway is not the same as trekking in
Nepal. Ecotourism is practiced in different ways in different
parts of the world, and is thereby applied to local conditions
(Edwards *et al.*, 1998). The input and support from the local
community is of utmost importance for a propitious ecotourism
development.

This chapter advocates an awareness of the fact that the ecotourism concept can be discussed on a theoretical as well as on an
operational level (how ecotourism is practiced). It is a utopia that
the research community would agree on one common definition,
although Fennell (2002, p. 4) claims that 'there appears to be a
growing level of comfort regarding what ecotourism is and how
it should be operationalized'. At the same time we have to accept

that the sets of principles derived from ecotourism definitions are area dependent and must be adapted. Finally, as in all theoretical concept discussions, we have to recognize the stance of WWF that 'while definitions can be useful, what is more important is the appropriateness and quality of action, not what it is called' (WWF International, 2001, p. 2).

References

Acott, T.G., La Trobe, H.L. and Howard, S.H. (1998). An evaluation of deep ecotourism and shallow ecotourism. *Journal of Sustainable Tourism* 6(3): 238–253.

Best Practice Tour (2000). *In Adventure Travel and Ecotourism.* Report prepared by The Economic Planning Group of Canada on behalf of the Canadian Tourism Commission, July.

Björk, P. (1997). Marketing of finnish eco-resorts. *Journal of Vacation Marketing* 3(4): 303–313.

Björk, P. (2000). Ecotourism from a conceptual perspective, and extended definition of a unique tourism form. *International Journal of Tourism Research* 2(3): 189–202.

Blamey, R.K. (1997). Ecotourism: the search for an operational definition. *Journal of Sustainable Tourism* 5(2): 109–130.

Boo, E. (1993). World Wildlife Fund's Involvement in Ecotourism Projects. *10th General Assembly*, Bali, Indonesia, 30 September–9 October. *Round Table on Planning for Sustainable Tourism Development.* World Tourism Organization.

Busby, G. and Rendle, S. (2000). The transition from tourism on farms to farm tourism. *Tourism Management* 21: 635–642.

Catalogue of Exemplary Practices and Adventure Travel and Ecotourism. Report prepared by Pam Wight & Associates on behalf of the Canadian Tourism Commission, March 1999.

Cater, E. (1995). Introduction. In Cater, E. and Lowman, G. (eds), *Ecotourism, a Sustainable Option?* John Wiley & Sons, Ltd., Baffins Lane, Chichester, pp. 3–17.

Ceballos-Lascurain, H. (1987). The future of ecotourism. *Mexico Journal* (January), 13–14.

Ceballos-Lascurain, H. (1991). Tourism, ecotourism and protected areas. *Parks* 2(3): 31–35.

Ceballos-Lascurain, H. (1996). Tourism, Ecotourism and Protected Areas. International Union for Conservation of Nature and Natural Resources, Gland, Switzerland.

Che, D. (2006). Developing ecotourism in First World, resource-dependent areas. *Geoforum* 37: 212–226.

Diamantis, D. (1999). The concept of ecotourism: evolution and trends. *Current Issues in Tourism* 2(2&3): 93–122.

Diamantis, D. and Westlake, J. (2001). Ecolabelling in the context of sustainable tourism and ecotourism. In Font, X. and Buckley, R. (eds), *Tourism Ecolabelling, Certification and Promotion of Sustainable Management*. CABI Publishing, Wallingford, UK, pp. 27–40.

Eber, S. (1992). *Beyond the Green Horizon. Principles for Sustainable Tourism*. WWF, UK.

Edwards, S.N., McLaughlin, W.J. and Ham, S.H. (1998). Comparative Study of Ecotourism Policy in the Americas – 1998. Inter-Sectoral Unit for Tourism Organization of American States. Department of Resource Recreation and Tourism College of Forestry, Wildlife and Range Resources, University of Idaho.

Fennell, D. (2001). A content analysis of ecotourism definitions. *Current Issues in Tourism* 4(5): 403–421.

Fennell, D. (2002). Ecotourism: where we've been; where we're going. *Journal of Ecotourism* 1(1): 1–6.

Fennell, D. (2003). *Ecotourism*. Routledge, London.

Figgis, P. (1993). Ecotourism: special interest or major direction? *Australia*, (February): 8–11.

Font, X. and Buckley, R.C. (2001). *Tourism Ecolabelling, Certification and Promotion of Sustainable Management*. CABI Publishing, Wallingford, UK.

Herbig, P. and O'Hara, B. (1997). Ecotourism: a guide for marketers. *European Business Review* 97(5): 231–236.

Hetzer, W. (1965). Environment, tourism, culture. *Links* (July), 1–3.

Heukemes, N. (1993). Living them to death? *Sustainable Tourism in Europe's Nature and National Parks*. Federation of Nature and National Parks of Europe (FNNPE).

Hunter, C. (1997). Sustainable tourism as an adaptive paradigm. *Annals of Tourism Research* 24(4): 850–867.

Hvenegaard, G.Y. and Dearden, P. (1998). Ecotourism versus tourism in a Thai national park. *Annals of Tourism Research* 25(3): 700–720.

Ingram, C. and Durst, P. (1987). *Nature Oriented Travel to Developing Countries*. FPEI Working Paper No. 28. Southeastern Center for Forest Economics Research, Research Triangle Park, NC .

Kane, M.J. and Zink, R. (2004). Package adventure tours: markers in serious leisure careers. *Leisure Studies* 23(4): 329–345.

Liu, Z. (2003). Sustainable tourism development: a critique. *Journal of Sustainable Tourism* 11(6): 459–475.

Long, V. (1993). Careful planning guides ecotourism development in Punta Lagu. *Business Mexico* 3(1): 23–27.

Marin, C. (1995). Charter for sustainable tourism. *World Conference on Sustainable Tourism*, Lanzarote, Spain.

Misra, S.K. (1993). Heritage preservation in sustainable tourism development. *10th General Assembly*, Bali, Indonesia, 30 September–9 October. *Round Table on Planning for Sustainable Tourism Development*. World Tourism Organization.

Orams, M. (1995). Towards a more desirable form of ecotourism. *Tourism Management* 16(1): 3–8.

Peattie, K. and Moutinho, L. (2000). The marketing environment for travel and tourism. In Moutinho, L. (ed.) *Strategic Management in Tourism*. CABI Publishing, Wallingford, UK, pp. 17–37.

Sæþórsdóttir, A.D., Gísladóttir, G., Grönningsaeter, G., Zettersten, G. and Högmander, J. (1998). Ekoturism i Norden. Exempel från Island, Norge, Sverige och Finland. Nord 1998: 13. Nordiska Ministerrådet, Köpenhamn, Danmark.

Saleh, F. and Karwacki, J. (1996). Revisiting the ecotourist: the case of Grasslands National Park. *Journal of Sustainable Tourism* 4(2): 61–80.

Shackley, M. (1996). *Wildlife Tourism*. International Thomson Business Press, Berkshire House, London, UK.

Simpson, K. (2001). Strategic planning and community involvement as contributors to sustainable tourism development. *Current Issues in Tourism* 4(1): 3–41.

Sirakaya, E., Sasidharan, V. and Sönmez, S. (1999). Redefining ecotourism: the need for a supply-side view. *Journal of Travel Research* 38: 168–172.

Valentine, P. (1991). Nature-based tourism. In Hall, M. and Weiler, B. (eds), *Special Interest Tourism*. Belhaven Press, London, UK.

Weaver, D. (1999). Magnitude of ecotourism in Costa Rica and Kenya. *Annals of Tourism Research* 26(4): 792–816.

Weaver, D. (2001). *Ecotourism*. John Wiley & Sons Australia, Ltd., Milton.

Weinberg, A., Bellows, S. and Ekster, D. (2002). Sustaining ecotourism: insights and implications from two successful case studies. *Society and Natural Resources* 15: 371–380.

World Tourism Organization (2001). Tourism Satellite Account: Recommended Methodological Framework. WTO.

WWF International (2001). *Guidelines for Community-Based Ecotourism Development*. WWF International.

Young, M. (1992). Ecotourism – Profitable conservation? *Proceedings of Ecotourism Business in the Pacific Conference*. University of Auckland, Auckland.

Ziffer, K (1989). Ecotourism: the uneasy alliance. Conservation International. Ernst & Young, Washington, DC.

Internet references

www.twnside.org.sg	TWN=Third World Network
www.esok.org/?q=node/view/32	Ecotourism in Kenya
www. wwf.com	WWF
www.ecotourism.org.au/	NEAP

CHAPTER 3

Ecotourism as a western construct

Erlet Cater

Introduction

The endorsement of ecotourism by the United Nations through the designation of 2002 as the International Year of Ecotourism (IYE) bears testament to the internationalization of an approach which is deeply embedded in western cultural, economic, and political processes. Concern was voiced from several quarters over the seeming legitimization of ecotourism by the UN, with Southern NGOs, in particular, expressing their concern that the floodgates would be opened to eco-opportunistic western exploitation. In a letter to Kofi Annan the Thailand-based Third World Network (TWN) expressed their view that:

> Because nature-based tourism is one of the world's most lucrative niche markets, powerful transnational corporations are likely to exploit the IYE to impose their own definitions of ecotourism, while people-centred initiatives will be squeezed out... Ecotourism's 'bad' policies and practices far outweigh the 'good' examples. We fear that the IYE, in combination with the globalization policies, will make things worse... We demand a complete review of ecotourism issues that take into consideration the political, social, economic and developmental conditions and the serious issues of globalisation.
>
> (TWN, 2001).

Vivanco (2002, p. 26) voiced concern that the IYE did not 'confront the structural inequalities that characterize ecotourism's origins and practice' and that it attempted 'to force people everywhere into the same cultural, economic and political mould'. How has ecotourism come to occupy such a centre-stage position globally? Both the TWN letter and the quote from Vivanco point to the main reason: ecotourism is but a process cast in a world where relationships of power are characterized by marked centre–periphery dominance. There is a lot to suggest that, because the origins of ecotourism lie in western ideology and values, and its practice is frequently dominated by western interests, the advocacy of ecotourism as a universal template arises from western hegemony. This is reflected in the institutionalization of ecotourism through influential and powerful, supranational organizations, western donor agencies, INGOs, NGOs, and industry alliances, often working in partnership which strengthens their influence yet further. An examination of these reveals how, and why, this has come about.

Ecotourism as cultural hegemony

The pervasive influence of western-envisaged ecotourism needs to be viewed against the backdrop of the global political economy. To paraphrase Blaikie (2000, p. 1043), who is examining the reasons for the global dominance of the neoliberal development agenda in general, 'the most powerful reasons why, in my view, are provided by political economy.... Theories, narratives, pol-icies and institutions – the global power-knowledge nexus – drive, and are driven by, global capital'. Jessop (2003, p. 16) describes how globalization involves the processes of both 'time-space distanciation' and 'time-space compression'. The former involves 'the stretching of social relations over time and space so that relations can be controlled or coordinated over longer periods of time ... and over longer distances, greater areas, or more scales of activity' while the latter involves 'the intensification of 'discrete' events in real time and/or the increased velocity of material and immaterial flows over a given distance'. So we can see that not only does western power and knowledge have a global reach, but also how that scope has become intensified, or deepened, and speeded up. The process is both circular and cumulative whereby centre–periphery dominance is both perpetuated and reinforced precisely because 'differential abilities to compress time and space become major bases of power and resistance in the emerging global order' (Jessop, 2003).

It is not surprising, therefore, that Euro-American paradigms of sustainability and development, and, very much associated with both of these, the western construct of ecotourism, have become all powerful and persuasive. Mowforth and Munt (2003) refer to the 'tripartite marriage' between sustainability, globalization and development. They claim that sustainability is 'a concept charged with power.... The crucial questions must remain: Who defines what sustainability is? How is it to be achieved? And who has ownership of its representation and meaning?' These questions therefore apply to sustainable tourism and hence to ecotourism. Global governance institutions play increasingly significant roles in mainstreaming sustainability as they 'involve the production, but more importantly the enforcement, of a global ideological framework' (Hartwick and Peet, 2003). This is particularly so with the case of environmental concern which, as Hartwick and Peet (2003) describe, was 'ideologically and institutionally incorporated into the global neoliberal hegemony of the late 20th century' such that 'the global capitalist economy can grow, if not with clear environmental conscience, then with one effectively assuaged'. This they describe as a process of neoliberal deflection which is evident in the 'legitimizing camouflage' as Rist describes it (cited in Mowforth and Munt, 2003) of the term sustainable development. Southgate and Sharpley (2002) describe the mainstreaming of sustainable development, lamenting that 'The perpetuation of sustainable development's underlying assumptions has achieved little more than justifying conventional top-heavy, interventionist approaches to environmental and developmental initiatives in much of the developing world, reinforcing public acceptance of sustainable development initiatives, and the institutions vested with responsibility for implementing it'.

This criticism is equally applicable to sustainable tourism. Bianchi (2004) highlights how 'international tourism development and indeed sustainable tourism discussions have been dominated by organizations with an implicit, and at times explicit, faith in neoliberal trickle-down economics and hostility to regulation'. Hall (2005) calls for an 'examination of the role of the supranational organizations such as the World Tourism Organization (WTO) and the World Travel and Tourism Council (WTTC) in enhancing the power and privileges of local elites in developing countries and their promotion of the myth of sustainable tourism'. The fact that the WTO achieved international legitimacy through its designation as a specialized agency of the United Nations in 2003, changing its acronym to UNWTO in 2005, is evidence of its global reach. Furthermore, we witness the deepening, or implosive phase as Hoogvelt (1997) describes it, of globalization as western-based electronic media instantly communicate awareness of WTO and WTTC initiatives across the globe. This is graphically illustrated by the promotion of the WTO/UNEP guide *Making Tourism Sustainable: a Guide for Policy Makers*, to be published in September 2005, by TravelWireNews (3 October 2005). The potential of electronic newsletters to intensify as well as consolidate the influence of western tourism ideology is evident when it is considered that by 2005 the US-based TravelWireNews and eTurboNews had a circulation of 214,000 to travel trade professionals and 7,300 journalists around the globe (having grown from 26,000, mostly US, subscribers at launch in 2001).

The declared purpose of the forthcoming WTO/UNEP publication is 'to provide tourism decision makers with guidance and a framework for the development of policies for more sustainable tourism, a toolbox of instruments that they can use to implement these policies... a basic reference book [which] provides a blueprint for governments to formulate and implement sustainable tourism policies'. Whilst it will draw on a research survey undertaken among WTO member states in 2003 and 2004 'to identify specific policies and tools applied in their territories that had effectively contributed to making their tourism sector more sustainable' this was obviously conducted within existing power structures both between and within nations. It is significant that the WTO refers to this forthcoming publication as 'a blueprint'. The title of the World Tourism and Travel Council's (WTTC) 2003 publication *Blueprint for New Tourism* even more explicitly spells out this notion of a universal template.

WTTC has consistently lobbied for the expansion of travel infrastructure, the liberalization of policies to encourage tourism industry growth and the removal of physical, bureaucratic and fiscal barriers to travel (Mowforth and Munt, 2003). As a strong advocate of self-regulation, WTTC launched its Green Globe scheme in 1994 which introduced standards for environmental management in travel and tourism in 1998. While it is not the intention of this chapter to enter into the heated debate surrounding tourism certification and accreditation schemes, it is pertinent to reflect that such endorsements 'may be used to further enfranchise the powerful tourism companies' (Honey and Rome, 2001). Detractors of the certification and accreditation process voice their concern that it is 'a method to exclude, to cartelise and to club so that the weak lose their autonomy and come under the hegemony of the strong' (Rao, 2001). Pleumaron (2001) calls for certification to be seen 'in the context of the parallel push for self-regulation by transnational tourism companies and big business associations such as WTTC and PATA'. Both of these views, therefore, reflect on the inherent structural inequalities at play.

So, it is against the backdrop of the global power-knowledge nexus (Blaikie, 2000) that we need to critically examine ecotourism as a western construct. Because it may be seen to both reinforce and be reinforced by western hegemony, as Duffy (2002, p. 156) suggests, 'like other neoliberal policies, ecotourism creates a series of problems'. We have considered the influence of supranational institutions above, and turn now to examine how ecotourism has been mainstreamed by other agencies with both a global reach and an intensifying influence.

It is strange to reflect that, until the early 1990s, tourism was seen as an inappropriate avenue for donor finance. With increasing recognition of the conservation/development nexus, and a growing engagement with the need to enhance rural livelihoods through sustainable resource utilization, western envisaged ecotourism captured the attention of international funding bodies as an attractive prospect. In 1992, for example, the International Resources Group (IRG) prepared a report for USAID on ecotourism as a viable alternative for the sustainable management of natural resources in Africa (IRG, 1992).

However, Mowforth and Munt (2003, p. 60) describe how environmental conditions and caveats which are placed on western loans and grants promote a greening of social relations which may be viewed as 'a kind of eco-structural adjustment where Third World people and places must fall in line with First World thinking'. This is particularly evident with the lending of supranational institutions such as the Global Environmental Facility (GEF) of the World Bank. The GEF is a financial mechanism that provides grants and concessional funds to recipients from developing countries and countries in transition for projects and activities that aim to protect the global environment. Webster (2003) describes how Russia's greatest protected areas (zapovedniks), which were strict scientific reserves during the communist era, have been opened to ecotourism as a result of a $20m grant from the GEF in 1996 for biodiversity conservation. He cites Ostergren's argument that 'the World Bank and the Russian government are making poor, unrealistic assumptions that succumb to the myth that nature can be protected through free market mechanisms'. Amongst the paradoxes with the GEF is the fact that the World Bank manages the fund (it is implemented by UNDP and UNEP) and yet the World Bank is simultaneously a massive promoter of energy and forest projects, and operates without adequate environmental safeguards effectively implemented in its lending. Ironically, the fund has been used to mitigate environmental problems arising from new projects funded by the World Bank and other institutions (Down to Earth, 2001). In Pakistan, the building of dams and barrages under the Indus Basin Project, funded by contributions from the World Bank and other donors, as well as necessitating the wholesale relocation of a considerable number of settlements, disrupted the distinctive livelihoods of the Indus boat people. GEF Small Grants Projects (SGP) funds have been allocated to an ecotourism initiative at Taunsa barrage to create alternative livelihoods for these boat people in a sanctuary for the Indus River Dolphin (GEF/SGP, undated).

Tickell, cited in Mowforth and Munt (2003, p. 151), highlights how control of GEF funds by the World Bank leads to the imposition of a neoliberal First World environmental agenda on the allocation of those funds. Furthermore, control is tightened yet further by the fact that, while the donor agencies oversee investment projects and administer funds, it is frequently the case that they link with major INGOs to implement conservationist policies. USAID, for example, frequently channels funding through the World Wildlife Fund. Seven ecotourism projects in the Russian Far East were funded by USAID through the WWF 'to develop infrastructure, partner Russian and American tour companies, involve indigenous populations in tourism services, and provide mobile equipment for camping in remote areas' (ee-environment, 2001). Ecotourism featured as one of the eight activity areas of WWF in Brazil in the year 2000, where WWF was the largest grantee of USAID. One of the most bizarre partnerships was that involved in the development of a community-based ecotourism enterprise in Gunung Halimun National Park (GHNP), Java, Indonesia. Membership of the initiating Consortium of Ecotourism Development in GHNP, as well as government and NGOs, included McDonalds Restaurant, Indonesia! Technical assistance and support to the project came from WWF, The Nature Conservancy and World Resources Institute, with funding from USAID (Joy, 1997).

The environmental agenda of the First World INGOs obviously reflects the views of their members or supporters. Thus 'Through membership of such organizations, or through a general empathy with their aims, the global concerns and consciousness of First World citizens are played out at a local scale; their "will" is imposed upon communities thousands of miles away' (Mowforth and Munt, 2003, p. 30).

Conservation International (CI) is a classic case in point. Supported by mega donations such as that of $261 million in 2001 by the cofounder of Intel, Gordon Moore, CI's mission is 'to conserve the Earth's living natural heritage, our global biodiversity, and to demonstrate that human societies are able to live harmoniously with nature' (Conservation International, 2004). CI's links with the World Bank lead them to adopt its approach of advocating corporate schemes, including tourism and ecotourism, which give total management control to the private or NGO sector. In doing so they fail to recognize the existence of village conservation movements opposing development projects or the rights of indigenous peoples (Mowforth and Munt, 2003, pp. 152, 278).

Lowe (2006) describes how in 1994 the Jakarta offices of CI (as well as those of WWF and TNC) had Euro-American administrators. While this situation had changed by 1997, so that Indonesian directors oversee domestic programs, the power of western ideology may still hold sway under the guise of 'conventional' wisdom adopted by professionals worldwide. Mowforth and Munt (2003) examine how tourism professionals comprised 'not just operators in the industry but consultants, journalists, tourism commentators, academics and charities' who are 'the opinion formers, the teachers, the advisers, even the ones who take decisions'. They cite the influence of a professional membership NGO with a dedicated ecotourism remit that has become increasingly international in its reach since its inception in 1990. The US-based The Ecotourism Society changed its name to The *International* Ecotourism Society (author's italics) in the year 2000. Overseas institutional membership of TIES (it also has individual professional members) listed by region of work or research of 103 in 1994 (The Ecotourism Society, 1995) increased to 443 by 2003 (The International Ecotourism Society, 2003). What is also quite telling, however, is that, whereas 119 North American institutions listed their region of work or research as North America in 2003, 195 gave their residence in North America, indicating that 76, or just under 40%, of North American member institutions have interests elsewhere in the world. Given that the institutional members also include other powerful First World interests such as CI, The Nature Conservancy, and WWF, it is inevitable that western-centric views are likely to prevail. Although, as Mowforth and Munt (2003) point out, the ethos of TIES is how to do ecotourism 'right', this is largely within existing power relations which may exacerbate and perpetuate inequalities.

While we need to recognize that hegemony is neither total nor static, but should be viewed as dynamic and evolving toward a 'stable equilibrium' (Johnston *et al.*, 1994), it is undeniable that the power relations described above currently give rise to a situation where western ideology concerning ecotourism is dominant and all powerful. Cohen (2002) echoes this concern with regard to the concept of sustainability in tourism development in general, arguing that it is open to misuses, 'not only in the obvious sense of misleading or fraudulent promotion, but in the more insidious sense of its use as an instrument of power in the struggle over rare and valuable environmental or cultural resources'.

The danger of pointing the finger of blame solely at the western world also needs to be recognised, however. Richter (1989) examines how many nation states in Asia, for example, have used tourism as a tool to elevate their status in international relations, and, as Teo (2002) argues 'in the discourse on global–local dynamics, it is propitious to ask whether such a view overlooks the role that national economies have moulded for themselves within the global capitalist framework'. In the month immediately following the catastrophic tsunami that hit the coastlines of the Indian Ocean on 26 December 2004 the significance that the region and individual countries affected attach to international tourism became immediately evident. Not long after the disaster the president of PATA declared 'If you want to help us, book your trip now', while the chairman of the Sri Lankan Tourist Board, launching the tourism 'Bounce-Back' campaign, announced under a month later 'the country is open for business in a big way' (Sri Lanka Tourism, 2005). If anything, however, these overtures serve to highlight the extent to which individual nation states are enmeshed in the global tourism industry. The Sri Lankan government's proposed US$80 million redevelopment of Arugam Bay on the east coast has met with resistance from local villagers. A local guest house owner declares 'We don't want mass tourism with luxury hotels. We would rather promote community-based tourism' (Raheem quoted in Tourism Concern, 2005). There is also concern that affected coastal populations throughout the region, faced with a loss of traditional livelihoods, may also be faced with being moved from where they lived to make way for tourism development as reconstruction proceeds (Tourism Concern, 2005). Hoogvelt's pointed observation that 'We may try to understand and improve the conditions of life of those who live within our world system, we cannot even think about those who live outside it' (Hoogvelt, 1985) has poignant resonance for those so blatantly excluded from the global economy.

Mowforth and Munt (2003) argue that it is with environmental conservation that tour companies and tourists have discovered the most effective method of exclusion, or 'inclusiveness'. This is clearly reflected in the trend towards elitism in ecotourism operations.

Ecotourism as an elitist construct

Whatever the calls for ecotourism operations to be basic and low key in theory, there is a marked tendency for it to translate into being expensive and exclusive in practice. Cohen (2002, pp. 272–273) examines how, as pristine, 'undiscovered' sites become increasingly more difficult to find, their rarity means that they constitute a 'new economic resource' and unspoiled sites harbouring particularly valuable natural or cultural attractions tend to become the most expensive ones.

Two recent contenders for a major tourism industry award for sustainable tourism initiatives bear witness to this fact. Cousine Island Resort, in the Seychelles describes itself as 'Seychelles' premier private island resort. This remote island can be reached only by private charter helicopter. . . Resort occupancy is limited to 10 guests'. The peak season rate for this exclusivity is US$1,280 per person per night (asiatravel, 2004). Tiger Mountain Lodge is situated 1000 feet above the Pokhara valley in Nepal. The 19-room lodge commands panoramic views of the Himalaya. As well as entering the 2003 Sustainable Tourism award, Tiger Mountain Lodge has won several awards including the Conde Nast Traveller magazine Ecotourism Award 2000, and Highly Commended Status for the Conservation International Ecotourism Excellence Awards 2000. Given the outstanding natural setting of the lodge, it is staggering, however, to find that 'There is a secluded swimming pool, in a strategic site that reflects the high mountains and drops away to the Bijaypur River below' (The Travel Mall, 2004). The exclusivity and exclusionary nature of both locations is evident when we find that Paul McCartney and Heather Mills spent their honeymoon at the former, while Princess Anne stayed at the latter in 2000.

While the environmental performance of such upmarket locales may be laudable, state-of-the-art eco-technology does not come cheap. The operator of Lao Pako ecotourism lodge, Lao PDR estimated that it would take at least 2 years to recover the outlay required to install imported solar panels and heavy-duty back-up batteries (W. Pfabigan, Lao Pako, 1997, personal communication). The gap between grassroots initiatives and locales backed by wealthy, often western, investors widens still further, and will only be accentuated by applying western standards of environmental performance in the certification schemes mentioned above.

It is undeniable that the visiting elite gain considerable social capital from visiting such exclusive locations. Inevitably, this may lead to the view that they are 'places to be collected, as if the people who live there are either irrelevant or at best incidental to the place' (Mowforth and Munt, 2003, p. 211). Rather than the essential requirement of active participation to generate local benefits the picture is frequently one of passive recipience or patronization. Even local inputs, such as agricultural products, are unlikely to meet the high-quality criteria demanded by an up-market clientele. Consequently 'the benefits accruing to the local community, even if significant relative to other sources of income, usually constitute only a fraction of the profits generated by the enterprise' (Cohen, 2002, p. 273). Furthermore, tourism to such rare and valuable sites may be environmentally sustainable, but effectively using the price mechanism to restrict numbers and thus guaranteeing low density and exclusivity restricts participation to a tiny minority of elite tourists. As Cohen (2002, pp. 273–274) points out, not only does this 'block access to such sites to the vast majority of potential visitors who cannot afford the costs' but also such discrimination excludes 'not only foreign visitors who cannot afford the price, but especially domestic ones'.

Ecotourism as a form of patronization

There has been considerable disappointment registered concerning the failure of ecotourism to deliver its promises in terms of locally realized benefits and enhanced local livelihoods. Wells and Brandon (1992) document how an analysis of

23 Integrated Conservation–Development Projects (ICDPs), most with ecotourism components, revealed that few benefits went to local people or served to enhance protection of adjacent wildlands. It is usually the case that active local participation is overwhelmingly confined to low-skilled, low-paid, often seasonal, employment. Also the gap between those who are so engaged and those not involved in tourism in the community is likely to widen. Entus (2002), for example, describes how pre-existing divisions of power may be engendered or exacerbated, leading to the formation of new business elites, who represent a small fraction of the local community. Nepal *et al.* (2002) show that a large lodge operator in the Annapurna region of Nepal will receive an annual income of over ten times that of a trekking porter and more than 40 times that of an agricultural labourer. Nyaupane and Thapa (2004) found in a survey of residents of the Annapurna Sanctuary Trail that 68% of respondents strongly agreed that income distribution was unequal in the area.

Benefits to the community at large by way of visitor donations may be viewed as tokenist patronization. For example, however well-meaning, the raising of funds from guests staying at Ol Donyo Wuas Lodge, Chyulu Hills in Kenya to cover medical expenses for members of the Maasai Group Ranch on which the lodge is located may be viewed as such, particularly when the lodge boasts of 'exclusive use of the 300,000 acre ranch which means approximately 17,000 acres per guest, so no worries about the crowds' (Ultimate Africa Safaris, 2004). This is especially so when local scouts are trained to patrol the area for 'bushmeat poachers', while guests can participate in shooting safaris – one rule for the rich, another for the poor. . .

Fundamentally, the idea that participation is a cure-all for political and social exclusion has been increasingly challenged. Mowforth and Munt (2003, p. 214) suggest that local participation may not be working, citing Taylor's view that this is because 'it has been promoted by the powerful, and is largely cosmetic..... but most ominously it is used as a "hegemonic" device to secure compliance to, and control by, existing power structures'. Participatory approaches are, in themselves, part of these power structures and consequently 'programmes designed to bring the excluded in often result in forms of control that are more difficult to challenge, as they reduce spaces of conflict and are relatively benign and liberal' (Kothari, 2001, p. 143). Walley (2004, p. 264) in her analysis of the 'social drama' of the Mafia Island Marine Park also draws attention to the fact that all that we are witnessing may be a repackaging of the status quo such that 'the merging of conservation and development agendas, the isolation of ecotourism as a development strategy, and the role of participation and transnational bureaucracies, are not ruptures, but rather build upon and work through existing and historical institutional structures and power relationships'.

The view that outsiders may have of traditional lifestyles may also be viewed as patronizing. In the same way that anti-developmentalists romanticize the lifestyles of indigenous peoples (Corbridge, 1995) so, too, may western-constructed eco-tourism assume an artificial, 'zooified' lifestyle on local populations, simultaneously assuming that the poor are happy as they are. This approach tends to ignore local peoples' aspirations for higher living standards founded on a clear understanding of the costs and benefits of development. As Brandon and Margoluis (1996) suggest, wholesale, unconditional acceptance of eco-tourism as a sole development strategy by local people is both unlikely and unrealistic. Poor households income needs are not fixed and they are likely to aspire beyond just holding their own economically. Consequently, they may divert to, or supplement with, other, less sustainable activities, particularly when the dimension of seasonality of tourism visitation is added into the equation. Furthermore, the romanticization of traditional ways of life by western ecotourists seeking 'otherness' frequently does not resonate with local attitudes. Christine Walley records a divergence of views, as locals were 'puzzled by the penchant of *wazungu* (Euro-American) visitors to Mafia go to "deserted" places and to prize photographs of peopleless landscapes... In short the people on Mafia did not share the romance for "nature" found among those who seek refuge from "modernity" in the natural environment' (Walley, 2004, pp. 140–144). In addition, those things which Mafia residents associated with poverty, for example cloth sails rather than outboard engines, were instead perceived as valuable forms of 'tradition' by many visitors, attractive precisely because of their difference from 'modern development' (Walley, 2004, p. 224). A fundamental issue here, as Hall and Tucker (2004, p. 8) highlight, is that such building of 'binary opposites is to make one dependent on the other. There cannot be consumption without production'.

One of the principles of ecotourism is that it should incorporate an educative component (Page and Dowling, 2002). However, while there is increasing recognition that indigenous knowledge is an important component of interpretation, it is undeniable that, once again, western views prevail and assume that First World conceptions of management are superior (Mowforth and Munt, 2003, p. 148). It is vital that it is recognized that education is a two-way process and that there is much to be learned from the long histories of ecological management undertaken by local indigenous communities. Indeed, it is necessary to recognize the inextricability of the natural and the cultural in eco-tourism localities (Hall, 1994). It is suggested, for example, that the islanders of Ono, Kadavu province, Fiji were more amenable to the concept of a no-take zone in the establishment of a marine protected area because it reflected their traditional practice of *tabu ni qoliqoli*, reserving a traditional fishing ground in order to increase the fish population for a traditional ceremony (WWF, undated).

Culture and ecology

So, we are faced with a situation where the dominant, western-centric, environmental imagination has given rise to what Vivanco (2002) calls ecotourism's 'universalistic and self-serving vision'. The danger of this ethnocentric bias is that it ignores the fact that there are 'multiple natures' constructed variously by different societies. As Macnaghten and Urry (1998, p. 95) declare 'there is no single "nature", only natures. And these natures are not inherent in the physical world but discursively constructed through economic, political and cultural processes'. Walley (2004, p. 14) draws attention to the dynamics of 'the ways in which ideas of development, nature, and participation are var-iously understood, appropriated, disputed and used'. Lowe (2006) describes how 'any understanding of nature will always depend upon processes of representation and the perspectives and actions of those claiming or attempting to represent such nature'. She goes on to argue that 'the knowledges, rationalities, and natures in Southern biodiversity conservation cannot be understood through the language of assimilation or adaptation in the tropics of a project that originated in more temperate climates'.

Sofield (1996) describes how in the Solomon Islands 'the trad-itions of the Melanesian villagers are so interlinked with their forests, coastal reefs and associated habitats that these features are regarded as their most important social and economic resources' and cites Baines observations in Fiji that the land, adja-cent reefs, and lagoons, and the resources therein, together with the people, constituted a single, integrated entity.

In attempting to engage with different constructs of nature by different societies, Walley (2004) asked men on Chole island, Mafia, Zanzibar, what they believed about 'nature'. Most of them, having been fishers at some point in their lives, gave detailed descriptions of fishing gear, of wind directions, and types of fish. Although this practical knowledge did not convert easily into a conception of 'nature', she points out that this does not automatically mean that they do not appreciate nature, recording, for example, how local boat passengers registered excitement on viewing a school of dolphins.

The crucial issue with western envisaged ecotourism is that it can fail to recognize, or downplays, the fundamentally divergent values and interests between the promoters and targets of ecotourism. The dominant ideology behind ecotourism of conservation-for-development may quite often not resonate with other, non-western, societies. As a North American indigenous person declares 'that is not necessarily consistent with our traditional view of guardianship and protection' (Taylor cited in Vivanco, 2002, p. 26). Wearing and McDonald (2002, p. 199) describe how:

The concept of conservation originates from a western world that is indeed very different from village life, and as such it represents a new time – new ways of thinking about the environment – that is foreign to the communities. The concept implicitly suggests that the environment should be thought of in terms of scarcity, or threats to scarcity; this being an understanding of the environment which is foreign to communities who have traditionally lived in an ecologically sustainable manner.

They go on to cite Flannery's observation that western notions of conservation often appear to be completely nonsensical to the local people in Papua New Guinea where 'the Melanesian world-view incorporates humans and animals, the seen and unseen, the living and the dead, in a way that is vastly different from the European outlook'.

Alternative views, which arise from a 'generally holistic (or cosmovision view) of nature held by indigenous peoples' (Colchester, cited in Mowforth and Munt, 2003, p. 154), mean that not only will there be a fundamental difference between how nature tourism, and hence ecotourism, is constructed in different societies, but also that indigenous communities may have a real problem with the effective commodification of nature through ecotourism.

With the burgeoning domestic and regional tourism in developing and transitional economies, it is increasingly evident that nature tourism is variously constructed by different societies and therefore there are multiple 'nature tourisms'. For example at Tiger Leaping gorge, Yunnan province, China, a new road was carved along the side of this deep gorge on the Yangtze, and 500 concrete steps constructed down to the river to facilitate visitation by a large number of domestic visitors (Cater, 2001). For these domestic tourists, the experience takes on the guise of a pilgrimage. Petersen (1995) documents how the Chinese domestic visitor's motivation is a voluntary cultural decision, akin to a pilgrimage to historical, cultural and political centres. Winchester (1996) substantiates this fact in his travelogue on the Yangtze; he describes the poetic identity of the river for the Chinese, reflected in literature, poetry, and art. Lindberg *et al.* (1997) document how levels of crowding are more tolerable to Chinese than to Western visitors. In addition, it must be recognized that Eastern cultures tend to favour human manipulation of nature in order to enhance its appeal compared to its preservation in a pristine state.

Another example is that of Mt Bromo National Park, Indonesia. Cochrane (2000, 2003) describes how group sizes for East Asian visitors averaged 20 and that for Indonesian tourists 15.5, compared with only 2.2 for non-Asian visitors. Most of the Indonesian visitors arrived in family groups or as small groups of friends, and 56% of those surveyed had been there before. A quarter of respondents gave recreation as their main purpose of visit. Cochrane points out that *taman nasional* (National Park in Indonesian) are not distinguished from other, more artificial, types of *taman*, such as amusement parks or urban parks. This is because the word *taman* normally means garden 'and for most people conjures up a heavily managed environment'. Consequently National Parks such as Mt Bromo 'are viewed principally as places for relaxation and general leisure, with concomitant expectations of amenities' (Cochrane 2003, pp. 119, 192). A study which surveyed domestic and foreign tourists in Nigeria similarly found that destination images held most by Nigerian domestic tourists involve recreation and leisure, while those of foreign tourists involved 'environmental education and appreciation' (Awaritefe, 2005).

Thus it can be seen that the construction of nature by different ethnicities may result in markedly divergent tastes and demands that do not conform to western views of ecotourism. While, as Weaver (2002) suggests, the extent to which Asian markets will be influenced by western models of ecotourism participation is unknown, he argues for peculiarly 'Asian' models of ecotourism that, for cultural reasons, deviate from the conventional western-centric constructs. Chung (2005) makes a similar call with regard to the conservation of architectural heritage, arguing that 'For effective implementation of conservation practice in the East Asian societies, it is necessary to develop conservation principles and methodologies that are more suited to their cultural and local conditions'. However, it is important here to draw attention to the fact that, while it is tempting to focus on East–West, or North–South distinctions, these generalizations may mask significant differences between and within individual nations. Moscardo (2004), for example, found that there was greater variation between Chinese and

Japanese visitors to the Great Barrier Reef than between these two groups and the other national cultural groups studied (from the UK and USA). In Taiwan, Hou *et al.* (2005) describe how the meaning and formation of attachment to a cultural tourism attraction for domestic tourists in Taiwan differed between visitors of the same ethnic group as the hosts and other Taiwanese ethnic groups.

One of the very few examples worldwide that is trying to introduce an expressedly non-western system of environmental protection into a threatened conservation area is the Misali Ethics Pilot Project of the Misali Island Conservation Programme, Zanzibar, Tanzania. Misali fishing grounds support more than 10,000 people and, additionally, its reef wall is a renowned scuba-diving location. In the light of the fact that mainstream environmental education was having little or no impact on the illegal fishing practices of local fishermen which were causing irreparable damage to the marine environment, The Islamic Foundation for Ecology and Environmental Sciences (IFEES) is laying down the foundation of Islamic environmental practice in Misali. Appropriate institutions are being established, based on the holistic *Sharia* code of living, which stresses that in Islam there is no separation from any one aspect of creation and the rest of the natural order (Khalid, 2004). The aim is also to produce an educational guide book to popularize the Islamic approach to environmental protection amongst Muslims as well as inform the international community of the breadth of the Islamic contribution to human welfare (IFEES, 2003).

An associated problem with western-envisaged ecotourism is that of the inevitable commodification of nature and culture whereby a financial value is attached to natural and cultural resources. As Hinch (2001) suggests, indigenous people have a much deeper connection with the land than non-indigenous people and consequently 'Because they do not treat land as a possession, they are very wary of treating it as a commodity, even in the purportedly benign context of ecotourism'.The knock-on effect is that, once a financial value has been attached in this way, should ecotourism fail, the expectations that are thus raised might push local populations into other, less sustainable, livelihood options. This indicates the importance of recognizing that, where ecotourism is being pursued as a strategy for development, it should take its place alongside a range of livelihood options for the community, rather than superseding these other activities (Scheyvens, 2002, p. 242).

Furthermore, we are frequently talking of the commodification of natural and cultural resources by outside interests which, not surprisingly, can be viewed as eco-imperialistic or eco-colonialist expropriation (Hall, 1994; Mowforth and Munt, 2003).

Expropriation of nature and culture

The Declaration of The International Forum on Indigenous People held in Oaxaca, Mexico, in March 2002 prior to the World Ecotourism Summit in Quebec of IYE 2002 expressed:

profound disagreement with the IYE's and ecotourism's most basic assumptions that define Indigenous communities as targets to be developed and our lands as commercial resources to be sold on global markets. Under this universalistic economic framework, tourism brings market competition, appropriates our lands and peoples as consumer products.

(Ascanio, 2002)

In Luzon, the Philippines, the Cordillera People's Alliance (1999, p. 3) echoes this concern, arguing that 'the Department of Tourism does not own "nature". Neither does it own the "culture" it so aggressively sells in international and national markets. The Cordillera region and its peoples' culture are not commodities; they are not for sale'. Pera and McLaren (1999) highlight how eco-tourism does not fundamentally alter the logic of capitalist development and that it represents the imposition of a new but familiar development threat on indigenous communities. 'Behind the rhetoric of sustainability, progress, and conservation lies a fundamental truth: like strip mining, cattle ranching, and other Western economic development strategies, ecotourism defines nature as a product to be bought and sold on the global marketplace'.

There is a call to reaffirm the *a priori* rights of Indigenous Peoples to their traditional lands, territories and resources and their values (Rao, 2002). The logical extension to this argument is that there is a need to recognize that:

Indigenous Peoples are not mere 'stakeholders' but internationally recognized holders of collective and human rights, including the rights of self-determination, informed consent and effective participation... Indigenous Peoples are not objects of tourism development. We are active subjects with the rights and responsibilities to *our* (author's italics) territories and the process of tourism planning, implementation, and evaluation that happen in them. This means we are responsible for defending Indigenous lands and communities from development that is imposed by governments, development agencies, private corporations, NGOs, and specialist.

(Ascanio, 2002)

As Pera and McLaren (1999) describe, such development under-mines traditional subsistence patterns, agriculture, community integrity, and economic self-reliance. Paradoxically, the consumptive orientation, largely sustainable, of indigenous people vs. the non-consumptive orientation of ecotourists also throws into sharp focus the fundamentally divergent values and interests between the consumers and targets of ecotourism. As Hinch (2001, p. 352) describes:

Given their traditional lifestyles and values, indigenous peoples are very protective of their right to harvest the resources in their territories... indigenous people have traditionally tended to harvest their resources in a sustainable fashion ... In contrast, most ecotourists explicitly seek out non-consumptive activities while traveling ... Given these contrasting perspectives, conflict is likely to occur should a group of ecotourists stumble across the harvesting of wildlife while they are visiting an indigenous territory.

Saarinen (2004, p. 446) highlights how, given the unequal power relations that are played out, 'the touristic idea and its representations of wilderness areas as places of aesthetic and scenic value may first contest ideologically and then displace in practical terms the local uses of nature as a resource for traditional livelihoods'.

Conclusions

From the plethora of definitions of ecotourism (Fennell, 2003; Page and Dowling, 2002) it is evident that it is a contested term in terms of operational definitions, subject to varying interpretations that are, however, almost without exception, rooted in western ideology. It is, therefore, at the grassroots level that contestation should occur. Silvern (cited in Simon, 2001) declares the need to reflect that there is no universal or unique understanding of development or the environment, and to appreciate that each culture articulates and deploys a particular view of nature and how it ought to be used. He points out that any taken-for-granted view of the natural world is the result of complex social interactions between differently empowered social groups. Therefore, if we uncritically accept western-constructed ecotourism as the be-all-to-end-all, we do so at our, and others', peril. It follows that ecotourism should be even more fundamentally contested in order to listen to different, distant, distanced, voices. Wearing and McDonald (2002, pp. 201–202) cite Prakash's call for 'a radical re-thinking of forms of knowledge and social identities authored and authorized by colonialism and Western domination' and they argue that, if ecotourism 'is to succeed in its goal of cultural and environmental integrity, it requires the development of theory that contains that same integrity'.

Of course, it must be recognized that the views expressed in this chapter are those of a privileged, western, academic. Blaikie (2000, p. 1037) questions the right of the author to represent the object of development rather than letting them 'represent themselves, tell their own authentic stories, and let them be heard above and over the master narrative of the author'. This fundamental challenge remains. The social appropriation of nature must be viewed in, and from, particular social, cultural, economic, and political contexts. Failure to do so will only result in continued disappointment, frustration, and resentment over the manifest shortfall between what ecotourism promises and what it delivers.

Acknowledgements

This chapter is almost entirely reproduced from an article first published in 2006 in the *Journal of Ecotourism* 5(1&2). I am grateful to the editor, David Fennell, and to the publishers, Channel View Publications, for permission to reproduce it here. It was based on a paper given at the Tourism and Leisure Pre-Congress meeting of the IGU and RGS/IBG, August 2005, and the author is also grateful for the helpful comments made by participants at that meeting as well as for the constructive observations of the three anonymous referees of the journal article.

References

Ascanio, A. (2002). *Turismo Declaracion de Oaxaca*. http://listserver. com.ar/pipermail/turismo/2002-August/000243.html

Asiatravel (2004). http://www.asiatravel.com/seychelles

Awaritefe, O.D. (2005). Image difference between culture and nature destination visitors in tropical Africa: case study of Nigeria. *Current Issues in Tourism* 8(5): 363–393.

Bianchi, R.V. (2004). Tourism restructuring and the politics of sustainability: a critical view from the European periphery (The Canary Islands). *Journal of Sustainable Tourism* 12(6): 495–529.

Blaikie, P. (2000). Development, post-, anti-, and populist: a critical review. *Environment and Planning A* 32: 1033–1050.

Brandon, K. and Margoluis, L. (1996). Structuring ecotourism success: framework for analysis. Paper presented at *the Ecotourism Equation: Measuring The Impacts*. International Society of Tropical Foresters, Yale University.

Cater, E. (2001). The space of the dream: a case of mistaken identity? *Area* 33(1): 47–54.

Chung, S.-J. (2005). East Asian values in historic conservation. *Journal of Architectural Conservation* 1: 55–70.

Cochrane, J. (2000). The role of the community in relation to the tourism industry: a case study from Mount Bromo, East Java, Indonesia. In Godde, P.M., Price, M.F. and Zimmermann, F.M. (eds), *Tourism and Development in Mountain Regions*. CABI, Wallingford, pp. 199–220.

Cochrane, J. (2003). *Ecotourism, Conservation and Sustainability: A Case Study of Bromo Tengger Semeru National Park, Indonesia.* Unpublished PhD Thesis, University of Hull.

Cohen, E. (2002). Authenticity, equity and sustainability in tourism. *Journal of Sustainable Tourism* 10(4): 267–276.

Conservation International (2004). Conservation International Home Page. http://www.conservation.org

Corbridge, S. (1995). Editor's introduction. In Corbridge, S. (ed.) *Development Studies: A Reader*. Edward Arnold, London, pp.1–16.

Cordillera Peoples Alliance (1999). Tourism in the Cordillera, HAPIT 6(2). http://www.inkarri.net/ingles/indioeng/fil31.htm

Down to Earth (2001). *The Global Environmental Facility. Down to Earth IFI Factsheet, 18.* http://www.dte.gn.apc.org/Af18.htm

ee-environment (2001a). *Y2K Problem.* http://www.ee-environment.net/missions/Russia/2001-Jul-13.doc

ee-environment (2001b). *USAID Helps Tourism Increase in RFE.* http://www.ee-environment.net/missions/Russia/2001-Jul-13.doc

Duffy, R. (2002). *A Trip Too Far: Ecotourism, Politics and Exploitation.* Earthscan, London.

Entus, S. (2002). 19 June 2002 Re: participative (business) community development. Discussion list (online). Available from trinet@hawaii.edu

Fennell, D. (2003). *Ecotourism: An Introduction*, (2nd edn). Routledge, London.

GEF/SGP (undated). *Profiles of GEF/SGP funded projects in Pakistan during Operational Phase.* http://www.un.org.pk/profilesgefsgpprojects.htm

Hall, C.M. (1994). Ecotourism in Australia, New Zealand and the South Pacific: appropriate tourism or a new form of ecological imperialism? In Cater, E. and Lowman, G. (eds), *Ecotourism: A Sustainable Option?* Royal Geographical Society and John Wiley, London and Chichester, pp. 137–157.

Hall, C.M. (2005). CMHall@business.otago.ac.nz, 11 October 2005. *The Ten Important World Tourism Issues for 2006*. Discussion list (online). Available from trinet@hawaii.edu

Hall, C.M. and Tucker, H. (2004). *Tourism and Postcolonialism.* Routledge, Abingdon.

Hartwick, E. and Peet, R. (2003). Neoliberalism and nature: the case of the WTO. *Annals American Academy of Political and Social Science* 590: 188–211.

Hinch, T. (2001). Indigenous territories. In Weaver, D. (ed.) *The Encyclopedia of Ecotourism.* CABI, Wallingford, pp. 345–357.

Honey, M. and Rome, A. (2001). *Protecting Paradise: Certification Programs for Sustainable Tourism and Ecotourism.* Institute for Policy Studies, Washington, DC.

Hoogvelt, A. (1985). *The Third World in Global Development.* Macmillan, London.

Hoogvelt, A. (1997). *Globalisation and the Postcolonial World.* Macmillan, Basingstoke.

Hou, J.-S., Lin, C.-H. and Morais, D.B. (2005) Antecedents of attachment to a cultural tourism destination: the case of Hakka and Non-Hakka Taiwanese visitors to Pei-Pu, Taiwan. *Journal of Travel Research* 44(2): 221–233.

IFEES (2003). *Activities Project Development: Zanzibar.* http://www.ifees.org/act_pro_zanzibar.htm

IRG (1992). *Ecotourism: A Viable Alternative for Sustainable Management of Natural Resources in Africa.* Agency for International Development Bureau for Africa, Washington, DC.

Jessop, B. (2003). *The Crisis of the National Spatio-Temporal Fix and the Ecological Dominance of Globalizing Capitalism.* Department of Sociology, Lancaster University, Lancaster. Available at http://www.comp.lancs.ac.uk/sociology/papers/Jessop-Crisis-of-the-National-Spatio-Temporal-Fix.pdf

Johnston, R.J., Gregory, D. and Smith, D.M. (eds), (1994). *The Dictionary of Human Geography.* Blackwell, Oxford.

Joy, R. (1997). Development of ecotourism enterprises in Gunung Halimun National Park, West Java, Indonesia. In Bornemeier, J., Victor, M. and Durst, P.B. (eds), *Ecotourism for Forest Conservation and Community Development.* FAO/RAP Publication: 1997/26;RECOFTC Report No.15, Bangkok, pp. 220–226.

Khalid, F.M. (2004). Islamic basis for environmental protection. In Taylor, B. and Kaplan, J. (eds), *Encyclopedia of Religion and Nature.* Continuum International, London.

Kothari, U. (2001). Power, knowledge and social control in participatory development. In Cooke, B. and Kothari, U. (eds),

Participation: The New Tyranny. Zed Books, London and New York, pp. 139–152.

Lindberg, K., Goulding, C., Zhongliang, H., Jianming, M., Ping, W. and Guohui, K. (1997). Ecotourism in China: selected issues and challenges. In Oppermann, M (ed.), *Pacific Rim Tourism* CABI, Wallingford, pp. 128–143.

Lowe, C. (2006). *Wild Profusion: Biodiversity Conservation in an Indonesian Archipelago*. Princeton University Press, Princeton.

Macnaghten, P. and Urry, J. (1998). *Contested Natures*. Sage, London.

Moscardo, G. (2004). East versus West: A useful distinction or misleading myth. *Journal of Tourism* 52(1): 7–20.

Mowforth, M. and Munt, I. (2003). *Tourism and Sustainability* (2nd edn). Routledge, London.

Nepal, S.K., Kohler, T. and Banzhaf, B.R. (2002). *Great Himalaya: Tourism and the Dynamics of Change in Nepal*. Swiss Foundation for Alpine Research, Zurich.

Nyaupane, G.P. and Thapa, B. (2004). Evaluation of ecotourism: a comparative assessment in the Annapurna Conservation Area Project, Nepal. *Journal of Ecotourism* 3(1): 20–45.

Page, S. and Dowling, R.K. (2002). *Ecotourism*. Pearson Education, Harlow.

Pera, L. and McLaren, D. (1999). *Fact Sheet on the International Year of Ecotourism*. http://www.kwia.be/toerisme/rtp.htm

Petersen, Y.Y. (1995). The Chinese landscape as a tourist attraction: image and reality. In Lew, A.A. and Yu, L. (eds), *Tourism in China*. Westview Press, Colorado, pp. 141–154.

Pleumaron, A. (2001). Message 171 Ecotourism Certification Discussion. http://groups.yahoo.com/group/ecotourism_certification/message/171

Rao, N. (2001). Message 14 Ecotourism Certification Discussion. http://groups.yahoo.com/group/ecotourism_certification/message/14

Rao, N. (2002). *Indigenous Peoples Interfaith Dialogue on Globalisation and Tourism*. http://www.world-tourism.org/sustainable/IYE/quebec/cd/statmnts/pdfs/rainde.pdf

Richter, L. (1989). *The Politics of Tourism in Asia*. University of Hawaii Press, Honolulu.

Saarinen, J. (2004). Tourism and Touristic Representations of Nature. In Lew, A.A., Hall, C.M. and Williams, A.M. (eds), *A Companion to Tourism*. Blackwell, Oxford, pp. 438–450.

Scheyvens, R. (2002). *Tourism for Development*. Pearson Education, Harlow.

Simon, D. (2001). Dilemmas of development and the environment in a globalising world: theory, policy and praxis.

Inaugural Lecture Series, Royal Holloway, University of London. Royal Holloway, University of London, Egham.

Sofield, T. (1996). Anuha island resort: a case study of failure. In Butler, R. and Hinch, T. (eds), *Tourism and Indigenous Peoples*. Thomson, London, pp. 176–202.

Southgate, C. and Sharpley, R. (2002). Tourism, development and the environment. In Sharpley, R. and Telfer, D.J. (eds), *Tourism and Development: Concepts and Issues*. Channel View, Clevedon, pp. 231–262.

Sri Lanka Tourism (2005). Tourism 'Bounce Back' Campaign to reach out Worldwide. Sri Lanka News, 11, 13th January 2005. Online document at http://www.contactsrilanka.org

Teo, P. (2002). Striking a balance for sustainable tourism: implications of the discourse on globalisation. *Journal of Sustainable Tourism* 10(6): 459–474.

The Ecotourism Society (1995). *International Membership Directory 1994*. The Ecotourism Society, North Bennington.

The International Ecotourism Society (2003). *2003 International Membership Directory*. The International Ecotourism Society, Washington, DC.

The Travel Mall (2004). *Nepal Tiger Mountain Pokhara Lodge*. http://www.nepal.travelmall.com/travelmall/hotel/Pokhara/Tiger + Pokhara+ Lodge

Tourism Concern (2005). *Post Tsunami Reconstruction and Tourism: A Second Disaster?* Tourism Concern, London.

travelwirenews (3 October 2005). *Making Tourism More Sustainable*. Available at http://www.travelwirenews.com/cgi-script/csArticles/articles/000063/006389.htm

TWN (2001). Cancel the year of ecotourism. An open letter to UN Secretary Kofi Annan *Earth Island Journal* 16(3). http://www.earthisland.org/eijournal/new_articles.cfm?articleID=237&journalID=48

Ultimate Africa Safaris (2004). Ultimate Africa travel and wildlife news archives http://www.ultimateafrica.com/feb04.htm (accessed February 2004).

Vivanco, L. (2002). Seeing the dangers lurking behind the International Year of Ecotourism. *The Ecologist* 32(2): 26.

Walley, C.J. (2004). *Rough Waters: Nature and Development in an East African Marine Park*. Princeton University Press, Princeton and Oxford.

Wearing, S. and McDonald, M. (2002). The development of community-based tourism: re-thinking the relationship between tour operators and development agents as intermediaries in rural and isolated area communities. *Journal of Sustainable Tourism* 10(3): 191–206.

Weaver, D. (2002). Asian ecotourism: patterns and themes. *Tourism Geographies* 4(2): 153–172.

Webster, P. (2003). The Wild Wild East. *The Ecologist 22/1/03.* http://www.theecologist.org/archive_article.html?article= 368&category=101

Wells, M. and Brandon, K. (1992). *People and Parks: Linking Protected Area Management with Local Communities.* World Bank, WWF and USAID, Washington, DC.

Winchester, S. (1996). *The River at the Center of the World.* Penguin, London.

WTTC (2003). *Blueprint for New Tourism.* WTTC, London.

WWF (undated). *Conservation in the Fiji Islands.* Online at http://www.wwfpacific.org.fj/fiji.htm

CHAPTER 4

Ecotourism and global environmental change

Stefan Gössling

Introduction

Like no other form of tourism, ecotourism is dependent on opportunities to observe, see or collect flora and fauna, and to visit particular landscapes or ecosystems. Consequently, global environmental change (GEC), including, for instance, increasing temperatures, changes in biogeochemical cycles or more frequent and intense weather extremes, is of great relevance for ecotourism as it will affect natural resources and species diversity. However, it is for several reasons difficult to assess the consequences of GEC for ecotourism. GEC is a process, which is currently felt mostly in the form of weather extremes, rather than linear change expressed in, for instance, increasing temperatures. Over the coming 40 years, temperatures and other weather parameters are likely to change substantially, as are other aspects of GEC, but the peak of these developments will not be felt for another four decades or so. Changes are also complex and potentially aggregating, which makes it difficult to predict their consequences for ecosystems and biodiversity. There is consensus, though, that landscapes will be fundamentally altered, also involving the loss of a wide variety of species (e.g. Sala *et al.*, 2000; Thomas *et al.*, 2004).

How will these changes affect ecotourism? At present, there seems little awareness of GEC as an ongoing phenomenon in industrial societies. Rather, GEC is seen to become relevant in the future, with few obvious, perceivable and unquestionably GEC-related alterations in the natural environment existing at this moment. How ecotourism will be affected by GEC is thus a question that lies partly in the perception of these changes by coming generations of ecotourists. Any understanding of the consequences of GEC for ecotourism demands an understanding of future changes in the physical environment and, more accurately, their effects on landscapes, landscape elements and species of relevance for ecotourism in comparison to the perception of these changes by future ecotourists. Based on these delimitations, the following chapter sets out to describe some of the expected changes in the natural environment going along with GEC, and attempts to draw a number of conclusions on the consequences of these changes for ecotourism.

Global environmental change

The nature of nature is change, and both GEC and species loss have always been going on. However, human activities have accelerated GEC, affecting land use, biogeochemical cycles, climate change, biota exchange and disturbance regimes such as tropical storms (e.g. Sala *et al.*, 2000; IPCC, 2001; WWF, 2005a). The consequences of some of the aspects of GEC are described in the following.

Temperature increase

Global average surface temperatures increased by 0.6 ± 0.2°C over the 20th century, and are, according to satellite data, now increasing by 0.15 ± 0.05°C per decade (IPCC, 2001). In the future, global warming is likely to accelerate, even though models do not allow for exact statements on the future of climate change, as there is a range of uncertainties concerning the parameters used, their interaction and feedback processes, as well as future emission levels of greenhouse gases. There is also still controversy over the cause and extent of natural climate variability in the past (Moberg *et al.*, 2005). Natural fluctuations, if underestimated in current models, might 'either amplify or attenuate anthropogenic climate change significantly' (Moberg *et al.*, 2005, p. 617). Climate models have so far suggested temperature increases in the range of 1.4–5.8°C by 2100 (IPCC, 2001), with a likely scenario of a 3°C warming by 2100 (Kerr, 2004, p. 932). Recent publications indicate, however, that temperature increases might become larger, with an upper range of 11.5°C warming by 2100 (Challenor *et al.*, 2005; Stainforth *et al.*, 2005). Any warming beyond 3–4°C is assumed to have adverse impacts for coastal resources, biodiversity, and marine and terrestrial ecosystem productivity (*cf.* Hitz and Smith, 2004), all of which are of importance for ecotourism.

Sea-level rise

One of the most important consequences of temperature increases will be sea-level rise, a result of the thermal expansion of the oceans and the melting of glaciers and ice caps. According to the IPCC (2001), the average global sea level has risen by between 0.1 and 0.2 m during the 20th century, and the IPCC's scenarios predict a sea-level rise of 0.9–0.88 m by 2100. Currently, the state of the West Arctic Ice Sheet (WAIS) is of great concern because its complete melting could raise global sea levels by approximately 7 m (Oppenheimer and Alley, 2004). While such a scenario would take long periods of time, there still is potential for a marked increase in the rate of sea-level rise due to accelerated ice loss. Sea-level rise can lead to the loss of coastal wetlands and biodiversity, and cause land inundation and coastal erosion (Nicholls, 2004; Zhang *et al.*, 2004). Clearly, all of these changes can affect ecotourism.

Land use change

Land use is changing at a global scale (Richards, 1990; Klein Goldewijk, 2001). A growing world population and diet changes associated with changes in living standards have contributed to the conversion of large areas of land from relatively natural states to agricultural land use and urban development. Development projects of various kinds can affect areas of importance for biodiversity, such as the Mediterranean coastline (GFANC, 1997). Land degradation adds to these changes, including deforestation, poor agricultural practices, industrialisation, pollution, salination, siltation, erosion, acidification and waterlogging. Often, development processes affect areas of high biodiversity, and consequently opportunities for ecotourism.

Precipitation patterns

Amount and intensity of global precipitation patterns have changed substantially in recent decades. According to the IPCC (2001), precipitation might have increased by 0.5–1% per decade in the 20th century over most mid- and high latitudes of the Northern Hemisphere continents, and by 0.2–0.3% per decade over the tropical land areas (10°N to 10°S). However, increases in rainfall in the tropics are not evident over the past few decades, and in the Northern Hemisphere sub-tropical land areas (10°N to 30°N), rainfall might have decreased during the 20th century by about 0.3% per decade. No changes have been observed over the Southern Hemisphere, and data are insufficient to establish trends over the oceans. Regarding the intensity of precipitation patterns, a 2–4% increase in the frequency of heavy precipitation events has occurred in the mid- and high latitudes of the Northern Hemisphere over the latter half of the 20th century. Heavy precipitation events can be a result of changes in atmospheric moisture, thunderstorm activity and large-scale storm activity. Globally, runoff is expected to increase by 4% given a 1°C global temperature rise, a result of more intense evaporation above oceans coupled to continental precipitation (Labat et al., 2004). However, there are increasing and decreasing runoff trends on intercontinental and regional scales. For instance, in Europe, models predict substantial changes in precipitation patterns (Xu, 2000). More intense precipitation, most of which is projected to occur in winter, will contribute to increased lake inflows, lake levels and runoff (Palmer and Räisänen, 2002). During the summer, drier conditions, exacerbated by greater evaporation, will reduce lake inflows and lake levels. Higher temperatures and decreasing water levels in summer may also affect thermal stratification, evaporation and species composition of lakes (Hulme *et al.*, 2003). Increasing river discharge has already been observed over much of the Arctic, with spring peak river flows now occurring earlier (ACIA, 2004). In the Northern latitudes, melting glaciers might also contribute to greater runoff. All of these changes could influence various forms of ecotourism.

Extreme climate and weather events

There is evidence that extreme weather events have become more frequent. Warm episodes of the El Niño-Southern Oscillation (ENSO) phenomenon, for instance, have been more frequent, persistent and intense since the mid-1970s, compared with the previous 100 years (IPCC, 2001). Furthermore, in some regions such as parts of Asia and Africa, the frequency and intensity of droughts have increased in recent decades. While these patterns seem connected to GEC, the IPCC points out that alterations in tropical and extra-tropical storm intensity and frequency are dominated by interdecadal to multidecadal variations, with no significant trends evident over the 20th century. Likewise, no changes in the frequency of tornadoes, thunder days or hail events were observed (IPCC, 2001). Weather events might potentially have serious consequences for species diversity and ecosystems, as these are affected by heat waves, heavy precipitation, cold extremes and storm events (Leemans and Eickhout, 2004).

Distribution and spread of diseases

GEC also leads to the distribution and spread of diseases. For instance, malaria is predicted to spread with climate change (Van Lieshout *et al.*, 2004), and there are concerns about the future distribution of ticks and mosquitoes and the diseases they carry (Lindgren and Gustafson, 2001; Ogden *et al.*, 2006). Disease-carrying vectors might be permanently established through climate change, and it seems clear that incidences of diseases or increased risks of infections might have substantial consequences for ecotourism.

Ecotourism and GEC

The importance of climatic and natural resources for many forms of tourism is well understood, and there is now a growing number of publications seeking to assess the interrelationships between GEC and tourism (for a biome/ecosystem-specific approach see

Gössling and Hall, 2005a; a bibliography of tourism and climate is provided by Scott *et al.*, 2005). Regarding climatic assets, changing weather parameters can have a direct influence on tourism behaviour as travel decisions are to a large extent based on images of sun, sand and sea, the availability of snow, etc., and thus on climate variables such as temperature, rain or humidity as well as their temporal patterns (e.g. Smith, 1993; de Freitas 2001, 2003; for a recent collection of conference papers see Scott and Matzarakis, 2004). Accordingly, it is expected that climate change will affect travel behaviour, both as a result of altering conditions for holidaymaking at the destination level and climate variables perceived as less or more comfortable by the tourists. The complexity of perceptions of weather parameters is, however, as yet not fully understood (*cf.* Gössling and Hall, 2006; Gössling *et al.*, 2006).

Changes in climatic assets might be only partially relevant for ecotourism, though, because natural resources appear to be of greater relative (i.e. in comparison to climatic resources) and absolute (i.e. in terms of travel motives) importance for eco-tourists (*cf.* Hvenegaard, 2002). Hence, ecotourism might be more seriously affected by GEC than other forms of tourism. More specifically, the attractiveness of natural resources for eco-tourism could be conceptualised as the combined quality of land-scapes (e.g. spectacular views), landscape elements (tourism and recreation based on a particular river, lake, forest or similar) or species (tourism based on species diversity or singular species, for instance whale watching) (see also Figure 4.1).

With regard to ecotourism, species diversity is clearly of great importance. Elephants, rhinos, whales, dolphins, but even a wide

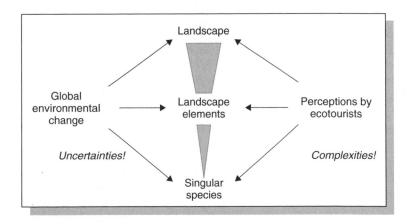

Figure 4.1
GEC and ecotourism

variety of reptiles or birds are examples of species attracting large tourist numbers (*cf.* Hall, 2005). Often, tourists may put great weight on the observation of singular species – bird watchers, for instance, are known to travel around the world to see a single rare bird species (Blondel, 2002). Biodiversity can also have an important symbolic function, as exemplified by moose in Sweden, kangaroos in Australia or lions in Africa. Clearly, countries and continents would lose much of their mythical power without these species. Even though the linkages between tourism and biodiversity seem clear, Hall (2005) reminds us that:

[…] the interrelationships between tourism and biodiversity are poorly understood in terms of empirical data, although the potential impacts of the loss of some charismatic species such as the polar bear (The Age, 2005), or African wildlife, or even entire ecosystems, such as the Great Barrier Reef (Fyfe, 2005), on tourism would be dramatic.

Generally, the relationship between ecotourism and biodiversity seems characterised by at least four aspects: First, species diversity is of greater importance for ecotourism than for other forms of tourism, as the observation of species is more often the main goal of the journey. Second, plant diversity has not the same importance as animal diversity, and within different animal taxa, megafauna, that is large, charismatic animals, are of greatest importance. Third, for some areas, diversity itself, that is the knowledge of visiting a biodiversity hot spot or an area rich in biodiversity, might be of greater importance than singular species. Finally, endemic biodiversity might be of greater importance than biodiversity in general. Should these suggestions hold true, this will be of importance for locations where tourism will be most affected by GEC-related biodiversity loss.

GEC threatens a large number of species. Currently, some 4,000 mammal, bird, reptile, amphibian and fish species are threatened with extinction, while about 600 species of animals are on the list of critically endangered species (UNEP, 2002). Extinctions are high, with an estimated 27,000–140,000 species being lost each year (Wilson, 1992; Pimm *et al.*, 1995). Future extinctions might even be larger in numbers, with the current speed of extinction through human intervention being 100–1,000 times faster than natural extinction rates (Martens *et al.*, 2003). By 2050, climate change alone is estimated to cause extinctions of 15–37% of the species existing within a wide range of taxa, such as plants, birds, reptiles and butterflies (Thomas *et al.*, 2004). Estimates vary in relation to the climate change scenario and assumptions concerning the species ability to disperse to new habitats (Thomas *et al.*, 2004). Species loss might be accelerated by land clearance, changing land use, changing biogeochemical cycles and pollution (Wilson, 1992; Sala *et al.*, 2000).

As discussed, a more sophisticated understanding of the consequences of GEC for ecotourism would have to consider the landscapes, landscape elements and species affected by GEC in the context of their respective importance for ecotourism. Given the lack of empirical data, this is not possible as yet, but it seems nevertheless clear that natural resources of importance for ecotourism will be affected in various ways, with some biomes, ecosystems and species being more susceptible to change than others. For example, northern environments are likely to be more affected by increasing temperatures than tropical ones because climate change will lead to more pronounced temperature increases in these areas (IPCC, 2001; ACIA, 2004). This could have substantial consequences for landscapes and landscape elements, but also for selected species of charismatic megafauna such as polar bears. Regarding tropical ecosystems, sea-level rise, weather extremes, siltation, coastal erosion and pollution, which are all taking place at a global scale (e.g. Wilkinson, 2004), could have negative consequences. Coral reefs, for instance, contain vast species numbers, which are threatened by GEC (Wilkinson, 2004; WWF, 2005b).

There are, as yet, few examples of natural resources altered or destroyed by GEC, and it is often difficult to judge how this affects visitation rates. The top of Mount Kilimanjaro, for instance, has now lost most of its snow cover, which, given its location close to the equator, has for centuries been the dramatic element of the mountain. It is not clear, though, whether visitation rates are affected by the retreat of the snow line. In contrast to such obvious changes, most GEC might indeed not become visible for another two decades. The situation is further complicated by the complexity of GEC perceptions. For instance, snow cover in mountainous areas in Europe has provided excellent skiing conditions in the period 2000–2005, and the perception of climate change as a threat is concomitantly low (e.g. Wolfsegger *et al.*, 2007). This largely ignores the fact that the reason for the exceptionally 'good' snow cover in recent years is with high probability a result of a changing Northern Atlantic Oscillation. In other words, climate change is unabated and progressing, but not observable in terms of less snow. Hence, it seems that there is a perception threshold that needs to be surpassed before (eco)tourists become aware of GEC (see also Gössling *et al.*, 2007). As for future perceptions of ecotourists with respect to GEC, there is substantial uncertainty. For instance, a child born in 2040 may grow up in a world largely deprived of its glaciers. It seems likely that this will affect aesthetic perceptions in the sense that the child will, as an adult tourist, put a lower amenity value on the existence of glaciers (Daniel Scott, personal Communication).

Another aspect of importance is the characteristics of eco-tourists. Weaver (2002) summarises the findings of various stud-ies on ecotourists by concluding that ecotourism markets seem mostly located in Anglo-America, western and northern Europe, and Australia/New Zealand. Ecotourists seem older than the population or tourists in general, even though this might depend on the ecotourism activity considered. Research also suggests that ecotourists are well educated and have relatively high per-sonal and household incomes. All of these parameters are likely to be of importance, as they might influence perceptions and decision-making. For instance, ecotourists might, as a result of their educational status, be more aware of GEC and be better informed about the state of the environment in their favoured destinations.

Furthermore, it is important to note that there are different types of ecotourists (Hvenegaard, 2002; Weaver and Lawton, 2002). For instance, Weaver and Lawton (2002) distinguish hard and soft ecotourists, with hard ecotourists showing higher degrees of biocentrism, reflected in higher levels of environmental com-mitment and support for enhancement sustainability, that is eco-tourism contributing to an improvement of sustainability through donations, tree planting and other activities:

Hard ecotourists are also associated with specialised, longer-duration travel in small groups, whereas soft ecotourists engage in ecotourism for short periods as part of a multipurpose itinerary, often involving larger groups. With respect to product support, hard ecotourists are purported to eschew most services and to frequent wild and remote destinations that require a significant amount of physical activity.

(Weaver, 2002, p. 20).

Clearly, hard ecotourists might thus be more susceptible to GEC, as they might be more critical of the nature resource base and its condition. Hard ecotourists might also be in a position to *see* envi-ronmental degradation, which is not necessarily the case with all tourists (see for instance Gössling *et al.*, 2007 for a case study of divers). Soft ecotourists, on the other hand, might put more emphasis on experiences (*cf.* Gössling, 2006). This implies that 'nature', which might largely be a cultural construction in the con-text of such tourism, is rather a playground than a 'scientific entity' (Hultman and Andersson-Cederholm, 2006), and GEC might not necessarily have an impact on the perception of these tourists.

It is generally difficult to say which landscapes, landscape elements or species are of greatest importance for ecotourism.

A review of articles published in the *Journal of Ecotourism* between 2002 and 2006, for instance, gives no clear indication of preferences. Ecotourists seem attracted by a wide variety of ecosystems in northern, temperate and tropical latitudes, are equally attracted by landscapes, landscape elements and particular species, seem to visit both non-protected and protected areas, have a wide variety of motivations, and are found all over the world. Consequently, it could be suggested that those environments threatened most by GEC will also be those where ecotourism is affected in the first place. Gössling and Hall (2005b) have provided a list of 'at risk' destinations in the context of tourism in general. The list might nevertheless be valid for ecotourism as well, even though uncertainties and complexities as outlined above should be held in mind (Table 4.1).

Table 4.1 Most at risk destinations

Land biodiversity loss	Marine biodiversity loss	Urbanisation
Polynesia/Micronesia	Polynesia/Micronesia	Coastal Mediterranean
Sundaland	Caribbean	Coastal southern China
California	Maldives	Coastal Malaysia
Mediterranean Basin	South China Sea	Coastal California
South African Cape region	Mediterranean	Florida
Water security	**Sea-level rise**	**Regime change/fuel**
South Africa	Mediterranean	Australia
Mediterranean	Gold Coast	New Zealand
Australia	Florida	Polynesia/Micronesia
Central America	Coastal China	South Africa
SW USA	Polynesia/Micronesia	East Africa
Warmer summers	**Warmer winters**	**Disease**
Mediterranean	European Alps	South Africa
California/Western USA	Pyrenees	Mediterranean
North Queensland	Rocky Mountains	Western, Northern Europe
South Africa	Australian Alps	USA
Western continental Europe	Eastern European alpine areas	Northern Australia

Source: Modified from Gössling and Hall (2005b).

Conclusions

This chapter has sought to outline the interrelationships between ecotourism and GEC. There is evidence that GEC is of particular relevance for ecotourism, and might become paramount on three different levels: landscapes, landscape elements and species. However, assessments of the consequences of GEC for ecotourism need to consider the perception of ongoing and expected changes by ecotourists. These perceptions are likely to be complex, translating into non-linear changes in behaviour (*cf.* Gössling and Hall, 2006). This means that constant change in one environmental parameter does not necessarily result in an equivalent change in tourist behaviour (*cf.* Gössling *et al.*, 2006). For instance, numbers of ticks have increased constantly in Sweden (Jaenson *et al.*, 1994), but it is less clear whether tourists will react to these changes or not, and whether decisions to no longer visit forests will be gradual or sudden.

Overall, there is strong evidence that GEC will affect ecotourism, as environmental resources including species diversity will be degraded, often to such a degree that the basis for ecotourism might disappear. Some of the countries and regions where such changes are most likely to be felt in the short-term future have been indicated in this chapter. However, the reaction of different types of ecotourists to these changes is not obvious. For instance, future ecotourists could replace one destination for another, or focus on another species. In contrast, the outlook of a species soon to become extinct might attract even larger ecotourist numbers. It could also be argued that future ecotourists will travel for experiences rather than particular landscapes, landscape elements or species. The future of ecotourism in the context of GEC thus remains uncertain, even though there is a link to the present: it is current generations deciding how the world is going to look like in the second half of this century, and which opportunities there will be for future ecotourists to experience unsullied landscapes and species diversity. Coming generations of ecotourists might have different perceptions of 'nature', but they are nevertheless likely to judge current generations for the decisions they have made to address – or not address – global environmental change.

References

ACIA (Arctic Climate Impact Assessment) (2004). *Impacts of a Warming Arctic: Arctic Climate Impact Assessment*. Cambridge University Press, Cambridge. www.acia.uaf.edu

Blondel, J. (2002). Birding in the sky: only fun, a chance for ecodevelopment, or both? In di Castri, F. and Balaji, V. (eds), *Tourism, Biodiversity and Information*. Backhuys Publishers, pp. 307–317.

Challenor, P., Hankin, R. and Marsh, B. (2005). The probability of rapid climate change. Paper presented at the *International Symposium on the Stabilisation of Greenhouse Gases*, Hadley Centre, Met Office, Exeter, February 1–3.

de Freitas, C. (2001). Theory, concepts and methods in tourism climate research. *Proceedings of the First International Workshop on Climate, Tourism and Recreation*, Porto Carras, Neos Marmaras, Halkidiki, Greece, October 5–10, 2001, pp. 3–20.

de Freitas, C. (2003). Tourism climatology: evaluating environmental information for decision making and business planning in the recreation and tourism sector. *International Journal of Biometeorology* 48(4): 45–54.

Fyfe, M. (2005). Too late to save the reef. *The Age*, February 12.

German Federal Agency for Nature Conservation (GFANC) (1997). *Biodiversity and Tourism: Conflicts on the World's Seacoasts and Strategies for Their Solution*. Springer Verlag, Berlin.

Gössling, S. (2006). Ecotourism as experience-tourism. In Gössling, S. and Hultman, J. (eds), *Ecotourism in Scandinavia. Lessons in Theory and Practice*. CABI Publishing, Willingford, pp. 89–97.

Gössling, S. and Hall, C.M. (eds) (2005a). *Tourism and Global Environmental Change. Ecological, Social, Economic and Political Interrelationships*. Routledge, London, pp. 1–34.

Gössling, S. and Hall, M. (2005b). Wake up! This is serious. In Gössling, S. and Hall, C.M. (eds), *Tourism and Global Environmental Change. Ecological, Social, Economic and Political Interrelationships*. Routledge, London, pp. 305–320.

Gössling, S. and Hall, M. (2006). Uncertainties in predicting tourist travel flows under scenarios of climate change. Editorial essay. *Climatic Change* 79(3-4): 163–173.

Gössling, S., Bredberg, M., Randow, A., Svensson, P. and Swedlin, E. (2006). Tourist perceptions of climate change: a study of international tourists in Zanzibar. *Current Issues in Tourism* 9(4-5): 419–435.

Gössling, S., Lindén, O., Helmersson, J., Liljenberg, J. and Quarm, S. (2007). Coral reefs, global environmental change, and the future of diving tourism in tropical environments. In Garrod, B. and Gössling, S. (eds) New frontiers in marine tourism: diving experiences, management and sustainability. Elsevier, to appear 2007.

Hall, C.M. (2005). Tourism, biodiversity and global environmental change. In Gössling, S. and Hall, C.M. (eds), *Tourism and*

Global Environmental Change. Ecological, Social, Economic and Political Interrelationships. Routledge, London, pp. 312–339.

Hitz, S. and Smith, J. (2004). Estimating global impacts from climate change. *Global Environmental Change* 14: 201–218.

Hulme, M., Conway, D. and Lu, X. (2003). Climate change: an overview and its impact on the living lakes. Report prepared for *the 8th Living Lakes Conference 'Climate Change and Governance: Managing Impacts on Lakes'*. Zuckerman Institute for Connective Environmental Research, University of East Anglia, Norwich, September 7–12, 2003.

Hultman, J. and Andersson-Cederholm, E. (2006). The role of nature in Swedish ecotourism. In Gössling, S. and Hultman, J. (eds), *Ecotourism in Scandinavia. Lessons in Theory and Practice*. CABI Publishing, Wallingford, pp. 76–88.

Hvenegaard, G.T. (2002). Using tourist typologies for ecotourism research. *Journal of Ecotourism* 1(1): 7–18.

IPCC (Intergovernmental Panel of Climate Change) (2001). *Climate Change 2001: The Scientific Basis*. Contribution of the Working Group I to the Third Assessment Report of the Intergovernmental Panel of Climate Change. Cambridge University Press, Cambridge.

Jaenson, T.G.T., Tälleklint, L., Lundqvist, L., Olsen, B., Chirico, J. and Mejlon, H. (1994). Geographical distribution, host associations and vector roles of ticks (Acari: Ixodidae and Argasidae) in Sweden. *Journal of Medical Entomology* 31: 240–256.

Kerr, R.A. (2004). Three degrees of consensus. *Science* 305: 932–934.

Klein Goldewijk, K. (2001). Estimating global land use change over the past 300 years: the HYDE database. *Global Biogeochemical Cycles* 15(2): 417–434.

Labat, D., Goddéris, Y., Probst, J.L. and Guyot, J.L. (2004). Evidence for global runoff increase related to climate warming. *Advances in Water Resources* 27: 631–642.

Leemans, R. and Eickhout, B. (2004). Another reason for concern: regional and global impacts on ecosystems for different levels of climate change. *Global Environmental Change* 14: 219–228.

Lindgren, E. and Gustafson, R. (2001). Tick-borne encephalitis in Sweden and climate change. *Lancet* 358: 16–18.

Martens, P., Rotmans, J. and de Groot, D. (2003). Biodiversity: luxury or necessity? *Global Environmental Change* 13: 75–81.

Moberg, A., Sonechkin, D.M., Holmgren, K., Datsenko, N.M. and Karlén, W. (2005). Highly variable Northern Hemisphere temperatures reconstructed from low- and high-resolution proxy data. *Nature* 433: 613–617.

Nicholls, R.J. (2004). Coastal flooding and wetland loss in the 21st century: changes under the SRES climate and socio-economic scenarios. *Global Environmental Change* 14(1): 69–86.

Ogden, N.H., Maarouf, A., Barker, I.K., Bigras-Poulin, M., Lindsay, L.R., Morshed, M.G., O'Callaghan, C.J., Ramay, F., Waltner-Toews, D. and Charron, D.F. (2006). Climate change and the potential for range expansion of the Lyme disease vector *Ixodes scapularis* in Canada. *International Journal for Parasitology* 36(1): 63–70.

Oppenheimer, M. and Alley, R.B. (2004). The Antarctic Ice Sheet and long term climate change policy. *Climatic Change* 64: 1–10.

Palmer, T.N. and Räisänen, J. (2002). Quantifying the risk of extreme seasonal precipitation events in a changing climate. *Nature* 415: 512–514.

Pimm, S.L., Russell, G.J., Gittleman, J.L. and Brooks, T.M. (1995). The future of biodiversity. *Science* 269: 347–350.

Richards, J.F. (1990). Land transformation. In Turner II, B.L., Clark, W.C., Kates, R.W., Richards, J.F., Mathews, J.T. and Meyer, W.B. (eds), *The Earth as Transformed by Human Action*. Cambridge University Press, New York, pp. 163–178.

Sala, O.E., Chapin III, F.S., Armesto, J.J., Berlow, E., Bloomfield, J., Dirzo, R., Huber-Sanwald, E., Huenneke, L.F., Jackson, R.B., Kinzig, A., Leemans, R., Lodge, D.M., Mooney, H.A., Oesterheld, M., Poff, N.L., Sykes, M.T., Walker, B.H., Walker, M. and Wall, D.H. (2000). Global biodiversity scenarios for the year 2100. *Science* 287: 1770–1774.

Scott, D. and Matzarakis, C.R. (2004). *Advances in Tourism Climatology*. Berichte des Meteorologischen Institutes der Universität Freiburg. Meteorologisches Institut der Universität Freiburg, Freiburg.

Scott, D., Jones, B. and McBoyle, G. (2005). *Climate, Tourism and Recreation: A Bibliography 1936–2005*. Faculty of Environmental Studies, University of Waterloo, Ont.

Smith, K. (1993). The influence of weather and climate on recreation and tourism. *Weather* 48(12): 398–403.

Stainforth, D.A., Aina, T., Christensen, C., Collins, M., Faull, N., Frame, D.J., Kettleborough, J.A., Knight, S., Martin, A., Murphy, J.M., Piani, C., Sexton, D., Smith, L.A., Spicer, R.A., Thorpe, A.J. and Allen, M.R. (2005). Uncertainty in predictions of the climate response to rising levels of greenhouse gases. *Nature* 433: 403–406.

The Age (2005). Polar bears' days may be numbered. *The Age*, February 3.

Thomas, C.D., Cameron, A., Green, R.E., Bakkenes, M., Beaumont, L.J., Collingham, Y.C., Erasmus, B.F.N., de Siqueira, M.F., Grainger, A., Hannah, L., Hughes, L., Huntley, B., Van Jaarsveld, A.S., Midgley, G.F., Miles, L., Ortega-Huerta, M.A., Townsend Peterson, A., Phillips, O.L. and Williams, S.E. (2004). Extinction risk from climate change. *Nature* 427: 145–148.

United Nations Environment Programme (UNEP) (2002). *Global Environmental Outlook 3: Past, Present and Future Perspectives.* UNEP, Nairobi.

Van Lieshout, M., Kovats, R.S., Livermore, M.T.J. and Martens, P. (2004). Climate change and malaria: analysis of the SRES climate and socio-economic scenarios. *Global Environmental Change* 14(1): 87–99.

Weaver, D. and Lawton, L. (2002). Overnight ecotourist market segmentation in the Gold Coast hinterland of Australia. *Journal of Travel Research* 40(4): 270–280.

Weaver, D.B. (2002). Hard-core ecotourists in Lamington National Park, Australia. *Journal of Ecotourism* 1(1): 19–35.

Wilkinson, C. (ed.) (2004). *Status of the Coral Reefs of the World: 2002.* Australian Institute of Marine Sciences, Townsville, Qld, Australia, 301 pp.

Wilson, E.O. (1992). *The Diversity of Life.* Norton, New York.

Wolfsegger, C., Gössling, S. and Scott, D. (2007). Climate change risk appraisal in the Austrian ski industry. *Tourism Review International*, accepted for publication.

World Wide Fund for Nature (WWF) (2005a). *The Implications of Climate Change for Australia's Great Barrier Reef.* http://www.wwf.org.au/News_and_information/News_room/viewnews.php?news_id=65 (accessed March 17, 2006).

World Wide Fund for Nature (WWF) (2005b). *Living Planet Report 2004.* http://www.panda.org/news_facts/publications/key_publications/living_planet_report/lpr04/index.cfm (accessed March 17, 2006).

Xu, C.-Y. (2000). Modelling the effects of climate change on water resources in central Sweden. *Water Resources Management* 14: 177–189.

Zhang, K., Douglas, B.C. and Leatherman, S.P. (2004). Global warming and coastal erosion. *Climatic Change* 64: 41–58.

CHAPTER 5

Ecotourism, energy use, and the global climate: widening the local perspective

Susanne Becken and
Matthias Schellhorn

Introduction

For the purposes of the International Year of Ecotourism, the United Nations World Tourism Organisation (UNWTO, 2001, p. 9) defined ecotourism as:

All forms of tourism in which the main motivation of tourists is the observation and appreciation of nature, which contributes to its conservation, and which minimizes negative impacts on the natural and socio-cultural environment where it takes place.

This definition has its focus at the destination level, where tourism-related impacts (both positive and negative) are of major concern. In 2001, UNWTO published *Sustainable Development of Ecotourism. A Compilation of Good Practices,* which provides a selection of case studies that demonstrate desirable standards underpinning the above definition. The sustainability of the cases studied is assessed in relation to their contribution to nature conservation and biodiversity, economic and social benefits, community involvement, educational features, and environmental practices during the development and operation phases of ecotourism. The latter makes reference to energy efficiency and the use of renewable energy sources, but the case studies as presented offer little or no detail on those aspects.

As the focus of UNWTO is on *local* biophysical and socio-economic impacts, macro-environmental issues and *global* effects are ignored. These broader issues include the future scarcity of fossil fuels and the global implications of burning transport fuels that produce greenhouse gas emissions. Emissions of anthropogenic greenhouse gases (most importantly carbon dioxide (CO_2)) add to the natural greenhouse effect and as a consequence lead to climate change. Climatic changes manifest among others as warmer air and water temperatures, more intense tropical storms, increased risk of extreme events (e.g. floods or droughts), and sea level rise. Predictions of the likelihood and magnitude of those changes are subject to some uncertainty, especially when trying to assess climate conditions at the micro-level. There is also uncertainty associated with the likelihood of the climate system to undergo abrupt and pervasive changes; such changes are termed 'surprises' and 'catastrophic changes' (US National Research Council, 2002).

All changes in the climate system pose significant flow-on challenges for tourism. The destinations likely to be most affected by climate change include already fragile environments such as small islands and alpine areas. In the case of coastal tourism, the physical challenges imposed by rising sea levels threaten the existence of entire and often dominant industry sectors. It is generally recognized that developing countries and their less diversified economies are more vulnerable to climate change than developed countries mainly due to reduced opportunities for adaptation and risk reduction measures (Becken and Hay, forthcoming).

The effects of climate change are particularly challenging to the niche ecotourism sector, which largely depends on pristine natural environments for its competitive consumer appeal. Many ecotourism operations are based in and around protected natural areas and often focus on particular aspects of the local flora or fauna. These, however, depend on the integrity of the ecosystem they inhabit. Climate change clearly has potential to alter significantly the abiotic (and as a consequence biotic) factors in those ecosystems and push species outside their tolerance level, leading to migration or extinction in a particular geographic area. Examples include the rising snowlines in alpine areas, higher water temperatures affecting coral reefs, and reduced precipitation levels in semi-arid and desert areas. All of these effects can potentially affect the successful operation of land- or marine-based ecotourism businesses.

While the dependency of ecotourism on stable environmental conditions is evident, the contributions of ecotourism to the depletion of global energy resources and the concomitant impacts on the global climate have received little attention. These macro-ecological considerations remain largely undocumented, not just by the UNWTO but also by academic ecotourism critiques (e.g. Duffy, 2002; Fennell, 2003). As discussed by Simmons and Becken (2004), ecotourism is often characterized by a substantial transport component, which results in high-energy consumption and considerable emission of greenhouse gases. Paradoxically, in many cases, ecotourism generates a larger 'carbon footprint' than other, more traditional forms of holiday such as resort-based tourism (Gössling, 2002; Gössling et al., 2003, Simmons and Becken, 2004). While these effects point at an inherent discrepancy between the conceptualization of ecotourism as 'green practice' and actual environmental performance, they also highlight the need for a closer look at global (rather than just localized) impacts of this important niche industry. The latter requires a broadening of our research agenda towards a more systemic and holistic analysis of new forms of tourism.

Ecotourism research: the reading glass approach

The opening quote to this chapter illustrates how ecotourism is commonly viewed as a 'caring partner for the environment'.

Indeed, conceptual links between ecotourism and conservation are well established in the literature, especially through a multitude of definitions that focus to varying degrees on the environmental performance of ecotourism operations (Orams, 1995; Fennell, 2003). This conceptual link to conservation draws justification partly from a wide body of research data, collected in abundant case studies documenting a manifold variety of operations labelled as ecotourism (see for example the above-mentioned compilation by UNWTO, 2001). While these studies often illuminate problems and issues at a local level, they fail to question ecotourism's environmental performance at a global scale and therefore its suitability as a conservation partner.

The growing significance assigned to ecotourism in the conservation context is best illustrated by international endorsements from multilateral organizations. The United Nations Environment Programme (UNEP, 2002), for example, devotes part of its website to tourism, and sees ecotourism development especially as a strategic conservation instrument, stating:

…ecotourism is of special interest to UNEP for its relationship with conservation, sustainability, and biological diversity. As a development tool, ecotourism can advance the … basic goals of the Convention on Biological Diversity.

UNEP's reference to the *Convention on Biological Diversity* (CBD) is noteworthy since the governing body of the CBD has clearly identified climate change as a major concern to the convention and one of the important crosscutting issues affecting its programmes. At its fifth meeting in 2000, the Conference of the Parties to the CBD identified 'Pollution and production of greenhouse gases, resulting from travel by air, road, rail, or sea, at local, national and global levels' as a risk to biodiversity and a specific area for detailed impact assessment (CBD, 2001–2005). Against this background, it seems astonishing that international organizations such as UNWTO and UNEP promote ecotourism as a conservation tool without reference to its global pollution potential.

The strategic demands placed upon ecotourism are far reaching and include expectations to be not only an efficient conservation tool but also an instrument for social change. This wider social goal resonates in recent activities of the UNWTO which, together with UNEP, has been appointed by the Commission on Sustainable Development to work on the implementation of Agenda 21 issues on tourism. The poverty reduction initiatives developed by UNWTO, for example, focus on ecotourism projects that are seen to have pro-poor potential. The document that outlines the 'Sustainable Tourism-Eliminating Poverty' (ST-EP) scheme, states this clearly:

We envisage that so called 'eco', 'responsible' or 'community' tourism based projects will be at the heart of this system. Why? Because the essence of such schemes must be community and people based actions which have issues such as poverty alleviation, social development, inclusion and the like at their core

(UNWTO, 2003, p. 7).

In recent years, various strategies for the development of poverty-stricken rural areas have advanced ecotourism in the form of community-based projects. Many of these projects have been funded by international donor organizations including development aid agencies, non-governmental organizations, and financial institutions such as the Asian Development Bank. The promise of financial returns to local communities and especially the poor provides justification for specific aid programmes, as well as international loans and donor grants.

Despite these endorsements and resulting expectations, the socio-economic potential and conservation benefits of ecotourism ventures have been widely questioned on empirical grounds. For example, there is little evidence to support the claim of long-term, self-sustaining viability of ecotourism projects. As Weaver (2002, p. 168) points out, ecotourism delivers the economic conservation incentive it is promoted for mainly through large visitor numbers and the associated incomes from entrance fees. Often such fee incomes outweigh those generated by community-based enterprises selling products and services. At the local level, therefore, ecotourism generally provides few entrepreneurial incentives and a rather limited economic stimulus. Promises of stable tourism incomes often prove unreliable, especially since tourism flows may reduce at any stage (for various, often unpredictable reasons). Questions therefore arise with regard to the overall development effectiveness of ecotourism (and therefore the sustainability of integrated conservation strategies that rely on ecotourism development).

Often noted is tourism's tendency to reinforce existing disparities of a social, economic, or spatial nature (Lübben, 1995; Brohmann, 1996; Scheyvens and Purdie, 1999; Richards and Hall, 2000; Borchers, 2002). In the case of Bali, a large part of the foreign exchange earnings generated by Indonesia's most successful tourism destination flows to the nation's capital, a fact that many Balinese have long resented (Richter, 1989). Weaver and Elliot (1996, pp. 205–217) note that the development of tourism often advantages those who are able to take up new opportunities because they have the economic power to do so while the poorest have very little or no benefit at all (Erb, 2001). The specific hierarchies at work in the global marketplace have become a key area of concern. Critics claim that these power relationships not only undermine less developed economies but also, within these, disadvantage those local people who lack power and opportunities (Scheyvens, 2002; Mowforth and Munt, 2003).

It appears that ecotourism in itself is not necessarily and always a recipe for successful development outcomes at a local level. As early as 1990, Boo noted that there are many caveats and pitfalls associated with ecotourism projects. Experience since has shown that such pitfalls can lead to an overall deterioration of a local situation both in terms of conservation and sustainable development.

We contend that the ambiguous nature of ecotourism development would become more apparent still if projects were considered in their true *global* context. So far, however, myriads of case studies treat ecotourism as an empirical research object to be investigated at the *environment where it takes place*. Typically, the researchers delineate this research environment themselves by setting case study boundaries. Based on our reading of ecotourism research, we argue that these boundaries are predictable in the sense that they almost exclusively focus on the locality where the ecotourism product is sold and consumed. Figure 5.1 illustrates this research approach through a series of magnifying glass symbols representing case studies that investigate the

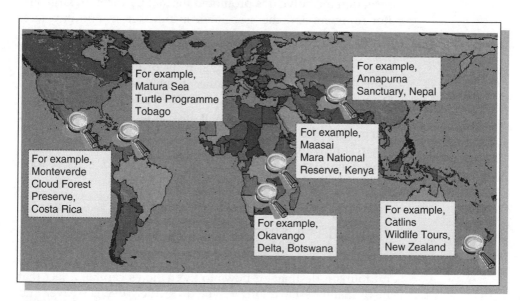

Figure 5.1
The reading glass approach to ecotourism

effects of ecotourism development *within* various individual destination localities. Since it reflects a micro-perspective, we describe such practice as the 'reading glass approach' to ecotourism research.

Without doubt, case studies make important and valuable contributions to our understanding of the growing ecotourism sector. We argue, however, that the micro-perspective they generally assume fails to capture the whole picture of ecotourism's performance in a global environment. Rather than accounting for ecotourism's heavy global footprint, the reading glass approach has led to an ill-conceived perception of ecotourism as a logical partner of conservation. To demonstrate the need for a widening of the current research perspective, we shall now discuss some key factors that link an ecotourism case study to global climate issues.

The paradox: local ecotourism with a global footprint

This section describes the magnitude of the global footprint associated with ecotourism travel and thereby highlights the need to consider those global impacts as part of ecotourism research no matter where it is located. We also consider possible control measures to reduce greenhouse gas emissions from international (ecotourism) air travel and discuss their potentially counterproductive development outcomes.

Global atmospheric impacts resulting from air travel

Greenhouse gas emissions from air travel have attracted increasing attention in recent years, partly as a result of the European Union's (Great Britain in particular) concern about the consequences of climate change and the growing contribution air travel is making to global emissions. Stabilization of CO_2 emissions will be difficult under the assumption of a continuously growing aviation sector. In the case of the UK, for example, the emissions from international air travel would make up 22%, 39%, or 67% of the national CO_2 budget in 2050 (depending on different growth rates of air travel at 3%, 4%, or 5%) (Lee *et al.*, 2005). There is also ongoing concern about the greater effect of emissions in the upper troposphere (about 10 km altitude) compared with surface travel (e.g. in relation to air contrails). Current research indicates that the effect of greenhouse gas emissions from aeroplanes could be about 2.7 times larger than CO_2 emissions alone (Penner *et al.*, 1999; Sausen *et al.*, 2005).

The World Tourism Organisation (2006) estimated over 808 million international arrivals for 2005. In 2000, 40% of those international arrivals were by air (Kester, 2002), and UNWTO predicts that long-haul travel (between distant world regions) will grow fastest. Environmental impacts will grow accordingly, unless major improvements in transport and aircraft technology are achieved. Ecotourists – as other tourists – increasingly travel by plane to reach their long-haul destinations. At the same time, ecotourism operations are increasingly taking place in developing countries, often in remote areas. The main markets for this long-haul ecotourism are relatively affluent tourists from Western countries, predominantly from North America and Europe (The International Ecotourism Society (TIES), 2000). Since the typical trip length for an ecotourism holiday is only between 8 and 14 days (TIES, 2000), fast and efficient transport modes are critical components of these vacations.

Popular ecotourism destinations[1] are, for example, Costa Rica, Trinidad and Tobago, Botswana, Kenya, Nepal, and New Zealand (see Figures 5.1 and 5.2). All of those, except New Zealand, are developing countries for which tourism is a major contributor to gross domestic product (GDP, see also Table 5.1), foreign exchange earnings, and employment. Even for New Zealand, tourism is one of the country's most important economic sectors, and a diversification from its traditionally dominant primary sectors. The ecotourism destinations listed above generate substantial intercontinental travel (Figure 5.2), mainly from North America and Europe, but also from Asia/Oceania (in the case of New Zealand). This origin-to-destination travel results in significant energy demand and greenhouse gas emissions. Return travel from London to Costa Rica, for example, produces about 2.5 tonnes of CO_2 per passenger travelling on a wide-bodied jet aircraft. In comparison, the per capita emissions of CO_2 in Costa Rica amount to only 1.2 tonnes annually (United Nations, 2001), so every tourist travelling to Costa Rica from Europe is responsible for more emissions than one Costa Rican in a whole year. Despite its simplified depiction, this example serves to highlight the unequal nature of travel to Third World destinations in general and the paradox of the 'eco' tourism label in particular.

Building on Gössling's (2002) estimate for CO_2 emissions associated with all tourist transport worldwide (1,263 million

---

[1]It is acknowledged that not every visitor to those destinations is an ecotourist. However, given the branding of these destinations, a substantial proportion of ecotourists compared to other tourists is assumed.

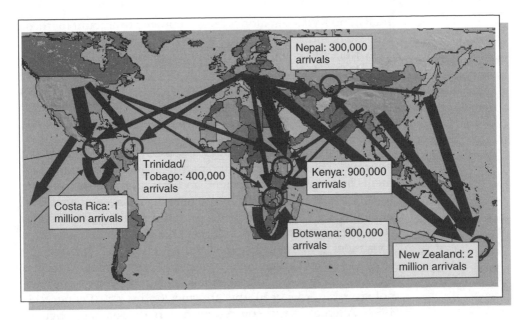

Nepal: 300,000 arrivals

Trinidad/ Tobago: 400,000 arrivals

Kenya: 900,000 arrivals

Costa Rica: 1 million arrivals

Botswana: 900,000 arrivals

New Zealand: 2 million arrivals

Figure 5.2
Selected ecotourism destinations and approximate tourist flows between these and their main markets of origin

tonnes in 2001) and assuming a share of ecotourism of 10%,[2] the cumulative emissions associated with ecotourism-related air transport would amount to about 88.4 million tonnes annually. This is similar to the annual total emissions by countries such as Belgium, the Philippines, or Greece. The above estimate does not take into account the greenhouse gas emissions produced as a result of the ecotourism operation itself, nor does it account for non-CO_2 emissions. The global environmental impact of ecotourism – as a result of transportation between origin and destination – is enormous and contradicts those conceptualizations of ecotourism that clearly require a low environmental impact from ecotourism holidays.

Reducing the impact of international aviation

Greenhouse gas emissions from international air travel are recognized in the Kyoto Protocol (Article 2, Paragraph 2 on bunker

[2]There is no global statistic on the size of the ecotourism market; estimates vary widely as they depend on the definition of ecotourism applied. More conservative estimates assume that ecotourists could make up 7% of international arrivals, whereas wider definitions lead to estimates of up to 30% (these would include nature tourism rather than just ecotourism) (TIES, 2000).

fuels), and Kyoto signatories are encouraged to account for those emissions and reduce them. However, they are reported separately from fuel consumed within national borders (IPCC, 1996) and do not form part of national emission reduction targets under the Kyoto Protocol. This means that so far countries have largely focused on reducing greenhouse gas emissions within their national borders rather than those associated with international travel.

Several measures are being discussed to reduce emissions from air travel. These include technological developments, improvements in air traffic management, and market-based instruments to control demand. Much improvement has been achieved in engine technology (about 40% over the last 40 years; Penner *et al.*, 1999); however, the development of new technologies often constitutes a trade-off between reducing fuel use and thereby CO_2, and water vapour emissions and NO_x emissions. The IPCC expects further reduction potentials from improved engine technology in the order of 10% by 2015 and 20% by 2050 (Penner *et al.*, 1999). Alternative fuel sources, such as hydrogen and ethylene, are being researched, but no short-term solution is expected.

In the short term, it is more likely that market-based instruments will lead to a reduction in air travel emissions. These can take various forms, such as a ticket surcharge, fuel, or emission levies, or the integration of aviation into national or global emission trading schemes. This last option is currently discussed by member countries of the European Union (Wit *et al.*, 2005). The advantage of an emission trading scheme is that it gives some assurance that the determined level of emissions would not be exceeded, and that savings are made where it is most economical.

Other forms of emission pricing, such as ticket surcharges, are highly controversial and least favoured by the airline industry. Assuming that such a price intervention would include CO_2 as well as non-CO_2 emissions (e.g. NO_x) and depending on the charge for emissions, the extra cost for a passenger flying the London–New York route could be in the order of €90 each way[3] (Whitelegg and Cambridge, 2004). Accordingly, in the case of the London–Costa Rica route, the price of an ecotour could increase by about €140. While these surcharges are hypothetical, the example serves to illustrate that regulatory pricing interventions may well affect consumer behaviour and, depending on price elasticities, reduce travel demand. It is unknown how higher ticket costs will affect specific markets

---

[3]Calculation based on the assumption of a surcharge of 0.3€ /kg kerosene for CO_2 and 14.31€ /kg kerosene for NO_x.

and destinations, but it is likely that tourists will at least to some extent substitute closer destinations for distant ones.

Local consequences of regulatory intervention

If greenhouse gas emissions from the aviation industry are regulated such that traffic volumes are reduced, this will affect those tourist destinations that depend on air travel for both tourists and supply of goods. Considering the growing volume of travel from rich to poorer countries, reduction in long-haul air travel will particularly affect Third World tourism accounts. A reduction in tourist arrivals is likely to result in economic losses (unless a destination achieves a shift from low-yielding to high-yielding forms of tourism). Substantial income losses could put at risk the long-term viability of long-haul travel and individual ecotourism destinations (e.g. the case studies in the reading glass approach). Particularly, less developed countries, which often rely strongly on ecotourism for their destination appeal and marketing mix, would suffer negative socio-economic consequences. As Table 5.1 illustrates the economic risk of losing tourism-related revenue and employment could be significant for the ecotourism destinations depicted in Figures 5.1 and 5.2.

The negative effects of reduced tourism flows would reach far beyond the material economy especially where ecotourism ventures are linked to conservation projects. As noted earlier, ecotourism is often promoted as a way of generating alternative benefits for local communities that traditionally rely strongly on harvesting natural resources. Where alternative income sources

Table 5.1 Economic indicators for the importance of tourism in selected ecotourism destinations for 2001 (WTTC, 2001)

Ecotourism destination	Tourism's contribution to GDP (%)	Tourism's contribution to foreign exchange earnings (%)	Proportion of employment generated by tourism (%)
Costa Rica	7.9	18.4	6.3
Trinidad/Tobago	4.1	17.8	2.0
Botswana	3.5	8.5	4.5
Kenya	4.3	17.9	3.3
Nepal	4.5	19.7	4.9
New Zealand	6.0	15.0	6.1

are sought, ecotourism is frequently seen as the only sustainable option. As Borchers (2002) pointed out, often, ecotourism is in fact, and arguably so, the only permissible resource use; hence, the increasing popularity of these particular niche market products as support activities for conservation projects.

International endorsement by organizations such as UNDP (discussed earlier) shows the significant expectations placed on ecotourism as a conservation support instrument. In light of our discussion of the effects of air traffic reduction, a new dimension of the ecotourism–conservation paradox becomes evident. Future regulation to improve environmental performance of the aviation transport sector may reduce atmospheric pollution on a global scale (and thus be in line with biodiversity conservation goals). At a destination level, however, such regulation could well reduce tourism incomes and therefore put additional pressure on non-renewable resources (and thus counteract local biodiversity protection efforts). The conservation–development nexus of ecotourism not only has far-reaching environmental implications but air travel's future regulation also poses a social dilemma of local–global complexity.

An open-systems approach

Based on our discussion of macro-scale environmental effects, we suggest that the current analytical perception of ecotourism should take a wider perspective. Our brief exposé of tourism impacts on the global atmosphere (and therefore biosphere) illustrates that the reading glass research approach that underpins most case studies is flawed. Ecotourism case studies usually resemble a closed system that pretends no connection with the outer world. This approach represents a convenient research agenda for those studies, which treat tourism as a localized (and thus easily delineated and analysed) phenomenon. Our overview of selected global effects demonstrates that it is important to open the closed system and include external aspects that are linked to the specific study in question. Most notably, this would include tourists' transport components and transit routes (see Figure 5.3), especially if researchers test environmental performance. Clearly, the resource efficiency of ecotourism cannot be measured in terms of destination impacts alone, but must account for the overall energy demand and emissions resulting from the various components of the wider tourism system.

The discussion of international air travel also showed that changes in global tourist flows as a result of climate change mitigation measures are likely to affect the viability of ecotourism

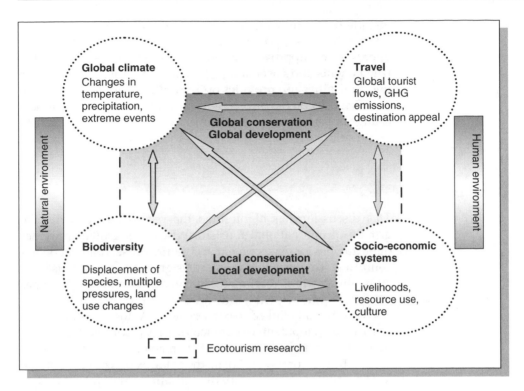

Figure 5.3
Open-system ecotourism research integrating local and global dimensions

operations for local communities. Therefore, there is a need to monitor those pricing effects and consider them in the planning process for future ecotourism developments. Figure 5.3 also shows other important relationships between ecotourism case studies and the wider environment. For example, as outlined in the introduction, the global climate – and any changes thereof – is highly relevant to ecotourism destinations. The global climate also affects the nature and distribution of international tourism flows (Hamilton *et al.*, 2005). Strong links also exist between the global climate and biodiversity, and likewise between the climate and socio-economic systems. Figure 5.3 illustrates that an open-systems approach to ecotourism research takes into consideration those multiple relationships, interactions, and dependencies. Such an approach also allows the integration of both global and local issues, and as a result provides an appropriate framework to address the complex paradox of global travel, energy use, greenhouse gas emissions, and conservation and development goals.

Viewed in this light, the 'environments where it takes place' referred to in the opening quote (UNWTO, 2001) do not just include the destinations visited, but all environmental systems affected by the supply of ecotourism products and services. An open-systems approach not only allows the assessment of the true benefits and costs of a particular ecotourism operation in question, but it also provides opportunities to identify potential risks imposed on the project by various external factors. Climate change impacts are one obvious example, but other relationships and resulting risks are conceivable and should be investigated.

Conclusion

This discussion has highlighted the paradox inherent in the growth of international tourism. While this growth provides opportunities for development and nature conservation in poorer countries, it is also the source of significant greenhouse gas emissions leading to climate change. This paradox becomes nowhere more evident as in the case of ecotourism, which is also conceptually linked to conservation. At the same time, eco-tourism development is characterized by complex interrela-tionships, multiple linkages, and far-reaching impacts. As is the case with other forms of tourism, the paradox of ecotourism mani-fests locally as well as globally and affects natural as well as human environments. Socio-economic considerations are cen-tral to the role of ecotourism as a development tool, especially where it is designed to support conservation projects by gener-ating income and/or non-material benefits for poor communities. Strategies to improve the energy efficiency of tourism trans-port, air traffic in particular, must take into account the intra-generational equity issues that arise if control measures reduce tourism flows from the rich world to less developed countries. Against the background of the millennium development target to halve worldwide poverty by the year 2015 as well as current protocols and proposals to improve energy efficiency, the call for a more inclusive and balanced discussion of these issues is not only timely but also a matter of urgency.

The current reading glass or closed-systems approach to eco-tourism research makes it very difficult or simply impossible to ascertain the balance between benefits and impacts generated by a particular project. Even if examined on a local scale, many ecotourism projects remain controversial. Adding a national or global component to the mix of indicators poses a new challenge, and bears the potential of gaining a more complete picture of the true value of an ecotourism project. The fact that tourism is an open system with multi-faceted, complex relationships, link-ages and concomitant effects on global environments should not be viewed as a threat by those practising sound research. Rather, it is a creative challenge best met by a holistic research approach based on an open-systems perspective akin to that underpinning ecological systems analysis.

The open-systems approach and the link to global issues clearly challenge the widely accepted conceptual link between ecotourism and nature conservation, as we cannot a priori assume their relationship to be symbiotic. The question must be asked: what size of 'carbon footprint' is acceptable to achieve unambiguous local benefits in (developing countries) ecotourism destinations? To answer this question, we need to change not only the way we perceive 'eco'-tourism but, importantly, also the way we approach tourism case study research in general.

References

Becken, S. and Hay, J. (forthcoming). *Tourism and Climate Change – Risk and Opportunities*. Channel View Publications, Cleveland.

Boo, E. (1990). *Ecotourism: The Potentials and Pitfalls*, vol. 2. World Wildlife Fund, Washington DC.

Borchers, H. (2002). *Jurassic Wilderness: Ecotourism as a Conservation Strategy in Komodo National Park, Indonesia*. Masters Thesis, University of Auckland, New Zealand.

Brohmann, J. (1996). New directions in tourism for Third World development. *Annals of Tourism Research* 23: 48–70.

CBD (2001–2005), Convention on Biological Diversity, Online, 2001–2005. Available at March 15, 2006, http://www.biodiv.org/default.shtml

Duffy, R. (2002). *A Trip Too Far. Ecotourism, Politics & Exploitation*. Earthscan, London.

Erb, M. (2001). Ecotourism and environmental conservation in Western Flores: who benefits? *Antropologi Indonesia* 66: 72–88.

Fennell, D.A. (2003). *Ecotourism*, (2nd edn). Routledge, London and New York.

Gössling, S. (2002). Global environmental consequences of tourism. *Global Environmental Change* 12: 283–302.

Gössling, S., Borgström Hansson, C., Hörstmeier, O. and Saggel, S. (2002). Ecological footprint analysis as a tool to assess tourism sustainability. *Ecological Economics* 43(2–3): 199–211.

Hamilton, J., Maddison, D. and Tol, R. (2005). Climate change and international tourism: a simulation study. *Global Environmental Change Part, A* 15(3): 253–266.

IPCC (1996). Revised 1996 IPCC guidelines for *National Greenhouse Gas Inventories*. Reporting Instructions. Available at February 1, 2003, http://www.ipcc-nggip.iges.or.jp/public/gl/invs4.htm

Kester, J.G.C. (2002). Preliminary results for international tourism in 2002, air transportation after 11 September. *Tourism Economics* 9(1): 95–110.

Lee, D.S., Lim, L.L. and Raper, S.C. (2005). The role of aviation emissions in climate stabilization scenarios. Poster at *Avoiding Dangerous Climate Change Conference*, 1–3 February, Exeter, UK.

Lübben, C. (1995). *Internationaler Tourismus als Faktor der Regionalentwicklung in Indonesien. Untersucht am Beispiel der Insel Lombok*. Reimer, Berlin.

Mowforth, M. and Munt, I. (2003). *Tourism and Sustainability. Development and New Tourism in the Third World*, (2nd edn). Routledge, London and New York.

Orams, M. (1995). Towards a more desirable form of ecotourism. *Tourism Management* 16: 3–8.

Penner, J., Lister, D., Griggs, D., Dokken, D. and McFarland, M. (eds) (1999). *Aviation and the Global Atmosphere*. A special report of IPCC Working Groups I and III. Published for the Intergovernmental Panel on Climate Change. University Press, Cambridge.

Richards, G. and Hall, D. (eds) (2000). Tourism and Sustainable Community Development. Routledge, London.

Richter, L.K. (1989). *The Politics of Tourism in Asia*. University of Hawaii Press, Honolulu.

Sausen, R., Isaksen, I., Grewe, V., Hauglustaine, D., Lee, D., Myhre, G., Koehler, M., Pitari, G., Schumann, Ul., Stordal, F. and Zerefos, C. (2005). Aviation radiative forcing in 2000: an update on IPCC (1999). *Meteorologische Zeitschrift* 14(4): 555–561.

Scheyvens, R. (2002). *Tourism for Development: Empowering Communities*. Prentice Hall, Harlow.

Scheyvens, R. and Purdie, N. (1999). Ecotourism. In Overton, J. and Scheyvens, R. (eds), *Strategies for Sustainable Development: Experiences from the Pacific*. UNSW Press, Sydney.

Simmons, D. and Becken, S. (2004). Ecotourism – the cost of getting there. In Buckley, R. (ed.), *Case Studies in Ecotourism*. CAB International, Wallingford, pp. 15–23.

The International Ecotourism Society (2000). *Ecotourism Statistical Fact Sheet*. Available at March 20, 2006, http://www.ecotourism.org/research/stats/files/stats.pdf

UNEP (2002). http://www.uneptie.org/pc/tourism/ecotourism/home.htm (accessed February 2006).

United Nations (2001). *Population, Environment and Development*. Population Division, Department of Economic and Social Affairs. Available at March 15, 2006, http://www.un.org/esa/population/publications/pdewallchart/popenvdev.pdf

UN World Tourism Organisation (2001). *Sustainable Development of Ecotourism. A Compilation of Good Practices.* World Tourism Organisation, Madrid.

UN World Tourism Organisation (ed.) (2003). *The ST-EP Initiative 2002/2003 Sustainable Tourism – Eliminating Poverty.* World Tourism Organisation, Madrid.

UN World Tourism Organisation (2006). *Tourism Facts.* Available March 12, 2006, www.world-tourism.org/facts/wtb.html

US National Research Council (2002). *Abrupt Climate Change – Inevitable Surprises.* National Academy Press, Washington DC.

Weaver, D. and Elliott, K. (1996). Spatial patterns and problems in contemporary Namibian tourism. *Geographical Journal* 162: 205–217.

Weaver, D.B. (2002). Asian ecotourism: patterns and themes. *Tourism Geographies* 4(2): 153–172.

Whitelegg, J. and Cambridge, H. (2004). *Aviation and Sustainability.* Stockholm Environment Institute. Available at January 20, 2005, www.sei.se

Wit, R., Boon, B., van Velzen, A., Cames, M., Heuber, O. and Lee, D. (2005). *Giving Wings to Emission Trading. Inclusion of Aviation under the European Emission Trading System (ETS): Design and Impacts.* Summary of draft final report. Available at June 02, 2005, www.ce.nl

World Travel and Tourism Council (WTTC) (2001). *Tourism Satellite Accounting Research. Estimates and Forecasts for Government and Industry.* WTTC, London.

Biosecurity and ecotourism

C. Michael Hall

Introduction: tourism and biosecurity

The world is an increasingly mobile place. Improvements in transport and communications technology, population growth, growth in per capita income, greater consumerism, deregulation and internationalisation of the world economic system, and moves towards 'free trade' have all encouraged greater mobility of goods, services, ideas, businesses and people. Tourism, along with labour and amenity migration, is an important part of the growth in the movement of people. However, increased movements of people across political and physical borders can have a number of unintended and unwanted consequences. Much of the focus is on the political, social and economic dimensions of illegal migrants. Yet arguably an even greater economic and social risk is the unwanted movement of diseases and pests that may affect humans directly or impact the environments on which they depend.

Many species are moved from one location to another as a result of trade. However, increased leisure travel, including the transport and infrastructure systems that support tourism and recreation, is increasingly acting as a vector for disease or undesirable flora and fauna, which in themselves may host or transport diseases (e.g. Russell, 1987; Carlton and Geller, 1993; Berkelman *et al.*, 1994; Wilson, 1995, 2003; Fidler, 1996; Ginzburg, 1996; Legors and Danis, 1998; Cookson *et al.*, 2001; Seys and Bender, 2001; Angell and Cetron, 2005; Steffen, 2005) (Table 6.1).

The protection of a country, region or location's economic, environmental and/or human health from harmful or undesirable organisms is referred to as biosecurity. 'Biosecurity involves preventing the introduction of harmful new organisms, and

---

Table 6.1 What is carried by humans when they travel

- Pathogens in or on body or clothes
- Microbiologic fauna and flora on body or clothes
- Vectors on body or clothes
- Immunologic sequelae of past infections
- Vulnerability to infections
- Genetic makeup
- Cultural preferences, customs, behavioural patterns, technology
- Luggage and whatever it contains, including food, soil, fauna, flora and organic material

Source: After Wilson (1995) and Hall (2005).

eradicating or controlling those unwanted organisms that are already present' (Biosecurity Strategy Development Team, 2001a, Sec. 1.3). Although tourism is a major focal point for biosecurity measures, particularly with respect to border control mechanisms in relation to agricultural protection, there is surprisingly little discussion of the significance of biosecurity measures in the tourism studies literature until very recently. Indeed, many in the tourism industry may be unaware of the role that tourism plays in biosecurity management beyond the perceived inconvenience they believe that tourists may encounter with respect to customs and biosecurity clearance (Pinfield, 2001). For example, even though New Zealand is a country with a very strong biosecurity strategy because of its relative geographical isolation and high degree of economic dependence on agricultural produce, of the 122 submissions received with respect to developing a new biosecurity strategy (Biosecurity Strategy Development Team, 2001b) only one came from the tourism industry (Biosecurity Strategy Development Team, 2002).

With respect to the tourism studies literature, several authors have noted the role of tourism as a factor in health and disease spread, and the potential for tourism to introduce diseases, pests and weeds into locations where they did not previously exist (e.g. Hall, 1992, 2003; Rudkin and Hall, 1996; Jay et al., 2003). Nevertheless, it must also be noted that in a number of countries, particularly those settled by European colonists, there is a long legacy of the deliberate introduction of alien species that are regarded as desirable from the perspective of hunting, fishing and other forms of tourism and recreation. For example, there is a long history of fish species being deliberately introduced from one location to another outside their previous range in order to enhance recreational fishing opportunities (Huckins et al., 2000) that often are now regarded as being an important element of nature-based tourism activities. In the case of the United States the stocking of wilderness lakes with trout began in the 1800s (Pister, 2001). This practice was followed for nearly a century with the singular goal of creating and enhancing sport fishing and without any consideration of its ecological ramifications. It was only in the 1960s that changes to practices started to occur when research indicated negative impacts on the native biota attributable to introduced species. As Pister (2001) notes, the necessity for wilderness fish stocking is now the subject of widespread debate in the United States especially in view of changing social values and priorities with respect to preserving the biodiversity of mountain lake ecosystems. Similar debates are also occurring in other countries such as Australia and

New Zealand where trout were introduced for purposes of sport fishing and the Europeanisation of the environment. However, the presence of such desirable fish species is often presented as part of the promotion of nature-based experiences even though they are exotics. Although the deliberate introduction of species is a significant point of debate between different stakeholders in nature-based tourism because of the tradeoffs between ecological impacts and economic and personal benefits (Huckins *et al.*, 2000), there is usually little debate over the damage caused by unplanned introductions of species.

Much of the concern over the introduction of alien species lies in their potential economic damage. Pimentel *et al.* (2000) estimated that the approximately 50,000 exotic species in the United States have an economic impact of US$137 billion per annum in terms of their economic damage and costs of control. Yet although such figures are staggering, they do not isolate the impacts of exotic introductions on tourism. One plant pest that has been accidentally spread by boating recreationists is Eurasian watermilfoil (*Myriophyllum spicatum*), an aquatic invasive weed that has been identified recently at a number of sites in the western United States including Lake Tahoe. Because Eurasian watermilfoil is easily spread by fragments, transport on boats and boating equipment plays a key role in contaminating water bodies. The weed has significant impacts on aquatic ecosystems, with associated economic affects on tourism and recreation uses. In a study of the value of a portion of the recreational service flows that society currently enjoys in the Truckee River watershed below Lake Tahoe, Eiswerth *et al.* (2000) calculated that the lower-bound estimates of baseline water-based recreation value at a subset of sites in the watershed ranged from US$30 to US$45 million per annum. Given such economic significance of water-based recreation the impacts from the continued spread of Eurasian watermilfoil in the watershed could be extremely significant and they suggested that even a 1% decrease in recreation values would correspond to losses of approximately US$500,000 per annum as a lower-bound estimate. Such results are important as there is only limited research on the economic impacts of alien species introduction specifically on the value of nature-based tourism.

More recently biosecurity issues have become a focal point for tourism concerns as a result of the impacts of disease control on tourist movement. Examples here include the impacts associated with the outbreak of foot-and-mouth disease in the United Kingdom in 2001, the SARS outbreak in 2003 and concerns surrounding the potential effects of an avian flu pandemic on international tourism flows (Sharpley and Craven, 2001;

Jay and Morad, 2003; Basili and Franzini, 2006). In addition, debate has started to emerge as to who should pay the costs of providing biosecurity, with government in many countries seeking to place the costs of provision on to carriers and/or passengers (e.g. Pinfield, 2001). For example, the New Zealand Parliamentary Commissioner for the Environment commented:

There is a strong case for some requirement on primary producers and other beneficiaries from the system to pay for some level of biosecurity protection, and for importers to pay for some element of biosecurity levy for increasing the risk to producers and the environment. But this argument is complicated by the fact that there is overlap in the benefits of biosecurity between private sector interests, such as those parts of the service industry that derive benefits from indigenous flora and fauna (e.g. ecotourism), and those of the public sector. In a broad economic sense, New Zealand is taking private risks with public externalities, but there is also a lack of risk transparency between private sector interests (2001, p. 62).

Ecotourism

The above general discussion on biosecurity and tourism have important implications for ecotourism. Although ecotourism does occur in a variety of environments it is more usually spatially concentrated in more peripheral regions that retain high natural values. The relative remoteness of such regions usually means that they have a relatively low proportion of introduced fauna and flora with the high degree of indigenous biodiversity usually being a drawcard for ecotourists. Nature-based tourism is ultimately based upon the factors that allow an area to display the characteristics of perceived and actual naturalness. These factors include accessibility, numbers of visitors and the relative naturalness as defined by distance from permanent human structures and ecological integrity. Ironically, the smaller the number of visitors, and the harder an area is to access, the higher is usually the perceived degree of naturalness (Figure 6.1). Such a situation therefore creates a number of difficult situations for tourism development, because if increasing number of tourists is the measure of success for nature-based tourism development so the greater the numbers of visitors so the lower the naturalness of the location will be as a result of impacts on the environment including trampling effects, the introduction of new species and the loss of existing biodiversity (Hall, 2004). In the case of New Zealand, for example, the Parliamentary Commissioner for the Environment (2001, p. 24) noted that indigenous biological assets were important to the tourism industry, because it 'relies

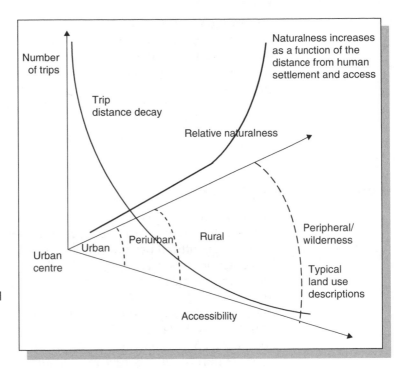

Figure 6.1
Tourism in peripheral areas: accessibility, naturalness and trip distance decay (Hall, 2004)

on the provision of natural experiences through the integrity of unique biological landscapes and the lack of threatening species'.

The potential impacts of biosecurity breaches on ecotourism are therefore several fold with respect to both the quality of the resource and attractions as well as impacting the ecotourist directly including:

1. The loss of the perceived naturalness of locations as a result of the introduction of exotic species and/or the loss of indigenous biodiversity.
2. The loss of indigenous biodiversity.
3. The loss of charismatic or attraction species as a result of competition with introduced species, habitat change because of exotic introductions or the introduction of disease.
4. Limits on tourist access or movement in order to control dispersal of exotics or diseases.

Given the supposed relationship between ecotourism and the conservation of the environment one could therefore likely expect there to be a substantial discussion in the ecotourism literature on the importance of biosecurity controls and how these should be integrated into business practices. However, there is not. Although there is an enormous literature on species range, conservation and tourism and travel's role in species dispersal from a biogeographical, biological conservation and environmental change perspective (Hall, 2006), this is not a literature that has actively been engaged in within the ecotourism literature or business community. Nevertheless, the sensitivity and vulnerability of many ecotourist destinations and attractions to species loss and/or environmental degradation means that biosecurity is an issue that the ecotourism sector needs to address.

Biosecurity management

Biosecurity measures occur at a number of different scales, all the way from the international level, such as agreements on the movement of agricultural produce through border controls, through to biosecurity practices at individual locations, such as farms. Biosecurity strategies can also be categorised in terms of their utility at the pre-border, border and post-border stages (Biosecurity Strategy Development Team, 2001a, 2001b; Green, 2001; Hall, 2005) (Table 6.2). However, it should be noted that the notion of a border here need not be a national border, for management purposes the border may be an administrative border, such as a government jurisdictional boundary or even a national park boundary. Similarly, border security strategies may utilise natural boundaries, such as watersheds, islands or specific natural environments.

Tourism is clearly a major area of biosecurity risk and is a focal point of border control activities, particularly in agriculturally based economies and regions. In Australia, a country with a long history of biological introductions (Pimentel *et al.*, 2000), the Australian National Audit Office (ANAO) (2001, p. 16) estimated that more than half of prohibited material carried by international airline passengers, entered Australia undetected. In Australia, there has been a marked increase in the number of interceptions of pests and diseases at the border, from around 3,500 interceptions in 1994 to over 10,000 in 1999 (ANAO, 2001). This may be due in part to increased international tourism and trade, but is also a likely result of improved biosecurity strategies with respect to surveillance, that is the more you look the more you find. Prohibited items, that is those considered having 'a high risk of carrying pests or diseases and which are seized, treated or re-exported', intercepted at Australian airports increased from 1,000 per month in 1998 to 4,000 per month in 2000, reflecting the impact of quarantine reform initiatives (ANAO, 2001, p. 25). Just as significant is the estimated leakage rate which measures the percentage of all items that have crossed the border but which still

Table 6.2 Pre-border, border and post-border biosecurity strategies

Pre-border
- Identifying threats to ecosystems and species.
- Profiling and modelling the characteristics of damaging or potentially damaging organisms and vectors.
- Identifying controls (in the country/region of origin) for selected organisms that pose a threat to destinations.
- Analysing and predicting risk pathways for unwanted organisms.
- Identifying and collating databases and expertise on unwanted organisms.
- Developing systems for rapid access to appropriate data.
- Developing import standards and compliance validation methodologies.
- Auditing exporting countries' compliance with destination biosecurity standards.
- Identifying and locating biosecurity-related risks to animal, plant and human health.
- Analysis of public attitudes and perceptions of biosecurity risks and barriers to biosecurity responses in visitor generating areas.
- Development of educational programmes in tourism source regions so as to reduce likelihood of introduction of unwanted organisms.
- Development of educational programmes for tourists and tourism businesses in both generating and destination regions so as to reduce likelihood of introduction of unwanted organisms.

Border
- Developing improved systems, including clearance systems and sampling methodologies, and technologies for intercepting unwanted organisms according to import standards.
- Developing border containment and eradication methodologies according to import standards.
- Developing profiles of non-compliance behaviour by individuals and firms to biosecurity requirements.

Post-border (includes pest management)
- Developing rapid identification techniques for unwanted organisms.
- Designing and developing methodologies for undertaking delimiting surveys for new incursions.
- Developing rapid response options for potential incursions of unwanted organisms.
- Analysis of public and business attitudes and perceptions of biosecurity risks and barriers to biosecurity responses in destination areas.
- Developing long-term containment, control and eradication strategies.

General
- Analysis of economic and political models for the management of biosecurity threats.
- Development of rapid-access information systems, collections and environmental databases on unwanted organisms.
- Improve export opportunities for 'clean' products, including service exports such as tourism.
- Development of industry and public biosecurity education programmes.

Source: After Hall (2003, 2005).

contain or possess seizable material. According to ANAO the leakage rates for airline passengers arriving in Australia have been relatively stable since 1998, at between 3% and 4%. Using these figures the ANAO in their audit of quarantine effectiveness in Australia estimate that 'in excess of half of the seizable material (or 300,000 items per year) carried by international air passengers breaches the quarantine barrier' (2001: 27).

From a tourism perspective biosecurity strategies occur at different stages of the trip cycle: decision-making and anticipation, travel to a tourism destination or attraction, the on-site experience, return travel and recollection of the experience. Each of these five stages will have different psychological characteristics with implications for how tourism organisations and businesses establish a relationship with the customer or, in the case of biosecurity, how biosecurity and quarantine organisations establish a relationship with the traveller and assists them in undertaking good biosecurity practice (Hall, 2003). As Fridgen (1984: 24) observed, 'people not only act in their present setting, they also plan for subsequent settings. People prepare to arrive in another setting to carry out preplanned behaviors'.

Central to appropriate tourism biosecurity practice is an improved understanding of biosecurity and quarantine. For example, improving awareness of biosecurity may lead to a decrease in the number of prohibited items which cross a border. In Australia the ANAO (2001, p. 24) noted that 'Awareness of quarantine amongst Australians intending to travel, or who have travelled recently, has improved markedly' since implementation of a national campaign to improve public understanding of, and commitment to, quarantine. Similarly, New Zealand has also developed a communications and education programme 'to emphasise the value of biosecurity and the role travellers can play in preserving New Zealand's unique flora and fauna' (Biosecurity Strategy Development Team, 2002, p. 11). Such measures apply not only to the international visitor but also to New Zealanders travelling abroad as 'incoming New Zealanders are responsible for 40% of border infringements by passengers' (Biosecurity Strategy Development Team, 2002, p. 11). As the 'issues paper' written as part of the development of a biosecurity strategy for New Zealand noted:

Because the actions of travellers and importers are key to successful biosecurity management, education and awareness programmes may have significant potential to provide low cost gains in biosecurity protection. Education is possibly the major risk management tool available for biosecurity. If the level of risk consistently presented at the border is lowered, facilitation could be improved and compliance costs and general inconvenience reduced. . . Programmes should encourage the general public to take personal accountability for protecting New Zealand's biosecurity. Attitude change may be the best way to reduce long-term risks in the face of increased trade and travel. . . Biosecurity agencies should work co-operatively with industries to develop messages and tools specific to the range of target audiences. The tourism industry is well placed to help to improve visitor awareness of the importance of biosecurity to New Zealand, and biosecurity messages could be inte-grated with tourism promotion campaigns.

(Biosecurity Strategy Development Team, 2001b, pp. 24–25)

Given such a policy agenda Hall (2003) investigated biosecurity issues with respect to New Zealand wine tourism in relation to customs passenger declarations and potential risk factors asso-ciated with clothing. Hall found that the majority of respondents did not perceive a vineyard or winery as being a farm which, it was argued, may lead to non-reporting on customs and agricul-tural forms. In addition, 45% of respondents believed that they had worn the same footwear on their last visit to a vineyard as they had on the visit where they surveyed, while 10% believed they were wearing another piece of clothing they had worn or carried with them on their previous vineyard visit. Significantly, Hall noted that consequent discussions with respondents sug-gested that with respect to clothing the 10% figure may have been substantially underestimated by a further 10–15%. Yet just as importantly such figures need to be put into a context in which approximately only 7% of New Zealand wineries had a biosecurity strategy at the time that winery visitor surveys were conducted (Christensen *et al.*, 2004).

In light of the biosecurity issues associated with the New Zealand wine industry the author has since gone on to examine some of the biosecurity measures of other New Zealand tourism sectors including nature-based tourism businesses and entre-preneurs. However, as with the wine tourism sector, the results of research with respect to nature-based tourism operators are more significant for what does not happen as what does with respect to biosecurity management. Participant observation was undertaken of self-identified ecotourism/wildlife businesses and tour operations associated with New Zealand's World Heritage, national parks and conservation estate over the period 2001–2005. Of the 18 different businesses studied not one enacted any proced-ure to ensure that customers did not introduce seeds or soil con-taminants into the conservation area, that is by ensuring that shoes and clothes were clean or by briefing people as to the importance of not introducing species themselves even though interpretation often commented on the damage wrought to New Zealand's environment by introduced species in general.

The observation is of even more concern given that Department of Conservation concessions for commercial operations on the Conservation Estate will often include procedures for good bio-security management practice, for example by getting guides to ensure that footwear is clean before entering protected areas.

As suggested above, the problem with such research is that it highlights the absence of procedures in a country in which the environment is an essential part of national branding with respect to tourism while nature-based tourism provides an important tourist activity in many rural and peripheral regions. While such businesses often proclaim the positive role that tourism can have in promoting conservation, they often fail to manage the dangers to the environment that tourism can also bring. Moreover, the lack of educative message with respect to biosecurity is also seemingly at odds with the education function that is also meant to be integral to ecotourism. The question clearly arises as to whether this is purely a New Zealand phenomenon. Unfortunately, the lack of research on ecotourism and biosecurity means that we do not know. However, the author would argue that in taking ecotourism tours or visiting ecotourism operations around the world he has never once been asked to ensure his shoes were clean or that he was not bringing in seeds on his clothing. Instead, such questions are asked at some national borders. Yet as we have seen such borders are permeable and operators at the local level cannot solely rely on them for the protection of the resources that keeps them in business, especially in countries that do not have the natural protection of being islands.

Conclusions

This chapter has highlighted the potential importance of biose-curity for ecotourism. People have been responsible for the intro-duction of alien invasive species throughout history and in all parts of the world. Species have been introduced both deliber-ately and accidentally. International tourism has long been recognised as a contributor to species dispersal and exchange. However, ecotourists arguably present substantial biosecurity risks to biodiversity and keystone species precisely because it typically occurs in peripheral areas that rely on a high degree of naturalness as part of their attraction to visitors.

Nevertheless, it is important to recognise that environmental change as the result of the natural dispersal and flows of species into ecosystems is a normal process. The issue that many envi-ronments face now is that the rate of such biotic exchange has increased dramatically in recent years as a result of global trade and tourism. There are two main reasons why the introduction of alien species is more difficult to deal with than many other serious environmental problems that may impact biodiversity and conservation strategies. First, it is very difficult to predict the impact of introduction of exotic species on ecosystems. The deliberate introduction of a species may result in the desired effects in terms of availability for amenity, but in many cases there is a negative impact on other species and even on the habitat and the results are often not as anticipated. Second, it is generally very difficult to reverse the introduction of a species. If an introduced species becomes securely established, experience shows that it is almost impossible to eradicate it from the ecosystem (Ministry of the Environment, 2001). In both cases the onus is on the ecotourism sector, along with other sectors to undertake precautionary measures to try and prevent such introductions, particularly as other dimensions of global environmental change such as climate change and land use change may magnify the negative impacts of any unwanted species introduction (Hall, 2006).

Although evidence is patchy it is suggested that ecotourism operations rely on customs and agricultural measures at national borders to provide biosecurity management. Although such measures are clearly significant, ecotourism operations also have a great role to play in minimising biosecurity risks. Given the dependency of ecotourism businesses on biodiversity and the conservation and education message that is meant to be at the core of ecotourism experience it is imperative that ecotourism become part of the vanguard of biosecurity management rather than a passive beneficiary.

References

Angell, S.Y. and Cetron, M.S. (2005). Health disparities among travelers visiting friends and relatives abroad. *Annals of Internal Medicine* 142(1): 67–72.

Australian National Audit Office (ANAO) (2001). *Managing for Quarantine Effectiveness: Department of Agriculture, Fisheries and Forestry – Australia*, The Auditor General Audit Report No. 47 2000–2001 Performance Audit. Commonwealth of Australia, Canberra.

Basili, M. and Franzini, M. (2006). Understanding the risk of an avian flu pandemic: rational waiting or precautionary failure? *Risk Analysis* 26(3): 617–630.

Berkelman, R.L., Bryan, R.T., Osterholm, M.T., LeDuc, J.W. and Hughes, J.M. (1994). Infectious disease surveillance: a crumbling foundation. *Science* 264: 368–370.

Biosecurity Strategy Development Team (2001a). *A Biosecurity Strategy for New Zealand, Strategy Vision Framework Background Paper for Stakeholder Working Groups.* Biosecurity Strategy Development Team, Wellington.

Biosecurity Strategy Development Team (2001b). *Issues Paper: Developing a Biosecurity Strategy for New Zealand: A Public Consultation Paper.* Biosecurity Strategy Development Team, Wellington.

Biosecurity Strategy Development Team (2002). *Developing a Biosecurity Strategy for New Zealand Submissions on the 'Issues Paper': A Summary Report.* Biosecurity Strategy Development Team, Wellington.

Carlton, J.T. and Geller, J.B. (1993). Ecological roulette: the global transport of non-indigenous marine organisms, *Science* 261: 78–82.

Christensen, D., Hall, C.M. and Mitchell, R. (2004). The 2003 New Zealand wineries survey. In *Creating Tourism Knowledge, 14th International Research Conference of the Council for Australian University Tourism and Hospitality Education, 10–13 February, School of Tourism and Leisure Management, University of Queensland, Book of Abstracts.* University of Queensland, Brisbane.

Cookson, S.T., Carballo, M., Nolan, C.M., Keystone, J.S. and Jong, E.C. (2001). Migrating populations – a closer view of who, why, and so what. *Journal of Emerging Infectious Diseases* 7(3) (Suppl, June): 551.

Eiswerth, M.E., Donaldson, S.G. and Johnson, W.S. (2000). Potential environmental impacts and economic damages of Eurasian watermilfoil (*Myriophyllum spicatum*) in western Nevada and northeastern California. *Weed Technology* 14(3): 511–518.

Fidler, D.P. (1996). ABA sponsors program on law and emerging infectious diseases. *Journal of Emerging Infectious Diseases* 2(4): 364.

Fridgen, J.D. (1984). Environmental psychology and tourism. *Annals of Tourism Research* 11: 19–40.

Ginzburg, H.M. (1996). Commentary – needed: comprehensive response to the spread of infectious diseases. *Journal of Emerging Infectious Diseases* 2(2): 151.

Green, W. (2001). *Review of Current Biosecurity Research in New Zealand.* Biosecurity Strategy Development Team, Wellington.

Hall, C.M. (1992). Tourism in Antarctica: activities, impacts, and management. *Journal of Travel Research* 30(4): 2–9.

Hall, C.M. (2003). Biosecurity and wine tourism: is a vineyard a farm? *Journal of Wine Research* 14(2–3): 121–126.

Hall, C.M. (2004). Seeing the trees in the forest: reflections on local connections for nature-based tourism. In Saarinen, J. and Hall, C.M. (eds), *Nature-Based Tourism Research in Finland: Local Contexts, Global Issues*, Finnish Forest Research Institute, Research Papers 916. Rovaniemi Research Station, Rovaniemi, pp. 9–18.

Hall, C.M. (2005). *Tourism: Rethinking the Social Science of Mobility*. Prentice-Hall, Harlow.

Hall, C.M. (2006). Tourism, biodiversity and global environmental change. In Gössling, S. and Hall, C.M. (eds), *Tourism and Global Environmental Change: Ecological, Economic, Social and Political Interrelationships*. Routledge, London, pp. 211–226.

Huckins, C.J.F., Osenberg, C.W. and Mittelbach, G.G. (2000). Species introductions and their ecological consequences: an example with congeneric sunfish. *Ecological Applications* 10(2): 612–625.

Jay, M. and Morad, M. (2003). Lessons for New Zealand from Britain's foot and mouth epidemic. *New Zealand Geographer* 59(1): 40–49.

Jay, M., Morad, M. and Bell, A. (2003). Biosecurity – a policy dilemma for New Zealand. *Land Use Policy* 20(2): 121–129.

Legors, F. and Danis, M. (1998). Surveillance of malaria in European Union countries. *Eurosurveillance* 3: 45–47.

Ministry of the Environment (2001). *Norwegian Biodiversity Policy and Action Plan – Cross-sector Responsibilities and Coordination, Report No. 42 to the Storting*. Ministry of the Environment, Oslo.

Parliamentary Commissioner for the Environment (2001). *New Zealand Under Seige: A Review of the Management of Biosecurity Risks to the Environment*. Office of the Parliamentary Commission for the Environment, Wellington.

Pimentel, D., Lach, L., Zuniga, R. and Morrison, D. (2000). Environmental and economic cost of nonindigenous species in the United States. *BioScience* 50: 53–65.

Pinfield, C. (2001). *Regulatory Issues in Biosecurity*. Treasury Working Paper 01/23. Department of Treasury, Wellington.

Pister, E.P. (2001). Wilderness fish stocking: history and perspective. *Ecosystems* 4(4): 279–286.

Rudkin, B. and Hall, C.M. (1996). Off the beaten track: the health implications of the development of special-interest tourism services in South-East Asia and the South Pacific. In Clift, S. and Page, S. (eds), *Health and the International Tourist*. Routledge, London, pp. 89–107.

Russell, R.C. (1987). Survival of insects in the wheel bays of a Boeing 747B aircraft on flights between tropical and temperate airports. *Bulletin of the World Health Organization* 65: 659–662.

Seys, S.A. and Bender, J.B. (2001). The changing epidemiology of malaria in Minnesota. *Journal of Emerging Infectious Diseases* 7(6): 993–995.

Sharpley, R. and Craven, B. (2001). The 2001 foot and mouth crisis – rural economy and tourism policy implications: a comment. *Current Issues in Tourism* 4(6): 527–537.

Steffen, R. (2005). Changing travel-related global epidemiology of hepatitis A. *The American Journal of Medicine* 118(10): 46–49.

Wilson, M.E. (1995). Travel and the emergence of infectious diseases. *Journal of Emerging Infectious Diseases* 1(2): 39–46.

Wilson, M.E. (2003). The traveller and emerging infections: sentinel, courier, transmitter. *Journal of Applied Microbiology* 94(Suppl): 1–11.

Ecotourism: pondering the paradoxes

James Higham and Michael Lück

Introduction

One of the most fundamental changes in human awareness over the last 50 years has been growing environmental consciousness and the realisation that humans are not free of environmental constraints (Dunlap, 1980; Hussey and Thompson, 2000). Ecotourism is one of the more prominent manifestations of this environmental awareness. It has long been argued that this growing environmental consciousness has had significant implications for tourism, and that ecotourism represents the vanguard of sustainable tourism. The counterview, however, is that ecotourism is a complex phenomenon that poses considerable challenges to the view that ecotourism approximates to sustainable tourism. The counterview sees ecotourism as little different to mass tourism (Wheeller, 1991), but that it takes place in environments that are arguably too precious to be exposed to the risks of tourism impact. This chapter explores some of the paradoxes of ecotourism, which pose considerable and as yet unresolved challenges to those who advocate for ecotourism.

The development context

Modern tourism development dates to the 1960s and the introduction of the passenger jet aircraft. Initially in Europe the development of 'mass tourism' involved the large-scale production and sale of organised package tours, mostly from Northern and Western Europe to the Southern European countries of Spain, France, Greece and Italy (Bramwell, 2004). It was during this time that the United Nations strongly advocated tourism as a 'smokeless' industry of great economic development potential for both developed and developing countries. As a result of the enormous growth of the tourism industry, combined with rising environmental consciousness during the 1960s and 1970s (McCormick, 1989), concern arose for the detrimental impacts that millions of tourists began to have on natural and cultural environments. In the late 1980s and early 1990s it was argued that 'responsible' tourism was a viable alternative to the increasingly widespread concerns associated with the growth of popular mass tourism (Krippendorf, 1986; Butler, 1992). This was partly because 'the public had become "tired" of the crowds, weary of jetlag, and awakened to the evidence of pollution' (Eadington and Smith, 1992, p. 6) and other forms of mass tourism impact.

Fennell (1999, p. 9) notes that alternative tourism encompasses a 'whole range of tourism strategies (e.g. "appropriate", "eco", "soft", "responsible", "people to people", "controlled", "small-scale", "cottage", and "green" tourism), all of which purport to offer a more benign alternative to conventional mass tourism'. In particular, the term 'ecotourism' found its way into the tourism vernacular during the 1980s and into increasingly wide use by industry, government and public bodies, conservationists, academics and tourists themselves. Initially ecotourism was seen to provide tourism experiences that were not detrimental to the natural and social environments of host regions (Cater and Goodall, 1992).

Over the past two to three decades a number of researchers and governmental bodies developed a plethora of definitions of ecotourism. Fennell (2001) and Diamantis (1999) investigated a number of definitions in terms of their content and in terms of trends and evolution of such definitions, respectively. Three of the main components of most definitions is that ecotourism takes place in natural, relatively undisturbed areas (Ceballos-Lascurain, 1987; Krippendorf, 1987a, b; Holmes, 1993; Valentine, 1993; Ballantine and Eagles, 1994; Eagles and Cascagnette, 1995; Weiler and Richins, 1995; Blamey, 1997; Fennell, 1999; Ross and Wall, 1999; Sirakaya et al., 1999; Weaver, 2001), tries to minimise the negative impacts on the local communities and the natural environment (Mathieson and Wall, 1982; Pleumarom, 1993; Valentine, 1993; Orams, 1995; Gilbert, 1997; Lindberg and McKercher, 1997; Acott et al., 1998; Honey, 1999; Fennell, 2003), and that it contributes to the conservation of those areas (Boo, 1990; Jones, 1992; Holmes, 1993; Valentine, 1993; Wight, 1993; Buckley, 1994; McArthur, 1997; Fennell, 1999; Honey, 1999; Ross and Wall, 1999). Despite these definitions, there are a number of challenges associated with ecotourism, not the least of which relate to the environmental contexts within which ecotourism takes place. In order to understand these challenges, it is important to understand a number of paradoxes inherent in the concept of ecotourism.

The paradox of ecotourism impacts

The development of ecotourism destinations inevitably brings with it a number of associated impacts. Critics argue that ecotourism promotes development and thus the destruction of natural resources (McLaren, 2003). Due to the fact that ecotourists tend to discover new and undisturbed areas, 'try to avoid the beaten track' and 'want to go to places where nobody else has set foot before them' (Järviluoma, 1992, p. 118), effects on the natural environment are more severe than, for example, urban tourist destinations. Paradoxically, therefore, whatever the intentions, ecotourism offers great potential to destroy the very resource based upon which it depends (Järviluoma, 1992; Gray, 1997; McLaren, 2003).

Weaver (2002) notes that the environmental impacts of ecotourism can be either deliberate or inadvertent. Deliberate costs are, for example, those costs that occur with the construction of an ecolodge. Even if sites are already developed to a certain extent, the construction of tourist facilities usually requires environmental modification, clear cuts and sealing of ground areas (Buckley, 2004). These impacts are usually foreseeable and seen as acceptable when kept small in scale and in limited areas (Weaver, 2002). Such deliberate impacts are often deemed to be more acceptable in less sensitive areas in order to divert possible negative impacts at adjacent sensitive areas. These sites are commonly referred to as 'sacrifice sites'. Of no less significance, inadvertent impacts include the disruption of wildlife behaviours, such a breeding behaviours and migration patterns, due to the development of tourist facilities and infrastructures and/or the mere presence of tourists at sensitive times or in critical ecological zones. It is inadvertent impacts that are particularly problematic to research and understand, but until these impacts are understood appropriate and sustainable tourism management will remain elusive (Lusseau and Higham, 2004).

The paradox of tourism and conservation

The debate as to whether or not tourism and conservation can exist in a relationship of symbiosis has been lengthy and protracted. In his earliest speculations, Budowski (1976) suggested that the desirable relationship of symbiosis is in practice the exception rather than the rule. More commonly a relationship of conflict, or coexistence moving towards conflict, prevails between the interests of the tourism sector and conservation groups (Budowski, 1976). So it remains an open question as to whether or not these competing ambitions can be reconciled. A universal ecotourism paradox is apparent in this instance. Ecotourism typically (although not exclusively) takes place in environments that are fragile, finite and valued primarily for conservation. Tourism competes for the use of these environments with largely incompatible interests in natural science, biodiversity protection (or enhancement), the protection of wild animal populations (often rare or endangered wildlife species), the protection of native flora and freedom from human demands.

Under these circumstances, the impacts of ecotourism are brought to bear in environmental contexts where many would consider the stakes are highest.

So while there may exist potential for ecotourism to serve the symbiotic interests of tourism and conservation, in most cases doubt exists as to whether conservation interests are adequately or genuinely served through ecotourism development. Recent research that addresses interactions between tourists and dolphins bears out these concerns. In locations such as Doubtful Sound, New Zealand (Lusseau, 2003) and Shark Bay, Australia (Bejder *et al.*, 2006), two of the most thoroughly researched populations of cetaceans in the world, evidence exists to suggest that tourist activities can have subtle impacts on animal populations that are barely possible to detect in the short or medium terms, yet likely to be biologically significant in the longer term. In the absence of scientific research and thorough insights into ecology of focal animal populations, the likelihood of a genuine relationship serving the mutual interests of tourism and conservation is difficult to foresee.

The paradox of ecotourism in 'pristine' environments

The notion that ecotourism is supposed to operate in natural areas, away from developed areas (Boyd and Butler, 1996) poses a considerable paradox. Ecotourism businesses require a minimum level of infrastructure in order to actually operate. Ecotourism venues exist in 'degrees of naturalness' but the very existence of tourism infrastructure usually exists at the expense of 'pristine' naturalness (Higham and Lück, 2002). In favour of naturalness and at the exclusion of an anthropocentric view, Boyd *et al.* (1995) attempted to map ecotourism areas in Ontario, Canada, using a Geographical Information System' (GIS) method. The results showed that only a few areas were suitable for ecotourism, because most areas in Ontario are located within some distance to major roads or other human constructs. Higham and Lück (2002) argue that this shows the value of GIS as a research tool, but highlights the inadequacy of many ecotourism definitions. A minimum of infrastructure is necessary to allow for viable ecotourism operations. In these instances definitions of ecotourism overlook the basic operational requirements of any ecotourism business and the bare necessities required to accommodate and provide for visitors. Thus the search for 'pristine' environments (if such a thing exists at all) is doomed to be futile as the very presence of tourists, and the demands that they place on environments in terms of transport, accommodation, service and entertainment, are brought to bear upon the environments in which they seek to achieve the eco-tourism experience (Brown and Hall, 2000). By implication, the more successful an ecotourism destination, if success is measured in terms of visitor numbers, the more it threatens its own future sustainability.

The paradoxes inherent in ecotourism as a form of entertainment

McKercher (1993) argues that the fundamental aim of eco-tourism operators is to entertain their visitors. This may require the manipulation and packaging of a 'saleable product' that will satisfy tour schedules, and in some instances the development of pseudo-events to guarantee the experience. This he describes as a *'necessary if somewhat distasteful aspect of the industry'* (McKercher, 1993, p. 12). Ultimately this packaging of experiences into pre-planned and highly structured itineraries leads to tired-ness, fatigue, boredom, disinterest and a lack of appreciation on the part of visitors.

While Duffus and Dearden (1990) argue that specialist or expert visitors may have a genuine interest in the subject of their atten-tion while on tour, they also suggest that those who follow, oth-erwise termed generalists or novices seek primarily to be entertained. In seeking to entertain, tour operators may readily succumb to providing the desired – as opposed to the most desir-able – visitor experience. In many cases this leads to visitor expe-riences taking exclusive priority over concerns for the impacts associated with those experiences.

The investigation of Scarpaci *et al.* (2003) into tour operator compliance with regulations on swim-with-dolphins tours in Port Phillip Bay, Australia after the government had introduced new regulations provides an excellent case in point. According to their findings operators ignore a number of rules, which potentially harasses and ultimately harms the mammals. Orams (2004) has directly addressed the all important question of whether or not tourists simply want to be entertained, and whether tourists who engage in the viewing of marine mammals in the wild ultimately just want to get as close as possible to the animals that they are able to view.

Thus a significant paradox emerges in that while ecotourism seeks to protect and conserve the animal populations that attract the interests (however fleeting) of tourists, the onsite experience is often one that brings visitors themselves into inappropriate contact and harmful interaction with those animals in the immediate interest of a close look. Individual tourists rarely recognise (and even when they do, very rarely carefully consider) the cumulative impacts of such short-term, self-interested behaviour or the non-compliance of tour operators. Thus, while a single drop of water cannot be held accountable for a flood, so tourists are rarely able to look beyond their own immediate visitor experience to the cumulative impacts of all tourists who visit a site over an extended period of time. All of those who individually seek to get as close as they can to animals are not held accountable for the cumulative impacts of many such actions over time.

The paradox of the ceaseless search for unspoilt places

Recreational succession, a concept first introduced by Stankey (1985), describes the cyclical patterns that often accurately describe tourism and recreation in natural areas. Stankey argues that pristine natural areas are 'discovered' by relatively exploratory visitors, who use the site for recreational purposes. These people can be described as 'expert/specialist' on Bryan's (1977) continuum of leisure specialisation. They are outgoing and self-confident, inquisitive and show a considerable degree of adventure and curiosity (Goeldner and Ritchie, 2003). According to Bryan (1977, 1979) these visitors are low in numbers, but have high interest in and good knowledge about the particular area. They are motivated by genuine interest and have minimal negative impacts on the site. With growing interest in a given site and subsequent increasing use, a gradual deterioration of the natural qualities of the area takes place (Orams, 1999). High initial visitor satisfaction and 'word of mouth' result in an increase in interest and demand. Subsequent visitor types, however, are typically less experienced according to Bryan's typology, such that at a certain point the site is too developed and popular for the taste of earlier visitors. The dynamics of visitor arrivals conceptualised initially by Bryan (1977) and subsequently by Duffus and Dearden (1990) highlight the importance of understanding visitor preferences for recreation and tourist experiences, and how they decide that their values have been compromised to the point that they are displaced. This phenomenon, termed 'recreational succession', takes places in association with phases of visitor displacement which has significant implications for tourism management (Figure 7.1).

It is important to understand these concepts when assessing ecotourism and its impacts. The majority of ecotourism definitions

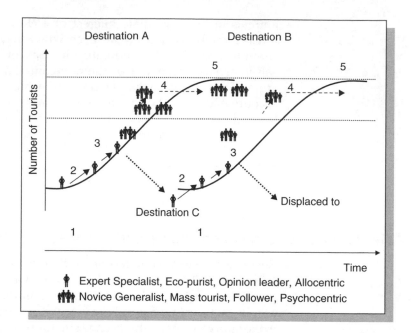

Figure 7.1
Recreational
succession and
displacement
(*Source*: Adapted
from Bryan, 1977;
Butler, 1980; Plog,
1991; Orams, 1999)

include a nature-based, a socio-cultural component and – since the Earth Summit in Rio de Janeiro 1992 – a sustainable development component (Diamantis, 1999). In addition, ecotourism is mostly associated with small-scale tourism (Gilbert, 1997; Lück, 1998; Fennell, 2003). The concepts discussed above all contradict the sustainability of ecotourism though. According to these models alternative tourists 'discover' places, sites and destinations. With recreational succession new areas evolve through phases from discovery and exploration, through development to stagnation and decline.

The ultimate goal of ecotourism – sustainability – is thus compromised in many cases in the short-term interests of economic development and employment. Cater (1993) argues that prime ecotourism attractions and sites are subject to concentrated use by ecotourists, who put the natural environment under stress, with overuse resulting in ecological degradation. Belize and Costa Rica are prime examples of this course of development. Once hailed as textbook cases for ecotourism, they offered visitor experiences that catered predominantly to 'ecotourists'. Both countries were relatively difficult to access from Europe. Tourists had to transfer in the United States, often with no same day connection which required a night in the United States. In the case of Belize the alternative option was to fly into Cancun/Mexico, and take a bus to Chetumal, and onto Belize City, which takes at least 8–9 hours. This relative inaccessibility was acceptable only for a certain type of tourist. However, after a dramatic increase in the popularity of ecotourism, it did not take long until both countries were served by European charter airlines, either with short-stop or direct services (Lück, 2002). This is just one manifestation of the continual succession of ecotourism destinations as they rise and ultimately fall in popularity.

The paradox of low-impact tourism and long-haul travel

An often neglected aspect of ecotourism arises from the fact that most research examines the costs and benefits from a macro- or destination perspective (see Becken and Schellhorn, this volume). The geographical settings of ecotourism destinations, and of ecotourist generating countries are important to consider. Thus, Flognfeldt (1997) divides the term ecotourism into 'destination eco-systems' and 'eco-route systems'. With the use of these terms, Flognfeldt clearly distinguishes between micro- or destination perspectives and macro- or whole trip perspectives. Cater (1993) notes that for various reasons, many Third World destinations are primary ecotourism destinations, while most ecotourists originate from more developed countries (MDCs). Thus, like any other tourist, in order to access their destinations of choice, most ecotourists travel by jet aircraft, most commonly on long-haul routes (Weaver, 2002; McLaren, 2003). Air travel is the least environmentally friendly form of travel, which contributes significantly to global warming. The ratios between energy consumption for travelling and the energy consumption for the stay at the destination are illustrated in Figure 7.2 (Gwinner, 2001). According to the World Wildlife Fund for Nature (McLaren, 2003, p. 92), air travel is likely to 'cause considerable environmental damage, and to have knock-on effects on the tourism industry itself'. Such environmental costs are in most cases not calculated or considered in parochial local accounts of ecotourism impacts. Weaver (2002) suggests that an extra-parochial approach would include actions from ecotour operators, for example, planting new vegetation in order to compensate for negative effects such as greenhouse gas emissions.

Airline companies are well aware of the negative environmental aspects of their day-to-day operations. With the knowledge of never being able to operate in an eco-friendly way, some attempt to support environmental projects or organisations, as suggested by Weaver (2002). Ansett Australia, for example, planted more than 500 trees at different points all over Australia as part of their environmental commitment associated with the 2000 Olympic Games in Sydney (Mieling, 2001). LTU International Airways, Germany's second largest charter carrier,

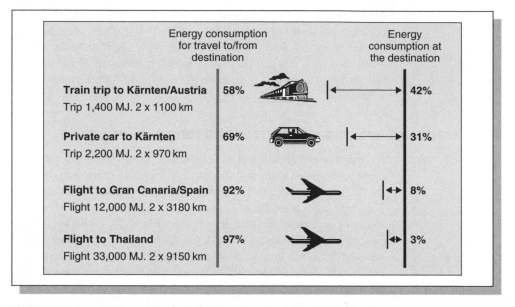

Figure 7.2
Ratio of primary energy use between the journey and the stay at the destination (country of origin: Germany) (*Source*: After Gwinner, 2001, p. 170)

supported high-calibre research on the effects of air travel on the atmosphere. In addition, for a number of years on flights from Germany to the Maldives, LTU distributed 'eco-bags' and encouraged their passengers to collect all inorganic waste products during their stay, and return them to the check-in, where they were collected, sorted and flown back to Germany for recycling or disposal (Lück, 2001). Ironically both of these airlines have subsequently encountered serious financial problems. Ansett went into receivership in 2003, while LTU was taken over by a new owner and these environmental initiatives were discontinued.

The paradox of transporting ecotourists to, at and between the sites of the visitor experience

Westwood and Boyd (2005) reviewed ecotourism definitions and subsequently argue that scenic flights adheres to many of the key elements of most definitions. It takes place in untouched nature and offers an educational component (in-flight commentary), while at the same time minimising the impacts due to limited contact with the setting. Finally, they argue that 'scenic flights are environmentally friendly as they discharge low levels of pollution, and create low levels of noise pollution for wildlife and other tourists' (Westwood and Boyd, 2005, p. 51). According to the World Watch Institute (WWI), aircraft, particularly helicopters and fixed wing aeroplanes, '... are the most energy-intensive means of carrying people and cargo' (McLaren, 2003, p. 92). While the WWI certainly refers particularly to large jet aircraft, it can still be maintained that small aircraft consume more fuel than, for example, a minibus. This is even more striking when the overall consumption is seen on a per passenger basis. According to Westwood and Boyd (2005), among the most popular aircraft types (fixed wing) are the Cessna 172 (4 seats including pilot) and the Cessna 206 (6 seats including pilot). The fuel consumption of these two types and the fuel consumption of a standard minibus (Toyota Hiace, 14 seats) are presented in Table 7.1. It is difficult to directly compare an

Table 7.1 Fuel consumption aircraft and minibus

	Seats (including pilot/driver)	Litres/hour	Litres/hour per passenger	Litres/100 km (longwheel/ super longwheel base)	Litres/ 100 kms per passenger
Cessna 172 Skyhawk	4	75% power: 30.28	7.57		
		65% power: 28.39	7.10		
Cessna 206 Stationair	6	75% power: 62.46	10.41		
		65% power: 54.13	9.02		
Toyota Hiace Petrol/Turbo Diesel	14			*Petrol*	
				Manual: 11.6/12.4	0.83/0.89
				Automatic: 11.6/12.6	0.83/0.9
				Turbo Diesel	
				Manual: 8.1/8.8	0.56/0.63
				Automatic: 8.4/9.6	0.6/0.69

Sources: Plane & Pilot (2006) and Toyota Australia (2006).

aircraft with a minibus, because one is measured by the hour and the other per 100 km.

However, it is clear that fuel consumption is much higher per passenger for a small aircraft. In addition, Ford has recently developed the first medium-sized commercial vehicle in Europe (Ford Transit) equipped with belt-driven integrated starter generator (ISG) technology. This hybrid solution is expected to save 15–25% of fuel during 'real world usage' (Ford, 2006).

Regarding noise pollution, Westwood and Boyd (2005) refer to a survey undertaken on three main hiking trails by the Department of Conservation (DOC), the Crown's agency for the management of New Zealand's conservation estate, in 1993. New Zealand's most famous track, the Milford Track, was significantly impacted by aircraft noise due to large numbers of flights between Queenstown and Milford Sound. DOC's survey revealed a 'high overall proportion (69%) of people on the Milford Track found aircraft activity to be disturbing' (Westwood and Boyd, 2005, p. 59). In a study on sperm whales in Kaikoura, New Zealand, Marrett (1992, in Constantine, 1999, p. 19) compared the noise levels of boats, helicopters and planes around whales. Marrett concluded that 'at a distance of 75 m from a whale on the surface, helicopters and planes were noisier than boats' (Constantine, 1999, p. 19).

The paradox of the ultimate ecotourist

Perhaps the definitive paradox associated with this phenomenon is that the ultimate ecotourist is one who stays at home (or close to home). The variety of impacts associated with ecotourism, both in terms of access to distant destinations as well as on-site impacts, brings with it a number of challenges. It remains vague and questionable whether many so-called ecotour operators and eco-attractions can be regarded as 'eco'. Surely many do comply with one or more ecotourism requirements, but ultimately harm the very environment that they operate in. Ecotourism, despite the rhetoric, contributes significantly to the degradation or destruction of the natural environment (Cater and Goodall, 1992).

One interesting variation is the notion of ecotourism taking place in urban environments. Dwyer and Edwards (2000) observe that as large cities continue to grow, city councils and local governments seek to meet the challenge of continually expanding cities in order to provide housing for growing urban populations on one hand, with the preservation of natural resources on the other. As this trend continues considerable and increasingly valued natural areas are located in urban or urban fringe areas. Dwyer and Edwards (2000) note the recreation and tourism potential of such areas. Higham and Lück (2002) argue that urban ecotourism can combat many of the problems associated with ecotourism and urban development. Firstly, environmental impacts can be kept to a minimum. There is no need to travel to and penetrate remote, relatively untouched natural areas. Cities offer well-developed transport and service infrastructures for local residents and tourists alike. Ecotourism in urban settings can contribute to the restoration of natural areas and/or the use of obsolete industrial sites. Conservational values can be restored and enhance the quality of the city while providing unique ecotourism experiences. Such projects can create habitats for endangered species and support the reintroduction of regionally extinct species (Higham and Lück, 2002). Under these scenarios, the ultimate ecotourist may seek out nature-based experiences that can be achieved in the absence of fast, long-haul travel.

Conclusions

Ecotourism is a travel phenomenon that is rife with contractions and paradoxes. Given these paradoxes it is understandable that many critics of ecotourism harbour grave concerns for the high and perhaps unrealistic ideals associated with this form of tourism. The term 'ecotokenism' has been coined in acknowledgement of the general lack of critical consideration associated with ecotourism development. This chapter presents one viewpoint on a range of paradoxes that may be associated with ecotourism. Until these paradoxes are adequately acknowledged, critically considered and satisfactorily addressed, the chorus of critical commentary on ecotourism that had grown in recent years will not abate.

It was noted at the start of this chapter that one of the most fundamental changes in human awareness over the last 50 years has been growing environmental consciousness and the realisation that humans are not free of environmental constraints. Milbrath (1984) notes that those who hold values aligned with the 'new environmental paradigm' (NEP) are in the vanguard of social change in response to growing concerns for the global environment. Those who hold values that are aligned with the NEP, according to Milbrath (1984), are perhaps slowly but surely influencing those whose values conform with the dominant social paradigm (DSP) so as to redirect society in the interests of environmental sustainability. Growing concerns associated with such global issues as peak oil and climate change appear to be adding pace to this redirection of society.

Perhaps the same scenario applies to ecotourism insofar as it will be the values of tourists themselves that will redirect ecotourism in the direction of sustainability. While many criticise ecotourism operators in terms of 'greenwashing' and 'ecotokenism', perhaps it is ultimately the values of visitors themselves that must change if ecotourism is ever to achieve its lofty ambitions. It is ultimately the visitor who chooses where they will travel, how they will travel there (and back) and how they will conduct themselves while on their travels (in all respects). It could be argued that only when tourists themselves begin to make the right decisions, and stand by those decisions as they relate to the paradoxes outlined in this chapter, will ecotourism finally have the potential to be a reality.

References

Acott, T.G., La Trobe, H.L. and Howard, S.H. (1998). An evaluation of deep ecotourism and shallow ecotourism. *Journal of Sustainable Tourism* 6(3): 238–253.

Ballantine, J.L. and Eagles, P.F.J. (1994). Defining Canadian ecotourists. *Journal of Sustainable Tourism* 2(4): 210–214.

Bejder, L., Samuels, A., Whitenhead, H., Gales, N., Mann, J., Connor, R., Heithams, M., Watson–Capps, J., Flaherty, C. and Kruetzen, M. (2006). Decline in relative abundance of bottlenose dolphins (*tursiops sp*) exposed to long-term disturbance. *Conservation Biology* 20(6): 1791–1798.

Blamey, R.K. (1997). Ecotourism: the search for an operational definition. *Journal of Sustainable Tourism* 5(2): 109–130.

Boo, E. (1990). *Ecotourism: The Potentials and Pitfalls*, Vol. 1. World Wildlife Fund, Washington, DC.

Boyd, S.W. and Butler, R.W. (1996). Managing ecotourism: an opportunity spectrum approach. *Tourism Management* 17(8): 557–566.

Boyd, S.W., Butler, R.W., Haider, W. and Perera, A. (1995). Identifying areas for ecotourism in Northern Ontario: application of a geographical information systems methodology. *Journal of Applied Recreation Research* 19(1): 41–66.

Bramwell, B. (2004). Mass Tourism, diversification, and sustainability in Southern Europe's coastal regions. In Bramwell B. (ed.). Coastal mass tourism: Diversification and sustainable development in Southern Europe. pp. 1–31. Aevedon: Channel View Publications.

Brown, F. and Hall, D. (eds) (2000). *Tourism in Peripheral Areas*. Channel View Publications, Clevedon.

Bryan, H. (1977). Leisure value systems and recreation specialization: the case of trout fishermen. *Journal of Leisure Research* 9: 174–187.

Bryan, H. (1979). *Conflict in the Great Outdoors: Towards Understanding and Managing for Diverse Sportsmen Preferences*. Sociological Studies No. 4. University of Alabama, Alabama.

Buckley, R. (1994). A framework for ecotourism. *Annals of Tourism Research* 21(3): 661–669.

Buckley, R. (ed.) (2004). *Environmental Impacts of Ecotourism*. CAB International, Wallingford.

Budowski, G. (1976). Tourism and environmental conservation: conflict, coexistence, or symbiosis. *Environmental Conservation* 3(1): 27–31.

Butler, R.W. (1980). The concept of a tourist-area cycle of evolution and implications for management. *The Canadian Geographer* 24: 5–12.

Butler, R.W. (1992). Alternative tourism: the thin edge of the wedge. In Smith, V.L. and Eadington, W.R. (eds), *Tourism Alternatives: Potentials and Problems in the Development of Tourism*. University of Pennsylvania Press, Philadelphia, pp. 31–46.

Cater, E. (1993). Ecotourism in the Third World: problems for sustainable tourism development. *Tourism Management* 14(2): 85–90.

Cater, E. and Goodall, B. (1992). Must tourism destroy its resource base? In Mannion, A.M. and Bowlby, S.R. (eds), *Environmental Issues in the 1990s*. John Wiley & Sons, Chichester, pp. 309–323.

Ceballos-Lascurain, H. (1987). The future of ecotourism. *Mexico Journal* January: 13–14.

Constantine, R. (1999). *Effects of Tourism on Marine Mammals in New Zealand*, Vol. 106. Science for Conservation Series. Department of Conservation, Wellington, New Zealand.

Diamantis, D. (1999). The concept of ecotourism: evolution and trends. *Current Issues in Tourism* 2(2&3): 93–122.

Duffus, D.A. and Dearden, P. (1990). Non-consumptive wildlife-oriented recreation: a conceptual framework. *Biological Conservation* 53: 213–231.

Dunlap, R.E. (1980). Paradigmatic change in social science. *American Behavioral Scientist* 24(1): 5–14.

Dwyer, L. and Edwards, D. (2000). Nature-based tourism on the edge of urban development. *Journal of Sustainable Tourism* 8(4): 267–287.

Eadington, W.R. and Smith, V.L. (1992). Introduction: the emergence of alternative forms of tourism. In Smith, V.L. and Eadington, W.R. (eds), *Tourism Alternatives: Potentials and Problems in the Development of Tourism*. University of Pennsylvania Press, Philadelphia, pp. 1–12.

Eagles, P.F.J. and Cascagnette, J.W. (1995). Canadian ecotourists: who are they? *Tourism Recreation Research* 20(1): 22–28.

Fennell, D.A. (1999). *Ecotourism: An Introduction*. Routledge, New York.

Fennell, D.A. (2001). A content analysis of ecotourism definitions. *Current Issues in Tourism* 4(5): 403–421.

Fennell, D.A. (2003). *Ecotourism: An Introduction* (2nd edn). Routledge, New York.

Flognfeldt, T. (1997). Eco-tourism in remote areas of Norway: just a green veneer? In Byron, R., Walsh, J. and Breathnach, P. (eds), *Sustainable Development on the North Atlantic Margin*. Thirteenth International Seminar on Marginal Regions, Ashgate, Aldershot, UK, pp. 239–248.

Ford (2006). *Ford Transit Diesel–Electric Hybrid Application Research Project Launched*. Retrieved April 3, 2006, from http://media.ford.com/article_display.cfm?article_id=17570

Gilbert, J. (1997). *Ecotourism means Business*. GP Publications, Wellington, New Zealand.

Goeldner, C.R. and Ritchie, J.R.B. (2003). *Tourism: Principles, Practices, Philosophies* (9th edn). John Wiley & Sons, Hoboken, New Jersey.

Gray, J. (1997, February). How green is your ecotour? *Sawasdee Inflight Magazine of Thai Airways International*.

Gwinner, R. (2001). Verkehrsmittel auf Diät setzen: Mit Megajoule der sparsamen Urlaubsanreise auf der Spur. In Kirstges, T. and Lück, M. (eds), *Umweltverträglicher Tourismus: Fallstudien zur Entwicklung und Umsetzung Sanfter Tourismuskonzepte*. Armin Gmeiner Verlag, Messkirch, pp. 169–173.

Higham, J. and Lück, M. (2002). Urban ecotourism: a contradiction in terms? *Journal of Ecotourism* 1(1): 36–51.

Holmes, J. (1993). Loving nature to death. *NZ SCIENCE Monthly* 4(3): 6–8.

Honey, M. (1999). *Ecotourism and Sustainable Development: Who Owns Paradise?* Island Press, Washington, DC.

Hussey, S. and Thompson, P. (2000). Introduction: the roots of environmental consciousness. In Hussey, S. and Thompson, P. (eds), *The Roots of Environmental Consciousness: Popular Tradition and Personal Experience*. Routledge, London, pp. 1–19.

Järviluoma, J. (1992). Alternative tourism and the evolution of tourist areas. *Tourism Management* 13(1): 118–120.

Jones, A. (1992). Is there a real 'alternative' tourism? Introduction. *Tourism Management* 13(1): 102–103.

Krippendorf, J. (1986). The new tourist – turning point for leisure and travel. *Tourism Management* 7(3): 131–135.

Krippendorf, J. (1987a). Ecological approach to tourism marketing. *Tourism Management* 8(3): 174–176.

Krippendorf, J. (1987b). *The Holiday Makers: Understanding the Impact of Leisure and Travel.* Heinemann Professional Publishing Ltd., Oxford.

Lindberg, K. and McKercher, B. (1997). Ecotourism: a critical overview. *Pacific Tourism Review* 1: 65–79.

Lück, M. (1998). Sustainable tourism: do modern trends in tourism make a sustainable management more easy to achieve? *Tourismus Jahrbuch* 2(2): 141–157.

Lück, M. (2001). Responsible tourism: does size really matter? *Tourismus Jahrbuch* 5(1): 215–226.

Lück, M. (2002). Looking into the future of ecotourism and sustainable tourism. *Current Issues in Tourism* 5(3&4): 371–374.

Lusseau, D. (2003). The effects of tour boats on the behavior of bottlenose dolphins: using markov chains to model anthropogenic impacts. *Conservation Biology* 17(6): 1785–1793.

Lusseau, D. and Higham, J.E.S. (2004). Managing the impacts of dolphin-based tourism through the definition of critical habitats: the case of bottlenose dolphins (*Tursiops* spp.) in Doubtful Sound, New Zealand. *Tourism Management* 25(5): 657–667.

Mathieson, A. and Wall, G. (1982). *Tourism: Economic, Physical and Social Impacts.* Longman, London.

McArthur, S. (1997). Introducing the National Ecotourism Accreditation Program. *Australian Parks and Recreation* 33(2): 30–34.

McCormick, J. (1989). *The Global Environmental Movement.* Belhaven Press, London.

McKercher, B. (1993). Some fundamental truths about tourism: understanding tourism's social and environmental impacts. *Journal of Sustainable Tourism* 1(1): 6–16.

McLaren, D. (2003). *Rethinking Tourism and Ecotravel* (2nd edn). Kumarian Press, Bloomfield, CT.

Mieling, T. (2001). Olympische Spiele – Grüne Spiele. In Kirstges, T. and Lück, M. (eds), *Umweltverträglicher Tourismus: Fallstudien zur Entwicklung und Umsetzung Sanfter Tourismuskonzepte.* Armin Gmeiner Verlag, Messkirch, pp. 151–166.

Milbrath, L. (1984). Environmentalists: Vanguard for a new society. State University of New York Press, Albany.

Orams, M. (1999). *Marine Tourism: Development, Impacts and Management*. Routledge, London, New York.

Orams, M. (2004). Why dolphins may get ulcers: considering the impacts of cetacean-based tourism in New Zealand. *Tourism in Marine Environments* 1(1): 17–28.

Orams, M.B. (1995). Towards a more desirable form of eco-tourism. *Tourism Management* 16(1): 3–8.

Plane & Pilot (2006). *Aircraft Specifications*. Retrieved April 3, 2006, from http://www.planeandpilotmag.com/content/specs/index.html

Pleumarom, A. (1993). What's wrong with mass ecotourism? *Contours* 6(3–4): 15–21.

Plog, S.C. (1991). *Leisure Travel: Making It a Growth Market ... Again!* John Wiley & Sons, New York.

Ross, S. and Wall, G. (1999). Ecotourism: towards congruence between theory and practice. *Tourism Management* 20(1): 123–133.

Scarpaci, C., Dayanthi, N. and Corkerin, P. (2003). Compliance with Regulations by 'Swim-with-Dolphins' Operators in Port Philip Bay, Victoria, Australia. *Environmental Management* 31(3): 342–347.

Sirakaya, E., Sasidharan, V. and Sönmez, S. (1999). Redefining ecotourism: the need for a supply-side view. *Journal of Travel Research* 38(November): 168–172.

Stankey, G. (1985). *Carrying Capacity in Recreational Planning: An Alternative Approach*. United States Department of Agriculture – Forest Service, Ogden, Utah.

Toyota Australia (2006). *Specification Summary*. Retrieved April 3, 2006, from http://hiace.toyota.com.au/toyota/vehicle/Content/0,4664,2176_762,00.html

Valentine, P.S. (1993). Ecotourism and nature conservation: a definition with some recent developments in Micronesia. *Tourism Management* 14(2): 107–115.

Weaver, D.B. (2001). Ecotourism as mass tourism: contradiction or reality? *Hotel and Restaurant Administration Quarterly* 42: 104–112.

Weaver, D.B. (2002). The evolving of ecotourism and its potential impacts. *International Journal of Sustainable Development* 5(3): 251–264.

Weiler, B. and Richins, H. (1995). Extreme, extravagant and elite: a profile of ecotourists on earthwatch expeditions. *Tourism Recreation Research* 20(1): 29–36.

Westwood, N.J. and Boyd, S.W. (2005). Mountain scenic flights: a low risk, low impact ecotourism experience within South Island, New Zealand. In Hall, C.M. and Boyd, S.W. (eds),

Nature-Based Tourism in Peripheral Areas: Development or Disaster? Channel View Publications, Clevedon, pp. 50–63.

Wheeller, B. (1991). Tourism's troubled times: responsible tourism is not the answer. *Tourism Management* 12(2): 91–96.

Wight, P. (1993). Ecotourism: ethics or eco-sell? *Journal of Travel Research* 31(3): 3–9.

CHAPTER 8

Against the current: striving for ethical ecotourism

Agnes M. Nowaczek,
Cesar Moran-Cahusac and
David A. Fennell

Introduction

Ecotourism, since its inception, has been a contentious concept both in study and practice because it challenges our ability to reconcile commerce and self-interest with more altruistic endeavours such as conservation and the well-being of others. Embedded in this reality is the belief that there are several critical issues which need to be addressed at various structural levels in attempts to move forward. First of all, the main components of ecotourism – conservation of the natural environment, land cultivation, culture and tradition, and local economic development – are in conflict for advantageous positioning as opposed to balanced coexistence. In the current scenario, what is most important often equals what is most profitable. Second, ecotourism philosophy is dominated by western thought, thus many valuable lessons can only be learned by deconstructing its meaning to find application in various socio-cultural contexts. Third, ecotourism ethics cannot pretend to operate via unethical frameworks of the global free-market economy and current political structures, which value completely different goals and objectives. How we manage these critical issues today will unquestionably dictate the possibilities for innately ethical ecotourism in the future. A framework is developed in the latter part of the chapter for the purpose of conceptualizing ecotourism according to three major geographical and temporal hierarchies. The broad aims of the chapter are discussed through various practical examples of ecotourism from South American markets.

Ethics wars for advantageous positioning

Ecotourism has many lofty goals that continue to be challenged by practices which vary considerably from the sub-field's theoretical basis. The goals of preserving the natural environment, cultivating land, preserving local cultures and traditions, and offering resident communities better options for improved livelihoods, are all connected and interdependent. The current tourism literature confirms that we cannot expect to meet these goals in separation. Social equity, environmental sustainability, local economic development, and cultural heterogeneity are all innately interlinked (Eichler, 2000). Where any of these relationships are omitted or ignored in practical terms, the ecotourism project is either unsuccessful or it creates problems for the local communities and the natural environments they depend on.

Ironically, nature as the main component of ecotourism, its reliance and benefits, is often compromised. The richest and most sensitive pristine areas are generally located in distant and difficult to reach world regions in the developing countries, and so by presenting an element of adventure and uniqueness they attract foreign tourists by default (West and Carrier, 2004). Air flights from the Northern to Southern Hemisphere where most of these hot spots are located, have a tremendous impact on the natural integrity of the area in terms of greenhouse gas (GHG) emissions, yet the ecological footprint of energy for infrastructure construction is not considered in ecotourism planning (Gössling *et al.*, 2002). It is a paradox that ecotourism projects which were originally created to protect natural and cultural resources are now contributing (among other factors) to global warming. By introducing unprecedented numbers of people and alien substances to the most delicate and remote areas of the planet, ecotourism has the potential to cause the destruction of what it was intended to protect.

Nonetheless, some measures have been taken to protect the natural integrity of habitats worldwide. In 1997, the Kyoto proto-col was signed to stop the risk of global warming and to promote the sequestration of anthropogenic carbon. Global warming reduction became an international task. To do so, this protocol promotes the development of carbon sequestration technologies and projects in order to reach certain global emission quotas by the year 2010. This effort has triggered the development of a mar-ket opportunity to buy and trade carbon credits. The maturation of this market can offer tourists the possibility of mitigating their travel impacts by voluntarily buying carbon credits to offset their travel carbon emissions – although voluntary carbon offsetting is still hampered by a lack of regulation. However, some can argue that carbon credits have been designed to the advantage of the wealthy societies who can counteract their air travel GHG emis-sions and in the process be able to have tax breaks, whereas they are not applied to alleviate local ailments caused by faulty tourism developments, particularly air travel.

Unfortunately, many of these sensitive areas lack control meas-ures, protective laws, or regulations. This condition provides an arena for regulatory manipulation by tour operators and power-ful stakeholders who are in charge of ecotourism projects, as opposed to local communities who the projects are intended to benefit. To minimize impacts, clearly defined and consensually developed operational standards must precede other scenarios, and all stakeholders must be held equally accountable. Such a scenario is only accomplishable in the presence of regulations supported by a strong political will of government, which is very unlikely in most developing countries. Moreover, the main drawback of this approach is that large-scale operators have better access to government, and by engaging in political manoeuvres at the local, regional, or national level, 'can persuade officials to make decisions that favour their interests' (West *et al.*, 2003).

The aforementioned philosophical and operational mindset has significantly altered the natural or cultural resource base to satisfy evolving interests in the visitor – whether these evolving interests are supply or demand driven is subject to further study. According to West and Carrier (2004), ecotourism can be so powerful that it shapes the natural world and its inhabitants in ways that contradict the values it is designed to represent. In this view, ecotourism does not lead to the preservation of valued ecosystems as much as to the creation of landscapes that form part of the Western idealizations of nature through market-oriented politics. This process results in a new product that satisfies the ecotourism market, the tour operator, and some of the key community members at the expense of the essence ingrained in these resources.

Another component which is innately ingrained in the ecotourism philosophy is the creation of benefits for resident communities and the hosts of ecotourism projects. These benefits may include the improved livelihoods of local people, the protection of natural and cultural resources, or the stimulation of local economic development – ideally, all of the above (Honey, 2002; Stem *et al.*, 2003). Although these goals are praiseworthy, they can contribute to a range of direct or indirect impacts on site. Ecotourism is also premised on the assumption that once engaged in the operation, a potential stream of revenues will stop locals from depleting natural resources (Wunder, 2000). In practice, however, local communities seldom possess the education and skills necessary to manage an ecotourism company, and often retreat to secondary positions. Additional advantage for ecotourism projects is that unlike extractive industries like oil or mining, they 'are not required to conduct social or environmental audits before they begin operations, or to commit to leaving improved environments and community development initiatives when they pull out' (Francis, 2005). This scenario presents a risk of involving communities in tourist schemes that might collapse, and where sustainable development goals proposed by the project are not expected to be verified or measured.

Not all stakeholders that are involved in ecotourism projects have, 'equal access to economic and political resources' (Reed, 1997, p. 567). The group that has more power will generally impose their interests in the planning process and at the stage of tourist product definition. In the long run, these 'power imbalances and legitimacy issues related to the stakeholders can inhibit both the initiation and the success ...' of the project

(Jamal and Getz, 1995, pp. 190–191). On the other hand, powerful local stakeholders whose fortunes are embedded in the growth and vitality of the region, or who have become more powerful due to their business relationship with the tour operator, have an influence upon community decision-making and policy formation. They may try to maintain their *status quo* and oppose anybody who threatens their position (Reed, 1997). In other words, such a scenario facilitates personal interests of those more powerful rather than collective benefits of the society or community as a whole.

Contrary to the pressures for short-term monetary profits from ecotourism ventures, the development of a successful tourist product requires a slow community building process due to the heterogeneous nature of these societies (Reed, 1997). It is very difficult to achieve the sustainable development of a community using ecotourism without the cooperative effort of all actors and identifying clear tangible benefits in the process. Otherwise, 'Even where ecotourism results in economic benefits for the local community, it may result in damage to the social and cultural systems thus undermining peoples' overall quality of life' (Scheyvens, 1999, p. 246). Contrary to international awards for successful ecotourism projects which are used as marketing tools in place of certification, a thorough stakeholder analysis along with market and product studies must form part of the process to ensure the least amount of damage.

Deconstructing the western meaning of ecotourism

In view of the aforementioned conflict over stakeholder goals, it is essential for researchers and operators to more closely examine the philosophical basis of ecotourism before embarking upon development of a project. Orams (2001) suggests that it is useful to consider the range of definitions offered in terms of represented conceptual approaches and frameworks, for if we are to understand the range of types of ecotourism we must first clarify what it entails. However, since the concept of ecotourism was first officially introduced and researched in western countries, it is not surprising that the same western ideologies found in broader society dominate the field of ecotourism. Along these lines,

… tourism is part of a socio-politico-cultural-power complex, within which developers and others quickly engage in small and large games of socio-cultural, environmental, and historical cleansing, as they promote and project some sociopolitical universes and chastise or omit other possible contending world views. Ecotourism has thus become

... a sponsored, commercialized cultural product, whereby it is deemed
appropriate to be an ecotourist

(Ryan *et al.*, 2000, p. 150).

Consequently, several limitations underline the basic assumptions ingrained in ecotourism research – one being that ecotourists are different from mass tourists and another that ecotourists are a heterogeneous group. The definition of ecotourism may be contextual, meaning that it may vary and be dependent upon specific settings and societies, as is the case of Poland and China where western generalizations do not hold true (Nowaczek and Fennell, 2002; Aramberri and Xie, 2003; Aramberri *et al.*, 2003; Fennell and Nowaczek, 2003). Research on Canadian or American ecotourists in different settings may not produce dissimilarities in these groups, as it might do if it involved local ecotourists. Furthermore, it has been suggested that an important trend in countries like North America and Northern Europe, where the international market demand for ecotourism is centred, is the trend of ageing populations (Wight, 2001). The changing nature of ecotourist demographics suggests that we should endeavour to stay on top of changing needs and expectations too.

To reflect the complexity of ecotourism research globally, the rates of growth estimates of ecotourism vary by destination, by country of origin and even by region, and may depend on activity (Wight, 2001). Weaver (1999) concludes that because of the concentrated nature of ecotourism activity within Costa Rica's and Kenya's protected areas, the generated direct impacts tend to be highly localized. Similarly, Cater and Lowman (1994) comment on the dangers associated with the development of ecotourism in Eastern Europe, including popularity of the concept, propaganda value for governments to be seen as greening the tourism development, and means of gaining access to development aid funds from the EU or the west. The authors point out that:

... too many projects are being developed based on Western European (or even North American) experience, despite the cultural and environmental circumstances and the nature of consequent pressures being very particular to the region itself. Indeed, there may be better lessons to be learned from the experience of the developing world ... In short, there is more than a slight danger of eco-ethnocentrism being superimposed on the application of ecotourism in Eastern Europe

(Cater and Lowman, 1994, p. 133).

Wylie (1994) proposes that there are many dimensions of ecotourism. It could be perceived as an activity, business, philosophy, marketing device, symbol, or a set of principles and goals. Because of this complexity, Orams (2001) believes that ecotourism as a concept should not be expected to provide a universal simple answer, but instead researchers should place emphasize on understanding different types of activity. Also, while Wallace and Pierce (1996) include a socio-cultural component within their discussion of ecotourism – with emphasis on the culture of local people and their relationship the land – the authors omit from the discussion the role of domestic ecotourists. A cross-cultural perspective, such as that employed by Wallace and Pierce (1996), could be enhanced by examining the tourism situation from domestic and international perspectives in appreciating the overall magnitude of the industry, especially if the focus were to extend outside predominant markets such as North America and Europe (see Fennell and Smale, 1992; Wallace and Smith, 1997; Lew, 1998; Nowaczek and Fennell, 2002).

Orams (2001) advises that the goal of ecotourism is sound and worthy despite the difficulty in achieving it in practice. The concept is not flawed, but rather it may reflect immaturity of the tourism management field and may need to further evolve the successful application of the concept. In terms of socio-cultural distinction, the author points out that, 'Part of this evolution involves the recognition of distinctive ecotourism typologies and types that utilize different habitats, attract different markets, and require distinctive planning and management measures' (Orams, 2001, p. 33). On a more theoretical level, Ryan *et al.* (2000) comment on the lack of research that attempts to examine ecotourism from a deconstructionist stance that seeks to understand its ritual and ideology. The authors state that ecotourism has its own anthropology of symbols and signifiers, and their study in Australia suggests that it may be culturally determined with the culture of consumerism where self-defined ecotourists gain an affective rather than cognitive experience.

Similarly, Cohen (1995) advocates that nature-based tourism is a cultural construct in which natural attractions are symbolically and physically marked off and regulated. Various cultural components and constructed views are selected within the natural area and presented to the tourist through acts of interpretation as institutionalized choices (Heron, 1991; MacCannell, 1992; Hollinshead, 1999). Cohen (2003) also comments on the need for research that would examine the dynamics of tourism at a destination within a broad context of linkages between local, regional, national, and international agents, or in other words, tourism in the context of local politics. The author advocates a deviation from the exclusive focus in studies of the host–tourist encounters on western tourists to that of the encounters between locals and domestic tourists, and those from other non-western and neighbouring countries (Cohen, 2003).

Ecotourism ethics in unethical frameworks

The philosophy of ecotourism is ingrained in ethical operation; however, it is often unsuccessfully translated into practice because it operates within an amoral atmosphere of more dominant paradigm initiated by the global free-market economy where profits dictate business decisions (McMurtry, 1998; Hall, 1999). Nevertheless, ethical business practices are valued by customers and do pay back in the long term – that is, new positions of Ethics Officers within companies (Maich, 2005), or outright public assessment (*Corporate Knights*, the Canadian Magazine for Responsible Business) – and so even small steps should be pursued. While the western approach to ecotourism may be inappropriate for some developing nations, certain practices (i.e. lessons from failures of the industrialized countries) should be encouraged so that other nations curb the learning curve of their own progress. The paradigm shift from locally to globally oriented thinking, although slow, may greatly assist in accepting these lessons. After all, there are possibilities for ecotourism ethics to work creatively within constricting paradigms.

Several movements to challenge unethical systems have been developed. The commitment of 182 governments to reform the tourism industry was officially formalized during the 1992 UN Earth Summit in Rio by signing Agenda 21 which stressed the importance of and sensitivity towards the Earth's ecosystems and indigenous people (Jenkins *et al.*, 2002). The French ministry of tourism also proposed the creation of World Committee on Tourism Ethics (Espaces, 1992, p. 60). Moreover, according to surveys of consumer opinion about travel conducted by the Association of British Travel Agents and Tearfund (one of United Kingdom's leading Christian relief and development agencies), the idea of more responsible travel is beginning to infiltrate the mainstream consumer market (Tearfund, 2000; Gordon, 2001; Goodwin, 2002). Despite the infancy of the topic area in tourism studies (i.e. 1990s), more authors are beginning to take a theoretical approach in addressing tourism ethics, especially in relation to business and environment, management, codes of ethics, and ethical frameworks (Hultsman, 1995; Przecławski, 1996; WTO, 1999; Fennell, 2006).

While there appears to be tacit support for responsible or ethical tourism from government, travel companies, NGOs, and various campaign groups, there is disagreement about what it should be and how to achieve it. For instance, Butcher (2002, 2003) criticizes the 'New Moral Tourism', and ecotourism in particular, for over-moralizing an experience that was designed to be free from evaluation and from other demands, focusing only on one's pleasure and relaxation. In contrast, others critique these trends in face of the global warming, environmental and cultural degradation, exploitation and poverty, and the spread of western values of materialism and capitalism (Prosser, 1998). Ecotourism is not sheltered from such criticisms (Orams, 1995; Jenkins *et al.*, 2002); however, while ecotourism is a small niche, responsible tourism is applicable to the mainstream travel industry. Even if ecotourism was environmentally and ethically sound, it may be economically unsustainable and so the most effective strategy promoted by our current market system may in fact lie with large-scale tourism projects (Prosser, 1998). At the broadest level, Cleverdon and Kalisch (2000) advocate for fair trade in tourism, such as through the advancements towards environmental responsibility, sustainable initiatives, open trading, attention to poverty, and community-based approaches.

Among the tools available for more ethical tourism, codes of ethics have emerged to influence attitudes and modify behaviour of various groups. Additionally, studies support that the intention to behave in an environmentally responsible way depends more on pro-environmental attitudes rather than on factual knowledge (Kotchen and Reiling, 2000; Nilsson and Küller, 2000). A study by Schwartz (2001) on the relationship between corporate codes of ethics and behaviour found that codes play a significant role in influencing the behaviour of corporate agents. Palmer (1997) suggests that while codes of ethics and charters are important in practice, they have an uneasy relationship with environmental ethics since they ignore the value of nature, independent of human use. Codes may actually serve to reduce moral standards if they are superficially used as a marketing tool or as means to avoid statutory regulations. As codes are used for various purposes, their uses range on a continuum from quasi-legal requirements through moral prescriptions to a marketing tool, and often all combine in any one code (Pritchard, 1998). If these voluntary codes are specific and action oriented, and further supported by plans of implementation and the monitoring and reporting of results, they can become a useful tool (Genot, 1995).

Ethical decision-making frameworks are another tool to guide researchers and practitioners in their understanding of ecotourists, operators, and the local populations at any given destination (Fennell and Malloy, 1995; Fennell, 2000). However, most of these frameworks exist within the business context (e.g. Schumann, 2001). Most interestingly, Quinn's (1997) study supports a link between personal ethics of owners and managers of small business (applicable to ecotourism) and their attitude towards ethical problems in business, or in other words business ethics. Previous models put forth by other researchers (e.g. Trevino, 1986) propose that the most influential factor which determines business behaviour of an ethical nature is personal ethics. Other authors also believe that principles of personal ethics (i.e. trustworthiness and honesty) are the first level of consideration in an ethical dilemma, overriding the levels of professional (i.e. impartiality, objectivity, confidentiality) and global ethics (i.e. global justice, social responsibility, environmental stewardship) (Quinn, 1997; Colero, 1997).

A company's ethical organizational culture is next in importance to personal ethics of its employees. Alongside the evolution of organizational structure from vertical to networks, there is dispersal of ethical and legal responsibility. In addressing this problem, Daboub and Calton (2002) advise managers to implement ethical values through their organizational culture to control the performance of their scattered employees, some of which may be in different countries and different organizations. Several studies support the importance of organizational culture, ethical leadership, and open communication (Lozano, 1996; Jose and Thibodeaux, 1999). In particular, Malloy and Fennell (1998) – based on the work of Schein (1985) – put forth a conceptual model portraying the moral development of organizational cultures from the 'market culture' of free-market economy to the 'principled culture' of holistic ethical understanding. The model implies that it is possible to evolve to a higher organizational culture, provided a standard of collective cognition is created for the employees (Malloy and Fennell, 1998). Along the lines of moral superiority, Fennell and Malloy's (1999) subsequent work found that ecotourism operators were more ethical in their practices than general tourism managers.

Many authors are pessimistic about the coexistence of ethics and the global market (e.g. Hall, 1999). While some suggest a necessary radical restructuring of the system, others point to the compromises of ethics which partially operate within the currently existing systems. For instance, Attfield (1998) blames the current inequitable international economic order for the majority of environmental problems, which she believes is unlikely to respond to ethical approaches unless it is radically restructured. Similarly, Stone (1993) sees technology as a framework of possibility, in other words what society is able to do, whereas ethics provides a framework of morality pointing to what society ought to do. Law, on the other hand, enables societies to carry out their ethical decision-making in practice. It seems that we have structured our laws according to what we are able to do, too anxious to weigh the ethical consequences of our choices. Such is the realistic perspective of Duffy (2002; see also Smith and Duffy, 2003) who sees ecotourism as part of the blue-green strand of environmental perspective which does not challenge the existing political, economic, and social structures to be fundamentally reorganized according to ethics, but instead operates within the current norms of the amoral market system. Moreover, the author suggests that ecotourism operates within 'green capitalism' where individuals, and not governments or the industry, take responsibility for environmental consequences (Duffy, 2002), thus relying on 'self-reflexivity' of the ecotourists who are thought to be more sensitive than mainstream tourists.

Incorporating ethics into ecotourism

Immediately applicable solutions to problems encountered in the ecotourism industry are few and limited. Figure 8.1 is an attempt to incorporate ethics according to three geographical/temporal and thematic hierarchies for the purpose of providing a better philosophical and operational connection in the development and management of ecotourism. The bottom part of the pyramid concerns locally and immediately applicable suggestions for incorporating ethics in ecotourism. Among the practical solutions within this realm is the inclusion of all stakeholders in the development of ecotourism product, such as thorough stakeholder analysis or 'social mapping' (Clark, 2002), which also takes into account their perceptions and values of the resource, and helps to build trust. This analysis may be in tune with Fennell's (2006) adaptation of the theory of reciprocal altruism ingrained in positive and trust-building tourist–host inter-actions, not necessarily between the same individuals but between the local and the continually changing visitor populations.

Also involving all stakeholders, another solution concerns the contextualization of the tour product, such as by developing an inclusive definition and sign system at major ecotourism attractions (i.e. educational information and codes of ethics), and mapping of the natural resources by the local people which displays their cultural, sacred, and biodiversity values. Additionally, land tenure and possessions in the area must be clearly defined through a legal tenure process and supported by government to avoid conflict between stakeholders. In the case of protected areas, governments have authority in deciding what development strategies should be implemented in the region (Epler-Wood, 2000). These strategies are promoted locally by different ministries and may be in conflict with the

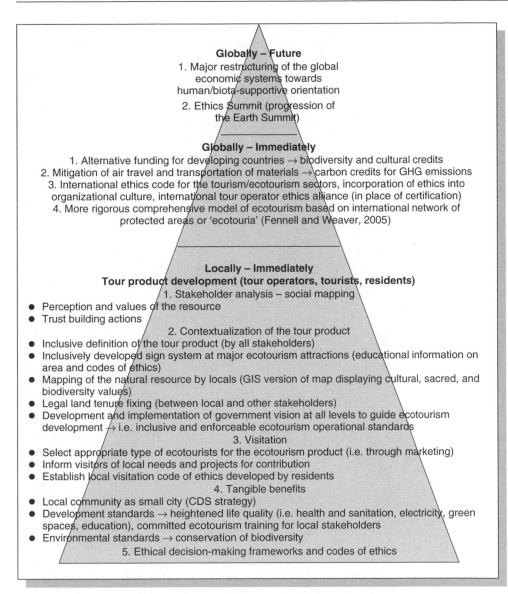

Globally – Future
1. Major restructuring of the global economic systems towards human/biota-supportive orientation
2. Ethics Summit (progression of the Earth Summit)

Globally – Immediately
1. Alternative funding for developing countries → biodiversity and cultural credits
2. Mitigation of air travel and transportation of materials → carbon credits for GHG emissions
3. International ethics code for the tourism/ecotourism sectors, incorporation of ethics into organizational culture, international tour operator ethics alliance (in place of certification)
4. More rigorous comprehensive model of ecotourism based on international network of protected areas or 'ecotouria' (Fennell and Weaver, 2005)

Locally – Immediately
Tour product development (tour operators, tourists, residents)
1. Stakeholder analysis – social mapping
- Perception and values of the resource
- Trust building actions
2. Contextualization of the tour product
- Inclusive definition of the tour product (by all stakeholders)
- Inclusively developed sign system at major ecotourism attractions (educational information on area and codes of ethics)
- Mapping of the natural resource by locals (GIS version of map displaying cultural, sacred, and biodiversity values)
- Legal land tenure fixing (between local and other stakeholders)
- Development and implementation of government vision at all levels to guide ecotourism development → i.e. inclusive and enforceable ecotourism operational standards
3. Visitation
- Select appropriate type of ecotourists for the ecotourism product (i.e. through marketing)
- Inform visitors of local needs and projects for contribution
- Establish local visitation code of ethics developed by residents
4. Tangible benefits
- Local community as small city (CDS strategy)
- Development standards → heightened life quality (i.e. health and sanitation, electricity, green spaces, education), committed ecotourism training for local stakeholders
- Environmental standards → conservation of biodiversity
5. Ethical decision-making frameworks and codes of ethics

Figure 8.1
Organizational framework for incorporation of ethics in ecotourism

development of an ecotourism project. In order to prevent detrimental policies at the regional and local levels, governments, tour operators, and communities cannot be disconnected from this process.

Other solutions revolve around the issue of visitation. Operational standards, including selection of appropriate type of ecotourists and development of local visitation code of ethics, may ease possible problems between different stakeholder groups. Where these are not implemented, tour operators may offer a variety of products and prices which can lead to high-end tourists at one end and mass tourists at another, thus dividing tour operators into rich and poor, and increasing the risk of running an operation that is likely to have detrimental impacts upon the natural resources and few profits for the local populations. The major challenge is to develop a plan for community involvement and empowerment, both in terms of resident participation in and ownership of the project, and fair distribution of benefits (defined beforehand) and costs (accounted for at the planning stage) from the ecotourism project. Initially, this can be achieved by providing practical and accessible ecotourism education and training in various fields (International Ecotourism Club, 2005). More meaningfully, having established a position of dialogue for the local populations, visitors can be readily informed of local needs and projects for their contribution.

Another means of ensuring ethical operation in practice is the provision of tangible benefits that can be measured or assessed in different ways. In effect, the community could be treated as a 'small city' in which urban issues like sanitation, solid waste management, water, green spaces, health, and education are fundamental for quality livelihoods. In a rural setting, for example, dry sanitation offers the potential to be a tangible benefit of the project. The improvement and reduction of children's early mortality due to gastrointestinal diseases could be an indicator of reaching a level of improved livelihood and can be easily measured. The linking of ecotourism to the development of a region follows what is called a city development strategy (CDS) where its goals and objectives are parallel to those of an ecotourism project seeking the sustainability of a community and protection of its natural resources (Cities Alliance, 2006). Therefore, the development standards for ecotourism may involve committed training for local stakeholders, while the environmental standards may include conservation of biodiversity. Finally, other means of ensuring ethical operation of an ecotourism project include the aforementioned codes of ethics and ethical decision-making frameworks, which guide the ethical decisions and behaviours of tour operators, visitors, and residents alike.

All of the above practical solutions to problems encountered in ecotourism are constrained by larger systems at work. Quite simply, it is impossible to rely on non-financial benefits from the economically ingrained operating world system, or to compete with other operators who ignore ethics at the expense of profit. To the contrary, Fennell and Weaver (2005) advocate implementation of more rigorous comprehensive model of eco-tourism based on international network of protected areas or 'ecotouria', believing it is fundamental in reaching more sustainable and ethical standards. Other international measures for incorporating ethics could include a global ethics code for the ecotourism sector (similar to that developed for tourism by WTO, 1999), incorporation of ethics into organizational culture of ecotourism companies, and establishment of international tour operator ethics alliance in place of certification which is often inconsistent and confusing. Moreover, besides carbon credits for mitigation of GHG emissions from air travel to eco-tourism destinations and transportation of materials, the eco-tourism sector could also promote biodiversity and cultural credits to provide alternative funding for developing countries, thus promoting their success in more sustainable operation.

Finally, at the very tip of the pyramid are solutions which are globally oriented towards the future. These solutions may be very controversial (politically, economically, socially, culturally, and spiritually) and thus fall outside mainstream thinking. They may involve major restructuring of the global political and economic systems towards a human/biota-supportive orientation, and by doing so, may be posing very real and direct practical implications for all nations and individuals alike – such as the Earth Summit has done. This growing body of research which openly challenges the operating global systems is discussed in more detail in the following section on future possibilities.

Future possibilities

Fortunately, a controversial body of research which introduces means to incorporate ethics as the key to global governance in any area is gaining momentum. Most recent examples from public media include Al Gore's book and now movie, entitled *An Inconvenient Truth* which exposes the consequences of global warming, or the bloc Quebecois lawsuit towards the Canadian government for not meeting the Kyoto agreement. From an academic perspective, Wenz (1996) introduces 'alternative politics' to the prevailing political system which is based on economic growth as central to human potential, and where 'practicality is determined by social, not physical, reality' (p. 164). His alternative is based on a smaller economy with less power over nature, including self-reliance and informal and personal arrangements in place of impersonal institutions. The author emphasizes the incompatibility of human values and the operating socio-politico-economic complex mega-structures which stand as blockades to alternative reality. He gives examples of abolishing slavery, civil rights, workers' rights, and womens' rights as having been impractical for generations in spite of appealing to common values (Wenz, 1996). The main challenge is to change slowly and painlessly, a complicated process of interrelated aspects that is compared to disengaging a bomb (Wenz, 1996, p. 165).

Similarly, Curtis (2003) proposes that sustainability is best achieved with the creation of local, self-reliant community economies, or in other words theory of eco-localism, contrary to the conventional pro-globalist perspective. The author describes this scenario as place-specific economy bounded in space by limits of community, geography, and natural resources. As scale is the key issue of economic sustainability, Morris (1996, in Curtis, 2003) concurs by suggesting that 'small is the scale of efficient, dynamic, democratic, and environmentally benign societies' (p. 90). However, the eco-localism theory requires reductions in technological throughput and in consumption, especially in wealthy societies. This alternative economic paradigm contends with local and international laws and regulations that under-mine it, and further it competes with, 'a hegemonic, market-oriented, profit-centered, consumerist, trade supremacist economic discourse' (Curtis, 2003, p. 100). On the contrary, eco-localism advocates a radical reorganization of economies across the globe to discourage globalization and to focus on a broader range of human values and environmental necessities than is present in policy (Curtis, 2003).

In attempts to reconstruct the political economies, some authors (i.e. Altvater, 1999; Dryzek, 1999) advocate ecological democracy (e.g. green parties). In supporting this idea, Miller (2003) emphasizes the role of complex, multidimensional global crises as the catalyst for a 'rising culture' (Capra, 1982) that may in turn stir humanity towards shifting of the entire belief system. The author believes that such global reform may only happen after the dynamics of oppression are made visible by decon-structing the 'politics of invisibility' (Miller, 2003). Norton *et al.* (1998) also point to the fact that current value systems convey inconsistencies between the short and long terms and between local and global goals, what others have referred to as 'social traps' (see Platt, 1973). The authors believe that once broad goals are established through a democratic process, they can be used to limit incompatible and unsustainable preferences at lower levels. Salleh (1997) also advocates for a strong socialist critique, urgent in the face of transnational corporate globalization, only now calling for politics that are gendered and ecologically literate.

However, she acknowledges that historical reorganization cannot emerge where people are disoriented and lack skills.

These new concepts of reality are supported by the Buddhist philosophy of 'sufficiency' (Theerapappisit, 2003), by the concept of smaller economies proposed by Wenz (1996), by the theory of 'eco-localism' suggested by Curtis (2003), and by prospects for 'ecological democracy' in reflexive reconstructing of the international political economy (Low, 1999). The above-mentioned share an inherent holistic perspective of 'the fundamental and inescapable interconnectedness of all life with everything on earth' (Hanh, 1988; Marietta, 1994; Paulo Freire in Crotty, 1998; Eichler, 2000, p. 6), as well as between various paradigms (Guba, 1990). In the view of natural limits where sufficiency replaces efficiency, Sachs (1999) proposes that limits can be productive, and lists new models of wealth: eco-intelligent goods and services, lower speeds and the plurality of time scales, shorter distances and the plurality of spaces, wealth in time rather than in goods, and well-being instead of well-having (pp. 197–212). The understanding of holism in the study of ecotourism should imply a consideration of the parts within a broader context of external political and economic forces, as well as other industries (Brown, 2000). Rather than aiming for the abstract construct of 'sustainable development' and 'social equity', the focus should be in reducing environmental unsustainability and social inequity (Eichler, 2000).

Conclusion

Much is needed to link current approaches to truly ethical scenarios in the near future – for ecotourism as much as for the overarching global system within which it operates. The first step lies in the development of an ethical and inclusive tour product which underscores multi-stakeholder discussions that could at some point take place on a global scale. The guiding framework represented in Figure 8.1 is not a panacea to reach sustainability, but it opens the door to the allocation of benefits to local stakeholders in helping to reach UN millennium development goals. Solutions that arise from such open discussions, such as the cultural and biodiversity credits proposed in this chapter, could be implemented immediately regardless of the overarching operating economic system, and provided ethics are implemented in the operation of the ecotourism sector. Further to this, it is argued that an interdisciplinary international conference organized around ethics and the creation of a blueprint for the restructuring of the market-based economy (i.e. ecological economics) on the basis of biodiversity and human objectives would provide the opportunity for ecotourism to demonstrate leadership in this new approach. Mechanisms which are not already at work offer logical progression of the Kyoto protocol and the Earth Summit, which integrate ethical objectives into all public debates and by doing so, demonstrate the problems with the free-market economy. Most importantly, insights and solutions gained from such a conference, ingrained in multi-stakeholder debates and research, could emerge as a blueprint for raising the ethical bar in politics, economics, and environmental affairs.

Singer (1981) made reference to the persistent widening of the circle of morality in society over time. If this persistence is to continue – and it needs to continue now more than ever – we need to take seriously the suggestions of those who would have us think differently. For ecotourism, enmeshed in the existent global market system which at present constrains our ability to operate *and benefit* through the implementation of ethical strategies, we will need to become much better at integrating theory and practice. If we fail in this regard, the metaphor used here of working against the current will constrain any attempts to secure an ethical ecotourism industry which could (and should) be a model for other forms of tourism development now and in the future.

References

Altvater, E. (1999). Restructuring the space of democracy: The effects of capitalist globalization and the ecologist crisis on the form and substance of democracy. In Low, N. (ed.), *Global Ethics and Environment*. Routledge, London.

Aramberri, J. and Xie, Y. (2003). Off the beaten theoretical track – domestic tourism in China. *Tourism Recreation Research* 28(1): 87–92.

Aramberri, J., Xie, Y. and Singh, S. (2003). Domestic tourism in Asia. *Tourism Recreation Research* 28(1): 34.

Attfield, R. (1998). Environmental ethics, overview. In Chadwick, R.F. (ed.), *Encyclopedia of Applied Ethics*, Vol. 2. Academic Press, San Diego, CA, pp. 73–92.

Brown, F. (2000). *Tourism Reassessed: Blight or Blessing?* Butterworth-Heinemann, Oxford.

Butcher, J. (2002). In Jenkins, T., Birkett, D., Goodwin, H., Goldstein, P., Butcher, J. and Leech, K. (eds), *Ethical Tourism: Who Benefits?* Hodder & Stoughton, London.

Butcher, J. (2003). *The Moralisation of Tourism: Sun, Sand … and Saving the World?* Routledge, London.

Capra, F. (1982). The turning point – science, society, and the rising culture. In Miller, A.S. (ed.), *Gaia Connections: An Introduction to Ecology, Ecoethics, and Economics* (2nd edn). Rowman & Littlefield Publishers, New York: Bantam New Age Books.

Cater, E. and Lowman, G. (eds) (1994). *Ecotourism: A Sustainable Option?* John Wiley & Sons, England.

Cities Alliance (2006). *City Development Strategies.* Retrieved May 29, 2006, from http://www.citiesalliance.org/activities-output/topics/cds/cds.html

Clark, T.W. (2002). *The Policy Process: A Practical Guide for Natural Resource Professionals.* Yale University Press, New Haven, CT.

Cleverdon, R. and Kalisch, A. (2000). Fair trade in tourism. *International Journal of Tourism Research* 2(3): 171–187.

Cohen, E. (1995). Contemporary tourism – trends and challenges: sustainable authenticity or contrived post-modernity? In Butler, R. and Pearce, D. (eds), *Change in Tourism, People, Places, Processes.* Routledge, London, pp. 12–29.

Cohen, E. (2003). Contemporary tourism and the host community in less developed areas. *Tourism Recreation Research* 28(1): 1–9.

Colero, L. (1997). *A Framework for Universal Principles of Ethics.* Crossroads Programs Inc. UBC Centre for Applied Ethics, University of British Columbia, Canada. Retrieved June 15, 2005, from www.ethics.ubc.ca/papers/invited/colero.html

Crotty, M. (1998). *The Foundations of Social Research: Meaning and Perspective in the Research Process.* SAGE, London.

Curtis, F. (2003). Eco-localism and sustainability. *Ecological Economics* 46: 83–102.

Daboub, A.J. and Calton, J.M. (2002). Stakeholder learning dialogues: how to preserve ethical responsibility in networks. *Journal of Business Ethics* 41: 85–98.

Dryzek, J. (1999). Global ecological democracy. In Low, N. (ed.), *Global Ethics and Environment.* Routledge, London.

Duffy, R. (2002). *A Trip Too Far: Ecotourism, Politics and Exploitation.* Earthscan, London.

Eichler, M. (2000). In/equity and un/sustainability: exploring intersections. *Environments* 28(2): 1–9.

Epler-Wood, M. (2000). *Meeting the Global Challenge of Community Development Participation in Ecotourism: Case Studies and Lessons from Ecuador.* USAID, The Nature Conservancy, and The Ecotourism Society.

Espaces (1992). Actualité, No. 118, October–November, p. 60.

Fennell, D.A. (2000). Tourism and applied ethics. *Tourism Recreation Research* 25(1): 59–69.

Fennell, D.A. (2006). *Tourism Ethics.* Channel View, Clevedon, UK.

Fennell, D.A. and Malloy, D.C. (1995). Ethics and ecotourism: a comprehensive ethical model. *Journal of Applied Recreation Research* 20(3): 163–183.

Fennell, D.A. and Malloy, D.C. (1999). Measuring the ethical nature of tourism operators. *Annals of Tourism Research* 26(4): 928–943.

Fennell, D.A. and Nowaczek, A.M. (2003). An examination of values and environmental attitudes among ecotourists: a descriptive study involving three samples. *Tourism Recreation Research* 28(1): 11–21.

Fennell, D.A. and Smale, B.J.A. (1992). Ecotourism and natural resource protection: implications of an alternative form of tourism for host nations. *Tourism Recreation Research* 17(1): 21–32.

Fennell, D.A. and Weaver, D. (2005). The ecotourism concept and tourism-conservation symbiosis. *Journal of Sustainable Tourism* 13(4): 373–390.

Francis, J. (2005). Post-tsunami tourism: the big test. *The Guardian Unlimited*. Retrieved February 25, 2005, from http://travel.guardian.co.uk/countries/story/0,7451,13906 10,00.html

Genot, H. (1995). Voluntary environmental codes of conduct in the tourism sector. *Journal of Sustainable Tourism* 3(3): 166–172.

Goodwin, H. (2002). The case for responsible tourism. In Jenkins, T., Birkett, D., Goodwin, H., Goldstein, P., Butcher, J. and Leech, K. (eds), *Ethical Tourism: Who Benefits?* Hodder & Stoughton, London.

Gordon, G. (ed.) (2001). *Tourism: Putting Ethics into Practice. A Report on the Responsible Business Practices of 65 UK-Based Tour Operators*. Tearfund, London.

Gössling, S., Hansson, C.B., Hoerstmeier, O. and Saggel, S. (2002). Ecological footprint analysis as a tool to assess tourism sustainability. *Ecological Economics* 43: 199–211.

Guba, E.G. (ed.) (1990). *The Paradigm Dialog*. Sage Publications, Thousand Oaks, CA.

Hall, C.M. (1999). Rethinking collaboration and partnership: a public policy perspective. *Journal of Sustainable Tourism* 7(3&4): 274–289.

Hanh, T.N. (1988). *The Heart of Understanding*. Parallax Press, Berkeley, CA.

Heron, P. (1991). The institutionalization of leisure: cultural conflict and hegemony. *Leisure in Society* 14(1): 171–190.

Hollinshead, K. (1999). Surveillance and the worlds of tourism: Foucault and the eye of power. *Tourism Management* 20(1): 7–24.

Honey, M. (2002). *Ecotourism and Certification: Setting Standards in Practice*. Island Press, Washington, DC.

Hultsman, J. (1995). Just tourism: an ethical framework. *Annals of Tourism Research* 22(3): 553–567.

International Ecotourism Club (2005). *Strengthening Ecotourism in Ecuador: Seven Recommendations*. Retrieved April 4, 2005, from http://ecoclub.com/gifee-es.html

Jamal, T.B. and Getz, D. (1995). Theory and community tourism planning. *Annals of Tourism Research* 22: 186–204.

Jenkins, T., Birkett, D., Goodwin, H., Goldstein, P., Butcher, J. and Leech, K. (2002). *Ethical Tourism: Who Benefits?* Hodder & Stoughton, London.

Jose, A. and Thibodeaux, M.S. (1999). Institutionalization of ethics: the perspective of managers. *Journal of Business Ethics* 22: 133–143.

Kotchen, M.J. and Reiling, S.D. (2000). Environmental attitudes, motivations, and contingent valuation of nonuse values: a case study involving endangered species. *Ecological Economics* 32: 93–107.

Lew, A. (1998). The Asia–Pacific ecotourism industry: putting sustainable tourism into practice. In Hall, C.M. and Lew, A.A. (eds), *Sustainable Tourism: A Geographical Perspective*. Addison Wesley Longman, Harlow, UK, pp. 92–106.

Low, N. (ed.) (1999). *Global Ethics and Environment*. Routledge, London.

Lozano, J.M. (1996). Ethics and management: a controversial issue. *Journal of Business Ethics* 15: 227–236.

MacCannell, D. (1992). *Empty Meeting Grounds*. Routledge, London.

Maich, S. (2005). Selling ethics at Nortel. *Maclean's* 118(4): 32.

Malloy, D.C. and Fennell, D.A. (1998). Ecotourism and ethics: moral development and organizational cultures. *Journal of Travel Research* 36(4): 47–56.

Marietta, E.M. (1994). *For People and the Planet: Holism and Humanism in Environmental Ethics*. Temple University Press, Philadelphia, PA.

McMurtry, J. (1998). *Unequal Freedoms. The Global Market as an Ethical System*. Garamond Press, Toronto, Ont.

Miller, A.S. (2003). *Gaia Connections: An Introduction to Ecology, Ecoethics, and Economics* (2nd edn). Rowman & Littlefield Publishers, New York.

Nilsson, M. and Küller, R. (2000). Travel behaviour and environmental concern. *Transportation Research* Part D, 5: 211–234.

Norton, B., Costanza, R. and Bishop, R.C. (1998). The evolution of preferences. Why 'sovereign' preferences may not lead to sustainable policies and what to do about it. *Ecological Economics* 24: 193–211.

Nowaczek, A.M. and Fennell, D.A. (2002). Ecotourism in post-communist Poland: an examination of tourists, sustainability and institutions. *Tourism Geographies* 4(4): 372–395.

Orams, M.B. (1995). Towards a more desirable form of ecotourism. *Tourism Management* 16(1): 3–8.

Orams, M.B. (2001). Types of ecotourism. In Weaver, D.B., Backman, K.F., Cater, E., Eagles, P.F.J. and McKercher, B. (eds), *The Encyclopedia of Ecotourism*. CABI Publishing, New York, pp. 23–36.

Palmer, C. (1997). *Environmental Ethics. Contemporary Ethical Issues*. ABC-CLIO, Santa Barbara, CA.

Platt, J. (1973). Social traps. *American Psychologist* 28: 641–651.

Pritchard, J. (1998). Codes of ethics. In Chadwick, R.F. (ed.), *Encyclopedia of Applied Ethics*, Vol. 1. Academic Press, San Diego, CA, pp. 527–533.

Prosser, R. (1998). Tourism. In Chadwick, R.F. (ed.), *Encyclopedia of Applied Ethics*, Vol. 4. Academic Press, San Diego, CA, pp. 373–401.

Przecławski, K. (1996). Deontology of tourism. *Progress in Tourism and Hospitality Research* 2: 239–245.

Quinn, J.J. (1997). Personal ethics and business ethics: the ethical attitudes of owner/managers of small business. *Journal of Business Ethics* 16: 119–127.

Reed, M. (1997). Power relationships and community based tourism planning. *Annals of Tourism Research* 24(3): 566–591.

Ryan, C., Hughes, K. and Chirgwin, S. (2000). The gaze, spectacle and ecotourism. *Annals of Tourism Research* 27(1): 148–163.

Sachs, W. (1999). *Planet Dialectics: Explorations in Environment and Development*. Fernwood Publishing, Halifax, NS.

Salleh, A. (1997). *Ecofeminism as Politics: Nature, Marx and the Postmodern*. Zed Books, New York.

Schein, E.H. (1985). *Organizational Culture and Leadership*. Jossey-Bass, San Francisco, CA.

Scheyvens, R. (1999). Ecotourism and the empowerment of local communities. *Tourism Management* 20(2): 245–249.

Schumann, P.L. (2001). A moral principles framework for human resource management ethics. *Human Resource Management Review* 11: 93–111.

Schwartz, M. (2001). The nature of the relationship between corporate codes of ethics and behaviour. *Journal of Business Ethics* 32: 247–262.

Singer, P. (1981). *The Expanding Circle: Ethics and Sociobiology*. Farrer, Straus & Giroux, New York.

Smith, M. and Duffy, R. (2003). *The Ethics of Tourism Development*. Routledge, London.

Stem, C.J., Lassoie, J.P., Lee, D.R., Deshler, D.D. and Schelhas, J.W. (2003). Community participation in ecotourism benefits: the link to conservation practices and perspectives. *Society and Natural Resources* 16: 387–414.

Stone, C. (1993). The Gnat is older than Man: Global Environment and human Agenda. Princeton: Princeton University Press.

Tearfund (2000). *Tourism – An Ethical Issue*. Tearfund, London.

Theerapappisit, P. (2003). Mekong tourism development: capital or social mobilization? *Tourism Recreation Research* 28(1): 47–56.

Trevino, L.K. (1986). Ethical decision making in organizations. *Academy of Management Review* 11: 601–671.

Wallace, G.N. and Pierce, S.M. (1996). An evaluation of ecotourism in Amazonas, Brazil. *Annals of Tourism Research* 23(4): 843–873.

Wallace, G.N. and Smith, M.D. (1997). A comparison of motivations, preferred management actions, and setting preferences among Costa Rican, North American and European visitors to five protected areas in Costa Rica. *Journal of Park and Recreation Administration* 15: 59–82.

Weaver, D.B. (1999). Magnitude of ecotourism in Costa Rica and Kenya. *Annals of Tourism Research* 26(4): 792–816.

Wenz, P.S. (1996). *Nature's Keeper*. Temple University Press, Philadelphia, PA.

West, P. and Carrier, J.G. (2004). Ecotourism and authenticity: getting away with it all? *Current Anthropology* 45(4): 483–498.

West, P.C., Fortwangler, C.L., Agbo, V., Simsik, M. and Sokpon, N. (2003). The political economy of ecotourism: Pendjari National Park and ecotourism concentration in Northern Benin. In Brechin, S.R., Wilshusen, P.R., Fortwangler, C.L. and West, P.C. (eds), *Contested Nature: Promoting International Biodiversity Conservation with Social Justice in the Twenty-First Century*. State University of New York Press, Albany, NY, pp. 103–115.

Wight, P.A. (2001). Ecotourists: not a homogeneous market segment. In Weaver, D.B., Backman, K.F., Cater, E., Eagles, P.F.J. and McKercher, B. (eds), *The Encyclopedia of Ecotourism*. CABI Publishing, New York, pp. 37–62.

WTO (1999). *Global Code of Ethics for Tourism*. Retrieved August 10, 2005, from http://www.world-tourism.org/code_ethics/pdf/languages/Codigo%20Etico%20Ing.pdf

Wunder, S. (2000). Ecotourism and economic incentives: an empirical approach. *Ecological Economics* 32: 465–479.

Wylie, J. (1994). *Journey Through a Sea of Islands: A Review of Forest Tourism in Micronesia*. USDA Forest Service Institute of Pacific Islands Forestry, Honolulu, Hawaii, HI.

CHAPTER 9

The role of sustainable tourism in international development: prospects for economic growth, alleviation of poverty and environmental conservation

Megan Epler Wood

Sustainable tourism in the new millennium

Tourism is a powerful, potential tool for economic development in lesser developed countries (LDCs). Gross revenues from the tourism industry increased 154% per year 1990–2000 in LDCs, more than double the rate of tourism growth in developed nations (Roe *et al.*, 2004, p. 7). It is the only service sector that provides concrete trading opportunities for all nations regardless of their level of development and it is the number one source of foreign exchange for LDCs, aside from petroleum (Diaz, 2001). Yet, it remains a low priority in the international development world (Christ *et al.*, 2003). It is often neglected because it is not viewed as a 'serious' development driver like agriculture or manufacturing and is therefore subjected to policies and priorities designed for other sectors (Roe *et al.*, 2004, p. 13). It is largely funded by international development agencies with funds not directly related to economic development, but rather as a subset of goals such as conservation of biodiversity or the promotion of corporate social responsibility.

There has been much less attention paid to its value in the international development world – perhaps because it is an unconsolidated industry that has few truly globalized players for large development agencies to work with. Its economic growth value has been difficult to quantify unlike commodities markets such as agriculture, textiles, or forest products (Hawkins *et al.*, 1995). But this chapter will demonstrate that increasingly tourism has better prospects for economic growth, lower environmental impacts, and more positive human development impacts than other industries in the poorest nations – particularly in rural areas where persistent poverty has been difficult to address. This chapter will therefore present that sustainable tourism has a very important role in the international development world that is growing and deserves increasing attention.

The facts supporting the review of tourism for its potential as an international development tool could not be stronger. It is the only service industry where there is a growing positive balance of trade flowing from the developed countries to the poorest nations, with 41 of the 50 poorest countries now earning over 10% of their exports from tourism. It is a principal export of 31 of the 49 LDCs and number one for seven (Roe *et al.*, 2004, p. 22), and it is in the top five exports for more than 80% of developing countries (Roe *et al.*, 2004, p. 19). In the larger group of developing countries, tourism represents as much as 66% of commercial services while in the developed world it represents only 36% (Sofield *et al.*, 2004, p. 2). The World Tourism Organization's research indicates that tourism's role in developing economies will continue to accelerate, becoming increasingly important in South America, Southern Africa, Southeast Asia, and Oceania (World Tourism Organization, 2006).

Ecotourism, the subset of sustainable tourism that focuses on responsible travel to natural areas worldwide, has been documented to have sustained positive economic impacts in regions of high ecological value (Lindberg *et al.*, 1998) because it attracts travelers interested in viewing wildlife and visiting parks. Ecotourism is defined by two primary objectives – 'to conserve natural areas and sustain the well-being of local people' (Lindberg *et al.*, 1998, p. 8). This chapter seeks to demonstrate that ecotourism development methodologies and analyses are entirely consistent with international development goals in economic growth, human development, and ecological sustainability. Though ecotourism projects and enterprises operate primarily in biodiversity zones and around natural areas – the case studies presented here demonstrate that ecotourism has a very strong role not only in conservation of natural resources, but also in the alleviation of poverty – particularly in rural areas.

International development and sustainable tourism

In order to assess how sustainable tourism can be appropriately positioned within the world of international development, it is important to summarize the goals – in brief – of the international development world and how they have evolved over the last 60 years.

The goal of international development is 'to achieve worldwide cooperation to solve international economic, social, cultural, and humanitarian problems' (United Nations Charter Article I, 2006). Since World War II, international development has been one of the primary functions of the United Nations, and the World Bank was formed shortly after the war to help finance international development goals set by the international community. Since then many international development institutions have been formed at both the national and international level supported by state funds and by non-government organizations (NGOs).

In the 1960–1980s, economic growth outcomes drove most decision-making in the international development world – and the development banks focused on the capitalization of large-scale industry projects and infrastructure without attention to environmental impacts, or incorporating environmental goals into projects (Clapp and Dauvergne, 2005).

The articulation of sustainable development as a goal of the international development community was led by the

Brundtland Commission in 1987. In their United Nations report, sustainable development was defined as 'meeting the needs of the present without compromising the ability of future generations to meet their own needs' (Brundtland Report, 1987, p. 24). This report has had an enormous influence on how international development is evolving, and it has been one of the most influential factors in ensuring that international development is not dominated solely by economic growth strategies alone. Increasingly, because of the Brundtland Report, international development agencies must provide indicators of success for a triple bottom line – economic growth, human development, and environmental preservation. But the progress toward incorporating all three indices has not been uniform as will be discussed here.

Efforts to incorporate human development goals more effectively into the international development process led to the definition of human development in 1990 as delivering greater access to knowledge, better nutrition and health services, more secure livelihoods, security against crime and physical violence, satisfying leisure hours, political and cultural freedoms, and sense of participation in community activities (UNDP, 2006a). The Human Development Index that is annually published by the United Nations Development Program monitors almost 200 indicators to determine how LDCs are meeting human development goals (UNDP, 2006c). Mahbub ul Haq (UNDP, 2006a) of Oxford University, the founder of the Human Development Index, states,

The human development school distinguishes itself from the economic growth school in that the latter focuses on expanding only one choice – income – while the former seeks to enlarge all human choices – social, economic, cultural, and political.

The Human Development Index has successfully provided an ongoing set of indicators that provide the international development community with valuable benchmarks to allow head to head comparison between economic development and human development results. The outcomes of these studies are clear; economic growth does not always result in an improvement of human development indicators. In fact, increasingly economic growth is simply contributing to an increasingly vast economic divide between the prosperous classes in LDCs and the poor (UNDP, 2006b).

Millennium development goals

To address the problem of persistent poverty and the growing economic divide in LDCs, the Millennium Development Goals

(MDG) campaign was launched in 2000. Proponents of this campaign explain that only one-sixth of the world's population has achieved high-income status through consistent economic growth, while two-thirds have achieved middle-income status. But one-sixth of humanity – or over 1 billion people are stuck in poverty (Millennium Project, 2006). MDG advocates seek to address the failure of economic growth approaches to help to alleviate poverty through the establishment of benchmarks to improve these inequities, including the eradication of extreme poverty and hunger by half, universal primary education, and halving the proportion of the poor without improved drinking water or proper sanitation (UN Millennium Development Goals, 2005). As Jeffrey Sachs (2005a) of Columbia University states,

Precisely because economic development can and does work in so many parts of the world, it is all the more important to understand and solve the problems of the places where economic development is not working (p. 51).

The Millennium Development project is set to meet its goals by 2015. Progress is charted annually, but investment from donor nations has not met the goals set by the campaign. The question of where the investment will come from continues to plague the process. While the EU has announced a timetable to reach 0.7% of gross national product (GNP) toward investment in the MDG goals, the US has avoided any such commitment (Sachs, 2005b). The lack of US commitment has to be cited as one of the chief barriers to further progress on this initiative. And there are problems with meeting goals particularly in rural areas, according to the campaign,

Progress has been far from uniform across the world – or across the Goals. There are huge disparities across and within countries. Within countries, poverty is greatest for rural areas
(Millennium Project, 2006).

Problems of addressing rural poverty strongly correlate to the rapid decline of the quality of environment in rural areas. The Millennium Ecosystem Assessment found that 60% of ecosystem services have been degraded worldwide, including fresh water, fisheries, air, and water and that the harmful effects of this degradation are borne disproportionately by the poor (Millennium Ecosystem Assessment, 2005). While it is well known that poverty and ecosystem degradation are strongly correlated, development initiatives often break into two schools – human development and environment. For example while the MDG initiative does address environment, it is one goal out of eight (Millennium Project, 2006).

Environmental indicators in international development

Environmental indicators for measuring the impacts of development on the environment have not yet been applied by the international development community, though there are a variety of indicators projects on the drawing boards. Throughout the 1980s, the development banks proceeded with financing large infrastructure projects without accounting for environmental impacts, and this caused well-documented problems such as the Polonoroeste colonization scheme in Brazil where a large highway into the Brazilian Amazon was financed in large part by the World Bank. This project has been cited as the primary cause of serious deforestation in Rondonia, Brazil, which increased from 1.7% to 16% in the 1980s (Clapp and Dauvergne, 2005).

The loss of natural capital in order to drive the growth of economies in developing countries has not slowed in many parts of the world despite the uproar over the investments of the World Bank in Rondonia and other projects causing the World Bank to pull out of Rondonia and establish a much more comprehensive environmental assessment program (Clapp and Dauvergne, 2005). Political leaders in developing countries frequently oppose efforts to stop large infrastructure for environmental reasons. For example, China proceeded with its Three Gorges Dam despite the lack of support from the international development world on environmental grounds (Qing, 1994), and in Asia in general, the push for growth continues to take a heavy toll on the environment. For example, in Southeast Asia 95% of forests with full biodiversity have been lost, financed largely by private corporations from North Asia (Clapp and Dauvergne, 2005). While some leaders in countries such as Malaysia argue that this is the necessary cost of economic development (*The Economist*, 1995), decision makers may not be considering the long-term economic impacts of degrading their natural capital.

Ecological economists argue that, 'selling natural assets and including the proceeds in the gross domestic product (GDP) is wrong on both economic and accounting grounds' (Serafy, 1997, p. 34). These economists strongly support the need for integrated resource accounting in the field of international development because it is vital for developing countries, with a heavy dependence on natural resources, to understand that economic accounting can lead to very destructive trade policies (Serafy, 1997). But integration of resource accounting has yet to come, because theoretical constructs are still being formulated that can accommodate the vast distinction between public and private good in the marketplace (Costanza and Daly, 1992).

Sustainable tourism

Sustainable tourism has been little considered throughout these global debates about achieving proper incorporation of natural capital and human development into international development goals. The UN World Tourism Organization (2005) released a declaration on *Harnessing Tourism for the Millennium Development Goals* in September 2005, stating that the United Nations needs to note:

the role that tourism plays in most developing countries, least developed and small island states, as the main – and sometimes the only – means of economic and social development on a sustainable basis with meaningful linkages to other productive sectors, such as agriculture and handicrafts.

While tourism is not an industry that is free from the problems caused by the drive for economic growth – it is a different industry where prices are not driven by a consolidated commodities marketplace but rather by the value of service, quality of the attraction, and the level of luxury of the infrastructure offered. These factors give sustainable tourism planners working for development agencies more latitude to work for not only economic growth, but also better labor standards, preservation of natural resources that serve as attractions, and environmental management of infrastructure for the purposes of creating a value-added development environment.

The experience of the author in sustainable tourism and ecotourism development projects in over 30 countries has led to a number of conclusions based on field experience. Tourism is frequently dependent on offering quality natural resources to succeed, often in rural areas – such as parks and protected areas or clean beaches, and the conservation of this natural capital is of great concern to their buyers, the tourists, who will pay more for a more pristine environment – clearly not the case in most commodity markets. Excellent service is expected and though labor is frequently seriously undervalued in the tourism market in developing countries (Riddle, 2002) – it is not confined by fixed pricing set for commodities – such as the coffee and banana markets which can drive labor prices down to unreasonable degrees. In fact, in tourism there is a strong argument for development agencies to invest in human resource training because it improves the competitiveness of the destinations, can lead directly to better profits of the company, and results in more tips directly to laborers. These more benign labor decision-making factors can lead to better human development outcomes, precisely because tourism is a service industry.

The industry also has unique characteristics that favor small and micro business in developing countries. It is an export market where the customer, the tourist, actually visits the country where the ser-vice is offered – making it one of the few globalized industries where small producers can sell directly to the end user. Micro and small enterprises can enter into the 'start-up' phases of the tourism industry with much less capital, and the markets are largely not controlled by large industry nor are they consolidated because of the great success of the Internet as a tool for marketing tourism. As a result, fixed pricing set by transnational buyers is not an issue in the tourism industry. Finally, the local entrepreneurial activity associated with the tourism industry is frequently in high biodiversity zones and in rural areas, where the Millennium Development project has stated poverty is often the most persistent.

The fact that tourism is a principal export of 80% of developing countries and the first source of foreign exchange for all of the 49 LDCs aside from petroleum (Diaz, 2001) is highly significant – and merits a much deeper discussion within the international development community about the value of putting more expertise and investment into sustainable tourism as a means to alleviate poverty, improve human development indicators, drive economic growth, and conserve natural resources upon which the well-being of the poor depends.

Enterprise development and sustainable development

The consolidation of wealth into the hands of just one-sixth of humanity has left those living traditionally on the land more and more isolated and without adequate human development options. Increasingly, those living at the top of the pyramid in the wealthy nations are using up the natural resources of the developing countries (Hart, 2005). The growth of the 'money economy' has essentially marginalized the traditional economy according to business analyst Stuart L. Hart of the Cornell University who points out that roughly 4 billion people or two-thirds of humanity live in a subsistence-oriented economy which has been adversely affected by globalization, ignored by the world of commerce, and victimized by corruption. They lack infrastructure, credit, collateral, and legal protection and they are increasingly suffering from pollution, depletion of natural resources, and forced dislocation (Hart, 2005).

For example, transnational mining has become increasingly controversial in countries with a very high poverty index such as Bolivia, the Philippines, and Papua New Guinea, because there are scores of cases of environmental pollution as well as ecological and social disruption that has had very negative human development impacts (Clapp and Dauvergne, 2005). Often miners displace indigenous people, the traditional economy almost always suffers, and revenues from these industries do not remain in local hands (Clapp and Dauvergne, 2005).

A growing school of thought rejects international development as a solution to addressing the needs of the poor and suggests a move toward more local, self-reliant economies. These thinkers suggest that, 'large scale industrialism is seen to encourage inequality characterized by overconsumption of the wealthy, while at the same time contributing to poverty and environmental degradation' (Clapp and Dauvergne, 2005, p. 12).

While extractive industries 'and other transnationals' environmental and social race to the bottom has led activists to reject all forms of global commerce, extractive industry performance is perhaps the worst example of the globalized economy. In fact, there is a high concentration of transnational corporations in mining, logging, and oil with very poor records of applying lower environmental and labor standards in developing countries (Clapp and Dauvergne, 2005).

While the global effort to address the inequities cited by MDG advocates may help to developing countries by addressing debt, health, and education, the problem of persistent poverty cannot be eliminated through social services alone. More wealth has to be generated and this cannot be achieved without the participation of the private sector. Hart suggests that the private sector may be the only sector of society that can raise the resources, develop the capacity, and achieve the global reach to make a more sustainable world (Hart, 2005):

Sustainable global enterprise thus represents the potential for a new private sector-based approach to development that creates profitable businesses that simultaneously raise the quality of life for the world's poor, respect cultural diversity, and conserve the ecological integrity of the planet for future generations (p. xlii).

Hart's analysis that private sector skills are needed to address global inequities fits well into the paradigm of using sustainable tourism and ecotourism as tools to achieve international development goals. His call for a new blend of private sector enterprise development that reaches into the traditional economy and provides local people with reasonable opportunity can easily be applied to the sustainable tourism field. And while his call is largely to transnational corporations to find business opportunities by servicing the poorest 5 billion people on earth – which he calls the bottom of the pyramid, sustainable tourism allows micro and small businesses in developing countries to play this role by encouraging those emerging from poverty to enter the globalized market of tourism – which is literally knocking on their door in many poor, rural regions of the world.

Ecotourism development strategies are almost always formulated in pockets of rural poverty in regions left behind by capital markets. It has been shown that the more natural resources a country has conserved, the more likely it is not advancing by standard economic development measures (Sachs and Warner, 1999). These rural, biodiverse nations are frequented by the extractive oil, mining, and logging industries which can leave a very negative environmental and human development legacy as will be explored in the upcoming case study on Ecuador.

In Ecuador, the ecotourism private sector has worked with nontraditional partners, including NGOs and community groups, to successfully build profitable enterprises that generate funds for these communities. In accordance with studies of the affected region, the funds are spent on health and education facilities in communities that have suffered from the environmental impacts of the extractive industries that have worked in the region (Drumm, 1998). The following case study on Ecuador discusses how these projects have evolved and provides an in-depth discussion of how ecotourism can be developed to address human development, environmental, and economic needs of the traditional economy.

Ecuador

Ecuador is a small country found on the Andean spine of South America that has some of the world's highest biodiversity. Sixteen hundred bird species are found there (17% of the global total), and some of the greatest tree and insect diversity recorded on earth (Koenig, 2004). There are large wilderness areas found in the country, which are well protected by the country's protected area system and by indigenous federations that are in control of millions of hectares of pristine rainforest within the Amazonian region, known as the Oriente (Epler Wood, 1998). But despite these favorable conditions, the Oriente is threatened by oil exploration and exploitation. The nation of Ecuador has retained all subterranean land rights and licenses third party oil operations to explore for oil and exploit it when found in any area that is not an official protected area.

Oil exploration began in the Oriente 30 years ago. The earliest example of oil exploitation in northern Ecuador was handled by Texaco beginning in 1973 (Koenig, 2004). In order to cut costs, Texaco made a decision to forgo re-injecting the toxic byproducts generated by their oil wells, placing such substances as benzene, arsenic, mercury, lead, and cadmium in unlined oil pits – a practice that was illegal in the US at the time. Many of the unlined pits ruptured and leaked into the surrounding watershed destroying local fisheries and contaminating the region's watery ecosystem. Cancer risks in the area have been found to be 30 times higher than normal, and an international class action suit against Texaco (now Chevron/Texaco) was filed in 1993. Expert witnesses for the trial have compared the scale of environmental damages caused by the ruptured waste pits in the Oriente to that caused by the melt down of the Chernobyl nuclear plant in Russia (Koenig, 2004). These experts testifying on behalf of the plaintiffs – who are the indigenous peoples from the excavation area – estimate the clean up will require as much as $6 billion USD not including any personal damages to local people (Koenig, 2004).

A group of Cofan – part of the local indigenous group who live near the Texaco oil wells – relocated in the 1980s, moving downriver to an uninhabited rainforest location called Zabalo. They fought for land and subterranean rights in their new location – rights they won with the help of Quito based environmental attorneys. There they began to invite tourists to visit and became one of the earliest communities in Ecuador to use ecotourism as an alternative livelihood that could contribute to their economic well-being and allow them to educate their children and pay for health care. Profits were handled communally and the management of the enterprise was carefully handled by a small, well-trained core group.

Despite their achievement, the large majority of Cofan, Secoya, and Siona people and the mestizo population located near the wells stayed, and there have been years of rancor over the role oil plays here and throughout the Oriente. This has caused unrelenting conflict between the government and self-reliant native communities – many of whom have turned to ecotourism as a means to develop their territories as an alternative to oil and other destructive extractive practices (Epler Wood, 1998).

This dramatic case of environmental destruction in Ecuador's highly biodiverse Amazonian landscape is an excellent example of where the global commodity market – in this case oil – has caused serious damage to the natural capital of the nation. And if that is not severe enough, during the period of excavation now being cited as an environmental disaster for the nation – Ecuador was experiencing an economic decline indicating that few local economic benefits were being derived (Sachs, 2005a).

From a human development standpoint, the indigenous people who lived in this region have seen their quality of life decline – many have health problems, access to education and health has not improved, and there are few options for them to consider. Yet, the oil economy continues to expand throughout the Oriente, because the nation of Ecuador receives a high rate of return on its oil fields and the oil economy contributes as much as 25% of total revenues to the national budget. Public debt has skyrocketed in the past, but is presently 45% of the GDP – largely due to the rising prices for oil (CIA World Factbook, 2006a).

The role of tourism in Ecuador's economic development process

The actual size of Ecuador's oil economy is very small in comparison to Venezuela, the US, or Canada. In 2003, the country produced just 420,000 barrels, which is worth an annual gross of $2.5 billion dollars. While oil remains the number one source of foreign exchange, tourism is number three (after foreign remittances) (Youth, 2006). In 2004 tourism was estimated to generate $367 million in revenues for the businesses throughout the country (Youth, 2006). In 2001, the government of Ecuador declared tourism an economic development priority of the nation and projected that by 2011 the nation will earn $1.6 billion from tourism. If this is achieved, the tourism economy is very likely to become the number one source of foreign exchange for the nation, as the oil economy is likely to decline in this time frame (Reinoso, 2003).

In a small country like Ecuador, with 45% of its people living in official poverty, and with vast parts of the country in large parks and reserves that represent some of the world's most vibrant examples of biodiversity – it is clear that ecotourism will grow as part of the nation's tourism growth strategy and can continue to expand and provide a growing economic development alternative to traditional peoples who are living on the land. At present the per capita GDP of Ecuador is $3,900, and rural communities, which make up 25% of the nation's population, live in the deepest poverty (Youth, 2006). These people receive few social and education benefits from the government, and viable economic alternatives that will actually lift them out of poverty are rare.

In this context, ecotourism offers a highly unusual, diversified means to spread economic development to rural and traditional peoples living far from major economic centers. Development is not achieved by environmentally harmful industrial activities that create a disempowered labor force (which frequently faces serious contamination in the workplace, such as oil excavation or banana production) but via a diversified small and medium enterprise business development model that includes community-owned cooperatives. Ecotourism in Ecuador has created many small business owners. It has generated profits at every level of society ranging from tour operators in Quito, to small hotels and historic inns in the Andes, to local agricultural cooperatives that produce crops and handicrafts for the tourism economy, to community-based ecotourism destinations in the jungles of the Oriente (Youth, 2006).

Examples from the Ecuadorian Amazon: the Oriente

The Cofan community that relocated five hours from the Texaco oil disaster developed an ecotourism economy in the 1990s that generated $500 per person per year for every member of their community (which is 25% of the average per capita income throughout the country in 2005). After experimenting with several private business profit sharing approaches, they established a community company in 1992 with ten Cofan associates who worked on the enterprise and in return earned a full partner percentage of the profits. All community members derived a smaller portion of the profits (the $500 per person figure) without becoming full time associates – by selling handicrafts in a cooperative store which was visited twice a week by a local tour company, and providing guided walks and visits to a traditional arts museum across the river from their village (Epler Wood, 1998).

Because Colombian narcotraficantes have infiltrated the porous border area between Ecuador and Colombia where the Cofan reside, tourists can no longer be safely accommodated in this area. While the Cofan are not presently offering ecotourism, they developed a model for community-based tourism that has become part of the fabric of Ecuador. Similar pioneering initiatives in the Oriente, such as the community tourism cooperative Ricancie, have inspired the development of over one hundred community tourism enterprises throughout the country. In 2001, the Ecuador Ministry of Tourism estimated there were 40 community managed ecotourism businesses in the Oriente alone, representing several hundred communities. Ricancie and similar community enterprises are dedicated to fostering 'respect of their natural resources and cultural heritage as a development alternative for their community members for now and in the future' (Reinoso, 2003, p. 27).

In the southeastern Oriente, a different model of ecotourism development was emerging that created a unique model of joint ownership between an indigenous federation and a private sector company. Kapawi was established in 1996 and is now considered to be the largest community-based ecotourism project in Ecuador. Unlike many community-oriented facilities, Kapawi targets the luxury market. It is found in a roadless area that can only be reached by light aircraft. It is located within Achuar territory and was formulated from its inception as a partnership project between OINAE (Indigenous Organization of Ecuadorian Achuar Nationalities) and Canodros, an Ecuadorian tourism company that specialized in Galapagos cruises.

In the 1980s, the Achuar were still living in a self-sustaining economy without outside commerce, but the influence of government, missionaries, and the interaction with other cultures was bringing many changes. By the early 1990s, an economist estimated that the need for monetary income was less than $300 per family per year, but the demand for outside cash revenue was beginning to grow rapidly as traditions changed and the demand for education and health care grew (Wunder, 1996, as cited in Epler Wood, M., 1998). While the Achuar had once lived via hunting, fishing, small farms, and gathering in the rainforest; logging, oil exploration, and intensive agriculture were all extremely likely forms of cash income for the Achuar in the future as they began to emerge into the global economy.

The territory leaders were keen to find alternatives to economic development that would avoid the destruction of their culture and ecosystem. A joint venture between the Achuar and Canodros was established to build and operate an ecotourism lodge that they would operate together for 15 years, at which time Canodros would withdraw all investment and allow the Achuar to manage the entire operation themselves. Until 2011, the Achuar are being trained in all activities to manage and market the lodge, and the lodge employs a majority of the Achuar people. A payment of $2,000 USD per month with 7% annual increases in rent for the land and a $10 entrance fee per person are paid by Canodros to OINAE until the agreement expires.

As of 2005, the reserve remains free of roads, and the community collects an average of $16,000 per year in entrance fees and $50,000 in rent. The lodge breaks even annually, but still produces little profit due to the costs of using private aircraft to transport the tourists and all their provisions into the site. OINAE is now looking into creating its own small aircraft service for the lodge and local residents to lower costs and increase revenues – as in 2011 the entire lodge and all its contents will be transferred to the OINAE (Youth, 2006).

Other examples in the central Oriente, which is more accessible by road and the easily navigable Napo River, also focus on providing income to traditional populations in outlying areas.

The Napo Wildlife Center provides 49% of its profits to the local Quichua community and 85% of its employees are from the local village (Youth, 2006). There is a strong focus on providing an underpinning of economic support for the local rural people in many projects of this kind throughout Ecuador – and it is this type of thinking that has made Ecuador one of the most dynamic examples of how ecotourism can become a nationally signifi-cant activity that supports conservation, and offers significant economic development returns for traditional people who have been left with few opportunities to move up the ladder in the globalized economy.

It is important to note that all of the projects cited here have gone through extensive internal consent-based processes and many are run by communities themselves. The RICANCIE proj-ect for example is managed by a group of eleven communities that are dedicated to (1) contributing to the family budgets of community members, (2) promoting participation of indige-nous women, (3) helping to prevent the out-migration of young indigenous people to cities, and (4) offering employment locally. All of the communities discussed in Ecuador have very little access to alternatives that will keep them on their land. Many have had contact with the devastating social and envi-ronmental impacts of the oil economy.

The ecotourism models referenced here have offered rural and traditional communities hope that economic development can be kinder and gentler. In Ecuador, where the divide between rich and poor is vast, companies like Canodros, located in the city of Guayaquil, have demonstrated that they seek fair and reasonable relationships with traditional community partners in the Oriente. In fact, companies in other parts of Latin America – such as Rainforest Expeditions in Peru – have cre-ated similar joint ventures. These 'build, operate, and transfer (BOT)' alliances between private companies and local commu-nities have proven to provide incentives for long-term relation-ships of mutual respect between partners which might never have existed given the vast geographic, social, and economic distance between the traditional economy of the rainforest in Ecuador and Peru and the cities of Guayaquil and Lima where these travel companies are headquartered.

As countries throughout Latin America seek to find develop-ment models that are not exploitative and benefit the growing numbers of poor in their societies, communities and businesses in Ecuador and Peru are creating models that reach deep into rural areas and traditional societies and bring them to the table of commerce in a fair and just manner. The 'BOT model' helps to build long-term national stability by partnering traditional corporations with traditional society. It can be a very significant and growing form of economic development that empowers local people in the most rural and remote parts of Latin America's landscape. While every ecotourism project is certainly not meeting these standards, ecotourism model projects in Ecuador are multiplying. They give local people a sense of optimism and an understanding that they are owners not employees, they help them to protect their natural and cultural heritage, and offer a reason to remain on the land.

Honduras

Tourism has been a focal point for economic development in Central America for well over a decade. The report *Centro America en el Siglo XXI – Una Agenda para la Competitividad y el Desarrollo Sostenible* (INCAE/CLACDS & HIID, 1999) names tourism as one of four 'clusters' of high potential for the region together with agribusiness, textiles, and electronics manufacturing. Honduras' close neighbor, Costa Rica, has long been known as one of the top tourism destinations in all of Latin America. Costa Rica earned $3.6 billion in foreign exchange from tourism in 2005 and demand was expected to grow 5.5% per annum, in real terms in the next 10 years (World Travel and Tourism Council, 2005).

Honduras is a small player in the tourism environment of Central America when compared with Costa Rica. The Honduran Institute of Tourism (IHT) estimates that tourism brought in $401 million in foreign exchange for Honduras in 2004, with 610,000 overnight visitors and 384,000 day visitors (IHT, 2004). Tourism is the third most important form of foreign exchange for the country after maquiladoras (textile factories in free trade zones) and remesas familiars (funds sent by family members living overseas), but three times more productive than any other industry including coffee or bananas (IHT, 2005) In terms of growth potential, tourism must be considered the number one growth industry of Honduras.

Honduras is one of the poorest countries in the Western Hemisphere with GDP per capita at US $2,900 per year. Economic growth is roughly 5% a year, but 53% people remain below the poverty line. It is estimated that there are more than 1.2 million people who are unemployed. The country is characterized by an extraordinarily unequal distribution between the rich and poor. The government is banking on free trade via the Central America Free Trade Act (CAFTA) and debt relief, which has been granted under the Heavily Indebted Poor Country

Initiative to lift it out of poverty. Debt as of 2005 was over 70% of the GDP (CIA World Factbook, 2006b).

The Honduras National Tourism Strategy

In December 2005, the government of Honduras presented a national strategy for tourism that gives high priority to tourism as an economic development engine for the country and projects governmental expenditures with donor support of $174 million for its implementation 2006–2016. The Honduran government is seeking to maximize the contribution of tourism to the economic prosperity of Honduras via securing reliable tourism growth, maximizing visitor spending, and reducing leakages. The National Sustainable Tourism Strategy is a 10-year long-range plan with many key concepts and ideas for the development of tourism in the nation. As of 2005, it was fully planned for implementation with budgets allocated for the Short Term (2006–2009) of $132,504,987 – 99% presently financed; Medium Term (2010–2014) $23,784,843 – 85% presently financed; and Long Term (2015–2021) $17,748,085 – 51% financed (Epler Wood for International Resources Group, 2005).

The National Tourism Strategy has designated three major tourism zones as high priority for tourism – Copan, Tela, and the Bay Islands. Copan is a major Mayan archeological site with over 25 years of tourism development history. The Bay Islands are found off the coast of Honduras and have been an important scuba diving destination for over 15 years. Tela is presently a small village on the North Coast, located on the Caribbean Sea. Many fine beaches are found in this part of Honduras, but there has been little significant waterfront development to date. The Tela Bay Project, which is being supported by the National Tourism Strategy loans, is a luxury resort complex project that will create the new Los Micos Beach & Golf Resort. According to the official master plan, Los Micos will occupy more than 300 hectares along over 3.2 km of the coastline and include up to seven 4 or 5 star hotels, 168 residential villas, a mall, casino, tennis, and equestrian centers, and an 18-hole golf course, among other amenities (Cuffe, 2006).

There was a judgment made by the national government that there needs to be support of 'critical' mass of tourism in Copan, on the Bay islands, and in Tela before further investment will be fruitful because:

● Copan and the Bay Islands are the most important destinations in the country, but both require significant new infrastructure and planning assistance in order to grow.

- Tela has been selected as the hub for tourism on the north coast to help spread the pressure away from the Bay Islands and Copan – which are already in significant environmental jeopardy until more infrastructure can be delivered to support growth.
- Honduras must see a return on its investment when it comes to accepting loans from such entities as the Inter-American Development Bank (IDB) and therefore must concentrate its investments in areas that are likely to attract investment and bring significant economic growth and deliver steady growth of foreign exchange (Ardila, 2005).

In short, the tourism strategies of the Honduran government are thoroughly researched and based on well-tuned strategies to deliver needed economic development returns to the national budget, partly to help offset the national debt. But these plans do not factor in how the growth in Tela will cause rapid unplanned development along the major road corridor between Tela and the international airport at La Ceiba, 60 miles away along an undeveloped coastal road. Sergio Ardila of IDB agreed that this corridor will be heavily affected by the tourism in Tela and confirmed that the region outside Tela is not receiving any support from the IHT (Ardila, 2005). He said this was not an oversight, but rather a limitation in the budget for the National Tourism Program. He predicted there would be no further potential for support of these areas via the IHT tourism development program.

Conservation and socioeconomic impacts of the national tourism strategy

The ramifications of the decisions made within the National Tourism Strategy are an excellent example of where international development institutions need to further fine-tune their investments to meet economic growth, human development, and ecological conservation goals. As will be discussed below, the North Coast is a very fragile, ecological corridor and the degradation of its watershed could have severe consequences for the poor living in this region.

The conservation of North Coast ecosystems of Honduras is an ecological challenge. Humid rainforest is found on a mountainous landscape within ten miles of the coast with numerous rivers flowing rapidly down a narrow flood plain and into mangroves before reaching the sea. This entire region receives very heavy rains from coastal storms and hurricanes. In 1998 the massive Hurricane Mitch hit the area with 180 mile per hour winds and then stalled right over the North Coast delivering 25 inches in 36 hours. Nearly ten thousand lives were lost, and the region was cut off from the outside world for months. The damage will take decades to repair (Heming, 2006, n.d.). These mountains are very vulnerable to ecological damage caused by flooding, as they have precipitous gradations and require extensive vegetative cover to protect them from serious landslides. With the increasing number of tropical storms and record number of hurricanes being recorded annually as of 2005, this region is in increasing jeopardy of annual flooding unless its watersheds are scrupulously protected. During the author's November 2005 visit, a relatively minor tropical storm named Gamma flooded the entire corridor and made it impossible to travel between La Ceiba and Tela. Rivers were well over their banks, entire sections of road were destroyed, and a bridge beyond Tela collapsed killing several travelers.

The protection of the watershed is not improving at present – though the USAID project for which the author was working – Project MIRA – is dedicated to improving this situation. According to Project MIRA documents, inappropriate farming, grazing, forestry, and other resource extraction practices, driven in part by poverty and in part by inadequate policies and enforcement safeguards, have caused soil degradation and accelerated erosion rates, especially since Hurricane Mitch. The water attenuation and retention capacity of the soils and vegetation has been reduced, resulting in increased flash floods and landslides. Projections indicate growing problems of endemic flooding, landslides, severe shortages of drinking water, scarcity, and contamination of water for productive uses (IRG, 2004).

There are four protected areas along the North Coast. Two are right in the Tela Bay project zone. The largest protected area in Honduras, Pico Bonito National Park, is just outside the Tela development zone. It protects 100,000 hectares of mountainous rainforest and operates without support of the national government, surviving on grants and the support of an ecotourism lodge, the Lodge at Pico Bonito. Given that tax dollars in Central America have traditionally been used almost exclusively for aggressive marketing of natural destinations without any investment in the management and protection of publicly managed natural areas, the case of Pico Bonito is not unusual (INCAE/CLACDS & HIID, 1999). But the issue is that this major protected area has not been factored in, from an ecological perspective to a major tourism project that will have large ecological impacts on the entire North Coast corridor – within which Pico Bonito is one of the most important, protected watershed zones.

In addition, the National Tourism Strategy has not created a plan for the North Coast to directly address poverty reduction for local communities – except for some Garifuna communities in the Tela area. Many small mestizo communities are living in the mountains between Tela and the La Ceiba airport. They are living with few social services, and infrastructure is minimal in much of this area. All of these communities are poor and lack the technical capacity or financing to develop land management protocols that will protect their land or their watersheds. They will be very vulnerable to speculators and developers who are likely to take a strong interest in this corridor. Local populations always lack the capacity to take advantage of the rapidly changing socioeconomic development environment that tourism represents. They are rarely given the tools to make effective decisions over the long-term that will bring greater cash resources to their communities, while defending their precious natural and cultural assets and avoiding the negative impacts that tourism development inevitably represents.

Small business based in La Ceiba is also at risk. The local businesses in La Ceiba were interviewed during the author's stay. She found that there is a promising community of small and medium enterprises that have managed to eke out a living on the North Coast, with a commitment to preserving the area – but that these businesses have few resources to do more than survive. At present there is an active river rafting economy, with four businesses operating on the Rio Congregal just outside La Ceiba – which offers some of the best river rafting in the Western Hemisphere according to the owner of Omega Tours, Udo Wittemann – a former German Olympian in rafting. Although the local rafting economy is being run by individuals who may love rivers and rafting, they are not sophisticated business people.

The danger of irresponsible tourism development flowing down the coast from Tela is extremely high, and the La Ceiba region may not have the opportunity to properly diversify a responsible home-grown tourism industry to protect their limited investment in the region. The local businesses have marginal profits and do not employ competitive business practices. Outside businesses with foreign investment will likely quickly take over in this vacuum and a strip development approach that does not respect local heritage or resources may well quickly emerge. If this 'strip' development mushrooms into the mountains there is a real danger of damage to the watershed. An unplanned tourism economy would likely be unregulated enough to cause damage to fragile river corridors that are already vulnerable to flooding during storms.

The consequences of rapid growth in this region can be viewed at any mass tourism coastal destination, such as Cancun. Cancun was once also limited to one coastal peninsula where large scale tourism development was to take place. It was also financed by development banks via the government of Mexico. Since its development in 1973, intensive urban hotel and condominium development now runs 200 miles down the Yucatan coast, and a major service industry and housing for workers with commercial strip development spreads inland about 50 miles.

After analyzing the status of the small businesses in the La Ceiba area, it was clear that the existing businesses needed donor support. They were presently all working to attract the same rafting market and undercutting each other's prices. There was little business cooperation, and few environmental, or social standards were being met as these businesses were all in the survival mode. Given the likely invasion of profiteers into the area, the local businesses needed a network of support to help them win a wide range of technical assistance for best practice and competitiveness in the North Coast region. The clustering of complementary ecotourism style businesses could have provided the economy of scale and cost-savings motivation to apply more best practice and competitiveness approaches in the long-term, but unfortunately the sustainable tourism component of the USAID project was cut entirely from Project MIRA.

The tourism development environment of Honduras represents both high potential and high risk. The danger of irresponsible tourism development flowing down the coast from Tela is extremely high, and the La Ceiba region may not have the opportunity to properly diversify and allow local players to develop their incipient ecotourism 'capital' into a real business opportunity in time. Local foundations managing vital public assets may not have the capacity in place to prepare for and manage the new influx of tourists. In addition, efforts to bolster local communities and develop their capacity to manage their land, defend it against speculation, and retain ownership of the local economy appeared to need much more serious consideration and work.

It is precisely this kind of scenario that gives tourism development a bad reputation. It becomes an aggressive economic scheme – similar to projects in Mexico – that can galvanize poor countries like Honduras into a better economic position at a national level – but there are many, many gaps with the technical analysis of the projects' short- and long-term social and environmental impacts. The ripple effect from 'planned developments' are often just not considered. Communities become disempowered in such scenarios and environmental impacts are not contained or appropriately planned for. And yet the technical capacity to create better projects is there. There is no question that a variety of very good investments could be made by donors to prevent all of the potential damage to the La Ceiba area – but the international technical will and investment in bilateral aid that is not dependent on loans – rarely is there to meet urgent needs such as those found in Honduras. It can only be hoped that more qualified technical support and development procedures will be used in future.

Conclusion

At present, macro-economic planning is leading to errors in countries like Honduras, leaving local people without means to organize appropriately to develop competitive business strategies in time. And despite efforts to preserve the ecosystem, the National Tourism Strategy of Honduras has left the largest most important protected area in the region without any funds to support itself, making it likely that the crucial watershed and biodiversity protection it provides will be under increasing threat.

In a country like Ecuador, there is more hope. Small and medium enterprises have been given a stronger incentive to lead, funds from development projects are beginning to flow into projects that partner private business with the traditional economy in the Oriente, and strategic alliances between business, governments, and NGOs at the destination level are beginning to help insure that appropriate regional planning takes place to prevent the inappropriate growth of tourism in sensitive ecosystems.

A wide variety of new initiatives can emerge that meet the goals of the global community if the focus of new investment in sustainable tourism is on the following:

1. Expanding sustainable tourism business opportunity and investment on a larger scale.
2. Increasing sustainable planning of tourism.
3. Targeting assistance to regions where traditional economies are in genuine need and the sustainable tourism economy can break new ground.

A great deal of outstanding work has already taken place that links larger scale business markets to local community enterprises. In the 'Practical Outputs of the Pro Poor Tourism Strategy' webpage there are excellent examples of how tourism operations can create stronger linkages with traditional community enterprises. The entire Pro-Poor Strategy has set the stage in every way for the thinking underpinning this chapter. It offers a myriad of realistic suggestions for improving how enterprises can connect to traditional community services and a realistic look at the obstacles (Pro Poor Tourism, 2005).

From both practical and technical viewpoints, sustainable tourism and ecotourism need to become a part of the international development lexicon – not sidelined as conservation or even pro-poor afterthoughts. Ecotourism with its focus on tourism to natural areas has particular advantage of helping with rural development in countries where poverty is extremely persistent and not responsive to alleviation through trade liberalization approaches.

Countries on the lowest end of the economic scale more and more frequently need highly expert advice in the development of socially responsible, sustainable tourism. The discipline of developing tourism for the purposes of economic development must become part of the larger economic development strategy approach that is applied to all nations. Until sustainable tourism and ecotourism is understood as an economic development tool and an industry, there will be confusion and inadequate expertise applied to the development of sustainable tourism and ecotourism projects by development agencies worldwide.

Slowly but surely tourism is being recognized as an international development tool of primary importance. The World Tourism Organization has become the United Nations World Tourism Organization. Increasingly schools, such as Columbia Business School and Duke are now including sustainable tourism and ecotourism in their social enterprise and globalization forums. The World Bank, the Dutch bilateral SNV, the UK Department for International Development, the IDB, and USAID are incorporating sustainable tourism and ecotourism into their portfolios. But the discipline of studying tourism as a form of international development is still in its infancy.

This chapter has sought to set out a framework where sustainable tourism can be appropriately studied in full for its international development potential. It is time that sustainable tourism and ecotourism are understood for their role in economic growth, human development, and conservation outcome. A thorough review of how well it is achieving international development goals in many more countries is urgently needed in order to set the standard for the development of new projects in the future that appropriately position the field of sustainable tourism in the planning and implementation process of international development agencies worldwide.

References

Ardila, S. (2005). Senior Economist IDB and Team Leader for National Tourism Program Loan, personal communication.

Brundtland Commission (1987). *Brundtland Report* [Electronic Version], p. 24. Retrieved September 11, 2006, from http:// www.are.admin.ch/imperia/md/content/are/ nachhaltige-entwicklung/ brundtland_bericht.pdf

CIA World Factbook (2006a) *Ecuador.* Retrieved September 12, 2006, from https://www.cia.gov/cia/publications/factbook/ geos/ec.html#Econ

CIA World Factbook (2006b) *Honduras.* Retrieved September 10, 2006, from https://www.cia.gov/cia/publications/fact book/geos/ho.html

CentroAmerica en el Siglo XXI – Una Agenda para la Competitividad y el Desarrollo Sostenible (1999). *Latinoamericano para la Competitividad y el Desarrollo Sostenible* (INCAE/CLACDS) & Harvard Institute for International Development (HIID).

Christ, C., Hillel, O., Matus, S. and Sweeting, J. (2003). *Tourism and Biodiversity: Mapping Tourism's Global Footprint.* Conservation International & UNEP, Washington, DC, p. 34.

Clapp, J. and Dauvergne, P. (2005). *Pathways to a Green World, the Political Economy of a Global Environment.* MIT Press, Cambridge, MA, p. 12.

Costanza, R. and Daly, H.E. (1992). Natural capital and sustainable development. In Harris, J.M., Wise, T.A., Gallagher, K.P. and Goodwin, N.R. (eds), *A Survey of Sustainable Development.* Island Press, Washington DC, pp. 37–46.

Cuffe, S. (2006, February 7). *Nature Conservation or Territorial Control and Profits? Upside Down World.* Retrieved March 15, 2006, from http://upsidedownworld.org/main/index.php? option=com_content&task=view&id=194&Itemid=0

Diaz, D. (2001). *The Viability and Sustainability of International Tourism in Developing Countries.* World Trade Organization. Geneva, Switzerland.

Drumm, A. (1998). *New Approaches to Community-Based Ecotourism Management: A Guide for Planners and Managers,* Vol. 2. In Lindberg, K., Epler Wood, M. and Engeldrum, D. (eds). The International Ecotourism Society, Washington DC.

Epler Wood, M. (1998). Meeting the Global Challenge of Community Participation in Ecotourism: Case Studies and Lessons from Ecuador. Working Paper No. 2. America Verde. The Nature Conservancy, Arlington, VA.

Hart, S.L. (2005). *Capitalism at the Crossroads.* Wharton School Publishing, Saddle River, NJ, p. xlii.

Hawkins, D., Epler Wood, M. and Bittman, S. (1995). *The Ecolodge Sourcebook for Planners & Developers*. The Ecotourism Society, North Bennington, VT.

Heming, J. (n.d.). *Hurricane Mitch Fact Sheet. Met Office*. Retrieved September 10, 2006, from http://www.metoffice. gov.uk/weather/tropicalcyclone/tcbulletins/mitch.html

Honduran Institute of Tourism (IHT) (2004). *Compendio Estadístico de Turismo*. Retrieved March 2, 2006, from http:// www.letsgohonduras.com/estadisticas/compendio-estadistico-2004-esp.pdf

Honduran Institute of Tourism (IHT) (2005). *Comparación del Turismo Entre los Principales Rubros de Exportación*. Retrieved March 2, 2006, from http://www.letsgohonduras.com/ estadisticas/otras_estadisticas/tabla-j.pdf

International Resources Group (IRG) (2005). International Watershed Resources Management, Standard 4.1.2 Report, Recommendations for Best Practices/Ecotourism Certification Programs. Honduras: USAID, p. 4.

International Resources Group (IRG) (2004). Technical Proposal Request for Proposal No. 522-04-016. Washington DC.

Koenig, K. (2004, Jan/Feb). *Texaco on Trial. Worldwatch Magazine*. Worldwatch Institute, Washington DC, pp. 10–19.

Lindberg, K., Epler Wood, M. and Engeldrum, D. (eds). (1998). *Economic Aspects of Ecotourism, A Guide for Planners and Managers*. The International Ecotourism Society, Washington DC, p. 8.

Logging On (1995, April 8). *The Economist*. Retrieved September 11, 2006, from MasterFILE Premier (EBSCO) database, p. 34.

Millennium Ecosystem Assessment (2005, March 30). Retrieved on September 10, 2006, from http://www.millenniumassess-ment.org/en/index.aspx

Millennium Project. (2006). Retrieved September 10, 2006, from http://www.unmillenniumproject.org/goals/index.htm

Pro Poor Tourism (2005). *Practical Outputs of the Pro Poor Tourism Strategy*. Retrieved September 10, 2006, from http:// www.propoortourism.org.uk/ppt_pubs_outputs.html

Qing, D. (1994). *Yangtze! Yangtze!* In Adams, P. and Thibodeau, J. (eds). Earthscan Publications Limited, London.

Reinoso, J.C. (2003). *Reestructuración de los productos de Ecoturismo Comunitario de RICANCIE, Propuesta de una Estrategia de Comunicación, Comercialización y Creación de Productos*, Unpublished Masters thesis. Universidad Autónoma de Barcelona, Spain, p. 27.

Riddle, D.I. (2002). *Services Export Capacity in Developing Countries* [Electronic Version]. *World Trade Organization*.

Retrieved September 9, 2006, from www.wto.org/english/ tratop_e/serv_e/symp_mar02_riddle_e.doc

Roe, D., Ashley, C., Page, S. and Meyer, D. (2004). *Tourism and the Poor: Analysing and Interpreting Tourism Statistics from a Poverty Perspective*, PPT Working Paper No. 16 [Electronic Version], pp. 7, 13. *Pro-Poor Tourism*. Retrieved September 9, 2006, from http://www.propoortourism.org.uk/16_stats.pdf

Sachs, J. (2005a). *The End of Poverty*. Penguin Press, New York, NY, p. 51.

Sachs, J. (2005b, September 16–22). No Time to Waste. *Guardian Weekly*, p. 2.

Sachs, J. and Warner, A.M. (1999). Natural resource abundance and economic growth. *Journal of Development Economics* 59: Oxford University Press, 2000.

Serafy, Salah El (1997). Green accounting and economic policy. In Harris, J.M., Wise, T.A., Gallagher, K.P. and Goodwin, N.R. (eds), *A Survey of Sustainable Development*. Island Press, Washington DC, p. 34.

Sofield, T., Auer, J., De Lacy, T., Lipman, G. and Daugherty, S. (2004). *Sustainable Tourism – Eliminating Poverty (ST–EP): An Overview* [Electronic Version]. Sustainable Tourism Cooperative Research Center, Gold Coast, Australia, p. 2. Retrieved September 12, 2006, from http://www.crctourism. com.au/CRCBookshop/Documents/FactSheets/ST~EP.pdf#s earch=%22Sustainable%20Tourism%20%E2%80%93%20Elimi nating%20Poverty%20(ST-EP)%3A%20An%20Overview%2C %20%22

United Nations Charter Article I (2006). Retrieved September 12, 2006, from http://www.un.org/aboutun/charter/

United Nations Development Programme (UNDP) (2006a). *Human Development Reports*. Retrieved September 10, 2006, from http://hdr.undp.org/hd/

United Nations Development Programme (UNDP) (2006b). *Human Development Reports*. Retrieved September 10, 2006, from http://hdr.undp.org/statistics/data/

United Nations Development Programme (UNDP) (2006c). *Human Development Reports*. Retrieved September 10, 2006, from http://hdr.undp.org/docs/statistics/indices/stat_fea ture_1.pdf

United Nation Millennium Development Goals (2005). Retrieved September 10, 2006, from http://www.un.org/ millenniumgoals/

World Tourism Organization (2005, September 13). *Harnessing Tourism for the Millennium Development Goals*. World Tourism Organization, New York, NY.

World Tourism Organization (2006). *Sustainable Tourism – Eliminating of Poverty*. Retrieved September 10, 2006, from http://www.world-tourism.org/step

World Travel and Tourism Council (2005). *Travel and Tourism Economic Research: Costa Rica*. Retrieved March 1, 2006, from http://www.wttc.org/2005tsa/pdf/1.Costa%20Rica.pdf

Wunder, S. (1996). Ecoturismo: Ingresos locales y Conservación: el caso de Cuyabeno, Ecuador. Quito, Ecuador. Ediciones Abya-Yala. In Epler Wood, Megan (1998). Meeting the Global Challenge of Community Participation in Ecotourism: Case Studies and Lessons from Ecuador. Working Paper No. 2. *America Verde*. Arlington, VA: The Nature Conservancy.

Youth, H. (2006 March/April). Ecuador: In Search of Natural Balance. *Worldwatch Magazine*. Worldwatch Institute, Washington DC, pp. 22–25.

Ecotourism and gender issues

Regina Scheyvens

Introduction

This chapter will examine gender issues pertaining to ecotourism, a subject that has received little serious attention from scholars to date:[1]

> ...while some critics of mass, large-scale tourism development have advocated the pursuit of small-scale, 'sustainable', 'alternative', 'responsible' or 'appropriate' tourism which is locally controlled, sensitive to indigenous cultural and environmental characteristics and directly involves and benefits the local population, gender considerations have yet to be placed centrally within such a debate (Kinnaird and Hall, 1996, p. 97).

Advocates of ecotourism have shown greater interest than have ecotourism scholars in women's involvement in ecotourism; however they seem to have an implicit belief that gender issues will be addressed if ecotourism is approached through a participatory planning approach in which community development is targeted. Here it is argued that a much deeper appreciation of the complex nature of 'communities' is needed before ecotourism ventures are implemented, and that direct efforts must be made to support poorer, less powerful groups, which often include women, if ecotourism is to be effective in meeting conservation and development goals.

In examining gender and ecotourism, this chapter focuses particularly on the situation of developing countries. Early, minimalist definitions of ecotourism focused on environmental sustainability while ignoring social and economic concerns, thus they were not appropriate for developing countries (Scheyvens, 2002; Weaver, 2005). In developing country contexts where there is no automatic separation of local peoples and the natural environments that have proven so attractive to tourists, it is insensitive – and perhaps amoral – to prioritise sustainably managed forms of tourism which promote nature conservation while neglecting the poverty of the people living in nearby communities. Advocates of ecotourism need to acknowledge the endorsement of the Millennium Development Goals by most countries and widespread support for campaigns such as 'Make Poverty History' and so ensure that poverty alleviation is central to ecotourism agendas in areas where poverty levels are high (Scheyvens, in press).

Fortunately contemporary definitions of ecotourism tend to be influenced by community development rhetoric and thus they are more comprehensive, incorporating the need for socio-cultural

---

[1] With a few exceptions, for example Dilly (2003) and Scheyvens (2000).

sustainability alongside environmental and economic goals (Weaver, 2005). A useful definition of ecotourism which incorporates conservation, development and education, is that provided by Ceballos-Lascuráin (1996):

Ecotourism is environmentally responsible, enlightening travel and visitation to relatively undisturbed natural areas in order to enjoy and appreciate nature (and any accompanying cultural features both past and present) that promotes conservation, has low visitor impact, and provides for beneficially active socio-economic involvement of local populations.

This definition and similar ones such as proposed by Fennell (2003) assert that community development is a central component of well-planned ecotourism. Looking at ecotourism practice, however, it is clear that governments, NGOs, conservation organisations and donors have often not met the requirements of the above definition. Specifically, there has been a primary focus on conservation, so that development opportunities for local communities often receive inadequate resources and attention and thus become sidelined:

It should come as no surprise that projects that seek to integrate the interests of conservation and development tend to place greater emphasis on conservation rather than the creation of an even balance between the interests of both in the various activities involved .... What often results is a tug-of-war process that ends up producing a 'conservationist' versus 'development' mindset.

(Effendi *et al.*, 2002, p. 3)

Despite the best efforts of many people committed to integrated conservation and development programmes, including those involving ecotourism in association with protected areas, it is clear that an outside-driven conservation agenda typically assumes priority over the development needs of local communities. This leads Butcher to conclude that NGOs and donors '...continue to fund ecotourism projects not on the basis of their long-term development potential, but principally on the basis of their environmental worth'. Consequently there are often 'limited development benefits instrumental to their conservation imperative' (Butcher, 2006, p. 308). Thus while ecotourism lodges or tours may be established as ventures to enable communities to receive a direct economic gain from a protected area, on many occasions these ventures are commercially not viable for a variety of reasons which may include a lack of business and marketing skills, remoteness and inadequate integration with other tourism products and services on the market (Goodwin, 2006).

While the rhetorie of community participation and empowerment is now firmly entrenched in certain documents pertaining to ecotourism in developing country contexts, comprehensive community development has remained elusive in practice. In particular, despite the best intentions of a range of agencies to target women through ecotourism ventures, ecotourism initiatives have struggled to ensure that women participate actively in decision-making regarding ecotourism planning and management while also sharing equitably in any benefits of ecotourism enterprises.

This chapter will now explain the logic behind connecting gender and ecotourism, before revealing challenges to achieving gender-sensitive ecotourism development. A case study of Indonesia's Gunung Rinjani National Park (GRNP) and associated ecotourism development highlights such challenges. This is followed by discussion of examples which show that, despite various constraints, it is possible to adopt an effective gender-sensitive approach to ecotourism development that can deliver real benefits for women, men and their communities as a whole.

Rationale for connecting gender and ecotourism

There are a number of clear reasons why any agency interested in promoting effective ecotourism should consider gender issues, even if their primary concern is not gender equity. In countries where socially prescribed roles mean that women and girls generally have greater interaction with the natural environment than men, women's cooperation is needed if that natural resource base, the resource upon which the ecotourism trade is dependent, is to be sustained. In many parts of the developing world, rural women and girls are responsible for collection of water, fodder and fuelwood, and in marine environments, for gathering shellfish. They are also involved in income-generating activities based upon the sale of forest products and crafts made from reeds and grasses (Deshingar, 1994). Furthermore, it is estimated that 60–80% of food production in Africa is carried out by women (James, 1995, p. 4). While some men also have a close connection with the environment through agricultural work, cattle raising and more sporadic activities such as hunting, in most developing countries more men than women now engage in paid employment and do not rely so heavily on the natural environment as do women.

In addition, where women's roles place them in close connection with the physical environment they develop specialist knowledge because of this work, as well as an interest in protecting the environment. Thus, argue Fortmann and Bruce (1993, p. 7), 'women, who as the hewers of wood, drawers of water and tillers of the earth suffer the most when soil erodes, water sources go dry, or trees disappear, are the natural constituency for environmental endeavours'. In such contexts it would seem logical that those responsible for projects which are based on sound management of natural resources, including ecotourism, should actively seek out women's involvement. However, in past development initiatives women's voices have often been sidelined as development consultants, researchers and government officers seek the opinions of headmen, chiefs, local elites and entrepreneurs, the vast majority of whom are men. Even male commentators from within developing countries are now calling for this situation to change:

…in order to translate the rhetoric of sustainable management of natural resources into reality, local people, including women, children, the elderly, and indigenous minorities, must be allowed to actively participate in the decision-making process. We have tended to vest too much power in our Traditional Leaders through traditional and cultural belief systems.

(Mulolani, 1997, p. 12)

Furthermore, deriving from their different roles and responsibilities, women's interests in terms of utilisation of natural resources are often different from those of men. Where women utilise natural resources which are necessary for local well-being, they need to be involved in decisions about ecotourism which may restrict access to such resources. For example, land beside a forest which is not suited to cattle grazing or commercial agriculture may be identified by men as an ideal location to be leased for a tourist lodge even though it is highly valued by women who collect broom grass and pottery clay at the site. They may make a reasonable income from the sale of products manufactured from these resources, and this needs to be weighed up against the likely revenue from a tourist lodge, which would require a lot of capital investment and may not return profits to the community until after several years of operation. Furthermore, if women are deprived of access to resources because of the development of ecotourism, and yet they do not receive any benefits from ecotourism, it is unlikely that they will have support for conservation of the natural resources upon which ecotourism is based (Sindiga, 1995).

In summary, it is important that gender is considered by proponents of ecotourism for three major reasons:

1. To promote good natural resource management which protects the key resource upon which ecotourism is based.

2. To ensure that ecotourism development benefits from the skills and knowledge of a broad range of community members. For example, the success of many ecotourism ventures rests on the roles that women often perform (in complement to men's roles) in terms of hospitality, cleaning, craft manufacture, and dance performances.

3. Gender equity is recognised as a basic human right: it is endorsed in the Millennium Development Goals and seen as a key principle by many donors who fund ecotourism initiatives in developing countries around the globe. According to this rationale, women and men should both participate in decision-making forums concerning ecotourism development and management, and they should share equitably in the benefits flowing from ecotourism initiatives.

A gender-sensitive approach to tourism can therefore be seen as in the interests of all tourism stakeholders, whether their main motivation is conservation, equity or business success.

Overview of issues surrounding women's participation in ecotourism endeavours

The following section considers the extent to which women have participated in and benefited from involvement in ecotourism, as well as ways in which this may lead to changes in gender roles and relations (see Table 10.1 for a summary of this information). Rather than primarily focusing on economic benefits from ecotourism, their development will be considered from social, political and psychological perspectives as well (Scheyvens, 1999).

Employment and income-generating opportunities

Many tasks traditionally carried out by women including food preparation, provision of accommodation and production of handicrafts can be turned into opportunities for income generation through ecotourism, both in the formal and informal sectors. The ability to earn an income through ecotourism has offered women opportunities for economic autonomy, allowed them greater influence over household decision-making and sometimes enhancing women's status in their communities. However the *nature* of ecotourism development in destination areas can have a marked impact on women's involvement in tourism such as whether they end up in poorly paid, servile

Table 10.1 Overview of positive and negative impacts that can result from women's involvement in ecotourism enterprises

Positive	Negative
• Formal and informal employment opportunities in areas in which women have existing skills (e.g. cooking, accommodation, crafts, cultural performance) • Employment in areas outside of normal gender stereotypes (e.g. guiding) • Economic independence means women can exercise more say over household decision-making • Women become involved in decision-making forums regarding ecotourism or natural resource management • Men accept that they need to engage in more domestic duties in order to support their income-earning wives • Opportunities for women to gain confidence from interactions with people from outside the local area • Where women are 'custodians of culture' they gain respect for the roles they play in continuing/reviving cultural practices • Increase in men's respect for their partners, leading to more egalitarian relationships	• The status and remuneration of women's jobs is often inferior to that of jobs held by men • When women's work is associated with their domestic responsibilities (e.g. cooking and cleaning) they receive no or little pay • Many women are expected to work a 'double day', meeting both the demands of formal employment and unpaid domestic duties. Women may feel that they are neglecting their children, and their religious or social obligations • 'Communal benefits' may be distributed to male heads of households, ignoring the needs of female-headed households and polygamous societies • Competition for ecotourism income between different groups in a community undermines social cohesion • Vested interests dominate park management boards, ecotourism associations and other decision-making bodies, making it difficult for women members to voice their opinions • Competition associated with ecotourism may exacerbate existing fissures within communities and lead to social disharmony

positions or whether they have the opportunity to manage their own ventures (Scheyvens, 2002). Shah *et al.* (2000, p. 38), for example, note that 'Women in destinations characterised by smaller hotels and lower levels of investment have proved themselves to be adept at managing small guesthouses and restaurants and running other small enterprises'.

However in the tourism literature in general, concerns are often raised about the types of employment opportunities available to women, with women shown to occupy predominantly lower-paid and lower-skilled positions, which are often associated with their domestic roles (Momsen, 1994; Bras and Dahles,

1999). This is particularly an issue for women from minority or migrant ethnic groups (Stonich *et al.*, 1995): 'Perhaps it is because the traditional *unpaid* labour of women in society in general is similar to their work in the industry that their condition seems to deserve no comment' (Richter, 1995, p. 76). Thus women have commonly been expected to perform tasks such as cleaning of lodges, preparation of guest accommodation and cooking as an extension of their unpaid work within the home. In addition to tourism sector employment, most women are still expected to continue to fulfil their domestic and community responsibilities, thus it has been suggested that tourism employment simply adds to the burden of women's already heavy workloads (Levy and Lerch, 1995; Goodwin *et al.*, 1998). In the Solomon Islands, for example, small-scale ecotourism lodges, which were established by families in the Marovo Lagoon area as part of a World Heritage Project, were seen by outside environmental groups as a favourable alternative to large-scale economic options, such as logging. However, it is largely women's unpaid labour that is used for the cleaning, cooking and laundry for guests staying in these lodges, and in addition the women still have to complete most of their domestic tasks as well as extending their food gardens so they can supply enough produce for both their families and their guests (Greenpeace Australia Pacific and Oliver, 2001).

Women often miss out on higher status and more lucrative employment opportunities in tourism because social norms restrict the type of economic activities in which women may engage. In both the Himalayan region and in Indonesia, for example, guiding is not usually an acceptable occupation for women (Wilkinson and Pratiwi, 1995; Cukier *et al.*, 1996; Lama, 1998). In 1992, local people from the fishing village of Pangandaran in Java who took tourists by canoe to a nearby game park could earn up to US$21 per trip, a very good income. However, of the 12 formal guides, none were women and of the 40 informal guides who worked during the peak season, only 5 were women. Many women felt they could not exploit this relatively lucrative economic opportunity because, 'Women being involved in guiding is not regarded favourably by villagers, the connotation being that such women are "prostitutes" interested in contacting foreign tourists' (Wilkinson and Pratiwi, 1995, p. 293).

In the Chiawa communal lands of Zambia which border the Zambezi River, the Chieftainess granted up to 20 tourism operators, mainly expatriates, the rights to lease land along the river banks and bordering the Lower Zambezi National Park. Her decision was based on the hope that this would bring much wanted investment and jobs to the region. While a small number of jobs were made available to local men, women were completely overlooked. One tour operator from the area cited several reasons why her company did not employ women:

- Staff need to be mobile, as they are often expected to move between the three camps the company owned along the river.
- Having women in the camps would encourage infidelity.
- Pregnancy/parental leave would be inconvenient.
- The company would have to provide accommodation for families, rather than individuals, as women would not want to leave all of their children to come to work (camps are often quite isolated and there is no public transport service in the Chiawa area).
- The presence of children and babies could annoy guests (Author's fieldwork, July 1998).

Such examples lead Sinclair (1997, p. 233) to conclude that: 'Tourism, *per se*, does not bring about a fundamental change in gender and race definitions and the structuring of work. Indeed, it frequently reinforces existing structures and work divisions'.

Community benefits

Besides individual income-earning opportunities, another way in which women can benefit from ecotourism development is through communal benefits, which are often built into community-based ecotourism ventures. In Zimbabwe's CAMPFIRE programme (Communal Areas Management Programme for Indigenous Resources), for example, communities collaborate with WWF to establish a 'sustainable cull' for animals on their communal lands. Then a limited amount of safari hunting (known as 'consumptive ecotourism') is allowed, with a majority of the profits going into a community development fund. Grain grinding mills purchased with CAMPFIRE monies have had particular benefits in easing the workloads of women, while the construction of classrooms is likely to lead to increases in the numbers of girls attending school, because parents do not like to send their daughters to school if this necessitates travelling some distance from home. In other cases, however, projects intended to benefit an entire community have inadvertently disadvantaged women. Thus in Masoka village, a decision was made to erect a 20 km electric fence around the settlement and cropping areas in order to control wild animals, whose numbers had increased under the CAMPFIRE scheme as community members were now reporting poachers. However, the limited number of gates put in the fence meant that women had to walk further to gain access to daily household requirements, specifically, water and fuelwood (Nabane, 1996). This is not surprising when considering the following observation about a game fence in another area of Zimbabwe: 'While the fence and its gates had been sited in painstaking consultation with villagers, only men had been involved in the formal consultations' (Fortmann and Bruce, 1993, p. 3).

Where CAMPFIRE communities have chosen to divide up part of their earnings from this consumptive ecotourism as household dividends, some anomalies have arisen as well. This money is generally paid to the household head, usually assumed to be a man, so women do not necessarily gain any control over CAMPFIRE revenues (Nabane, 1996). In some CAMPFIRE areas, however, local campaigners have managed to secure dividends for women. In Kanyuriria Ward, women argued that because they have to deal with the consequences of greater numbers of wildlife as they work in fields which wildlife have destroyed, married women should be registered in their own right so that they would be entitled to receive CAMPFIRE dividends. In another ward, women insisted that in a family of three wives, a common occurrence in the polygamous societies of southern Africa, each should be registered as a separate household. In another case, a divorced mother successfully convinced men and women in her area that divorced women with children should also share in the distribution of financial revenue from wildlife utilisation (Fortmann and Bruce, 1993).

Social and psychological impacts of ecotourism

Ecotourism is often reliant on a combination of attractive natural and cultural features. Interestingly, women are often at the centre of efforts to preserve aspects of culture. For example, in the Langtang Ecotourism Project in Nepal, women are the 'keepers of cultural traditions and knowledge' because many men find employment in towns or with trekking parties and are away from home for long periods of time (Lama, 1998). Women maintain traditions and therefore build strong communities through supporting religious functions, producing handicrafts, using natural medicines, speaking local dialects, wearing traditional dress and performing traditional songs and dances. Where these roles are valued by their wider communities, this can lead to enhanced social cohesion among local people and also psychological empowerment for women.

Psychological and social disempowerment can also occur, however, if tourism work interferes with women's community roles and their spiritual development, leading to reduced social interaction with their wider community and feelings of guilt.

In the Solomon Islands' Marovo Lagoon, for example, women were often physically isolated from their friends because the guest lodge operated by their family was located on a small island in the lagoon, away from other villagers. Here women assisting their families to run lodges felt they were forced to neglect God as they did not have the time to spend at church or in prayer groups (Greenpeace Australia Pacific and Oliver, 2001). Women involved in the Bouma ecotourism initiative in Fiji similarly felt that the project had led to competition and conflicts between different interest groups in their communities, and they were sufficiently distressed with the ensuing social disruption that they complained to programme officials that they wished the ecotourism venture had never come to their community (Ministry of Foreign Affairs and Trade, 1995, pp. 34, 39).

Decision-making roles

In ecotourism ventures which occur at the community level, there is often a need for a community-based decision-making forum which can convey community interests and act on behalf of the community, or for community representatives to sit on broader decision-making bodies with multiple stakeholders. Such forums may be an existing traditional or government institution, or it may be a specially formed grouping such as a park management board. Gender bias in community forums is a common problem (Joekes *et al.*, 1996), leading Moore (1996, p. 29) to identify '...gendered patterns of exclusion from "public" forums empowered with constructing "community" opinion'. While donors and other groups have often insisted that women are represented on decision-making forums regarding protected area management or on community-based ecotourism forums, and women have sometimes been empowered with greater voice in their communities, overall the results have not been great. Representation of women in such decision-making structures beyond the village level is notoriously poor both because of societal attitudes about appropriate roles and behaviour for men and women (Lama, 1998), and because of what Moore (1996) calls 'sexual policing' of women's movements.

Thus in many cases the vested interests in communities resist attempts to actively involve women in decision-making. In Fiji, women involved in the Bouma ecotourism project faced discrimination from some landowners (all men) who claimed that only landowners should gain revenue from the project and be involved in its management. Consequently, some women were not even aware of proposals for ecotourism development in their community, even though discussions had been taking place for some time (Ministry of Foreign Affairs and Trade, 1995). Similarly, in the Sua Bali sustainable village tourism initiative in Indonesia, the female owner-manager was not able to promote as much local participation in her venture as she would like simply because as a woman, she could not be actively involved in village discussions in the traditional village council, the Banjar. Her lack of voice in the Banjar, a forum dominated by richer males who were very suspicious about her successful tourism venture, made it difficult for the manager to achieve her aim of a '...mutual, careful, coexistence ... between the village (its culture and the natural surrounding) on the one side and Sua Bali on the other' (Mas, 1999, p. 110).

Changes to gender roles and relations

In communities where women are involved in operating ecotourism ventures or providing goods to services to tourists, their increased earnings and demonstrated management skills often lead to both greater respect for women and a reconsideration of gender role stereotypes (Greenpeace Australia Pacific and Oliver, 2001). For example, many of the lodges for trekkers in Dhampus, Nepal, are managed by women and they are often more economically successful than the traditional livelihood in the area, agriculture. With the growing popularity of trekking, women have to rely upon the cooperation of their whole families, thus men have been found to be engaging in a much wider spectrum of work than previously, including kitchen work (Gurung, 1995). A greater sharing of the workload and appreciation of the value of domestic work has often occurred in these situations. In addition, when a women's group in Dhampus raised funds to build 500 m of trail, used by both trekkers and villagers, men could see the benefits this provided the wider community and thus they felt compelled to allow their wives to attend community meetings, even if this meant the men had to take on domestic roles while the women were absent (Gurung, 1995).

Now that an overview of gendered impacts of ecotourism has been provided, this chapter moves on to take an in-depth look at an ecotourism venture in Indonesia which attempted to support community development. It will particularly consider how well gender issues were addressed.

Gunung Rinjani National Park case study

The Indonesia island of Lombok lies to the east of Bali. Over the past decade Lombok has been promoted as a 'Beyond Bali' destination, and has become increasingly known for its beaches, as well as the majestic volcanic peak of Gunung Rinjani. Gunung Rinjani and the surrounding forests provide a diverse environment in which unique flora and fauna thrives. There are numerous rare plants, over 66 species of birds and 8 species of mammals. The National Park is around $410\,km^2$, and prior to its protection it had a range of designated purposes, from a permanent production forest to a multipurpose area.

Conflicting agendas: conservation, subsistence and tourism

Forty-two villages with a population of 344,478 are located on the boundaries of the Rinjani park (David *et al.*, 2005). The most common activity is subsistence agriculture, but as up to 70% of families are landless, many encroach on the park's boundaries to meet their livelihood needs, utilising forest products or burning sections of forest to make gardens. It is quite possible for tourists to Lombok to be oblivious to this poverty however:

Visitors to Lombok often perceive Gunung Rinjani as a topical idyll. Palm-lined paddies surround the villages on the flanks of the volcano, oxen do much of the ploughing, and the fields are full of men and women in colourful sarongs. But appearances are deceptive. There is considerable poverty in the area, particularly among the indigenous Sasak people .... Access to health care and education are inadequate, especially for women; illegal logging threatens the forests; and water must be shared among a great many people and enterprises

(David *et al.*, 2005, p. 11).

The status of women in this area of Lombok is of particular concern. Around 40% of women work as agricultural labourers and illiteracy levels are the highest in the country. There are significant rates of abandonment because husbands frequently leave their wives to marry teenage girls, mostly leaving children with the mother. Commonly landless women and children illegally extract timber from the forest, walking up to 10 km into the forest early in the morning and returning with a 25–40-kg bundle of fuelwood which will be sold for around one dollar (World Neighbors, *ca.* 2002). World Neighbors thus declares that 'Population pressures combined with landlessness are probably the two single major threats to the Rinjani ecosystem' (World Neighbors, *ca.* 2002, p. 2).

Thus while the Indonesian government, conservation organisations and donors have all shown an interest in ensuring conservation of Rinjani's rich ecosystem, the reality is that their interests often conflict with those of other stakeholders such as villagers and also tourism entrepreneurs.

Gunung Rinjani is believed to be sacred and thus it is a site of pilgrimage for some domestic tourists, and a site of recreational trekking for both domestic and international visitors. The trek itself takes people from villages into the forest through to the mountain top, passing waterfalls and hot springs along the way. While over 7,000 international visitors came to the GRNP in 1990, numbers have since fluctuated widely and declined overall due to a range of factors including the East Timor crisis in 1999, riots on Lombok in 2000, bomb blasts in Bali and Jakarta in 2002 and SARS. However domestic tourism is very strong, constituting over 90% of arrivals. The National Park accommodated 148,252 domestic tourists in 2004 (David *et al.*, 2005, p. 12).

NZAID funding for the national park and ecotourism development

Between 1999 and 2005, NZAID (the New Zealand Agency for International Development) provided almost NZ$3 million to fund ecotourism development in the GRNP. NZAID's first foray into alternative approaches to tourism in a protected area began in 1988 with support for another Indonesian park, the Ujong Kulong National Park. In the proceeding years NZAID had supported ecotourism projects in countries such as Fiji, the Solomon Islands, China and Cambodia, typically adopting a model of encouraging strong community participation in such endeavours. It is not surprising then that support for GRNP was founded on the idea of three interlocking concepts: conservation, community engagement and tourism. With regard to the second element, the specific objective was:

Fostering community development on park boundaries by bringing benefits to rural women and men in recognition of the link between national conservation goals and local development goals.

(David *et al.*, 2005, p. 8)

NZAID could not provide assistance to all of the communities surrounding the National Park, thus it chose to focus on two villages at the gateway to the main trekking route: Senaru and Sembalun Lawang. They were home to a mixture of indigenous Sasak people who practice traditional customs, known as *adat*, as well as migrants from lowland areas who had been brought in over time to 'develop' the area (David *et al.*, 2005, p. 12). As noted after an extensive participatory rural appraisal (PRA) exercise in these communities in 2000, the people living in the area who had least access to and control over resources and who therefore deserved most support from the NZAID programme were the Sasak commoners, as well as some poorer groups of migrants (McKinnon and Suwan, 2000). There was also need for attention to women's development. At this stage few women had gained formal employment in tourism enterprises associated with Gunung Rinjani such as guiding or working in homestay accommodation: '...nearly all tourism/trekking related activities and job opportunities are monopolised by men' (McKinnon and Suwan, 2000, p. 24). Those women employed were often young relatives of the homestay owner who barely received any pay during quiet months. While male employees were free to take temporary leave to earn extra cash when jobs as porters or guides arose, the female employees did not have this opportunity (McKinnon and Suwan, 2000).

NZAID assistance to GRNP came in two phases. The first, from 1999 to 2002, aimed to support development and protection of the National Park. At the end of this phase, an independent researcher cited it as a very good example of sustainable tourism development which demonstrated high levels of community involvement (Fallon, 2003, p. 154). In the second phase, from 2003, NZAID provided specific funding to the Rinjani Trek Ecotourism Programme, which had a focus on developing local capacity to continue the management of the Rinjani Trek (David et al., 2005, p. 8). With the narrowing of the project focus, the community engagement element weakened and this had particular implications for women's involvement in the project:

During the transition phase the inputs from the community development consultants were discontinued and a local person was engaged part-time to support small business development. The gap in community development expertise reduced the capacity of the programme to continue the engagement, facilitation and follow-up role the community development staff had played in Sembalun Lawang and Senaru. In particular this affected the work with women's groups, which needed considerable facilitation, and the capacity of the programme to pick up on and to respond to sensitive issues concerning the Senaru and Sembalun Lawang adat communities. The relatively strong focus during the first stage on promoting transparency and accountability at the level of community-based organisations also weakened. As a consequence, much of the strong and effective community development work that began in the early years of this programme has not been sustained.
(David et al., 2005, p. 65)

Consequently the impact of this project on poverty alleviation has been far less than would be expected considering the money invested in it. While substantial efforts were made to establish a management board and ensure the long-term sustainability of the trek, only 2.4% of funding was spent on community development. It is not surprising, therefore, that a review found 'the programme didn't have sufficient presence in the communities' (David *et al.*, 2005, p. 56), a situation which led to miscommunication and a lack of transparency. While entrepreneurship has been stimulated, the benefits are concentrated in the hands of a few. Thus although 817 individuals can be said to have benefited from the two phases of the project, over 600 of these are 'non-economic beneficiaries' (with increased knowledge, skills and confidence), 253 received 'limited economic benefit' (mostly from participation in a savings and loan scheme) and there have only been 43 individuals and their families who have experienced significant economic benefits from the project (David *et al.*, 2005, p. 60).

Gendered impacts of the programme

While many women received training through the programme, especially in guiding, production of snack foods, business management and craft manufacturing, few went on to gain direct employment or to start income-generating ventures as a result of this.

The case of female guides is interesting as, similar to many other countries, guiding is traditionally seen as a man's activity. In this programme however they decided to train women in 'soft trekking', that is, to guide people on half-day panorama trips, village trips to visit traditional houses or rice field trips of 1–2 hours. In this way they would not be competing with men for custom and they would not need to stay away from home (the trek up and down Gunung Rinjani takes several days). However the 2005 review of the programme revealed that female guides felt their role was not being promoted sufficiently and thus there was little uptake of the tours. In addition, women noted that the trek organisers still tended to give the soft trekking jobs to male guides, perhaps because women's English skills were not so good and they lacked confidence. The female guides also felt that when they were employed, the travel agent guides only passed on to them a small proportion of their actual tips (e.g. they felt that if Rp. 50.000 was given by guests, only Rp. 5.000 was returned to the female guides). Most of those women trained to be guides are thus not active, and they are not encouraged to become more active because there is limited demand for female guides. For the few female guides who do find employment, however, there have definitely been positive spin-offs:

The female guides are a product of the Programme that is excellent and interesting in the field of tourism. The village women have begun to become courageous and promote tourism in Senaru, while before they were very shy meeting people from outside the village and were afraid to leave the village (summary of self-reflection by female guides and snack-makers, Senaru-David *et al.*, 2005, p. 21b).

Another enterprise established to bring benefits to women was snack-making to produce foodstuffs that could be sold to trekking parties. Two snack-making groups were formed in Senaru and one in Sembalun. Women took part in training on production of snacks and financial administration, plus they received working capital and equipment for their businesses. Sales have not been great, however, as most of the trek organisers are from the main town on Lombok, Mataram, and they come equipped with all of the food and equipment which their guests need. Furthermore, the women received training in making 'wet' sweet snacks which did not last, whereas the traditional dry snacks such as *kriprik* (crackers) had a much longer shelf life. While most snacks were made using bananas, in 2005 bananas were not available because of a disease which affected banana trees in the area. For such reasons many women have left the groups and returned to agricultural work. For example, of the two groups in Senaru, one broke up and another has only four of the original ten members left. The groups feel frustrated that there has been a lack of ongoing support from programme staff:

The group's members perceive that facilitation and guidance from the Programme staff is insufficient, nobody provides motivation to develop the business. The active members only wait for orders. If there are no orders they don't produce (Summary of self-reflection by female guides and snack-makers, Senaru-David *et al.*, 2005, p. 21).

There was also evidence of ethnic and class discrimination within the snack-making groups. In one group, the members of the traditional *adat* community were not involved in making the food products but were instructed to clean the equipment (David *et al.*, 2005, p. 20b). In another group, the chairperson of the group was the wife of the Babinsa (person in charge of village security). She expected the group to work for long hours making snacks in her house, paying them in snacks and rice rather than cash. The group members became frustrated because they felt they were neglecting the needs of their children by being away from home for so long, and meanwhile they had to deal with the anger of husbands who felt the snack-makers' earnings were not sufficient for the effort that was expended. The members felt exploited by the chairperson, so they left the group. They felt their problems could have been solved, however, with better support from programme staff: 'The impression is that the Project only establishes groups who are then left on their own, not supervised and monitored' (David *et al.*, 2005, p. 32b).

However it is promising that the programme has resulted in the empowerment of certain women. In particular, there is a successful women's weaving group which has revived traditional weaving in the area and turned it into a profitable enterprise. As a consequence, women are receiving more respect from their families and communities. Young women are once again learning to weave, members have received training in business management and how to package their products to make them attractive to buyers and they are marketing their own products and using innovative designs:

...the people are proud that the weaving industry which was abandoned and almost forgotten was resurrected again, and the people benefit from it. As a result, new weavers appear, a new generation has picked up the tradition, and an almost lost art has been saved and is being conserved .... The weaving industry has emancipated the women. Previously women never left the village; they had not the courage to speak to outsiders. But presently they leave the village, dare to interact and deal with outsiders and speak up. The members are already marketing their own products in Mataram and Senggigi. They have learned to develop their own weaving patterns, motifs and colouring, creating variation (summary of self-reflection by the weaving group – David *et al.*, 2005, p. 35b).

The income raised by these women has led to a change in the household division of labour, with women not needing to work in the fields any more and men helping out more within the home (David *et al.*, 2005, p. 39). In fact, women have been able to support their husbands' farming activities by purchasing inputs such as seeds and fertilisers, and paying for farm labour:

The husbands appreciate this very much and accept that their wives now have less time for them and their children, so many domestic chores are taken over by men.... The husbands start to help in the home, bathing the children, preparing what is needed for school, and cooking the food. Husbands used to become angry if their wives didn't make breakfast and coffee, now they care for themselves without waiting for their wives (Summary of self-reflection by the weaving group – David *et al.*, 2005, p. 35b).

With her earnings, the leader of the Sembalun Lawang women's weaving group was able to send her son to university, and other members of this group cited a variety of benefits including their ability to send children to school, improve their homes and invest in gold jewellery (David *et al.*, 2005, pp. 39–40).

Analysis

While NZAID's support for the GRNP and associated eco-tourism development has yielded a variety of benefits, including enhanced capacity of park's staff to manage the natural environment, the establishment of an innovative park management board with representation from a variety of stakeholder groups, and training for hundreds of residents of the two programme villages, its effectiveness in delivering tangible, ongoing benefits to the community – and especially to women – have been somewhat less than could be hoped for a NZ$3 million development intervention. Certainly some female guides and members of the weaving group are earning reasonable incomes and have been considerably empowered by their experiences; however many others have yet to see a positive impact of the programme in their lives.

While women were targeted for assistance and training was made available to many women, it was difficult for them to turn newly acquired skills into effective income-generating enterprises. The female guides, for example, were often passed over in favour of male guides, and many of the women felt that they lacked the confidence required and had inadequate English skills so they could not be effective guides. Class issues also came to the fore when the labour of one group of snack-makers was exploited by the chairperson of their group. In the case of revival of the traditional skill of weaving, however, a number of women experienced a significant improvement in their income and also in their status as there was widespread respect for this tradition. Gender roles were challenged and husbands were more willing to assist women with domestic work.

Many of the problems associated with ineffective interventions stem more broadly from the insufficient attention paid to community development. Thus, for example, there was a high rate of attrition of women involved in guiding and snack-making groups as indicated above due to a lack of ongoing support and facilitation, and the programme's inability to address conflicts which arose between different groups. Women's own evaluations of the programme repeatedly called for 'intensive facilitation' of groups and activities for women, stressing that they had little experience of running a business or dealing with outsiders, and that they needed more confidence before running enterprises on their own. In this context, providing training for a few months and then arranging for intermittent appearances by programme staff was not an effective strategy.

It was interesting to note, however, that in cases where women did earn a good income from their forays into guiding or weaving, a shift in gender roles was welcomed or at least accommodated by both men and women. Meanwhile in cases where the returns were poor, such as with the snack-making group, there was significant resentment from husbands about the time that women were spending away from home.

Ensuring gender-sensitivity in community ecotourism ventures

Even in apparently well-planned ecotourism ventures like the GRNP discussed above it can be very difficult to ensure widespread benefits to community members. In this light it is not surprising that a number of authors have become increasingly cynical about the potential for ecotourism to bring broad-ranging benefits to local communities. Manwa (2003, p. 45), for example, writes that wildlife-based tourism in Zimbabwe maximises benefits to the power brokers within communities while the 'hidden stakeholders, the very poor and women who are the traditional users of resources' miss out. Increasingly tourism researchers are recognising the complexity of power relations at play within communities and between communities and outside interest groups, and the consequent difficulty of promoting community development through ecotourism (Campbell, 2002; Wearing and MacDonald, 2002; Jones, 2005). Thus, for example, based on research in a community-based rural ecotourism project in Gales Point Manatee Belize, Belsky asserts that '...strategies such as ecotourism are often based on simplistic images and generic models that ignore politics' (Belsky, 1999, p. 641). She insists that we must understand the politics of ecotourism development within communities, including the complex interplay of power in class and gender relations: this influences participation in management of ecotourism and conservation initiatives, benefit-sharing and the support for conservation practices.

The challenges to implementing gender-sensitive ecotourism discussed above suggest the need for approaches which: (a) provide ongoing, comprehensive support to women; (b) involve both women and men; (c) provide communal benefits to ensure a broad spread of the benefits of ecotourism; (d) establish effective and representative decision-making forums; and (e) involve comprehensive data gathering at the community level, as well as participatory monitoring and evaluation. Some guidelines on how this can be done are provided below.

Targeting, mentoring and empowering women

Strenuous efforts are often made to engage indigenous groups/ minority ethnic groups and women in tourism endeavours through PRA exercises, consultation forums and training. However these efforts are sometimes disjointed and piecemeal. Thus while women may be targeted for a training exercise, this does not necessarily result in the training being directed into a viable enterprise: sometimes because women are balancing multiple roles, other times because society will not necessarily support women acting outside their traditional roles. In other cases women may be provided with a certain percentage of the seats on a decision-making forum, but cultural norms make it difficult for them to express their ideas and concerns.

Women involved in the Gunung Rinjani programme and others have stated clearly that they need more ongoing support, suggesting that it could be useful to engage a local facilitator such as a consultant or member of a partner NGO, to play a mentoring role. They could, for example, ensure that women are aware of opportunities to collaborate with private sector interests, help them to iron out problems that arise with their small business enterprises, ensure women have sufficient training in the areas required, provide information on how to access loans and information, and even monitor women's participation in public meetings concerning ecotourism to ensure they are able to speak out on issues of concern to them.

Women and men together

While targeting women can be a useful strategy in ensuring that women do not miss out on opportunities presented by eco-tourism development, it can be a problematic strategy if it does not address broader gender concerns. In Dilly's (2003) research in Guyana, for example, targeting of women in response to out-migration of men from the community had helped to undermine the formerly egalitarian gender relations among the Makushi. In this case, it would have been more beneficial for the community as a whole if ecotourism opened up new opportunities for both women and men, as this could have reduced the out-migration rates of men (Dilly, 2003).

Creative solutions are often needed to overcome constraints to women's participation in ecotourism, and these solutions can include working together with men. In Tanzania, the Netherlands bilateral donor, SNV, made efforts to involve women in guiding tourists by establishing an all-female team of guides. However the women were less outgoing than the men, they only managed to attract nine tourists in their first year, and the tourists were not happy with the standard of their tours. In the following year, the two best female guides were encouraged to collaborate with two male guides and seeing how the men worked encouraged the women to have more confidence and develop some flair in their newly learned trade. Consequently they attracted 300 tourists, all of whom were satisfied with the quality of their guides (Leijzer, 2003).

The Mountain Institute (TMI) in Nepal, which works on community-based mountain tourism in the Himalayan region, actively seeks to gain men's support for women's involvement in mountain tourism, holding community discussions at which the roles and responsibilities of women in tourism, and the unique skills women bring to tourism, are highlighted (Lama, 1998). That way there is less resistance from men to initiatives to involve women in study tours, committees and planning workshops.

Communal benefits

While it can be difficult to ensure income-earning opportunities for a wide range of individuals through ecotourism development, communal benefits should always be built into ecotourism planning to ensure a spread of benefits among all sectors of a community. In some cases, for example, communities have been happy with ecotourism development and have consequently been supportive of conservation efforts not because they have earned cash from ecotourism, but because ecotourism has led to improvement of roads and communications infrastructure in their area, it has led to better access to markets or improved water and electricity supplies or it has resulted in greater social stability by providing employment for young people who had previously had to migrate out of the area to find work. Such communal benefits can help to reduce women's workloads and provide new economic opportunities to them outside of tourism.

Research examining the dispersal of benefits at Tarangire National Park in Tanzania found that it was more equitable to develop communal projects such as schools, dispensaries, roads and wells, than to provide cash rewards (World Bank Group, 1997, cited in Parker and Khare, 2005, p. 41). In a similar way, park authorities can collect a levy from each tourist (e.g. 10% of the park entry fee) which is directed into a development fund accessed by surrounding communities. As long as women are fairly represented on the committee which decides on the use of these funds, it is likely that they will be used in ways which benefit a wide spectrum of the local community. In cases where dividends are paid to households, however, as in the CAMPFIRE programme discussed earlier, it is important to ensure that female-headed households, divorced women and women in polygamous relationships are not excluded.

Communication and decision-making

Too often there is poor communication between various stake-holder groups to the extent that the majority of community members do not fully understand the intentions and function of an ecotourism project. This can seriously jeopardise community-based ecotourism ventures. Women and men may need to be empowered, in terms of having access to a wide range of information about their options and the confidence to take part in discussions and negotiations, *before* they can effectively decide whether, and how, to pursue involvement in ecotourism. As Akama (1996, p. 573) argues,

...the local community need to be empowered to decide what forms of tourism facilities and wildlife conservation programmes they want to be developed in their respective communities, and how the tourism costs and benefits are to be shared among different stakeholders.

It will be a positive step forward, and an advancement on many wildlife management programmes, if agencies supporting locally based ecotourism recognise that the 'local community' and 'stakeholders' referred to by Akama must include women.

It is important, in the first instance, to inform broad sectors of communities about a proposed ecotourism project. For example, in order to reach women this may involve holding meetings at times of day when women are able to attend, or, if women are constrained from attending public meetings, providing information to women at meetings of their religious group or when they gather at the health centre once a month for mother and child checkups. The second step is to establish or utilise existing decision-making forums which ensure representation of different interest groups from within the community including women, indigenous groups, youths and traditional leaders. It may also be appropriate to include government and private sector groups. Once established, there must be good communication between this forum and the wider community and regular reporting to the community in order to ensure sharing of information and transparency of operations. This can help to avoid the types of conflicts which often arise due to confusion over (a) who is in control of a project and (b) who should share the project's benefits.

Data collection, monitoring and evaluation

It is not sufficient for outside organisations, be they donors, governments or conservation organisations, to assume that adopting a participatory planning approach to ecotourism will ensure that they will meet the needs of the local people (Stronza, 2001). Before any planning starts, there needs to be an in-depth understanding of local communities and their hetero-geneous make up and interests. Many problems with commu-nity ecotourism ventures stem from the fact that there is inadequate understanding of local populations: their history, politics and culture. It is thus vital to ensure that adequate time and resources are devoted to social profiling (e.g. through PRA techniques or Participatory Learning and Action) of commu-nities in order to identify factors such as: (a) who are the most poor and vulnerable groups; (b) who owns and controls resources; (c) what are the needs and motives of various groups within the community; and (d) concerns deriving from religious/ethnic/ gender/class inequalities (e.g. the role of elites).

Once an ecotourism programme is in place, it is critical that regular monitoring and evaluation is carried out in order to see if development objectives are being achieved. In Palawan vil-lage in the Philippines, for example, a group of women who had started a boat business with their husbands which involved taking tourists around nearby islands and reefs, wanted to ensure that their practices were both sustainable and equitable. Thus together with a partner NGO they set up a participatory monitoring and evaluation system which includes collection of data on gender issues such as the distribution of labour and revenue within households involved in the tour boat business (Mayo-Anda *et al.*, 1999).

Conclusion

Community involvement in ecotourism in developing coun-tries can be very positive in terms of promoting development in economically marginalised regions, encouraging sustainable use of natural resources and enhancing the control of local people over development in their surrounding area. However, communities are complex entities with various factions and it can therefore be difficult to implement effective community development in practice. In addition, ecotourism is not a gen-der neutral activity which automatically benefits women. At times their work is seen as merely an extension of their domes-tic roles and thus it is poorly paid or unpaid; cultural con-straints make it difficult for women, whose livelihood activities are often directly reliant on the natural resource base, to speak up even if they do have positions on natural resource management or ecotourism decision-making forums; certain employment is seen as only suitable for men; and preservation of natural resources in the name of ecotourism may mean that women lose access to resources important to their survival and well-being.

While the cultural positioning of women continues to pose constraints to women's involvement in ecotourism ventures, such constraints can be successfully challenged. It is very important, as the GRNP case study showed, to provide women with strong, ongoing support, mentoring and facilitation if they are to fully benefit from the opportunities presented by ecotourism development. In addition, it can be valuable to find creative ways of addressing gender issues which target communities will accept: taking a confrontational position is rarely successful (Leijzer, 2003). Where new training, employment and decision-making opportunities are to be opened up to women, men need to be informed and efforts made to gain their support for this broadening of women's roles and responsibilities. There is much to learn from examples such as TMI in Nepal which insists on equitable involvement of local women in all employment, study tours and training schemes, but which also include awareness-raising activities for men.

In order to address the needs of target communities any outside organisation must have a deep understanding of these communities, necessitating research into the history and culture of the people. When this information is available, appropriate strategies that are tailored to the specific nature of gender roles and relations in different societies can be devised. Thus, for example, the idea of reviving a dying tradition through formation of the weaving group in Gunung Rinjani was most appropriate, leading to development of new skills, boosting women's confidence in dealing with outsiders, giving women money to invest in school fees or in agricultural inputs for their husbands, and resulting in an increase in their status within their own communities. Building communal benefits into an ecotourism programme can also be an effective way of targeting women as long as they have a say over how any funds are spent: some good examples include the purchase of labour-saving grinding mills and the construction of classrooms with ecotourism revenues, positive developments for both women and girls. Such cases show that, with careful planning and in-depth understanding of communities, there is potential for ecotourism to promote equitable, sustainable development for marginalised Third World peoples.

References

Akama, J. (1996). Western environmental values and nature-based tourism in Kenya. *Tourism Management* 17(8): 567–574.

Belsky, J.M. (1999). Misrepresenting communities: the politics of community-based rural ecotourism in gales point manatee, Belize. *Rural Sociology* 64(4): 641–666.

Bras, K. and Dahles, H. (1999). Massage, miss? Women entrepreneurs and beach tourism in Bali. In Dahles, H. and Bras, K. (eds), *Tourism and Small Entrepreneurs – Development, National Policy, and Entrepreneurial Culture: Indonesian Cases*. Cognizant Communications, New York, pp. 35–51.

Butcher, J. (2006). A response to 'building a decommodified research paradigm in tourism: the contribution of NGOs' by Stephen Wearing, Matthew McDonald and Jess Ponting. *Journal of Sustainable Tourism* 14(3): 307–310.

Campbell, L. (2002). Conservation narratives and the 'received wisdom' of ecotourism: case studies from Costa Rica. *International Journal of Sustainable Development* 5(3): 300–325.

Ceballos-Lascuráin, H. (1996). *Tourism, Ecotourism and Protected Areas*. International Union for the Conservation of Nature, Gland, Switzerland.

Cukier, J., Norris, J. and Wall, G. (1996). The involvement of women in the tourism industry of Bali, Indonesia. *The Journal of Development Studies* 33(2): 248–270.

David, R., Sekartjakrarini, S. and Braun, A. (2005). *Gunung Rinjani National Park Project: Rinjani Trek Ecotourism Programme, Lombok – Indonesia: A Participatory Evaluation*. NZAID, Wellington.

Deshingar, P. (1994). *Integrating Gender Concerns into Natural Resource Management Policies in South Africa*. Working Paper 6. Land and Agriculture Policy Centre, Johannesburg.

Dilly, B.J. (2003). Gender, culture and ecotourism: development policies and practices in the Guyanese rain forest. *Women's Studies Quarterly* 31(3/4): 58–75.

Effendi, E., Suhandi, A. and Jihadi, F. (2002). *Project Impact Assessment of the NZODA Gunung Rinjani National Park Project*. Greenomics, Indonesia.

Fallon, F. (2003). After the Lombok riots, is sustainable tourism achievable. *Journal of Travel and Tourism Marketing* 15(2/3): 139–158.

Fennell, D. (2003). *Ecotourism: An Introduction*. Routledge, London.

Fortmann, L. and Bruce, J. (1993). *You've Got to Know who Controls the Land and Trees People Use: Gender, Tenure and the Environment*. Occasional Paper NRM 1/1993, Centre for Applied Social Science, University of Zimbabwe, Harare.

Goodwin, H. (2006). Community-based tourism: failing to deliver? *id21 Insights* 62: 6 (available online: www.id21.org/insights).

Goodwin, H., Kent, I., Parker, K. and Walpole, M. (1998). *Tourism, Conservation and Sustainable Development: Case Studies from Asia and Africa*. Wildlife and Development Series No. 12. International Institute for Environment and Development, London.

Greenpeace Australia Pacific and Oliver, P. (2001). *Caught Between Two Worlds: A Social Impact Study of Large and Small Scale Development in Marovo Lagoon, Solomon Islands*. Greenpeace Australia Pacific, Suva.

Gurung, D. (1995). *Tourism and Gender: Impact and Implications of Tourism on Nepalese Women – A Case Study from the Annapurna Conservation Area Project*. Mountain Enterprises and Infrastructure Discussion Paper, 95/03. International Centre for Integrated Mountain Development, Kathmandu.

James, V.U. (1995). Introduction: sustaining women's efforts in Africa's development. In Jones, V.U. (ed.), *Women and Sustainable Development in Africa*. Praeger, Westport, CT, pp. 1–14.

Joekes, S., Green, C. and Leach, M. (1996). *Integrating Gender into Environmental Research and Policy*. Institute for Development Studies University of Sussex, Brighton.

Jones, S. (2005) Community-based ecotourism – the significance of social capital. *Annals of Tourism Research* 32(2): 303–324.

Kinnaird, V. and Hall, D. (1996). Understanding tourism processes: a gender-aware framework. *Tourism Management* 17(2): 95–102.

Lama, W.B. (1998). CBMT: Women and CBMT in the Himalaya. Submitted to the *Community-Based Mountain Tourism Conference*, as posted on the Mountain Forum Discussion Archives on 5-08-99: http:www2.mtnforum.org/mtnforum/archives/document/discuss98/cbmt/cbmt4/050898d.htm. Downloaded 23-09-98.

Leijzer, M. (2003). Sustainable tourism background paper. *Reference Guide on Sustainable Tourism* (CD ROM) SNV Netherlands Development Organization, The Hague, The Netherlands.

Levy, D. and Lerch, P. (1995). Tourism as a factor in development: implications for gender and work in Barbados. *Gender and Society* 5(1): 67–85.

Manwa, H. (2003). Wildlife-based tourism, ecology and sustainability: a tug-of-war among competing interests in Zimbabwe. *Journal of Tourism Studies* 14(2): 45–54.

Mas, I. (1999). Sua Bali: a pilot project on sustainable village tourism on Bali. In Hemmati, M. (ed.), *Gender and Tourism:*

Women's Employment and Participation in Tourism. Report for the United Nations Commission on Sustainable Development, 7th Session, April 1999, New York. United Nations Environment and Development Committee of the United Kingdom, London, pp. 101–112.

Mayo-Anda, G., Galit, J. and Reyes, A. (1999). The women's hand in a boatmen's cooperative: organizing the Honda Bay tour boat operators in Palawan, Philippines. In Hemmati, M. (ed.), *Gender and Tourism: Women's Employment and Participation in Tourism*. Report for the United Nations Commission on Sustainable Development, 7th Session, April 1999, New York. United Nations Environment and Development Committee of the United Kingdom, London, pp. 90–100.

McKinnon, J. and Suwan, Y. (2000). Gunung Rinjani National Park Project: PRA Report – Participatory Rural Appraisal in Senaru and Sembalun Lawang, June 2002.

Ministry of Foreign Affairs and Trade (1995). *NZODA Support for Eco-Tourism in Fiji: A Report of a Study, March 1995*. Development Cooperation Division, Ministry of Foreign Affairs and Trade, Wellington.

Momsen, J. (1994). Tourism, gender and development in the Caribbean. In Kinnaird, V. and Hall, D. (eds), *Tourism: A Gender Analysis*. Wiley, Chichester, pp. 106–120.

Moore, D.S. (1996). *A River Runs Through It: Environmental History and the Politics of Community in Zimbabwe's Eastern Highlands*. NRM Series, Occasional Paper. University of Zimbabwe, Centre for Applied Social Sciences, Harare.

Mulolani, D. (1997). Traditional democracy? *Resource Africa* 1(4): 8.

Nabane, N. (1996). *Lacking Confidence? A Gender-Sensitive Analysis of CAMPFIRE in Masoka Village*. Wildlife and Development Series No. 3, International Institute for Environment and Development, London and Africa Resources Trust, Harare.

Parker, S. and Khare, A. (2005). Understanding success factors for ensuring sustainability in ecotourism development in southern Africa. *Journal of Ecotourism* 4(1): 32–46.

Richter, L. (1995). Gender and race: neglected variables in tourism research. In Butler, R. and Pearce, D. (eds), *Change in Tourism: People, Places, Processes*. Routledge, London, pp. 71–91.

Scheyvens, R. (1999). Ecotourism and the empowerment of local communities. *Tourism Management* 20(2): 245–249.

Scheyvens, R. (2000). Promoting women's empowerment through involvement in ecotourism: experiences from the Third World War. *Journal of Sustainable Tourism* 8(3): 232–249.

Scheyvens, R. (2002). *Tourism for Development: Empowering Communities*. Prentice-Hall, Harlow.

Scheyvens, R. (in press). Exploring the tourism-poverty nexus. *Current Issues in Tourism*.

Shah, K., Gupta, V. and Boyd, C. (eds) (2000). *Tourism, the Poor and Other Stakeholders: Experience in Asia*. Overseas Development Institute and Tourism Concern, London.

Sinclair, M. (ed.) (1997). *Gender, Work and Tourism*. Routledge, London.

Sindiga, I. (1995). Wildlife-based tourism in Kenya: land use conflicts and government compensation policies over protected areas. *Journal of Tourism Studies* 6(2): 45–55.

Stonich, S., Sorensen, J. and Hundt, A. (1995). Ethnicity, class and gender in tourism development: the case of the Bay Islands, Honduras. *Journal of Sustainable Tourism* 3(1): 1–28.

Stronza, A. (2001). Anthropology of tourism: forging new ground for ecotourism and other alternatives. *Annual Review of Anthropology* 30: 261–283.

Wearing, S. and McDonald, M. (2002). The development of community based tourism: re-thinking the relationship between intermediaries and rural and isolated area communities. *Journal of Sustainable Tourism* 10(2): 21–35.

Weaver, D.B. (2005). Comprehensive and minimalist dimensions of ecotourism. *Annals of Tourism Research* 32(2): 439–455.

Wilkinson, P. and Pratiwi, W. (1995). Gender and tourism in an Indonesian village. *Annals of Tourism Research* 22(2): 283–299.

World Neighbors (*ca.* 2002). Three Year Program Plan: Rinjani Integrated Re/NRM Program. http://www.globalgiving.com/pfil/441/projdoc.doc (accessed 20 July 2006).

CHAPTER 11

Ecotourism, CSR, and the fourth dimension of sustainability

Pamela Wight

Introduction

It has long been understood that ecotourism activities need to consider economic, environmental, and social dimensions, all fundamental considerations for sustainable development, and that an ethical component is involved (Wight, 1993a). However, in the wider business community, it was environmental considerations which first emerged and became evident through various types of corporate reporting. Only more recently have other tools incorporated the social and other dimensions. This chapter provides the context for changing approaches in industry, tourism, and ecotourism, and the parallels between ecotourism and corporate social responsibility (CSR) via its fourth ethical dimension, or quadruple bottom line (QBL). Issues in CSR and its application to ecotourism operations are discussed, and questions raised about the transferability of CSR to ecotourism, in addition to the current focus on reporting in CSR, and on performance in ecotourism.

Context

Moves to sustainability, triple bottom line, and CSR in industry

The last decade and longer has seen increasing prominence given to integrating environment, economy, and society in a move towards sustainable development. But only recently has there been recognition that sustaining natural capital (environmental goods and services) is the basis for all economic, built and social systems, and that the tourism system, like ecosystems, is dynamic and depends on natural capital. Tourism has a responsibility to invest in ecosystem services. One action suggested by the IUCN is that biodiversity concerns should be mainstreamed into business planning and operations, including via 'the use of tools such as "triple bottom line (3BL)" accounting and sustainability audits' (Mainka et al., 2005).

Historically, companies were understood primarily in economic terms, but environmental aspects became the priority of leading edge companies in the late 1980s. In 1992, Agenda 21 called on industry to report their environmental records. Although tourism was not addressed in Agenda 21, it has gradually become more involved in sustainable development activities, but mainstream tourism business initiatives continued to tend to focus on *environmental* responsibility. By contrast, in ecotourism there was earlier recognition that sustainability goals incorporated environment and economy and society, and Wight (1993a) developed an ecotourism model in which these underpinning principles fit, as well as a central, ethical dimension.

Through the 1990s the greening of the marketplace emerged in investment, awareness of irresponsible environmental behaviour, desire to contribute to more sensitive purchases and activities, and a growing interest in 'green' products of all types. The ethically active consumer market in developed countries is assessed to be between 12% and 30% (OCA, 2006). In 2001, seven ecotourism market studies revealed market interest (varying by country of origin) in contributing to local development in destinations, minimizing environmental impact, respect for local traditions and lifestyles, and conservation (WTO, 2001). Similarly, there was varied interest by the travel trade in ethical codes of conduct, charters of responsible tourism, respect for local customs, and company contributions to conservation and local development. However, while responsible travel features may be *expected* by a proportion of consumers, they may not necessarily be *requested* when booking travel packages (EplerWood *et al.*, 2003; Dodds and Joppe, 2005). This makes the role of the tour operator extremely influential in moving the industry supply chain towards sustainable tourism.

The concept of the triple bottom line (3BL) was coined in relation to company environmental reporting (Elkington, 1997; SustainAbility, 1997). It refers to companies communicating effectively with stakeholders about economic prosperity, environmental quality, and social justice (Wheeller and Elkington, 2001) and rapidly gained recognition as a business performance framework measure. 3BL is a management principle aimed at creating long-term shareholder value by seizing opportunities and managing risks of doing business. The 3BL movement puts profit alongside concern for environment and people, creating what is said to be a 'win–win–win' situation. It is a common reporting tool in transnational companies (TNCs) and has been discussed as both a planning and reporting mechanism, and a decision-making framework – an internal management tool and external reporting framework (Dwyer, 2005).

UNEP's Global Environmental Outlook, GEO 2000, suggested action to encourage large industries to help small and medium enterprises (SMEs) with voluntary actions and implementing 3BL accountability. Its Global Reporting Initiative (GRI) enabled companies to prepare 3BL reports through an international framework to standardize Sustainability Reporting Guidelines across various sectors. Business leaders in 3BL reporting are solid Fortune 100 companies, and 3BL is rapidly spreading. But its adoption throughout the tourism industry does not seem especially high.

Globalization, UN guidelines and compacts, organized activism, socially responsible investment growth, and threats of regulation have generated the CSR movement. As in 3BL, CSR companies strive to address three dimensions of sustainability (Earthwatch *et al.*, 2002), but CSR is broader than simply 3BL accounting and reporting. CSR covers responsibility to *internal* stakeholders; and responsibility to *external* stakeholders including relations with state agencies, and with the society in which it operates. Although CSR has many different definitions, a useful one is, 'a company's commitment to operating in an economically, socially and environmentally sustainable manner, while recognizing the interests of its stakeholders, including investors, customers, employees, business partners, local communities, the environment and society at large' (CBSR, 2006).

Experience with environmental initiatives suggests that going beyond legal compliance can contribute to a company's competitiveness. For example, the UK government sees CSR as good for society and good for business, and UK business leaders look at CSR as an investment in a strategic asset or distinctive capability rather than an expense (Pearce, 2003). CSR is increasingly seen as a source of business opportunities – in identifying new markets, improving reputation, and maintaining public support (Goldberg, 2001). In 2003, 80% of CEOs of 900 global corporations believed 'sustainability' is or soon will be vital to their profitability, and 71% said they would consider sacrificing short-term profits to move their company towards sustainability (Savitz and Webster, 2006).

CSR is currently promoted by TNCs, but there has been little uptake by SMEs or the tourism sector. The European Commission (EC) suggests CSR is relevant in all sectors and types of companies, from SMEs to others – 'its wider application in SMEs including micro-businesses is of central importance, given that they are the greatest contributors to the economy and employment' (EC, 2001, p. 8). This is particularly relevant in tourism and ecotourism, where SMEs comprise the largest portion of enterprises.

3BL and CSR in tourism

The World Tourism Organization's (WTO) comprehensive Global Code of Ethics for Tourism, endorsed in 1999, does not appear to have been adopted by the private sector. The WTO (2002) examined 104 global voluntary initiatives for sustainable tourism, and suggested that while they had not yet had a significant impact on the mass market, voluntary initiatives reveal tremendous potential to move the industry towards sustainability, but not without careful nurturing and support from key industry partners. Nearly all tourism entities put forward their *own* specific programmes and initiatives, rather than adhering to broad CSR policies or reporting guidelines, and focus largely on the environment.

A World Bank Group study of several industries found the tourism sector was the least developed in terms of CSR initiatives and codes of conduct. It felt 'the tourism industry appears to be virtually unmonitored regarding CSR initiatives, and claims of eco-friendly practices ... appear to be more marketing schemes than actual policies' (Smith and Feldman, 2003, p. 27). Subsequent study concluded that the tourism industry was just beginning to develop and adopt codes of conduct, with virtually no effective monitoring or implementation mechanisms anticipated for several more years (Smith and Feldman, 2004). Those tourism companies considered to be at the forefront of CSR were major corporations such as airlines, hotel chains, and cruise lines. While large, these are hardly representative of the majority of tourism (or ecotourism) operations, although they may provide leadership to the overall tourism industry.

Tour operators have been regarded as the weakest link in sustainable tourism stewardship (Miller and Twining-Ward, 2005) but there have been considerable efforts to change this through the Tour Operators' Initiative (TOI) promoting responsible tourism through the Tour Operators' Sector Supplement for use with GRI guidelines (UNEP, 2002). Operators are urged to be accountable for 'the new 3BL', and TOI equates 3BL with CSR: 'This whole approach is corporate social responsibility or CSR' (TOI, 2002, p. 1). TOI relates the CSR approach to customer satisfaction, environmental protection, and a positive contribution to development: 'CSR adds value through product differentiation and increased quality, as well as by preventing the degradation of the very base of the tourism experience, i.e., natural and cultural heritage' (TOI, 2002, p. 1). They indicate that CSR actions need to be integrated throughout the tourism supply chain, and subsequently reported.

TOI asks tour operators to describe joint actions taken with suppliers to support improvements in their environmental and social performance, as well as ways they recruit local residents for management, cooperate with groups at the destination, etc. It was hoped that through improved disclosure, tour operators could help influence the tourism industry to be more sustainable. While worthwhile, in the 4 years since the launch, the number of operators has only increased from 15 to 20 members. However, their supply chains do represent a significant number of travellers, staff, and businesses. Also, some of the larger TOI operators have demonstrated that with improved 'sustainability' and reporting they can enhance their business performance, and have been able to influence their smaller network partners.

One CSR company is *forum anders reisen*, a German Alternative Travel Forum, founded in 1998 (EPS, 2000). Members are agents and tour operators who aim to support sustainable tourism both practically and politically. Stringent membership criteria relate to being ecologically justifiable, economically feasible, and ethically and socially just to local communities. They have many restrictions on travel (particularly air) and members undertake not to offer travel to particularly sensitive areas. An independent monitoring system includes regular input and random sampling by a monitoring committee. Its membership increased dramatically in the first 2 years, with members representing a turnover of DM 100 million.

First Choice comprises four holiday sectors: mainstream holidays, specialist holidays, activity holidays, and online destination services. They have produced an 'Environment and People' report (2005) using the framework and indicators suggested by the GRI. This is published with their Annual Report and Accounts which have financial and corporate governance information. They are using this first independently verified report as a basis for multi-stakeholder consultations to decide the content of future annual reports. They developed an Environmental Management System (EMS) using ISO 14001. Part of their sustainable development policy commits to being open, honest, and realistic about environmental and social impacts, targets and achievements (corporate transparency). Their contributions to responsible tourism relate to:

- *Customers*: Satisfaction, product quality, data protection, health and safety, access to all.
- *Staff*: Developing and retaining great people, positive workplace, relevant rewards, engaging staff.
- *Destination communities and local environment*: Protecting the environment, sharing wealth and benefits locally, fair working conditions along the supply chain, preventing sexual exploitation, education, and influencing customers and industry partners.
- *Responsible operations*: Minimizing impacts on environmental and community impacts of aviation emissions, other travel, purchasing decisions, natural resource use, and disposal.

Despite such examples, CSR actions in tourism tend to be *ad hoc*, and there has been even less information on CSR in ecotourism. The WTTC *et al.* (2002) indicate that the tourism industry has been trailing trends already mainstreamed in other industries, and that social responsibility and corporate citizenship will become future issues of strong concern to tourism.

Ecotourism

CSR parallels ecotourism's four dimensions (QBL)

CSR and ecotourism have certain similarities. Wight (1993a) described ecotourism principles in terms of their *internal* environmental operations and resources (i.e. within operations) and their *external* practices (i.e. relationship with the local community and wider society, as well as with surrounding natural and cultural resources). This perspective parallels the subsequent description of the *internal* dimension of CSR (internal company practices primarily involving employees and environment) and the *external* dimension (local communities, other stakeholders, and natural environment) (EC, 2001).

Another similarity is with CSR's recently introduced ethical dimension and stakeholder dialogue. Wight (1993b) first introduced the concept of ethics in ecotourism, expanding this in a model illustrating principles of ecotourism within sustainability goals (Wight, 1993a), including participatory planning and ethical and behavioural responsibilities (to the natural and socio-cultural environments both internal and external to the operation). In CSR performance expectations, organizations commit to meeting stakeholder expectations on economic, environmental, and social performance, as well as ethical and transparent governance policies and procedures (Five Winds, 2006). Wight's 1993 model is also similar in general construct to their CSR model (Figure 11.1) which includes the three dimensions plus the central integrative area of transparent corporate governance including information about ethical and social activities. This can be referred to as a fourth dimension or QBL.

The Earthwatch Institute *et al.* (2002) have drawn parallels between sustainable development, sustainable finance, sustainable business, and biodiversity objectives, only in that they have environmental, economic, and social dimensions – 3BL. But CSR and ecotourism have the explicit additional fourth dimension or values, including transparency in governance and operations, stakeholder consultations, and responsible, ethical behaviour (QBL).

This concept of QBL may be expanded beyond businesses, to governments or other organizations. The ethical issues are an important addition. Sustainability may be described as striving for social, environmental, economic, and ethical responsibility.

It is not surprising that the broader corporate community is recognizing that ethics plays a role, since 'environment is one of those cross-cutting issues which involves science and ethics … in the form of responsibility for the well-being of future generations' (Isaacs, 2006). Broader than 3BL reporting and accounting, CSR's fourth dimension revolves around ethical responsibilities

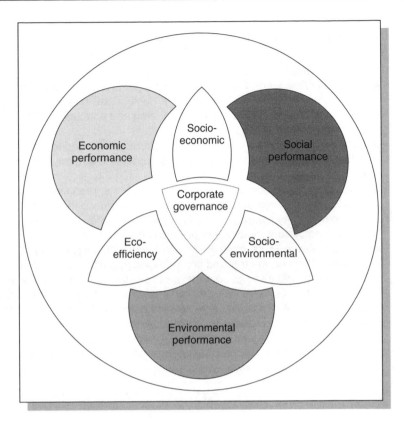

Figure 11.1
CSR in a sustainable enterprise (*Source*: Five Winds, 2006, based on Ranganathan, 1998)

related to stakeholder involvement, external monitoring and verification, public private partnerships, supply chain management, and more recently incorporating international labour and human rights, anti-corruption, and the global poverty reduction agenda (Utting, 2005a, p. 1). Most definitions of CSR now include four components:

- *Commitment of business* (operating so as to add value to society).
- *Benefits to society/stakeholders* (communities, employees, other stakeholders).
- *Environmental performance* (environmental management and performance).
- *Ethical behaviour* (including society's expectations of acceptable business practice).

These categories parallel ecotourism goals, dealing with the internal and external dimensions of an enterprise, as well as

---

Table 11.1 Ethical behaviour in ecotourism enterprises

Ethical practices

- *CanoeSki Discovery*: Prepared and implements a document on 'Wilderness Environmental Ethics and Responsible Ecotourism' for staff and guests.
- *Remote Passages*: Assists in local research and enables clients to contribute to the research.
- *Mariner Cruises; Fundy Tide Runners; Quoddy Link Marine*: Adhere to Codes of Ethics developed to foster trust between operators and ensure ethical wildlife viewing.
- *Chockpaw Expeditions*: Listen to client comments, read evaluations, meet regularly to address improvements, and keep files on clients so they know their history when re-booking. They review all complaints with staff and clients, and *always* offer another equivalent trip *whether or not* the complaint is justified.
- *Niagara Nature Tours*: Interpreters carry domestic ginger plus pocket-knife in their pockets. When on the trail and find wild ginger, guides cut a little piece of ginger from their pocket sample, so each guest can taste it, but examine and smell the wild rhizomes. 'Guests see by example that we do not dig up the plants to let them taste it, then we can explain the ethics of edible wild harvesting'. Everything shown in nature talks and displays is collected ethically, leading to a discussion of collecting ethics. They volunteer for many local causes highlighting local issues, forwarding donations, speaking to media, and enabling staff to volunteer for social, environmental, and conservation causes.

---

with ethical practices, stakeholder empowerment, and institutional governance. With such similarities, it raises the question why CSR has not made more inroads into SMEs in tourism and ecotourism.

QBL and CSR in ecotourism enterprises

A study of best practices in ecotourism was designed to obtain information about multiple dimensions of operations. Unlike most best practices studies which use case studies, this benchmarking study systematically examined a wide range of aspects of ecotourism operations, including transparency/ethical aspects (Pam Wight and Associates, 1999). It found that there is a substantial variation between ecotourism enterprises – while some operations address all QBL dimensions, a number do not. A key finding was that a range of ethical behaviours were found. Examples of ethical practices are provided in Table 11.1.

Although there are many examples of QBL in ecotourism, and there are parallels between CSR and ecotourism, there are very few examples of CSR in ecotourism. This may be because of the emphasis on *reporting* in CSR. One example is at Turtle Island Resort, Fiji, which has been operating a small luxury resort for over 25 years, and enabled local islanders to co-establish two budget lodges via interest-free loans. The resort management have a mission and business philosophy revolving around CSR. This involves meeting community needs in education and health, and enabling guests to contribute. It has recently become a leading proponent of 'Traveller's Philanthropy', believing this to be a response to their guests' desire to engage with and meet community needs (IFC, 2004). Examples of their programmes (beyond local staffing and purchases) include:

- Supporting a community foundation providing health care, education, and employment.
- Supporting job creation programmes and skills transfer, for locally owned businesses.
- Building an island school for village children.
- Providing specialist health clinics using overseas volunteer specialists and building a modern medical facility.
- Creating a regional tourism association to assist in destination planning, marketing, and guidelines.

Turtle Island believes in benchmarking and evaluating performance: 'The difficulty in measuring what you are achieving is knowing where you are on the sustainability continuum at a particular time' (BEST, 2002, p. 4). So they conduct independent audits of impacts via environmental audits (three since 1994) and socio-cultural audits (two since 1998).

Rain Forest Expeditions (RFE) illustrates QBL in ecotourism. RFE manages two ecolodges in Peru, and demonstrates a very strong commitment to sustainable community development and the cultivation of local indigenous leadership (IFC, 2004). Some activities include:

- Support for a research station and five staff.
- Hiring and training community guides.
- Supporting an ethnobotanical centre.
- Fostering community micro-enterprises, helping to obtain grants and technical support for a craft micro-enterprise, and product purchase for lodge sales.
- A full-time community outreach manager who assists with community development initiatives.
- Profit sharing and management agreement with the local community, with shared participation in all decision-making.

- Tracking expenditures, grants, and profits spent in the local community.
- Tracking tourism impact on wildlife.
- Conducting household surveys to obtain community opinion on key issues, including satisfaction with RFE.
- Sharing 60% of profits with the community in return for land equity and labour in lodge construction.

RFE tracks their social, economic, and environment impacts, but not in the form of a CSR. They go beyond community participation to community empowerment. From the outset, they have had an ethical approach to distributing benefits to the local community, as a just entitlement for community involvement in their operations – not simply as a matter of largesse or philanthropy, which is an increasingly contentious approach (Utting, 2000a; Justice, 2003; Scholte, 2003). RFE also has very transparent decision-making – all their policies, work procedures, infrastructure, marketing strategies, and itineraries are approved by the community's Ecotourism Committee before implementation. The following sections may cast light on why CSR has not made greater inroads into ecotourism operations.

Critical issues

Issues in CSR

Moves towards 3BL and CSR by industry seem beneficial, but there are also a number of actual or potential issues. For example, the uptake of CSR is currently very low. Even in non-tourism sectors, CSR involves only a fraction of the 70,000 TNCs, their 700,000 affiliates and millions of suppliers. In November 2005, fewer than 5,000 companies produced company reports, about 700 claimed to use the GRI guidelines, but only 68 companies used them systematically (Utting, 2005a).

Various terms are confused with CSR, including 3BL, responsible business, social responsibility, corporate sustainability, corporate responsibility, stewardship, sustainability in economic activities, sustainable growth, sustainable action, corporate citizenship, business/corporate ethics, sustainable value, core values, or even sustainability. Many definitions of CSR exist, often beneficial to the authors (e.g. business commitment to contributing to sustainable *economic* development; WBCSD, 2000; World Bank, 2006). Given this, it is little wonder that one finds a range of interpretations among companies.

The question 'what is being sustained' is also relevant in the context of these varied definitions. A UK government report indicates sustainability is 'capacity for continuance over the long term' but rarely mentions *what* is to be continued (Pearce, 2003, p. 34). It discusses 'a strong business case for corporate sustainability' without discussing whether this means 'sustaining corporations' or 'the contributions of corporations to sustainable development'. We notice that 'sustainability' is thrown into many different report titles or chapters like a magic tag. The RWE Group even says: 'Sustainability means the planned development of our corporate business strategy'! (2006, p. 2).

Fiksel (2003) indicates 75% of US companies claim to have adopted sustainable business practices – mainly for enhanced reputation, competitive advantage, and cost savings. Norman and MacDonald (2003) are unsurprised to find prominent TNCs without traditions of social responsibility now supporting CSR, especially when trying to shake off a reputation for irresponsible practices. These reports may then become greenwashing propaganda, with more manipulation than accounting to stakeholders.

There is a tendency to assume that any references to the three dimensions in 3BL (or CSR) are consistent with sustainability or sustainable development (Gray and Milne, 2004). But adding environmental and social criteria to financial reporting, while potentially improving the reporting, does not necessarily make the reporting about sustainability, nor the firms about being sustainable (Milne and Ball, 2005). We would not go as far as Norman and MacDonald who say the concept of 3BL turns out to be a 'good old-fashioned Single Bottom Line plus Vague Commitments to Social and Environmental Concerns' (2003, p. 13). But we would suggest a need for specific actions (performance) and careful consideration of what indicators should be used across the tourism sector, especially to SMEs such as ecotourism enterprises.

CSR is a voluntary initiative. Organizations emphasize that companies must be free to choose how they respond to community needs (EC, 2001, 2006; WTTC, 2002). The GRI, Global Compact, and European Union (EU) emphasize voluntary approaches, dialogue and best practice learning, rather than monitoring compliance, complaints procedures, enforceability, penalties, or answerability to different stakeholders. Agencies themselves are torn between the voluntary nature of CSR, and the need to develop more rigorous standards, at the same time realizing the lack of homogeneity among sectors and within tourism.

The emphasis on 'voluntary' is precisely the paradox highlighted by Morhardt (2001), who suggests that the extent to which companies participate in CSR reporting is likely related to financial self-interest. If perceived competitive advantage is behind

CSR reports, then this might relate to the change in report scores over time by the same companies, as they modify their reporting activities to increase perceived advantage.

Mazurkiewicz (2004) shows companies that support voluntary approaches to environmental standards are often involved in *resisting* external regulations, and says there is definitely a need to extend government regulations in developing and emerging economies. Von Moltke and Kuik (1998) agree, saying that there has been government intervention in all replacements of environmentally damaging products by those less damaging. Government leadership in 3BL is apparent in New Zealand and Australia, and for CSR in Canada and Europe, especially the UK. There is likely need for further government involvement in CSR adoption among SMEs and in tourism. The WTTC *et al.* (2002) see roles for both CSR and government. They feel it is the responsibility of companies to place sustainable development issues at the core of their management structure and encourage corporate citizenship, whereas it is the responsibility of governments to develop mechanisms to support SMEs in the adoption of sustainable good practice, and policies to create incentives for CSR in tourism. CSR can be seen as complementary to government regulation, because CSR relies on influence (market-based drivers) while the public sector relies on regulatory approaches (Mazurkiewicz, 2004).

Sagafi-nejad (2005) and others highlight the polarized perspectives about CSR: voluntary approaches are strongly supported by industry and associations and even by the UN; while critics of the Global Compact argue that voluntary initiatives are well-meaning but toothless, and a vehicle for public relations (PR) benefits, and that government policy or regulations are needed. Discussions on voluntary vs. mandatory approaches have been useful in questioning the rather utopian discourse on CSR and highlighting issues. However, polarized debate (e.g. voluntary vs. regulatory, best practice vs. greenwash) diverts attention from other approaches, including more attention to the interface between voluntary and legalistic (soft and hard) approaches, co-regulation (multi-stakeholder initiatives and partnerships for standards), or articulated regulation (coincidence of regulatory approaches to be mutually reinforcing) (Utting, 2005b).

Since ecotourism companies are most likely to be SMEs, incentives for CSR adoption are likely necessary. However, often initiatives (e.g. company codes of conduct, certification schemes, or partnerships) are designed by northern interests (whether governments, non-governmental organizations (NGOs), or corporations). It is important that all types of initiatives for developing countries incorporate southern interests in the decision-making processes that affect them. One of the issues is that CSR is a micro-level tool, whereas the macro-dimension is the broader environment (policy, institutional, and political) in which CSR operates. Unless this broader context is examined, the efforts of CSR may be undermined due to a disabling environment, particularly in developing countries. What is important is how the various approaches (voluntary, legalistic, rights based, etc.) can be articulated and synergistic, or at least made less contradictory.

In terms of content, some authors feel a 3BL claim is not sound unless there is an agreed methodology that allows adding and subtracting data to arrive at a net sum – a social bottom line – and ask 'what use bottom lines without a bottom line?' (Norman and MacDonald, 2003). This is a rather extreme view, and rather like saying that only quantitative data have value. On the other hand, an airline CEO recently stated 'businesses must make business decisions; they should exercise a moral responsibility to destinations only where the figures stack up' (WTTC, 2005, p. 8). SMEs in tourism may rightly be hesitant to move in this direction.

Morhardt (2001) also raises issues related to the fact that corporate commitment often celebrates and encourages employee activities on their own time, from working with local community organizations, to community cleanups, to supporting environmental organizations. Also, the legitimacy of such extramural activities is supported by recognized standards (e.g. National Academy of Engineering, GRI guidelines, ISO 14031 environmental performance evaluation guidelines). While employee contributions may be part of a solution, they may be only a very small part – rather like having recycling opportunities in *guest* rooms only, without integrating measures at back-of-house and throughout external operations.

The Brundtland Report linked the term eco-efficiency (doing more with less) with environment, and this was taken up at Agenda 21, and by WBCSD, and a number of companies have since changed internal practices (which actually make more money for corporations through eco-efficiencies). This does not necessarily invalidate eco-efficiency activities. Indeed, many more environmental activities could be undertaken in the interests of increased profitability, or at least with additional cost savings as an ancillary benefit Morhardt (2001). But while it is beneficial to see corporations consuming less and reducing waste and pollution, it is equally important to note that such eco-efficiencies alone do not address the deeper and wider issues related to sustainability (Figure 11.1). Eco-efficiency is 'not a strategy for success over the long term, because it does not reach deep enough' (McDonough and Braungart, 1998). It lacks transformational power.

Business and accounting observers have concluded that many CSR reports do not have high quality or completeness, and vary from region to region. For example, while EU reports tend to have 3BL information, it is rare for US companies to include *economic* impacts; and while the majority of US companies almost entirely avoid external assessment, in the EU, external assurance is high (Context, 2006). Regarding CSR standards, Von Moltke and Kuik (1998) point out that EMS almost inevitably reflect the resources and attitudes of those involved in their development, and that to assess the economic impact of voluntary standards, it is essential to identify those who have contributed to their development and their interests. Similarly, Utting (2005b) refers to self-appointed entities undertaking CSR standard-setting and regulatory action with limited accountability. De Regil (2006) feels that the GRI's multi-stakeholder working groups represent only current practitioners of the GRI framework, excluding other stakeholders. The adequacy of input from smaller stakeholders and SMEs in developing guidelines and standards needs to be questioned, particularly since the value of CSR to SMEs is also in question.

The EC (2001) notes that there are many organizations developing standards for social accounting, reporting, and auditing, each with different standards, examining process or performance, voluntary and mandatory, single to multiple issues, with only a handful covering all CSR issues. The variety of competing frameworks, standards, and standard-setting bodies have no measuring and reporting comparability. Corporations currently select their own reporting system (e.g. AccountAbility 1000, ISAE 3000, SA 8000, ISO 140000, GRI, European Framework of Quality Management, etc.). Morhardt (2001) reviewed three major systems of reporting and found that due to design differences, high scores in one do not necessarily mean high scores in the others. Also, corporations may be at different stages in CSR, so comparability across time, enterprises, and sectors may be impossible.

These scoring systems all measure the *number* of topics and the *depth* of discussion, not company *performance*. Thus a high score does not necessarily reveal a high level of performance. Companies which are environmentally responsible and benign (e.g. many ecotourism operations) may therefore not need to discuss a large variety of topics, but may score low if they focus on *relevant* topics; while companies which add topics irrespective of relevance or performance, can improve their scores through topic manipulation (Morhardt *et al.*, 2002). Reports may also cherrypick stakeholder issues and topics to report on, while key issues arising from corporate activity remain unaddressed (e.g. social justice and equity; labour issues; development scale, limits, and constraints; externalities; or future generations).

Such issues are central to sustainability. Similarly, Utting (2000b) illustrates the paradox of how specific TNCs are lauded for their 'best practices' (which may be relatively superficial) while these same companies are also identified as bad practitioners in more fundamental ways.

Hawken felt it is critical that the meaning of sustainability not get lost in the trappings of corporate speak (2002). Corporations using various terms such as social responsibility or sustainability often do not address deeper issues which are key to sustainability. Recently, key industry leaders are addressing some issues omitted from earlier reports (e.g. climate change), but it is essential that businesses don't mask deeper structural issues with superficial changes – 'an honest report … would detail the externalities borne by other people, places, and generations' (Hawken, 2002). One of the problems may be that sustainability is essentially a *systems* level concept, not an *organizational* one (Dyllick and Hockerts, 2002; Gray and Milne, 2004).

Ecotourism enterprises, scale, and resource issues

SMEs make up the largest section of the world's marketplace, so incorporating CSR into SMEs is of interest, because corporate responsibility is an issue that involves the whole supply chain. European SMEs don't currently feel pressures from consumers or corporations, but they are influenced by supply chain pressures from larger enterprises, regarding environment and quality, and probably social activities (Hillary, 2003). Europe is now focusing on the need to adapt the CSR concept, practices, and instruments to suit the specific situation of SMEs. However, SMEs are not homogenous, even within the tourism sector, and represent a huge range of sub-sectors, suppliers, and service providers. CSR issues may be exacerbated in ecotourism.

SMEs, due to their size, have more restrictions than larger enterprises, including knowledge, staff, finances, and capabilities. These difficulties become greater in the already fragmented tourism sector, and are increased in the ecotourism sector. For example, an ecolodge study found that financing was extremely difficult to obtain for ecolodges, despite the fact that green fund managers wished to support conservation-oriented projects, because ecolodges were considered very risky investments due to small margins, high vulnerability to externalities, complex operations in remote locations, need for sophisticated market knowledge, and frequent local competition. In addition, such loans required monitoring, and reporting requirements and costs were too high for the businesses (EplerWood *et al.*, 2003).

The financial sector is said to have a role in sustainable development, including taking environmental considerations into account in their lending practices. But this sector has shown little interest in long-term perspectives, nor in links between environmental performance and investment performance (Goldberg, 2001). Many respondents to the ecolodge survey said banks are unable or unwilling to measure and to understand the value of a 3BL philosophy, yet *after* lodges became successful, banks which had previous rejected them were very ready to fund them (IFC, 2004). This is doubly ironic, since banks and lending institutions are moving to strong involvement in 3BL/CSR activities themselves, yet take an economics-only perspective for loans, and don't account for the 3BL activities of the prospective operator. Since ecolodges usually take 3–5 years to reach profitability, and even successful 3BL ecolodges experienced financial difficulties at start-up, it seems valid to question how realistic it is to expect annual reporting, with attendant costs, according to sophisticated international standards, particularly since ecolodges were found to require technical assistance for many aspects of operations *besides* 3BL reporting.

Goldberg (2001) felt it was a special challenge for smaller organizations to prepare and issue full GRI reports, and considered they might find it more practical to adopt a phased or incremental approach to implementation. He felt that the GRI should consider creating an abbreviated reporting framework to address the needs of SMEs, initially focussing on disclosure of legally required issues, or easily available data. It is telling that few of the most successful ecolodges are involved in 3BL or CSR reporting, and most do not have a system in place to evaluate their performance (IFC, 2004).

North-centric consultation and decision-making processes often characterize multi-stakeholder initiatives such as the GRI, with key developing country stakeholders (e.g. trade unions) poorly represented or absent. Additionally, there is an assumption that anything improving social or environmental standards in TNC supply chains or SMEs must be good for development. Utting (2005b, p. 5) feels this approach:

can ignore key development issues, priorities and realities in developing countries; certain stakeholders; and the fact that raising social and environmental standards implies costs that may constrain enterprise development and employment generation, and that CSR supply chain management may be a way for TNCs to pass costs on to suppliers. It also tends to ignore more fundamental structural issues associated with corporate power and certain competitive and fiscal practices of TNCs that are implicated in the broader problem of underdevelopment.

The impact of CSR initiatives in TNCs may result in the squeezing out of SMEs in developing countries, and certainly, there has been little evidence of support by TNCs throughout their supply chain – rather, a devolution of responsibility and costs. Leading authors feel CSR needs to become more south-centred, considering costs, indigenous approaches, and pressures specific to developing countries (Mazurkiewicz, 2004; Nelson *et al.*, 2005; Utting, 2005b). The majority of ecotourism enterprises are SMEs in developing countries, thus further questions arise about the applicability of CSR.

Although 3BL/CSR reports have recently blossomed, it is still unclear whether a natural audience exists for these reports beyond sustainable development advocates (Fiksel, 2003). In ecotourism, where enterprises are usually small scale, without concerned shareholders, one questions whether there is a significant demand for such reports.

Ecotourism enterprises emphasize performance, not reporting

Over 100 ecolodges surveyed have a very positive environmental *performance* overall, but only 40% have an ongoing system to identify environmental impacts and review environmental performance, and less than a quarter (22%) have an annual written *review* of environmental performance (IFC, 2004). This potentially questions whether most ecolodges can clearly understand their impact on the environment. In other words, while environmental *performance* was high, systems and *reporting* were low. A more detailed survey of 15 model ecolodges found that 3BL strategies were variable: some businesses integrate 3BL into all aspects of operations, while others use more philanthropic approaches. But ecolodges which take an integrated and focused approach to environmental and social sustainability are convinced they benefit economically from a 3BL approach (EplerWood *et al.*, 2003). In addition, ecolodges that are associated with a larger ecotourism business have a greater likelihood of being financially sustainable than one operating in isolation. This indicates that the small-scale nature of ecotourism operations and ecolodges is not necessarily helpful for overall sustainability.

Although there are parallels between ecotourism and CSR, unfortunately in industry overall, the question of why some business sectors are accepting CSR 'has less to do with a new-found ethical concern among corporate executives for the environmental and social condition of the planet, than with economic, political and structural factors' (Utting, 2000b, p. viii) including competitive advantage and reputation management. He further points out 'strictly speaking, the notion of responsibility is restricted to the realm of ethics and principles and not concrete actions or outcomes' (2000b, p. 4). Thus in CSR discussions, there is now interest in the notion of corporate social *performance*, which includes outcomes and impacts.

RFE is considered a model ecolodge. They keep track of their positive and negative social and environmental impacts but not within one 'system'. For example, economically, they use accounting software to track expenditures within the local community, as well as grants/donations and profits they distribute. Environmentally, they have researchers tracking tourism's impact on key wildlife and wildlife encounters. But their system of tracking social impact has varied – they had 5 years of systematic research via a university researcher, 2 years of further analysis, and more recent bimonthly household surveys designed to obtain community opinions on key issues including satisfaction with the operation. Thus while they have very good indicative information and feedback, they comment, data tracking has three problems:

- it is *expensive*;
- *organizationally* SMEs have a difficult time tracking profits, commissions, and satisfaction levels, never mind community satisfaction or ecosystem change indicators; and
- it is *difficult* in terms of identifying appropriate indicators for a range of issues, topics, and impacts (K. Holle, 2006, personal communication).

The cost and complexity of reporting and auditing systems is a disincentive to SMEs. If exemplary operations such as RFE are tracking progress on a variety of fronts, and are on a genuine self-improvement course, must there be the added burden of external sustainability *reporting* too? Questions may be: Who are the audiences for ecotourism reporting? And if ecotourism operations are *implementing* the principles and goals of ecotourism or QBL, is *reporting* also a necessity? And if it is, where are the models that are adapted for SMEs? And where should such reporting be published, if it is to serve a useful purpose? This author also wonders if ecotourism SMEs are generally even aware of the trend to global reporting, if they have the knowledge to compile a report, whether or not they feel reporting is in their interests, and whether or not guidelines for all SMEs can be readily used by the ecotourism industry.

Conclusion and future possibilities

Almost 15 years after the Earth Summit, many corporate leaders now recognize that the environment, social, and economic development are not always in conflict. A number of companies are adopting sustainable development as a management framework to build long-term value in line with shareholder and societal expectations. The tourism industry has been slow on the uptake of new approaches to business, although recent drivers of sustainability are evident in the TOI. The World Ecotourism Summit (2002, p. 2) recognized that ecotourism has provided leadership in introducing sustainability practices to the tourism sector, and emphasized that it should:

continue to contribute to make the overall tourism industry more sustainable, by increasing economic and social benefits for host communities, actively contributing to the conservation of natural resources and the cultural integrity of host communities, and by increasing awareness of all travellers towards the conservation of natural and cultural heritage.

While leadership ecotourism enterprises have been based on QBL for well over a decade in terms of performance, they have not moved in the direction of sustainability *reporting*, as have other enterprises. But the latter have tended to be large corporations, whilst ecotourism operations are SMEs with little shareholder presence or image issues, and few resources for the kinds of time-invested activities that sustainability reporting involves. For that matter, many ecotourism operations are currently unlikely to know about sustainability reporting trends.

There are a number of issues surrounding CSR, including the fact that it is fairly fragmented and uneven, and the number of companies which have taken a lead is very small. In the general business marketplace, key researchers indicate that CSR is 'here to stay', while others feel it is at a crossroads, or might fade. Rather than supporting or dismissing CSR, a transformational scenario might be more likely (Raskin *et al.*, 2002; de Regil, 2005; White, 2005). Transformation would need to address many of the issues around CSR in industry, as well as specific issues related to SMEs and to the ecotourism sub-sector. A transition would require a revised concept of progress; the active engagement of civil society; and new corporate policies, behaviour, and values.

The success of voluntary initiatives such as CSR will depend largely on its institutional setting – the macro-environment within which CSR companies (and most ecotourism enterprises) operate. Perhaps, too, the development agenda needs to include better *integration* of voluntary approaches such as CSR with government regulation and other approaches. The concept of sustainable development goes far beyond environmental protection. Welford (1997 in Utting, 2000b) stated that companies contributing to sustainable development need to be active in six areas: environmental performance, empowerment of employees, economic performance, ethics, equity, and education. A similarly comprehensive approach may be needed to integrate and articulate various approaches to sustainable development, to enable CSR to succeed.

We are, on the one hand, encouraged by the take-up of CSR approaches to performance and reporting, as they may promote improvements in business reporting and probably actions, but we are concerned that CSR and related concepts are increasingly confused with and seen as 'sustainability'. We need to be cautious that CSR is not used as a greenwashing tool, nor as a distraction from tackling externalities and addressing the deeper issues of sustainability.

A commitment to principles is not commitment to performance, and benchmarking environmental *reports* is not benchmarking environmental *performance* (SustainAbility, 1996; Utting, 2005a). However often company reports mention corporate responsibility, or sustainable development in their texts, substantial movement in this direction is slow. Perhaps companies engaged in CSR need to move toward corporate *accountability* and focus on corporate social *performance*. It is ironic that while ecotourism has led the tourism industry in sustainability approaches and QBL performance, now that mainstream tourism industry is beginning to re-focus on how to achieve and report on sustainability, ecotourism enterprises seem to be lagging in reporting, due to particular challenges. Despite this apparent paradox, CSR is not a straightforward tool to be adopted without addressing some of the concerns touched on earlier. The additional challenges for SMEs (e.g. pressures of time, cost, skills, report size, audit standards) also need to be addressed.

Leading companies may be involved in a paradigm shift, which includes regarding environmental and social issues as company-wide responsibilities, and where transparency and stakeholder dialogue become a norm. The challenge is to create a commonly respected CSR framework, which also allows detailed assessment of business practices. This process will involve CSR innovations, as well as a shift from narrow, technical approaches, to a holistic, systemic, and more responsive approach.

References

BEST (Business Enterprises for Sustainable Tourism) (2002). *Turtle Island Resort: To Be a Vital Resource to Its Community*. The Conference Board and WTTC. 3, 1.

CBSR (Canadian Business for Social Responsibility) (2006). Website: www.cbsr.bc.ca/

Context (2006). *Reporting in Context: Global Corporate Responsibility Reporting Trends*. Context, London.

de Regil, Á. (2005). *The Future of CSR Will Mirror the Health of Society: Pondering the Evolution of CSR*. The Jus Semper Global Alliance, November.

de Regil, Á. (2006). *Living Wages: The GRI's Missing Link*. The Jus Semper Global Alliance, March.

Dodds, R. and Joppe, M. (2005). *CSR in the Tourism Industry? The Status of and Potential for Certification, Codes of Conduct and Guidelines*. Prepared for CSR Practice Foreign Investment Advisory Service Investment Climate Department, World Bank Group, June.

Dwyer, L. (2005). Relevance of triple bottom line reporting to achievement of sustainable tourism: a scoping study. *Tourism Review International* 9(1): 79–94.

Dyllick, T. and Hockerts, K. (2002). Beyond the business case for corporate sustainability. *Business Strategy and the Environment* 11: 130–141.

Earthwatch Institute (Europe), IUCN, and World Business Council for Sustainable Development (2002). *Business & Biodiversity: The Handbook for Corporate Action*. Switzerland.

EC (European Commission) (2001). *Promoting a European Framework for Corporate Social Responsibility: Green Paper*. Directorate-General for Employment and Social Affairs, Luxembourg, July. http://europa.eu.int/comm/employment_social/soc-dial/csr/greenpaper_en.pdf

EC (2006). *Implementing the Partnership for Growth and Jobs: Making Europe a Pole of Excellence on Corporate Social Responsibility*. http://ec.europa.eu/enterprise/csr/policy.htm

Elkington, J. (1997). *Cannibals with Forks: The Triple Bottom Line of 21st Century Business*. Capstone Publishing, Oxford.

EplerWood International, Pam Wight & Associates, and Jeanine Corvetto (2003). *A Review of International Markets, Business, Finance & Technical Assistance Models for Ecolodges in Developing Countries*. For IFC/GEF, January. http://www.ifc.org/ifcext/enviro.nsf/AttachmentsByTitle/fly_EBFP_EcolodgeEplerwood/$FILE/Ecolodges-EplerWood.pdf

EPS (Environmental Conservation Services GmbH) (2000). *German Initiatives Towards Sustainable Tourism*. Federal Ministry for the Environment, Nature Conservation and Nuclear Safety, Bonn.

Fiksel, J. (2003). Revealing the value of sustainable development. *Corporate Strategy Today. Making the Business Case About the Near Future*. AHC Group, New York, 7/8, pp. 28–36.

First Choice (2005). *Environment and People Report 2005*. First Choice Holidays PLC.

Five Winds (2006). Sustainability and CSR. Web page: www.fivewinds.com/services/services_SustainabilityCSR.cfm

Goldberg, E. (2001). *Profit, People, Planet Policy Issues & Options Around Triple Bottom Line Reporting*. Prepared for the Ministry for the Environment, New Zealand, February.

Gray, R. and Milne, M.J. (2004). Towards reporting on the triple bottom line: mirages, methods and myths. In Henriques, A. and Richardson, J. (eds), *The Triple Bottom Line: Does It All Add Up?* Earthscan, London, pp. 70–80.

Hawken, P. (2002). McDonald's and Corporate Social Responsibility? April 25. http://www.foodfirst.org/archive/media/press/2002/mcdresponsibility.html

Hillary, R. (2003). Starting small: Europe's SMEs and social responsibility. *CSR Magazine, Corporate Social Responsibility Magazine in Europe* 3(2): 4–7, October.

IFC (International Finance Corporation) (2004). *Ecolodges: Exploring Opportunities for Sustainable Business*, Washington. http://www.ifc.org/ifcext/enviro.nsf/Content/EBFP_Ecolodge

Isaacs, C. (2006). Destroying Canada's international environmental reputation. *Gallon Environment Letter*, HR Edition, 11(39), April.

Justice, D. (2003). The Role of the United Nations in Corporate Accountability and International Regulation. *UNRISD Conference of Corporate Social Responsibility and Development: Towards a New Agenda?* Geneva, 17–18 November.

Mainka, S., McNeely, J. and Jackson, B. (2005). *Depend on Nature: Ecosystem Services Supporting Human Livelihoods*. IUCN – The World Conservation Union, Switzerland, June.

Mazurkiewicz, P. (2004). *Corporate Environmental Responsibility: Is a Common CSR Framework Possible?* DevComm-SDO, World Bank. Presented with the *IAIA Conference* in Vancouver, May. http://siteresources.worldbank.org/EXTDEVCOMMENG/Resources/csrframework.pdf

McDonough, W. and Braungart, M. (1998). The next industrial revolution. *The Atlantic Monthly*, October.

Miller, G. and Twining-Ward, L. (2005). *Monitoring for a Sustainable Tourism Transition: The Challenge of Developing and Using Indicators*. CABI, Cambridge.

Milne, M.J. and Ball, A. (2005). Examining the triple bottom line: from soothing palliatives and towards ecological literacy. Presentation at the *16th International Conference on Social and Environmental Accounting Research (4th Australasian CSEAR)*, Geelong, Victoria, 30 March–1 April.

Morhardt, J.E. (2001). Scoring corporate environmental reports for comprehensiveness: a comparison of three systems. *Environmental Management* 27(6): 881–892.

Morhardt, J.E., Baird, S. and Freeman, K. (2002). Scoring corporate environmental and sustainability reports using GRI 2000, ISO 14031 and other criteria. *Corporate Social Responsibility & Environmental Management* 9: 215–233.

Nelson, V., Martin, A. and Ewert, J. (2005). What difference can they make? Assessing the social impact of corporate codes of practice. *Development in Practice* 15(3&4). www.developmentinpractice.org

Norman, W. and MacDonald, C. (2003). Getting to the bottom of 'triple bottom line'. *Business Ethics Quarterly* 14(2): 243–262.

OCA (Office of Consumer Affairs) (2006). *Corporate Social Responsibility: An Implementation Guide for Canadian Business.* Industry Canada, Ottawa.

Pam Wight and Associates (1999). *Catalogue of Exemplary Practices in Adventure Travel and Ecotourism.* Canadian Tourism Commission, Ottawa.

Pearce, B. (2003). *Sustainability and Business Competitiveness. Measuring the Benefit for Business Competitive Advantage from Social Responsibility and Sustainability.* Forum for the Future's Centre for Sustainable Development with DTI, December. www.csr.gov.uk

Raskin, P., Banuri, T., Gallopin, G., Gutman, P., Hammond, A., Kates, R. and Swart, R. (2002). *Great Transition: The Promise and Lure of the Times Ahead.* A Report of the Global Scenario Group. Stockholm Environment Institute, Boston.

RWE Group (2006). *Corporate Responsibility Report 2005.* www.rwe.com/responsibility

Sagafi-nejad, T. (2005). Should global rules have legal teeth? Policing (WHO Framework Convention on Tobacco Control) vs. good citizenship (UN Global Compact). *International Journal of Business* 10(4): 363–382.

Savitz, A. and Weber, K. (2006). *The Triple Bottom Line: How Today's Best-Run Companies Are Achieving Economic, Social and Environmental Success – and How You Can Too.* Jossey-Bass. Website: http://www.wiley-vch.de/publish/en/books/forthcomingTitles/BA00/0-7879-7907-4/?sID=ed7b009ed36ae9ec1e43b571d8f31915

Scholte, J.A. (2003). The role of the United Nations in Corporate Accountability and International Regulation. *UNRISD Conference of Corporate Social Responsibility and Development: Towards a New Agenda?* Geneva, 17–18 November.

Smith, G. and Feldman, D. (2003). *Company Codes of Conduct and International Standards: An Analytical Comparison. Part I of II: Apparel, Footwear and Light Manufacturing, Agribusiness, Tourism.* The World Bank Group, International Finance Corporation.

Smith, G. and Feldman, D. (2004). *Implementation Mechanisms for Codes of Conduct*. The World Bank, International Finance Corporation.

SustainAbility (1996). *Engaging Stakeholders* Executive Summary. United Nations Environment Programme. http://www.enviroreporting.com/others/unep_eng.htm?&username=guest@enviroreporting.com&password=9999&groups=ENVREP

TOI (Tour Operators Initiative) (2002). *Improving Tour Operator Performance: The Role of Corporate Social Responsibility and Reporting*. TOI, Association of British Travel Agents, Tearfund. http://www.abtamembers.org/responsibletourism/csr_guide.pdf

UNEP (2002). Tour operators launch new performance indicators to promote environment friendly tourism. Press Release 13 November. London/Nairobi. http://www.grida.no/newsroom.cfm?pressReleaseItemID=30

Utting, P. (2000a). UN-business partnerships: Whose agenda counts? Paper presented at seminar on *Partnerships for Development or Privatization of the Multilateral System?* Organised by the North–South Coalition, Oslo, Norway, 8 December, UNRISD. www.unrisd.org.

Utting, P. (2000b). *Business Responsibility for Sustainable Development*. Occasional Paper No. 2, January, UNRISD, Geneva.

Utting, P. (2005a). Beyond social auditing: micro and macro perspectives. Presentation at the EU Conference on *Responsible Sourcing: Improving Global Supply Chains Management*, Brussels, 18 November.

Utting, P. (2005b). *Rethinking Business Regulation: From Self-Regulation to Social Control*. Technology, Business and Society Programme Paper No. 15, UNRISD, September.

Von Moltke, K. and Kuik, O. (1998). *Global Production Chains: Northern Consumers, Southern Producers, and Sustainability*. Prepared for UNEP. Institute for Environmental Studies, Vrije University, Amsterdam.

WBCSD (2000). *Corporate Social Responsibility: Making Good Business Sense*. World Business Council for Sustainable Development, January.

WES (World Ecotourism Summit) (2002). *Quebec Declaration on Ecotourism*. http://www.world-tourism.org/sustainable/IYE/quebec/anglais/quebec-eng.pdf

Wheeller, D. and Elkington, J. (2001). The end of the corporate environmental report? Or the advent of cybernetic sustainability reporting and communication. *Business Strategy and the Environment* 10(1): 1–14.

White, A. (2005). *Fade, Integrate or Transform? The Future of CSR*. Business for Social Responsibility, August.

Wight, P. (1993a). Sustainable ecotourism: balancing economic, environmental and social goals within an ethical framework. *Journal of Tourism Studies* 4(2): 54–66.

Wight, P. (1993b). Ecotourism, ethics or ecosell? *Journal of Travel Research* 31(3): 3–9.

World Bank (2006). DevComm CSR Program. Development Communication Division definition of CSR: http://web.worldbank.org/WBSITE/EXTERNAL/TOPICS/EXTDEVCOMMENG/EXTDEVCOMSUSDEVT/0,,contentMDK:20243787~menuPK:509009~pagePK:64146915~piPK:64146896~theSitePK:423901,00.html

WTO (2001). *The Italian Ecotourism Market; The Spanish Ecotourism Market; The French Ecotourism; Market; The British Ecotourism Market; The German Ecotourism Market; The Canadian Ecotourism Market; The US Ecotourism Market.* Market studies commissioned for IYE2002. World Tourism Organization, Madrid.

WTO (2002). *Voluntary Initiatives for Sustainable Tourism.* World Tourism Organization, Madrid.

WTTC (2002). *Corporate Social Leadership in Travel & Tourism.* World Travel & Tourism Council, London, November.

WTTC (2005). *Realizing the Potential.* World Travel & Tourism Council, London, October.

WTTC, IFTO, IH&RA, and ICCL (2002). *Industry as a Partner for Sustainable Development: Tourism.* UNEP.

Part Two

Critical issues in ecotourism policy, planning and management

Scaling ecotourism: the role of scale in understanding the impacts of ecotourism

C. Michael Hall

The concept of scale is one of the key ideas in the social sciences. Unfortunately, its importance for understanding tourism phenomena, and ecotourism in particular, has been seriously neglected. Scale is an important issue in understanding tourism because it raises issues as to what scale of analysis should tourism be examined and as to how findings at one scale can be related to another (Burt, 2003). These are not merely academic concerns. Given the claims that are often made regarding the environmental friendliness, or otherwise of ecotourism (see Chapter 1), the scale at which ecotourism is examined becomes critical for ascertaining its affects and therefore its actual contribution with respect to such matters as conservation, and community and economic development.

Tourism presents a range of interesting issues with respect to understanding the role of scale. Although as a phenomen on tourism is recognised as occurring over successive stages in time and space: home – transit region – destination – transit region – home (Fridgen, 1984; Hall, 2005a), the vast majority of tourism research is undertaken at 'destinations' and research sites within destinations, which in themselves are also not comparative homogenous units (Hall, 2005b) (Figure 12.1). Extremely limited research is undertaken in the 'home' location of tourists, primarily with respect to travel decision-making, while the effects of tourism mobility in transit regions are negligible. This leads Hall (2005b) to ask the question, 'How well can we generalize from the specific to the general in tourism when we know that the evidence on which many of our papers are based are not only spatially specific but also time specific in relation to the stages of the travel process?'

Relegating the analysis of tourism to destinations, albeit often for pragmatic research reasons, clearly raises issues in ascertaining

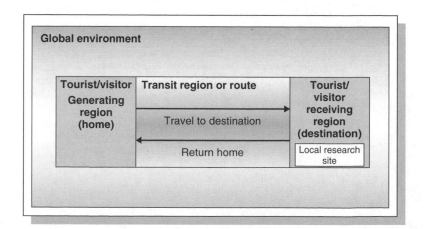

Figure 12.1
Geographical elements of a tourist system

tourism impacts. In the case of the economics of tourism it has long been acknowledged that there is often a failure to delimit implications of the size of the regional economy that is to be studied – the smaller the area to be analysed, the greater will be the number of 'visitors' and hence the greater is the estimate of economic impact (e.g. Burns *et al.*, 1986). Yet such concerns apply not just to the economic impacts of tourism, including ecotourism, but also to the social and environmental impacts. The selection of boundaries for studying the affects of tourism is critical. For example, widely used tourism management monitoring and evaluation frameworks such as carrying capacity, Environmental Impact Assessment (EIA), Limits of Acceptable Change (LAC), Recreation Opportunity Spectrum (ROS) and the Tourism Optimisation Management Model (TOMM) focus on the local destination or activity environment rather than on the larger impact of tourism activity. Nevertheless, with respect to long-distance tourism, for example, more than 90% of a typical journey's contribution to climate change comes from the transport component and particularly aviation (Gössling, 2000) in getting to and from the destination or the study site in which tourists are intercepted by researchers. Similarly, in the New Zealand context Becken *et al.* (2003) noted that energy use, and therefore emissions as well, is clearly dominated by transport accounting for approximately 70% of the total energy use of international and domestic travellers in the West Coast of New Zealand's South Island. Therefore, by only studying what happens at a destination or a specific site rather than over an entire trip it is likely that there will be a gross underestimate of the environmental, and other, impacts of tourism (Høyer, 2000; Olsthoorn, 2001; Gössling, 2002; Gössling *et al.*, 2002; Gössling and Hall, 2006). Such a situation provides a serious challenge to the environmental credentials of ecotourism. As Gössling (2002, p. 200) argued, 'even ecotourism projects often seem to ignore the global environmental aspects of travel. Ecotourism may thus be sustainable on the local level (in the sense that it puts a minimum threat to local ecosystems through the conversion of lands, trampling, collection of species, etc.), but it may in most cases not be sustainable from a global point of view'.

Unfortunately, the resolution at which many studies of ecotourism operate tends to be extremely localised in both time and space whether it be with respect to consumption, that is the potential for ecotourism to change visitor values, or production, that is the contribution of ecotourism to the conservation of a specific species or to income for a particular community (see Twynam *et al.*, 1998). Studies of the impacts of tourism on specific species for example tend to focus on local populations rather than over the complete range of the species. Similarly, studies of ecotourism operations tend to focus on the day-to-day operations of the operation rather than the supply and distribution channels within which they operate and, perhaps just as significantly the life cycle of the business, its operations and physical infrastructure. It is extremely rare for a clear boundary to be drawn around an ecotourism study area so as to be able to identify and calculate the inputs and outputs of the system. Moreover, the frequent focus on a relatively few target species or charismatic megafauna in studies of the conservation and environmental dimension of ecotourism also often means that broader biodiversity and ecological understandings of the role of tourism remain relatively unknown (Fennell, 1999; Hall, 2006a).

Although the relativities of localisation and globalisation are appropriate for understanding many social, political and economic relations (Herod, 2003) they are not helpful in generating a clear understanding of environmental impact by connecting tourism activities to environmental quality. This is particularly the case given that it has been long recognised that 'the generalizations made at one scale of analysis do not necessarily hold at another, and that conclusions derived at one scale may be invalid at another' (Burt, 2003, p. 211). Nevertheless, such generalisations have often been undertaken with respect to the conservation values of ecotourism, and often at the highest level with organisations such as the World Tourism Organization and the United Nations Environment Programme. As Gössling et al. (2002, p. 200) commented, 'Existing concepts [of tourism and the local environment] are thus insufficient to make clear statements about the sustainability of particular forms of travel or the sustainability of certain destinations'.

There is clearly a strong relationship between the spatial and temporal scales involved in studies of tourism. In general, through the sciences and social sciences, as spatial scale increases, so does the time scale of interest (Burt, 2003). However, in tourism the temporal and spatial scales with respect to tourism phenomenon tend to be limited (Hall, 2004) (Figures 12.2 and 12.3). The correlation between spatial and temporal scales of analysis is not always maintained but, as Burt (2003) notes with respect to issues of scale in the physical environment, in general terms, short-term studies tend to focus on process dynamics whereas longer-term studies are more likely to involve statistical analysis of form and structure. The temporal and spatial scales at which studies are conducted also have implications for understanding causality (Schumm and Lichty, 1965). At the shortest time scale, processes operate within an essentially fixed environment.

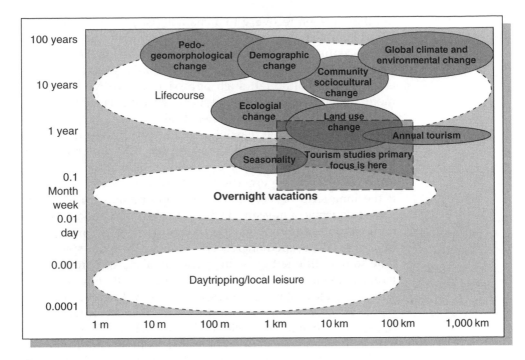

Figure 12.2
The influence of temporal and spatial resolution on assessing mobility-related phenomenon (Hall, 2004)

Figure 12.3
Scale in tourism analysis: primary foci in socio-economic systems, biodiversity and climate research in terms of research outputs (Hall, 2004). Shading indicates the extent to which certain scales of analysis have been studied

Socio-economic systems	Biodiversity	Climate
International	Global	Macroclimate
Supranational	Continental	
National	Biome	
Regional	Bioregion	
	Landscape	
Local	Ecosystem	
Family	Stand/field/communities	Mesoclimate
Individual	Individual species	Microclimate

Over the longer term, properties that were fixed at the shorter times cale now become variable. As Burt (2003, p. 212) comments, 'Process now controls form and a "steady-state equilibrium" may be identified. Large events may perturb the system but there is then recovery to a characteristic form'. Such ideas have begun to influence tourism, including with respect to better conceptualising ideas of sustainable tourism (Farrell and Twinning-Ward, 2004). Indeed, systems thinking has long influenced tourism although such approaches have tended to be more metaphorical than analytical (McKercher, 1999; Hall, 2000, 2005b; Russell and Faulkner, 2004).

Arguably one of the reasons why tourism studies has failed to reap the benefits of a systems approach to understanding tourism's relationship to the environment is that tourism does not have a workable ergodic hypothesis. A system is ergodic if the long-term observation of a single motion leads to the same frequency of measured values as the observation of many motions with different starting points. In ecology an ergodic hypothesis is an expedient research strategy that links space and time so that different areas in space are taken to represent different stages in time (Bennett and Chorley, 1978). For example, with respect to ecological succession whereby different locations within an area at one point in time are taken to represent the sequence of changes in species composition that would occur in that area over longer periods of time. In tourism studies possibly the nearest that exists to an ergodic hypothesis is the concept of a tourist area cycle of evolution (Butler, 1980, 2006) that is often described as a tourism, destination or resort cycle of evolution (Papatheodorou, 2004). However, its capacity to explain the trajectory of tourist area development on the basis of single location, short-term studies is extremely limited, if not non-existent in its initial form although it does provide a useful heuristic device, although subsequent reinterpretations of the model may provide the basis for a more quantitative approach that does have greater predictive capacities (e.g. Coles, 2006; Hall, 2006b).

The lack of a workable ergodic hypothesis as well as insufficient appreciation of the role of scale in drawing conclusions from research presents a substantial problem in drawing insights on the environmental dimensions of ecotourism at anything other than single case scale, as for example seeking to understand environmental implications at a regional, national or global scale. There is therefore a need to understand the detail of process mechanisms as indicated by small-scale studies as well as larger-scale studies that help us understand how broader, complex environmental systems within which tourism is situated actually operate. Yet the vast majority of small-scale studies of ecotourism, which nearly all studies of the impacts of ecotourism are (see Twynam et al., 1998; Carr and Higham, 2001; Weaver, 2003 for meta-reviews of ecotourism literature), do not pay adequate attention to issues of representation and sampling or the need for more nested studies, in order to be able to generalise the results of such small-scale studies at the larger scale. And where such generalisation is attempted (e.g. Gössling, 2002), the results of such studies do not necessarily support the notion that ecotourism is necessarily any friendlier to the environment than mass tourism. Indeed, where the study of ecotourism is stretched over space and time so as to include all aspects of the consumption and production of the tourism experience it seems likely that at the aggregate level there is little difference between different forms of tourism particularly as travel time increases (Gössling and Hall, 2006).

For example, with respect to long-distance travel to sites that are simultaneously 'mass' and ecotourism destinations the environmental impacts of the flight there in terms of energy consumed and emissions will be the same regardless of the activities engaged at the destination. There may be at destination differences between 'mass' and ecotourists depending on the willingness to engage in low energy/low pollution activities and the type of accommodation (see Becken *et al.*, 2003). However, because of the location of many ecotourism activities in more peripheral locations that have higher degrees of naturalness and environmental amenity (Hall and Boyd, 2005), it may well mean that the ecotourist consumes further energy and generates more emissions in order to be transported to such a location rather than the more sedentary mass tourist. Such a scenario therefore means that an analysis of the environmental contribution of each tourist on a site only basis would conclude that the tourism activities of the ecotourist would be more environmentally beneficial. Yet if a system wide analysis was conducted little difference in overall environmental impact would be noted with the ecotourist possibly even contributing higher levels of greenhouse gas emissions because of their transport requirements. Both will have contributed to global-scale emissions that have local effects on the quality of the environment and on the welfare of specific species but these are environmental impacts that are not considered in local assessments of the environmental impact of ecotourism.

Such considerations are not merely academic musings but indicate the kind of research that needs to be undertaken before the environmental contribution of ecotourism can be fully accounted for. They also raise very practical questions about the type of audit that needs to be conducted of ecotourism operations, especially when such practices are related to ecolabelling (Synergy and World Wildlife Fund (WWF), 2000; Font and Buckley, 2001; Global Ecolabelling Network, 2004).

Auditing is an increasingly important aspect of assessing the sustainability of ecotourism and other tourism businesses. However, arguably, auditing has become more significant for

Type of audit	Local	Regional	Scale National	Supranational	Global
Compliance	--------				
Site	------				
Corporate	------				
Issues	---				
Associate	--				
Activity	---				

Figure 12.4
Scale of analysis
with respect to
audits

ecotourism than many other sectors because it is explicitly used as a component of accreditation schemes, such as Green Globe, that may not only assess the environmental friendliness of firms and destinations but also can contribute to a 'green' image and may be also utilised in marketing and promotional activities (Font and Buckley, 2001; Buckley, 2002). Although the monitoring of environmental conditions appears as a logical and self-evident activity for any tourism business that is positioned as an ecotourism operation in practice they are very difficult to undertake with any degree of thoroughness, primarily because of the difficulties in obtaining adequate information. Such difficulties are not just technical but also relate to the time and financial cost in gathering such information. Acceptable quality standards are not only difficult to define but may vary from firm to firm, destination to destination, jurisdiction to jurisdiction and between different accreditation schemes. Therefore, potentially creating confusion in the minds of both producers and consumers of ecotourism product.

Different types of audits also have different assessment requirements over different scales of analysis in relation to the supply and distribution chains of ecotourism operations (Figure 12.4). These include:

- *Compliance audits*, which seek to ensure that accreditation (e.g. ecolabelling programmes) and/or regulatory standards are not being breached.
- *Site audits*, that examine specific locations which might previously have been identified as problem areas with respect to environmental or other standards.
- *Corporate/organisational audits*, which examine the performance of an entire business or agency. This may be with respect to integrated audits that examine environmental and social aspects of organisational performance as well as economic performance, for example the notion of a 'triple bottom line'. From an environmental perspective such reviews can ensure

that there is sufficient support for environmental issues within an organisation.

- *Issues audits*, which seek to ensure that an operation has responded to specific environmental issues. For example, an operation's policies with respect to using timber from sustainable forests or purchasing local products. More recently, issues audits for ecotourism companies have extended to also include social dimensions such as human rights, for example for international firms there are some locations where they will not go because of the rights records of specific countries such as Myanmar or China.
- *Associate audits*, in which an organisation's contractors, agents and suppliers through the supply and distribution chain are vetted with respect to their environmental and/or other standards.
- *Activity audits*, which evaluate organisational policy in activities that cross business boundaries, particularly over distribution and transport networks.

The most common type of audits – common, site and corporate are primarily local in implementation or, in the case of corporate audits, internal to the organisation. However, issues, associate and activity audits have the potential to be much broader in scale. In all of the audits the key question is the extent to which the audit captures the travel of the customer rather than just the consumptive and productive activities of the organisation *per se*. Yet given that as a service industry tourism is primarily defined by its consumers, then it seems logical that such an element was included in any assessment of the environmental dimensions of tourism. One mechanism by which this could be undertaken is through greater use of ecological footprint analysis.

Ecological footprint analysis estimates how much of the biophysical output of the earth is required to meet the resource consumption and waste absorption needs of an individual or a given community, region, state or continent (Rees, 1992). Ecological footprint studies sometimes compare the estimated demand for land/water ecosystems with the readily available supply (e.g. domestic productive land) to determine whether the study population and region could be self-sufficient (Rees, 1992, Wackernagel and Rees, 1996). Such analyses show that many developed countries are running significant 'ecological deficits' with the rest of the world (Senbel *et al.*, 2003). Significantly, studies of the ecological footprint of tourism incorporate the travel of consumers to and from the destination. Although such studies are extremely limited in tourism when they are undertaken the results have substantial implications for the supposed environmental benefits of tourism. Gössling *et al.*'s study of the ecological footprint of tourism in the Seychelles noted that although 'high-value tourists might generate the largest foreign exchange earnings per capita ..., but they also seem to be characterised by the highest resource use per capita' and concluded, 'Environmental conservation based on funds derived from long-distance tourism remains problematic and can at best be seen as a short-term solution to safeguard threatened ecosystems' (2002, p. 209). Gössling *et al.* (2002) reported that long-distance travel was the biggest contributor to the ecological footprint of tourism on the island. Other studies of the ecological footprint of locations have also concluded that transport and hence tourism are some of the major contributors to ecological consumption (e.g. Collins *et al.*, 2006).

Gössling *et al.* (2002) conclude that 'in order to become more sustainable, destinations should seek to attract clients from close source markets' (209):

From a global sustainability and equity perspective, air travel for leisure should be seen critically: a single long-distance journey such as the one investigated in this survey requires an area almost as large as the area available on a per capita basis on global average. This sheds new light on the environmental consequences of long-distance travel, which have rather seldom been considered in the debate on sustainable tourism. Taking these results seriously, air travel should, from an ecological perspective, be actively discouraged (2002, p. 210).

Such a conclusion, while most appropriate in terms of environmental conservation, presents a major challenge for many ecotourism operations. This chapter has emphasised that in order to ascertain the full impacts of ecotourism and therefore judge the actual contribution of ecotourism to the environment then a much broader analysis in time and space needs to be conducted. However, to do so may likely derive not only results that many will not want to acknowledge but also the solutions. Unfortunately, some of the locations that most depend on the contribution of ecotourism to local community and economic development are also the most peripheral and therefore distant with respect to source markets. In these locations ecotourism may well be one of the few development options available. In such circumstances there may well be a need to acknowledge that while economically significant ecotourism is likely to have a nett negative impact with respect to the environment. The story in short is therefore given the energy and emissions costs of ecotourism it may even have a greater negative impact than other alternative forms of economic development. The challenge for operations is to reduce such costs while for researchers it is to utilise studies that fully appraise the impacts of ecotourism on a global as well as a local basis.

Acknowledgements

An earlier version of this chapter was presented as a paper 'Scale and the problems of assessing mobility in time and space', at the Swedish National Doctoral Student course on tourism, mobility and migration, hosted by the Department of Social and Economic Geography, University of Umeå, October 2004. The comments received at the workshop are greatly acknowledged as are the comments of Dieter Müller and Stefan Gössling on earlier versions of this work.

References

Becken, S., Simmons, D.G. and Frampton, C. (2003). Energy use associated with different travel choices. *Tourism Management* 24: 267–277.

Bennett, R.J. and Chorley, R.J. (1978). *Environmental Systems: Philosophy, Analysis and Control*. Methuen, London.

Buckley, R. (2002). Tourism ecocertification in the International Year of Ecotourism. *Journal of Ecotourism* 1(2/3): 197–203.

Burns, J.P.A., Hatch, J.H. and Mules, F.J. (eds) (1986). *The Adelaide Grand Prix: The Impact of a Special Event*. The Centre for South Australian Economic Studies, Adelaide.

Burt, T. (2003). Scale: upscaling and downscaling in physical geography. In Holloway, S.L., Rice, S.P. and Valentine, G. (eds), *Key Concepts in Geography*. Sage Publications, London, pp. 209–227.

Butler, R.W. (1980). The concept of a tourist area cycle of evolution: implications for management of resources. *Canadian Geographer* 24: 5–12.

Butler, R.W. (ed.) (2006). *The Tourism Life Cycle*, 2 vols. Channelview Press, Clevedon.

Carr, A.M. and Higham, J.E.S. (2001). *Ecotourism: A Bibliography*. Department of Tourism, University of Otago, Dunedin.

Coles, T.E. (2006). Enigma variations? The TALC, marketing models and the descendents of the product life cycle. In Butler, R.W. (ed.), *The Tourism Life Cycle: Conceptual and Theoretical Issues*. Channelview Publications, Clevedon, pp. 49–66.

Collins, A., Flynn, A., Weidmann, T. and Barrett, J. (2006). The environmental impacts of consumption at a subnational level: the ecological footprint of Cardiff. *Journal of Industrial Ecology* 10(3): 9–24.

Farrell, B.H. and Twinning-Ward, L. (2004). Reconceptualizing tourism. *Annals of Tourism Research* 31(2): 274–295.

Fennell, D. (1999). *Ecotourism*. Routledge, London.

Font, X. and Buckley, R.C. (eds) (2001). *Tourism Ecolabelling: Certification and Promotion*. CABI, Wallingford.

Fridgen, J.D. (1984). Environmental psychology and tourism. *Annals of Tourism Research* 11: 19–40.

Global Ecolabelling Network (2004). *Introduction to Ecolabelling*. Global Ecolabelling Network, Ottawa.

Gössling, S. (2000). Sustainable tourism development in developing countries: some aspects of energy-use. *Journal of Sustainable Tourism* 8(5): 410–425.

Gössling, S. (2002). Global environmental consequences of tourism. *Global Environmental Change* 12: 283–302.

Gössling, S., Hansson, C.B., Hörstmeier, O. and Saggel, S. (2002). Ecological footprint analysis as a tool to assess tourism sustainability. *Ecological Economics* 43: 199–211.

Gössling, S. and Hall, C.M. (eds) (2006). *Tourism and Global Environmental Change*. Routledge, London.

Hall, C.M. (2000). *Tourism Planning*. Prentice-Hall, Harlow.

Hall, C.M. (2004). 'Scale and the problems of assessing mobility in time and space', Paper Presented at the *Swedish National Doctoral Student Course on Tourism, Mobility and Migration*, hosted by Department of Social and Economic Geography, University of Umeå, Umeå, Sweden, October.

Hall, C.M. (2005a). *Tourism: Rethinking the Social Science of Mobility*. Prentice-Hall, Harlow.

Hall, C.M. (2005b). Time, space, tourism and social physics. *Tourism Recreation Research* 30(1): 93–98.

Hall, C.M. (2006a). Tourism, biodiversity and global environmental change. In Gössling, S. and Hall, C.M. (eds), *Tourism and Global Environmental Change: Ecological, Economic, Social and Political Interrelationships*. Routledge, London, pp. 211–226.

Hall, C.M. (2006b). Space-time accessibility and the tourist area cycle of evolution: the role of geographies of spatial interaction and mobility in contributing to an improved understanding of tourism. In Butler, R.W. (ed.), *The Tourism Life Cycle: Conceptual and Theoretical Issues*. Channelview Publications, Clevedon, pp. 83–100.

Hall, C.M. and Boyd, S. (2005). Nature-based tourism and regional development in peripheral areas: introduction. In Hall, C.M. and Boyd, S. (eds), *Tourism and Nature-based Tourism in Peripheral Areas: Development or Disaster*. Channelview Publications, Clevedon, pp. 3–17.

Herod, A. (2003). Scale: the local and the global. In Holloway, S.L., Rice, S.P. and Valentine, G. (eds), *Key Concepts in Geography*. Sage Publications, London, pp. 229–247.

Høyer, K. G. (2000). Sustainable tourism or sustainable mobility? The Norwegian case. *Journal of Sustainable Tourism* 8(2): 147–160.

McKercher, B. (1999). A chaos approach to tourism. *Tourism Management* 20: 425–434.

Olsthoorn, X. (2001). CO2 emissions from international aviation: 1950–2050. *Journal of Air Transport Management* 7: 87–93.

Papatheodorou, A. (2004). Exploring the evolution of tourism resorts. *Annals of Tourism Research* 31(1): 219–237.

Rees, W.E. (1992). Ecological footprints and appropriated carrying capacity: what urban economics leaves out. *Environment and Urbanisation* 4(2): 121–130.

Russell, R. and Faulkner, B. (2004). Entrepreneurship, chaos and the tourism area lifecycle. *Annals of Tourism Research* 31(3): 556–579.

Schumm, S.A. and Lichty, R.W. (1965). Time, space and casality. *American Journal of Science* 263: 110–119.

Senbel, M., McDaniels, T. and Dowlatabadi, H. (2003). The ecological footprint: a non-monetary metric of human consumption applied to North America. *Global Environmental Change* 13: 83–100.

Synergy and World Wildlife Fund (WWF) (2000). *Tourism Certification*. WWF, Godalming.

Twynam, D., Johnston, M., Payne, B. and Kingston, S. (1998). *Ecotourism and Sustainable Tourism Guidelines: An Annotated Bibliography*. The Ecotourism Society, North Bennington.

Wackernagel, M. and Rees, W. (1996). *Our Ecological Footprint*. New Society Publishers, Gabriola Island.

Weaver, D.B. (ed.) (2003). *The Encyclopedia of Ecotourism*. CABI, Wallingford.

CHAPTER 13

Defining critical habitats: the spatio-ecological approach to managing tourism–wildlife interactions

James Higham and
David Lusseau

Introduction

The management of tourism impacts upon wildlife presents a critical but complex tourism research domain. This is a field of study that is yet to be adequately addressed by the research community (Higham, 2001). It is apparent, however, that significant contributions in this area have been achieved in recent years (Shackley, 2001). From this body of research it is clearly evident that scientific methodologies are required to provide reliable and detailed insights into the impacts that tourist may bring to bear upon focal wildlife populations, and that such insights are needed to provide a baseline for the development of appropriate and effective management responses and strategies (Constantine, 1999). In most cases, both in New Zealand and elsewhere, commercial and recreational engagements between wild animal populations (individuals and/or groups) and tourists take place where animals are most predictably located and/or where concentrations of wildlife may be found. In such cases, these interactions are more likely to occur where critical behaviours take place, and where wildlife populations are most likely to have to tolerate, and perhaps accommodate otherwise unacceptable levels of stress associated with the presence of tourists (Higham, 1998). As such it may be desirable to manage tourist–wildlife engagements based on an understanding of critical behaviours and the spatial ecologies where these behaviours take place, either exclusively or predominantly (Lusseau, 2003a). The management of wildlife–tourism in this manner requires that critical behaviours are understood, and that the habitats where these behaviours take place are identified and adequately protected (Lusseau and Higham, 2004).

Wildlife–tourism and impact management

The New Zealand tourism industry is heavily dependent upon nature as a key resource. The forms of nature-based tourism that exist in New Zealand are varied, and include outdoor recreation pursuits (e.g. tramping and climbing), adventure (e.g. rafting, jet boating and heli-skiing) and ecotourism activities (those that generally centre on learning and conservation goals). The commercial development of adventure and ecotourism activities is a notable feature of the period from 1985 to the present (Higham *et al.*, 2001). Within this context, a substantial component of the tourism sector in New Zealand has come to focus on wildlife as a key attraction. Dickey (2003) demonstrates that ecotourism development has taken place rapidly during the last decade. Her analysis of commercial ecotourism businesses in New Zealand highlights two trends: (1) the rapid expansion of commercial eco-tourism businesses particularly in the coastal and marine context and (2) increasing pressure of commercial tourism development in association with wildlife populations. These trends highlight the priority that needs to be placed on developing sustainable wildlife–tourism management practices.

It is difficult to assess the impact of human activities on populations of wildlife animals. Strict methodologies are necessary to interpret responses to anthropogenic impacts objectively. For the past 10 years there has been increasing interest in studying the effects of tourism activities on wildlife species (Constantine, 1999; Orams, 1999). However, most studies tend to examine only one aspect of wildlife–tourist engagements and therefore fail to capture complex interrelationships between variables. In the context of tourist interactions with marine mammals, for example, a critical challenge is understanding the relationship between acoustic communication and behavioural state (Lusseau and Higham, 2004). Furthermore, few studies have been developed to understand the long-term impacts associated with human disturbance of wildlife species. Most studies tend to be short term in focus and attempt to demonstrate wildlife responses to interactions with tourists.

Thus, in terms of boat-based interactions with marine mammals, Blane and Jaakson (1995), Barr (1996) and Novacek et al. (2001) demonstrate that schools of animals tend to tighten when boats are present. Other studies have demonstrated active avoidance in response to human interactions as demonstrated in the case of marine mammals by changes in movement patterns (Edds and MacFarlane 1987; Salvado et al., 1992; Campagna et al., 1995; Bejder et al., 1999; Novacek et al., 2001), increases in dive intervals (Baker et al., 1988; Baker and Herman, 1989; Blane, 1990; MacGibbon, 1991; Janik and Thompson, 1996; Lusseau, 2003a) and increases in swimming speed (Blane and Jaakson, 1995; Williams et al., 2002). These signs of avoidance can be a result of not only the presence of boats, but also boat manoeuvring patterns, such as sudden changes in boat speed or rapid approaches (MacGibbon, 1991; Gordon et al., 1992; Constantine, 2001; Lusseau, 2003a). Few studies have been able to address the biological significance of wildlife responses to tourist activities.

Understanding biological significance

There are several apparent features of wildlife–tourism interactions in New Zealand. Firstly it is evident that wildlife–tourist interactions generally take place in locations dictated by the presence and/or abundance (concentrations) of focal wildlife populations. Thus, in the case of most colonial nesting sea bird populations, including rare and/or engaged species (e.g. Albatross, yellow-eyed penguins), tourist interactions generally take place at nesting sites, which can result in significant localised impacts if not carefully managed. Further to this end, it is evident that research into tourist-induced impacts at these sites must move beyond the apparent tolerance of individuals or groups of animals (Mills, 1990; Robertson, 1993a; Higham, 1998). These are sites where critical behaviours take place (e.g. such behaviours as nest building, incubation, chick rearing, fledging and moulting). Many of these behaviours require animals to tolerate human presence because flight is either a last option (e.g. abandoning a chick) or not an option at all (e.g. moulting). Clearly tolerance of animals can mask impacts that may be biologically significant (Higham, 1998).

Another notable feature of wildlife–tourism interactions is that little is known about the biological consequences of observed avoidance responses. Fortunately research efforts are beginning to address this knowledge gap. For example, Robertson (1993b) notes that Albatross chicks that are observed by tourists from the Richdale Observatory (Taiaroa Head) demonstrate behaviours that are distinct from chicks with natal nests that lie beyond the view of visitors in the observatory. The former leave the natal nest at an earlier age, move further from the natal nest, and fledge from the colony at an earlier age when compared to the latter (Robertson, 1993b). These distinct behavioural patterns were considered by Robertson to represent avoidance responses. However, the critical question that remains unanswered is what, if any, are the biological consequences of these responses? The same question applies when a dolphin spends 10 s longer underwater on average when a boat interacts with it (Lusseau, 2003a) or if a whale demonstrates reduced surface time between dives when boats are present (Gordon et al., 1992). It is possible to speculate on such consequence, but it is preferable to relate the effects of the responses observed to standardised parameters such as the energetic budget of the species to assess their biological significance.

Relating the effects observed to their energetic cost would allow the establishment of simple and appropriate management responses, through such initiatives as the establishment of guidelines and quotas. Any such management interventions should, according to Duffus and Dearden (1990), acknowledge the site-specific nature of tourist–wildlife engagements, incorporating the nature of the user (type of tourism development), focal (and incidental) wildlife species and the ecology of the site where interactions take place. Thus management approaches that are applied at different locations must be appropriate to:

1. different wildlife species,
2. different local populations of animals,
3. different settings where interactions take place,
4. different tourism development contexts.

It is critical that such insights are achieved and appropriate management initiatives applied before the development pressure of the tourism industry reaches levels that cannot be sustained.

Defining critical habitats

A logical extension to this context is to develop understandings of critical habitats based on behavioural data. Defining critical habitats through the analysis of behavioural data is the basis of a proposed 'spatio-ecological approach' to managing wildlife-tourist interactions. This requires the development of research methodologies that capture:

1. wildlife responses to anthropogenic impacts;
2. the impacts of wildlife responses in terms of energetic budget;
3. the definition of ecological zones, if they exist, where critical behaviours are most likely to take place.

This chapter proposes a seven-step methodological approach that is designed to allow researchers to explore and define critical habitats (Table 13.1) as part of the process of designing appropriate wildlife–tourism management initiatives.

Table 13.1   Seven-step approach to defining critical habitats

Step 1 Definition of individual and group behaviour states
Step 2 Development of a database of observed behaviours
Step 3 Definition of critical behaviours
Step 4 Definition of critical and important regions
Step 5 Assessment of temporal variations of behavioural observations
Step 6 Delineation of appropriate and effective management interventions
Step 7 Monitoring critical behaviours and long-term site stability

Step 1: The definition of individual and group behaviour states

Initially the definition of individual and group behaviour states needs to be undertaken, preferably in a way that mitigates researcher impacts. Behavioural states should be mutually exclusive and cumulatively inclusive (as a whole they described the entire behavioural budget of the wildlife population). Scan sampling of individuals within the population should be preferred to focal group sampling because of the observer bias inherent to the latter technique (Altman, 1974; Mann, 2000). The scan sampling of individual animals provides the required detail of data collection that affords insights into the relationship between individual animal behaviours and the collective behaviour of the population.

Step 2: The development of a database of observed behaviours

The development of a database of observed behaviours should include the position of individuals and groups when observations take place, date, time and behavioural state. Observed behaviours are plotted on a map which is divided into quadrats. The size of the quadrats must maximise both the number of quadrats that contained sightings and the number of sightings per quadrat, while maintaining a detailed representation of the site ecology of the species. The number of sightings in different behaviour states are recorded and standardised by the total number of sightings in each quadrat/region. The percentage of time spent in different behavioural states can then be calculated for each quadrat/region in the study area. The collection of observational data must record both the presence and absence of tourist activities.

Step 3: Definition of critical behaviours

Critical behaviours may be defined as those behaviours that are most sensitive to interactions with tourists. They are represented by any individual of collective behaviours that tend to be discontinued when tourists are present, or with particular aspects of tourist conduct (e.g. noise levels, visitor behaviour, manoeuvring of vehicles/vessels).

Step 4: Definition of critical and important regions

A critical region may be defined as a location that is predominantly used for critical behaviours. An important region is an area where critical behaviours are often observed. The overall behavioural budget of the population should be used to define 'predominantly' and 'often'. Values are biologically meaningful if they are based on the total behavioural budget of the population.

Step 5: Assessment of temporal variations of behaviour observations

It is necessary that data collection accommodate the assessment of temporal variation of behavioural observations. Temporal variation relates to seasonal changes in the proportion of time engaged in critical behaviours in given regions. Differences between proportions of time spent engaged in critical behaviours should be tested on the basis of seasonality.

Step 6: Delineation of appropriate and effective management interventions

This step involves the identification of critical spatio-ecological zones that most need to be protected. Management interventions then need to be established that maximise the protection of critical habitats, and the viability/sustainability of tourism operations. Such rules may include the designation of zones where visitor operations are precluded (critical regions), the issuing of operator permits to allow appropriate levels of visitor activity in important regions, and the designation of buffer areas of appropriate range so as to make practical the protection of critical and important regions. Such initiatives should be developed in consultation with commercial tourism operators so as to incorporate elements of business viability.

Step 7: Monitoring critical behaviours and long-term site stability

Longitudinal data collection is required to monitor changing patterns of behaviour and critical ecologies beyond the annual seasonal time frame. An understanding of geographical and/or ecological factors is necessary to ensure that proposed areas represent critical habitats, as opposed to short-term preferred locations for certain behaviours.

This methodology allows locations where focal animals engage in critical behaviours to be identified. It also allows detailed insights into the probable effectiveness of visitor management initiatives to be achieved. It provides baseline information to guide management interventions and, if necessary, wildlife protection measures (e.g. sanctuaries) to be established precisely where and when they are likely to be most effective. The intended outcome should be minimisation of wildlife–tourist interactions in locations and/or at times when members of the focal wildlife population are most likely to be engaged in critical behaviours.

Discussion

In the past, the establishment of wildlife–tourism businesses, and the designation of wildlife sanctuaries, has relied primarily on abundance information. This information is based on locations where members of a population are predictably present, and/or where concentrations of individual animals are greatest (Dawson and Slooten, 1993; Buckingham *et al.*, 1999; Thompson *et al.*, 2001). The goal in these cases is to:

1. achieve the highest probability that tourists will be able to observe members of a wildlife population at the location; and/or
2. protect locations with high concentrations of animals in order to decrease the probability of exposure to anthropogenic impacts.

Thus the viewing of many colonial nesting bird species takes place at the very sites where these species are most predictably located and perhaps, therefore, where critical behaviours are most likely to be exposed to potential tourism impacts.

It is argued here that the designation and management of such sites should specifically use or, at the very least, incorporate behavioural information. The sensitivity of animal populations to anthropogenic impacts is known to be dependent on behaviour (Lusseau, 2003b; King and Heinen, 2004; Rees *et al.*, 2004). Thus, some behavioural states are more susceptible to anthropogenic impacts than others. In the New Zealand context marine mammals and seabird populations have been to the fore in terms of commercial tourism developments centred on wild animal populations. In the case of bottlenosed dolphins it has been demonstrated that resting and socialising behavioural states are those that are most likely to be discontinued when engagements with tourist vessels take place (Lusseau, 2003b). In the case of seabird populations the various behaviours associated with nesting (adult animals) and natal nest stages (chicks) appear to be critical or important behaviours (Department of Conservation, 1992; Robertson, 1993a, b, c; Peat, 1997). The less critical behaviours take place in marine environments (e.g. feeding) rather than at nesting colonies. This point is captured by boat-based tour operators, such as Monarch cruises (Dunedin), Black Cat (Akaroa) and Pelagic Bird Tours (Kaikoura). The challenge, therefore, is to identify locations where critical behaviours take place, and to protect these ecological zones (or parts thereof) through the establishment of sanctuaries or the close management of tourist activities that take place in or adjacent to those zones.

This management approach should allow benefits to both wildlife populations and commercial tourism operators to be captured. In terms of the former, it protects areas where behaviours that are especially sensitive to interactions with tourists take place. Where necessary it would eliminate interactions in regions where critical behaviours occur. It allows critical ecologies to be protected and ensures that limited interactions take place in ecological regions deemed to be important. Such information can also be used and applied to other non-tourism anthropogenic impacts of relevance to the wildlife population (e.g. transport, communications, utilisation of natural resources). For example, in response to the impacts of recreational set netting, this approach has been effective in reducing Hector's dolphin (*Cephalorhynchus hectorii*) by-catch in gillnets around Banks Peninsula (East Coast of New Zealand's South Island) (Slooten *et al.*, 2000), a location where Hector's dolphins are concentrated (Dawson and Slooten, 1993).

It is also necessary that such tourism management initiatives do not compromise the viability of commercial tourism operations. Management approaches must establish clear operational benefits associated with the establishment of protected critical zones, and the issuing of permits to allow operators to enter important ecological regions under stated conditions. It may be argued that operators might also benefit from increased intrinsic economic values associated with visitor use of ecological regions in which sustainable management approaches can be scientifically demonstrated. Clearly social science research techniques are required to ensure that management approaches are workable in terms of the commercial and practical realities of operating a tourism business. A third party should also benefit from such an approach; management agencies that are commonly charged with a dual mandate of protecting wildlife populations while fostering visitor experiences in areas designated for conservation.

This approach is reflected in work that is currently taking place in the international context. Whittington *et al.* (2004) show that behavioural reactions to road density and road usage in wolves can be related to the use of significant extra energy when wolves are travelling. This extra-expenditure can then be related to the carrying capacity of the ecosystem in terms such as how many more preys wolves need to eat to meet the extra energy cost (Lusseau, 2004). This can help managers to decide where roads may be developed and where they should not be developed, and how to most effectively regulate the use of existing roads given that the wolves' prey also react to road presence and use. Lusseau (2004) therefore provides an example of how behavioural studies can help better refine spatial management of an ecological area.

Other studies have been able to relate changes in habitat use as well as avoidance of previously preferred areas in response to increases in tourism impacts (Baker *et al.*, 1988; Salden, 1988; Corkeron, 1995). In these instances spatio-ecological management responses have proved effective. The Robson Bight–Michael Bigg Ecological Reserve in Canada has contributed to minimising boat interactions with killer whales (*Orcinus orca*) in that area (Kruse, 1991; Williams *et al.*, 2002). Marine mammal sanctuaries have been established in other locations to regulate and minimise interactions between humans and marine mammal species that are the subject of tourist interest. Examples include (1) manatee (*Trichechus manatus*), Crystal River National Wildlife Refuge, Florida, created in 1983; (2) humpback whale (*Megaptera novaeangliae*), Stellwagen Bank Sanctuary, Maine, created in 1989 (3) humpback whale, Hawaiian Islands Humpback Whale Sanctuary, Hawaii, created in 1997.

Conclusions

It is argued in this chapter that an understanding of spatial ecology is critical to the effective management of wildlife–tourist interactions. If sustainable development in the field of wildlife-based ecotourism is to be taken seriously, it is necessary that research employing rigorous scientific techniques is undertaken, and that the findings of scientific research are acted upon. A growing appreciation of behaviour change in wildlife populations due to interactions with tourist now exists. Less is known about the biological significance of behaviour changes, and herein lies a critical challenge for environmental and social scientists. Recent research demonstrates that it is necessary to understand and manage the disruption of critical behavioural states in order to mitigate significant consequences for the energetic budget of an animal population. This information provides an important starting point for the delineation of critical habitats based on the collection and analysis of spatio-ecological data. Based on such analyses it is possible to develop management responses that are likely to be most effective in mitigating the effects of tourism activities on wildlife populations. Such an approach can be undertaken in a way that does not jeopardise, but may significantly enhance the sustainability of commercial wildlife–tourism operations.

References

Altman, J. (1974). Observational study of behaviour: sampling methods. *Behaviour* 49: 227–267.

Baker, C.S. and Herman, L.M. (1989). *Behavioural Responses of Summering Humpback Whales to Vessel Traffic: Experimental and Opportunistic Observations*. Final Report to the National Park Service, Alaska Regional Office, Anchorage, AK.

Baker, C.S., Perry, A. and Vequist, G. (1988). Humpback whales of Glacier Bay, Alaska. *Whalewatcher* Fall: 13–17.

Barr, K. (1996). *Impacts of Tourist Vessels on the Behaviour of Dusky Dolphins (Lagenorhynchus obscurus) at Kaikoura*, MSc Thesis, Department of Marine Sciences, University of Otago, Dunedin, New Zealand.

Bejder, L., Dawson, S.M. and Harraway, J.A. (1999). Responses by Hector's dolphins to boats and swimmers in Porpoise Bay, New Zealand. *Marine Mammal Science* 15(3): 738–750.

Blane, J.M. (1990). *Avoidance and Interactive Behaviour of the Saint Lawrence Beluga Whale (Delphinapterus leucas) in Response to Recreational Boating*, MA Thesis, University of Toronto, Toronto, Ont.

Blane, J.M. and Jaakson, R. (1995). The impact of ecotourism boats on the Saint Lawrence beluga whales. *Environmental Conservation* 21(3): 267–269.

Buckingham, C.A., Lefebvre, L.W., Schaefer, J.M. and Kochman, H.I. (1999). Manatee response to boating activity in a thermal refuge. *Wildlife Society Bulletin* 27(2): 514–522.

Campagna, C., Rivarola, M.M., Greene, D. and Tagliorette, A. (1995). *Watching Southern Right Whales in Patagonia*. Unpublished Report to UNEP, Nairobi.

Constantine, R. (1999). Effects of tourism on marine mammals in New Zealand. *Science for Conservation* 106. Department of Conservation, Wellington, New Zealand, 60 pp.

Constantine, R. (2001). Increased avoidance of swimmers by wild bottlenose dolphins (*Tursiops truncatus*) due to long-term exposure to swim-with-dolphin tourism. *Marine Mammal Science* 17(4): 689–702.

Corkeron, P.J. (1995). Humpback whales (*Megaptera novaeangliae*) in Hervey Bay, Queensland: behaviour and responses to whale-watching vessels. *Canadian Journal of Zoology* 73: 1290–1299.

Dawson, S.M. and Slooten, E. (1993). Conservation of Hector's dolphins: the case and process which led to establishment of the Banks Peninsula Marine Mammal Sanctuary. *Aquatic Conservation: Marine and Freshwater Ecosystems* 3: 207–221.

Department of Conservation (1992). Royals keeping out of the limelight. *Otago Daily Times* September 26: 21.

Dickey, A. (2003). *Commercial Ecotourism in New Zealand: A Spatio-temporal Analysis*, Unpublished Dissertation Thesis, Department of Tourism, University of Otago, Dunedin, New Zealand.

Duffus, D.A. and Dearden, P. (1990). Non-consumptive wildlife-oriented recreation: a conceptual framework. *Biological Conservation* 53: 213–231.

Edds, P.L. and MacFarlane, J.A.F. (1987). Occurrence and general behaviour of balaenopterid cetaceans summering in the Saint Lawrence Estuary, Canada. *Canadian Journal of Zoology* 65: 1363-1376.

Gordon, J., Leaper, R., Hartley, F.G. and Chappell, O. (1992). *Effects of Whale Watching on the Surface and Underwater Acoustic Behaviour of Sperm Whales Off Kaikoura, New Zealand*. Department of Conservation Science and Research Series, No. 52.

Higham, J.E.S. (1998). Tourists and Albatrosses: the dynamics of tourism at the Northern Royal Albatross Colony, Taiaroa Head, New Zealand. *Tourism Management* 19(6): 521–533.

Higham, J.E.S. (2001). Managing Ecotourism as Taiaroa Head Royal Albatross Colony. In Shackley, M. (ed.), *Flagship Species: Case Studies in Wildlife Tourism Management*. The International Ecotourism Society, Burlington, VT, pp. 17-31 (0-905488-31-8).

Higham, J.E.S., Carr, A. and Gale, S. (2001). *Ecotourism in New Zealand: Profiling Visitors to New Zealand Ecotourism Operations*. Research Paper No. 10. Department of Tourism, University of Otago, Dunedin, New Zealand.

Janik, V.M. and Thompson, P.M. (1996). Changes in surfacing patterns of bottlenose dolphins in response to boat traffic. *Marine Mammal Science* 12: 597–602.

King, J.M. and Heinen, J.T. (2004). An assessment of the behaviors of overwintering manatees as influenced by interactions with tourists at two sites in central Florida. *Biological Conservation* 117: 227–234.

Kruse, S. (1991). The interactions between killer whales and boats in Johnstone Strait, B.C. In Norris, K.S. and Pryor, K. (eds), *Dolphin Societies: Discoveries and Puzzles*. University of California Press, Berkeley, CA, pp. 149–159.

Lusseau, D. (2003a). Male and female bottlenose dolphins (*Tursiops* spp.) have different strategies to avoid interactions with tour boats in Doubtful Sound, New Zealand. *Marine Ecology Progress Series* 257: 267–274.

Lusseau, D. (2003b). The effects of tour boats on the behavior of bottlenose dolphins: using Markov chains to model anthropogenic impacts. *Conservation Biology* 17(6): 1785–1793.

Lusseau, D. (2004). The energetic cost of path sinuosity related to road density in the wolf community of Jasper National Park. *Ecology and Society* 9(2): r1. Available online at http://www.ecologyandsociety.org/vol9/iss2/resp1

Lusseau, D. and Higham, J.E.S. (2004). Managing the impacts of dolphin-based tourism through the definition of critical habitats: The case of bottlenose dolphins (*Tursiops spp*) in Doubtful Sound, New Zealand. *Tourism Management* 25(5): 657–667.

MacGibbon, J. (1991). *Responses of Sperm Whales (Physeter macrocephalus) to Commercial Whale Watching Boats Off the Coast of Kaikoura*. Unpublished Report to the Department of Conservation, University of Canterbury, Christchurch, New Zealand.

Mann, J. (2000). Unraveling the dynamics of social life. In Mann, J., Connor, R.C., Tyack, P.L. and Whitehead, H. (eds), *Cetacean Societies: Field Studies of Dolphins and Whales*. University of Chicago Press, Chicago, IL, pp. 45-64.

Mills, R.G. (1990). *Royal Albatross Nest-Site Selection*, BSc Hons. (Zoology) Dissertation Thesis, University of Otago, Dunedin, New Zealand.

Novacek, S.M., Wells, R.S. and Solow, A.R. (2001). Short-term effects of boat traffic on bottlenose dolphins, *Tursiops truncatus*, in Sarasota Bay, Florida. *Marine Mammal Science* 17(4): 673–688.

Orams, M.B. (1999). *Marine Tourism: Development, Impacts and Management*. Routledge, London.

Peat, N. (1997). Royal treatment for Taiaroa Head chicks. *Otago Daily Times (Wednesday Magazine)* June 4: 21.

Rees, E.C., Bruce, J.H. and White, G.T. (2005). Factors affecting the behavioural responses of whooper swans (*Cygnus c. Cygnus*) to various human activities. *Biological Conservation* (doi.10.1016/j.biocon.2004.05.009) (in press).

Robertson, C.J.R. (1993a). Effects of nature tourism on marine wildlife. *Proceedings of the Marine Conservation and Wildlife Protection Conference*, Auckland, May 1992.

Robertson, C.J.R. (1993b). *Development of the Royal Albatross Colony and Increasing Tourist Activity at Taiaroa Head, New Zealand*. Department of Conservation Science and Research Series, Wellington, New Zealand.

Robertson, C.J.R. (1993c). *Assessment of Tinted Glass for Public Observatory, Taiaroa Head Nature Reserve*. Conservation Advisory

Science Notes, No. 42. Department of Conservation, Wellington, New Zealand.

Salden, D.R. (1988). Humpback whales encounter rates offshore of Maui, Hawaii. *Journal of Wildlife Management* 52(2): 301–304.

Salvado, C.A.M., Kleiber, P. and Dizon, A.E. (1992). Optimal course by dolphins for detection avoidance. *Fishery Bulletin* 90: 417–420.

Shackley, M. (ed.) (2001). *Flagship Species: Case Studies in Wildlife Tourism Management*. The International Ecotourism Society, Burlington, VT.

Slooten, E., Fletcher, D. and Taylor, B. (2000). Accounting for uncertainty in risk assessment: case study of Hector's dolphin mortality due to gillnet entanglement. *Conservation Biology* 14(5): 1264–1270.

Thompson, P.M., Van Parijs, S. and Kovacs, K.M. (2001). Local declines in the abundance of harbour seals: implications for the designation and monitoring of protected areas. *Journal of Applied Ecology* 38: 117–125.

Whittington, J., St. Clair, C.C. and Mercer, G. (2004). Path tortuosity and the permeability of roads and trails to wolf movement. *Ecology and Society* 9(1): 4. Available online at http://www.ecologyandsociety.org/vol9/iss1/art4/print.pdf (free to download).

Williams, R., Trites, A.W. and Bain, D. (2002). Behavioural responses of killer whales (*Orcinus orca*) to whale-watching boats: opportunistic observations and experimental approaches. *Journal of Zoology* 256: 255–270.

CHAPTER 14

Ecotourism and wildlife habituation

Eric J. Shelton and James Higham

Introduction

Pilot's Beach, situated at the entrance to Otago Harbour, near Dunedin, New Zealand, is visited by tens of thousands of tourists every year. Many are budget travellers; the beach has free and unregulated daytime access. Many originate from the increasing number of cruise ships that visit the harbour. Some arrive in limousines, driven by liveried chauffeurs. A very small number travel in the same vehicle in which Queen Elizabeth travelled on a state visit many years ago. In order to 'do' Pilot's Beach, each of these visitors must pick his or her way past numerous New Zealand fur seals (*Arctocephalus fosterii*) scattered over the landing area. These non-breeding males affect indifference to the tourists' presence; sleeping, or resting on their backs with flippers in the air. In such circumstances animals often are described as being habituated to humans.

There is now a well-established academic tradition of how nature-based tourism may be considered (Garrod, 2006). For the sake of the following discussion we will not differentiate between ecotourism, nature-based tourism and wildlife tourism, although these activities undoubtedly possess different motivations and modes of practice. This tradition comprises Shackley (1996), Higginbottom (2004) and Newsome *et al.* (2004). In each of these contributions to the field the concept of habituation is accepted uncritically, as a unitary phenomenon, and is presented as a negative possible consequence of human–wildlife interaction. Here we argue that this global and stable behavioural descriptor, habituation, is not the most useful way to formulate most observed lack-of-response to visitors and that for optimal management of nature-based tourism a more fine-grained behavioural and temporal approach is required.

Considerations of habituation in ecotourism usefully may consider environmental variables, guiding practice, species-level variables and characteristics of individual animals. Some species contain individuals who demonstrate a well-established response of inquisitiveness to humans or signs of human activity. Gulls are a ubiquitous example. It is reasonable to suppose that some foraging or exploratory event involving humans resulted in food becoming available (a discussion of the contingent and non-contingent dimensions of inquisitiveness is beyond the scope of this chapter). Not often, though, are gulls the focal species of ecotourism, and the formation of superabundant, human-dependent populations, for example of Black-backed gulls (*Larus dominicanus*) at municipal landfills, is of little concern to visitors. Of interest is how best to approach the task of analysing the behaviour of species of tourist interest.

Applied behaviour analysis, based on the notion of stimulus control and situated within learning theory, is well suited to provide a formulative framework for those human/wildlife interactions that are of interest to tourism operators. In wildlife tourism the term habituation frequently is used to describe not only any situation where wildlife tolerate the presence of humans without any obvious signs of physiological or behavioural response but also when animals investigate garbage or approach people (Newsome *et al.*, 2005). Our position is that, to be as useful as possible, consideration of habituation should be distinguished from analysis of foraging or increased approach behaviour, even though the three phenomena regularly occur together (Davis *et al.*, 2002). Park managers in North America attempt to educate the public not to engage in behaviours that will merge habituation and approach-for-food, particularly in the case of deer (The National Park Service, 2006) and bears (Davis *et al.*, 2002). It seems desirable that ecotourism operators actively address separately likely habituation or other conditioning to humans as part of their business plan or concession application. In order to illustrate the tourism management benefits of applying a behavioural formulation to what is commonly called habituation we present below accounts of several typical tourist–wildlife interactions of which we have firsthand knowledge.

Everyday tourist/wildlife interactions in southern New Zealand

Southern New Zealand boasts an appealing range of *charismatic megafauna* and supports a number of ecotourism and nature-based-tourism operators who contribute significantly to the area's tourism industry. Interactions between visitors and various species of wildlife are common and, since in New Zealand there is unrestricted public access to many beaches and almost all of the conservation estate, the vast majority of these interactions involve visitors who are not part of any organised group. It will prove useful for us to accompany a typical tourist couple as they travel along the south coast, encountering on their journey various species with which they form a relationship, however fleeting.

Horst and Gabi are in their mid-twenties and hail from Cologne. The couple have each recently finished university study and are spending 3 months over the southern summer exploring New Zealand. Gabi studied animal behaviour as part of her psychology degree and is particularly interested in how the concept of stimulus control can be used to explain the behaviour of wildlife. In particular, Gabi is keen to observe instances where an initial rate and/or magnitude of approach–avoidance responses have decreased over multiple exposures to the point where an individual animal or group of animals could fairly be described as being habituated to human presence. Horst has visited New Zealand once before, when he joined a 7-day trip to the sub-Antarctic islands and explored Fiordland on another seven-day cruise, including Doubtful Sound and Dusky Sound.

On arriving in Auckland the couple purchased a small van, already fitted out in a rudimentary way for cooking and sleeping, from another young German couple who were about to return home. Although Horst and Gabi do not consider themselves affluent the exchange rate between Euros and New Zealand dollars means that they can travel throughout the country, live simply and purchase almost as many of the available nature-based tourism products as they wish. Still, nothing is quite so rewarding for them as visiting sites independently and experiencing close encounters with wildlife. Although Horst and Gabi have studied the latest *Lonely Planet*, a popular source of information and itinerary planning for visitors to southern New Zealand (Shelton and Duval, 2004), and regularly go online to *Thorntree*'s Australia, New Zealand and Antarctica thread, still they find that they have not allocated enough time to the southern sector of their journey. After visiting the *i-site* visitor information centre at Oamaru Horst and Gabi realise that ideally they would like to observe Little Blue penguins (*Eudyptula minor*) that evening, visit the Moeraki penguin recovery and rehabilitation centre the next day and spend the three subsequent days on Otago Peninsula, touted in the promotional material they have collected as the 'ecotourism capital of New Zealand'. From here the couple plan to travel via the Southern Scenic Route through to the Catlins region. This itinerary will offer these tourists ample opportunities to experience many of the species that comprise the local and regional nature-based tourism product. Also, Horst and Gabi will be able to observe the behaviour of the same species of wildlife in multiple settings.

Little Blue penguins have bred at what is now Oamaru Harbour for centuries. Over 150 years of European settlement they have colonised the local quarry, nested in abandoned cars and raised their clutches of chicks under the floors of private dwellings, commercial premises and an art gallery. Horst and Gabi arrived at the viewing grandstand in plenty of time. The birds were still offshore, forming large noisy rafts. The landing area was well illuminated, using a wavelength that was comfortable for the birds, and the guide was using a public address system to explain what was going to happen. In response to some as-yet-unknown cue the first raft of penguins rushed ashore, moving quickly through the surf and across the exposed littoral margin and then slowing as the birds reached vegetation.

It is challenging to speculate about why exposure to the littoral margin induces massed rushing. There has been no risk of predation in this area, certainly none avoidable by grouping and rushing, for nearly 200 years. The birds are clearly under stimulus control, proximity to the landing site, but the grouping and rushing response seems to be sufficiently hard wired that it is unavailable to modification despite millions of unchallenged landings over many generations of birds. This failure to habituate to the coastline has no obvious evolutionary cost to the species. The lighting, public address system and grandstand full of people do not deter the birds from landing where they have, in recent history, always landed. This lack of avoidance behaviour has not changed over time but seems to be characteristic of this species of penguin. Gabi is convinced that the Little Blue penguins of Oamaru do not demonstrate habituation of approach or avoidance behaviour.

After leaving Oamaru Horst and Gabi drove south on the main highway for about 20 min and turned off to visit the Moeraki penguin treatment and rehabilitation centre, by the lighthouse. On the day they visited there were two Yellow-eyed penguins (*Megadyptes antipodes*), one Snares crested penguin (*Eudyptes robustus*), an Erect-crested penguin (*Eudyptes sclateri*) and one Fiordland crested penguin (*Eudyptes pachyrhynchus*), all receiving treatment for conditions ranging from exhaustion and starvation to bite wounds from barracuda. Every one of the birds was alert to the sounds of humans approaching and each came out to stand close to the wire mesh of the enclosures, ready to be fed. Gabi was curious to know how tame the birds became and whether there was ever any difficulty returning them to the wild once they had recovered; their having become so used to human contact.

The answer was yes and no. As soon as the birds were fit to be released they began to show signs of restlessness though, once released, rarely returned to the breeding population (McKinlay *et al.*, 2004). Being placed back in the sea was not a strong enough stimulus to trigger a return to whatever home range they had been collected from, injured, or driven from by storms. While in Auckland Horst and Gabi had visited *Antarctic Encounter and Underwater World* and seen the Adelie penguins (*Pygoscelis adeliae*) transferred there from Antarctica. These birds had seemed well settled into their new home, and approached whatever staff member came to feed them. That setting, though, approximated as closely as possible the

Antarctic environment that the birds were used to, there were enough birds to induce normal social behaviour and every effort was made to ensure that the birds came to perceive staff as sources of food, rather than being indifferent towards them. Still, questions formed in Gabi's mind about exactly what controlled approach/avoidance behaviour in different species of penguin in the three settings she had experienced. At Moeraki the Yellow-eyed penguins had seemed the most unresponsive to human proximity. Gabi looked forward to observing the behaviour of this species again, on Otago Peninsula, in a quite different setting.

Dunedin was only an hour down the road and Horst and Gabi already had planned their itinerary. On the first day the couple intended taking a short cruise on the *Monarch* to view sea birds and marine mammals, a guided tour of the Royal Albatross colony at Taiaroa Head, a short visit to Pilot's Beach and a guided tour of a Yellow-eyed penguin reserve at *Penguin Place*. As they board the *Monarch* Horst spotted a Little Blue penguin swimming within 3 m of the moored boat seemingly oblivious to the vibration of the engine or the noise of the passengers on deck. This species really did seem to ignore human presence across settings. Gabi was still not convinced that this behaviour illustrates habituation though, since the Little Blue had not demonstrated decreasing avoidance behaviour, but seemed to be have been tolerant of humans right from first contact. This intrinsic tolerance characterised the three species of shag that the *Monarch* sailed close by. Taiaroa Head is the only place where Spotted shags (*Stictocarbo punctatus*), Stewart Island shags (*Leucocarbo chalconotus*) and Little shags (*Phalacrocorax melanoleucos*) all nest in the same area and individual shags of all three species go about their business of diving, surfacing and warming with outstretched wings just as they do anywhere else on the coast.

Despite repeated exposure to *Monarch*'s passing near to where they perch the proximity that these birds will tolerate, although satisfyingly close for the tourists, does not seem to have changed over 20 years and several generations. The balance between intrinsic tolerance and socially learned tolerance has not been explored. Some other bird species, specifically New Zealand dabchick (*Poliocephalus rufopectus*), have been shown to habituate to passing boats (Bright *et al.*, 2003). Horst noted that an intense stare was enough to cause a shag to dive or fly from its perch on a channel marker. The tolerance of human proximity clearly was to certain behaviours only. As *Monarch* passed a series of gun emplacements, dating from the Russian expansionism scares of the 1880s and refurbished to rebuff Japanese expansionism in World War Two, the skipper told of a solitary adult male New Zealand sea lion who had positioned himself there the previous autumn, swimming out, charging and sometimes biting the passing kayaks of a commercial operator. At other times of the day this individual hauled out on nearby Te Rauone beach where he tolerated close approaches by visitors. No one was sure why this sea lion's agonistic approach behaviour was limited to this one site, only 300 m from where he displayed indifference. Repeated exposure to kayakers, at this time of year, did not decrease what was almost certainly some kind of territorial behaviour. This seasonality of response strength to kayaks made Gabi wonder if habituation also may have a temporal aspect. Perhaps a later encounter with another species would clarify this point.

An adult Elephant seal (*Mirounga leonine*) weighing about three tonnes was hauled out on a rock ledge about a metre above the current tide mark. The skipper explained that the seal landed on the ledge at high tide, slept for 12 h, and then rolled back into the water on the next tide. Gabi was interested to note that the seal showed no sign of noticing the boat; its eyes remained closed. Given that the seal was effectively confined to the rock ledge no elements of the seal's approach or avoidance behavioural repertoire were available to it, awake or asleep. The ledge seemed the choice of an animal singularly confident of remaining unmolested. Estimating that the seal was about 4 years old, and assuming it most likely hailed from sub-Antarctic Campbell Island, then the only human contact it could plausibly have had was limited to juvenile exposure to two or three groups of visitors per year to North West Bay. Horst recalled how, when he had visited North West Bay on Campbell Island, juvenile Elephant seals had approached his tour party and investigated them at close range. This Taiaroa Head adult's lack of interest very probably reflected a decreasing exploratory behaviour as a consequence of maturation rather than through repeated exposure to humans. The encounter did raise an issue of interest, what are the naturally occurring contingencies and physiological processes that operate to reduce exploratory behaviour during maturation from neonate through juvenile to adult? Repeated non-consequential exposure to a range of human behaviours needed to be situated somewhere in this process.

Monarch passed on through Taiaroa Head and when about a kilometre offshore was approached from the stern by a Buller's mollymawk (*Diomedea cauta eremita*) who soon departed after an investigatory fly past. The skipper explained that this opportunistic approach behaviour was generalised from the birds' habit of following fishing boats whose crews were gutting offshore.

A Giant petrel (*Macronectes giganteus*) responded to *Monarch*'s presence in a similar way. A couple of Northern Royal albatross (*Diomedea epomophora sanfordi*) glided past without deviating to investigate. These birds had fed nearly at the coast of South America and were returning to feed their chicks after some days away. Gabi was intrigued at how the *Monarch* had acted as a stimulus for approach for individuals of two species but not for the third. Despite daily exposure to the boat, and never having been fed, the exploratory approach behaviour persisted. Perhaps the mollymawks and the petrel simply could not distinguish *Monarch* from a fishing boat or, with so little energy needing to be expended to complete an investigation, perhaps approaching every boat just in case gutting commenced was an optimal feeding strategy.

On the return journey into Otago Harbour *Monarch* nudged to within 2 m of the rocky outcrop populated by breeding female fur seals and their young pups. Neither mothers nor pups showed any behavioural reaction to the boat. Gabi was confident that here was an example of habituation in a natural setting but when the skipper explained that *Monarch* and its passengers had been a part of each pup's experience since the day it was born, she reconsidered. With such early exposure, in the presence of an unresponsive mother, and to the extent that avoidance behaviour is socially acquired, the pups may never have perceived *Monarch* as a stimulus for flight. Presumably pups varied in their post-weaning exploratory audacity and some, having moved around the site once in the presence of humans with no ill-effects, would begin to include indifference in their behavioural repertoire. Each uneventful visit would reduce the discriminative value of humans. The mothers were more problematic. Those adult females who had been born at the colony could conceivably have retained their neonate indifference but those recruited from other colonies, for example the one at Sandfly Bay where they had exhibited an avoidance response to human approach, would be good candidates for illustrating socially acquired habituation through their peers modelling indifference. The complexities of seal habituation to human approach, including the confounding effect of probable previous exposure, have been investigated (van Polanen Petel, 2005). This author suggests that a species-specific approach utilising Proportional Odds Regression Modelling (PORM), to generate impact contour maps for individual settings, offers a promising approach to managing human/wildlife interactions optimally.

Once ashore Horst and Gabi visited the nearby *Royal Albatross Centre*. Visitor interaction with Northern Royal albatross at Taiaroa Head is closely monitored (Higham, 1998) and tourists are confined to a soundproof hide glazed with reflective glass. The intention clearly was that the nesting birds remain unaware of human presence. Of course the birds, when in the air, have a clear view of the tens of thousands of visitors annually to the colony, and frequently are exposed to close attention from conservation staff, including handling. As Horst watched the birds' responses to staff handling them during weighing and measuring he was struck by the persistence of their defensive use of their beaks, in just the same way as the albatross he had seen previously on Campbell Island. Despite having been handled periodically over the years since their hatching these birds did not seem to have habituated to this particular human behaviour. Horst was well aware of the issue of scale. Although there had been no apparent change in the gross motor component of the birds' defence rituals there may well have been reductions in human-induced physiological arousal. Such physiological information most usually is collected using a data recorder disguised as an egg but in this case such an approach cannot be justified since the number of breeding albatross at the colony is low and artificial eggs are used only to keep birds, who have lost their own egg for any reason, on the nest when otherwise they may abandon it.

A 200-m walk down the hill brought Horst and Gabi to Pilot's Beach. True to form several New Zealand fur seals were stretched out on the rock platform asleep. Gabi sat down near one and gingerly inched towards its face. The seal must have been conscious of her scent at this range but remained unresponsive. Horst stepped back to capture the moment on camera and in doing so brushed against a seal lying behind him. The seal lifted its head and gave a gruff bark, then settled back to sleep again. Gabi and Horst agreed that this behaviour was worthy of study. These non-breeding apparently placid males, while content to ignore visitors walking by them on land, regularly showed ritualised aggression to swimmers in the shallow water of the same beach. Also, every now and then a particular seal would display aggression on land, quickly being dubbed by ecotourism operators as a 'bad tempered' or 'cranky' individual. This range of behavioural responses to the presence of humans militates against describing the animals as habituated. Rather, such variability begged the question: which individual animals or groups of animals would respond in what fashion to what kind of tourist behaviour in what contexts? Other individual seals in this setting, or these individual seals in other settings may not be so sanguine. Still, Pilot's Beach, where a particular set of contingencies operated to induce decreasing gross behavioural responsiveness, on land, to a fairly narrow set of visitor behaviours, in a group of seals who shared non-breeding status, provided good evidence of spatially and temporally bounded habituation. The responsiveness of physiological processes within individual seals, the role of developmental maturation and the influence of vicarious or social learning through the observation of calm conspecifics remain unexamined, although available for formulation.

After leaving Pilot's Beach Horst and Gabi drove their van about 2 km to *Penguin Place* where a previously unregulated beach habitat has been transformed into a penguin conservation area and ecotourism product. Visitors moved through shoulder-high trenches and then occupied underground hides in order to observe Yellow-eyed penguins at close range. Approach/avoidance was at the discretion of the individual penguin. On this trip several penguins individually approached the observation slit in the hide, and looked directly in at the visitors, before heading to their nests. Gabi was satisfied that approach behaviour had not habituated but avoidance behaviour may well have decreased over the years, as the guide reported new recruits to the colony became less timid with time. Horst volunteered that approach behaviour could easily be misattributed. The impact of humans on this most phlegmatic but inquisitive of penguins is the subject of ongoing study (Seddon *et al.*, 2004). The birds' possible increased tolerance of humans at one end of another still unregulated beach, Sandfly Bay, has been noted (Shelton and Lubcke, 2005), based on several thousand unstructured guiding observations. Measuring penguin habituation using solely approach/avoidance behaviour is inappropriate since physiological arousal fluctuates independent of observable behaviour (Ellenberg and Mattern, 2004) and the relationship varies between penguin species (Ellenberg *et al.*, 2006).

This poor fit between observable behaviour and internal state is not confined to penguins. The behaviour of fantails/ *piwakawaka* (*Rhipidura fuliginosa*) is typically misleading. Visitors often encounter the situation where they are walking along a bush track and suddenly numerous fantails appear and flutter tantalisingly close-by. Many visitors assume that it is their presence that has attracted the birds and offer up a finger for them to alight upon. The proffered finger is almost always ignored. What is in fact attracting the fantails are the small flies that have risen from the leaf litter as a result of human disturbance. Fantails feed on-the-wing and this explains the darting about in proximity to humans. The attraction to visitors in the bush is indirect in that people act as a discriminative stimulus for a likely disturbed forest floor, and consequent available prey. The New Zealand wood pigeon/*kereru* (*Hemiphaga novaseelandiae*), in the south, frequents some urban areas, particularly Dunedin city, and can appear to be indifferent to everyday human activity. Closer analysis reveals seasonal variations in the species' tolerance of humans. During late July and early August *kereru* are at their minimum body weight and are reduced to eating relatively unpalatable fare, for example coarse leaves. As the *kowhai* (*Sophora* spp.) begin to flower the pigeons gorge themselves, characteristically stripping branches of many new shoots, leaves and flowers, and as they do so move outward until a branch has been bent almost to breaking point. Being large, heavy birds *kereru* inevitably lose height as they commence flight, and must complete a swooping arc before heading off in the desired direction. It is at the point of flight that the birds' seasonal variation in avoidance behaviour is manifest. Undisturbed, the pigeon will climb back along the branch until it reaches a suitably elevated position. If visitors happen to be passing when the bird is close to the ground, and pay no attention, then the gorging pigeon will accommodate their proximity. If, however, the visitors stop, or stare directly at the bird, it will take flight even though this involves a clumsy manoeuvre. As the season progresses, and food becomes more abundant, *kereru* increasingly favour branches higher up in trees, and rarely then respond to human activity around them.

Rather than describing urban-dwelling *kereru* as habituated to humans it is clearly more useful to elucidate precisely what role people are playing as discriminative stimuli. People minding their own business, presumably measured by their unmodified patterns of movement, uninterrupted chatter and non-bird-directed gaze, act as discriminative stimuli for approach tolerance. A sudden silence, ceasing walking or bird-directed gaze acts as stimuli for flight. The paradox for the ecotour operator who intends that visitors experience pigeons close-up is that the best advice to be given is to ignore them. Natural settings do not offer the frequency of close contact that would be required to attempt deliberately to manipulate the birds' existing responses. These two examples illustrate a more general concern with how humans can best interact with multiple species of birds in urban areas (Blumstein *et al.*, 2005).

Another case of misattribution involves a local cetacean. On Horst's last visit he had encountered Bottlenose dolphins (*Tursiops truncatus*) in Doubtful Sound, in Fiordland. These marine mammals had entertained the visitors on the tour boat with their bowriding and leaping out of the water. Every one of the visitors told Horst that they believed the dolphins engaged in this behaviour by choice. Power boats, though, act as a stimulus for dolphins not to rest; that is, bowriding and leaping are more likely to be under stimulus control and therefore not the result of choice. There are clear potential negative impacts of decreased resting on this species, including a disrupted energy budget and likely compromised reproductive success (Higham and Lusseau, 2004; Lusseau and Higham, 2004). Repeated exposure to craft does not seem to reduce the strength of the dolphins' approach responses and this situation clearly demonstrates the difficulties inherent in referring to stable or increasing approach behaviour as habituation. Management strategies should, in this case, explore ways of *inducing* habituation; that is, reducing the dolphin's responsiveness to the presence of tourist vessels. The deliberate induction of habituation as a positive management tool has received little attention. One attempt to have the proposition considered (Shelton et al., 2004) was received unsympathetically by an audience of biological scientists and wildlife managers, on the grounds that habituation, (as commonly misunderstood) *by definition*, was undesirable. Yet, deliberate habituation is used in the laboratory.

In New Zealand, avian fauna provides considerable raw material for ecotourism. This fauna is under acute and chronic threat from introduced predators. A major conservation focus is *Restoring the Dawn Chorus* (Department of Conservation, 2006). In order to achieve this objective it is crucial to understand the reproductive processes of the primary pests. This understanding requires live capture from the wild and subsequent study of these individuals in captivity. 'Stoats (*Mustela erminea*) are one of New Zealand's most destructive predators and are implicated in the continuing decline of native bird species' (O'Connor et al., 2006). Captive study requires these predators to be acclimatised to the laboratory. This acclimatisation involves the individual stoat habituating to the sounds of human activity and then recognising the sounds associated with food presentation and treating them as a cue to feed rather than as a cue to flee. Could exposure to humans, in the wild, ever be beneficial to a species? One promising observation, that repeated exposure to tourists appeared to lower corticosterone levels in marine iguana (Romero and Wikelsi, 2002), and that this outcome may be beneficial to this animal, creates another cell in the response-to-humans matrix. Lowering corticosterone production in response to human interaction, compared with animals who have no human interaction, demonstrates sensitisation, the opposite of habituation. In this case the sensitisation may legitimately be labelled *paradoxical sensitisation*. Of course one study is inconclusive but it does raise an intriguing possibility. If robust, this finding implies that chronic sub-optimal physiological processes may be a naturally occurring phenomenon.

Discussion

In this chapter we have utilised the not at all far-fetched conceit of Horst and Gabi's search for evidence of habituation: 'a decrease in the strength of a response after repeated presentations of a stimulus that elicits that response' (Mazur, 2006). This discussion is predicated on the proposition that ecotourism operators who are committed to providing a sustainable nature-based product will be interested to know how their activities may be influencing the environments in which they do business. The inherent tensions between business practice and sustainability in nature-based tourism have been well described (Fennell, 2003; McKercher, 1993a, 1993b, 1998; Newsome *et al.*, 2005). As nature-based products are offered in more and more remote places it becomes more and more likely that any given individual animal will encounter humans, engaged in particular behaviours, at some stage of its life. The animal may approach the human, as many neonates and juveniles of many species do. If, on repeated exposure to this particular human behaviour, this approach behaviour decreases, and is not replaced by escape/avoidance behaviour, then the animal may accurately be described as being habituated to the human behaviour to which it has been exposed, in a particular setting. If the animal increases its escape/avoidance response then it has become sensitised to this human behaviour in this setting.

This habituation/sensitisation process is dynamic, and may reflect the hormonal balance of the individual animal at the time of exposure to the particular human behaviour. If the individual animal demonstrated indifference to the human behaviour right from the start then habituation is not the best term to use to describe the situation; tolerance or resilience may be more useful. Similarly, animals may respond to human activity through increases in physiological processes, commonly grouped under the term *arousal*. Decreasing physiological arousal upon repeated exposure indicates habituation, increased arousal indicates sensitisation. We have tentatively labelled the unusual situation where an initially high level of arousal may be reduced by exposure to human activity *paradoxical sensitisation*. It is possible also for wildlife to decrease one response to human presence, for example fleeing, but to increase another response. Chimpanzees' activity rates in Kibale Forest, Uganda, habituate to the presence of increasing numbers of observers but vocalisation increases (Johns, 1996).

It is useful at this point to address two issues. Firstly, why is it important to specify what human behaviours, in what settings and at what times that individual animals may habituate to, and avoid the simpler descriptor; habituation to humans? Habituation to humans, by definition, involves decreased vigilance in response to human presence, decreased communication of alarm upon coming across humans and decreased avoidance of, or fleeing from, humans. The argument then is that habituated animals are made vulnerable in that habituation to one potential predator, *Homo sapiens*, will induce a generalised reduction of predator-preparedness (Beale and Monaghan, 2004). We argue that this concern evaporates when habituation is more usefully formulated. If habituation is related to spatially and temporally constrained specific human behaviours, rather than simply to human presence, then it is reasonable to hypothesise that individual animals will retain predator-preparedness outside of these parameters. Discriminating between human behaviours is consistent with laboratory-based enquiry that has demonstrated that many species have the ability to discriminate even between individual human beings performing the same behaviours (Davis, 2002). Predator-preparedness training in birds, in common with exploratory behaviours (Huber *et al.*, 2001), can occur through social learning. For example adult Sandhill cranes teach predator-preparedness by modelling vigilance and predator-response even to unrelated captive-reared conspecific chicks (Heatley, 1995). There is debate about how possible habituation to human activity acquired while in captivity, for example in a rehabilitation facility, should be managed. A fine-grained analysis is available addressing the issue of how much deliberate training-for-release should take place, what such training should comprise and exactly how humans should be involved in its delivery (Bauer, 2005).

It is reasonable to suppose that habituation can be socially learned also in natural settings, and be passed on in a sophisticated rather than generalised way. Different species teach their offspring different sensitivities. For cliff-dwelling birds visited by tourists, size-of-party has been reported to have species-specific effects (Beale and Monaghan, 2005). It is not unreasonable to suggest that certain species may teach their young not to respond to a particular wildlife guide, acting within certain behavioural limits. A photo of Prince Charles crouching within a metre of a nesting albatross and its chick at the Taiaroa Head colony (New Zealand Department of Conservation: Te Papa Atawhai, 2005) may well have been possible only because the prince was accompanied by a guide familiar to the bird.

The second issue that needs to be addressed is one of management. If, as we argue, many behaviours of many species can be brought under stimulus control, then what happens to the *wild* in *wild*life? The application of stimulus control techniques to the management of human behaviour is widely reported in the Applied Behaviour Analysis literature. Using the nuanced approach to habituation outlined above it is conceivable that wildlife managers and visitor managers could cooperate to apply behavioural technologies to structure almost completely the nature of human/wildlife interactions site-by-site, species-by-species and taking into account time of day and time of year. This level of management, although common in captive settings, if applied to natural settings would challenge directly Horst and Gabi's motivation for visiting such sites in the first place. Nonetheless, our position is that, in certain cases, the conservation outcomes available using such an approach may be justified.

References

Bauer, G. (2005). Research training for releasable animals. *Conservation Biology* 19(6): 1779–1789.

Beale, C. and Monaghan, P. (2004). Human disturbance: people as predation-free predators? *Journal of Applied Ecology* 41: 335–343.

Beale, C. and Monaghan, P. (2005). Modeling the effects of limiting number of visitors on failure rates of seabird nests. *Conservation Biology* 19(6): 2015–2019.

Blumstein, D., Fernandez-Juricic, E., Zollner, P. and Garity, S. (2005). Inter-specific variation in avian responses to human disturbance. *Journal of Applied Ecology* 42(5): 943–953.

Bright, A., Reynolds, G., Innes, J. and Waas, J. (2003). Effects of motorised boat passes on the time budget of New Zealand dabchick, *Poliocephalus rufopectus*. *Wildlife Research* 30: 237–244.

Davis, H. (2002). Prediction and preparation: Pavlovian implications of research animals discriminating among humans. *Institute for Laboratory Animal Research* 43(1): 19–26.

Davis, H., Wellwood, D. and Ciarniello, L. (2002). *'Bear Smart' Community Program: Background Report*. British Columbia Ministry of Water, Land and Air Protection, Victoria, BC.

Ellenberg, U. and Mattern, T. (2004). The most timorous of all? Impact of human disturbance on Humboldt penguins. *New Zealand Journal of Zoology* 31: 120–121.

Ellenberg, U., Mattern, T., Seddon, P.J. and Jorquera, G.L. (2006). Physiological and reproductive consequences of human disturbance in Humboldt penguins: the need for species-specific visitor management. *Biological Conservation* 133(1): 95–106.

Fennell, D. (2003). *Ecotourism: An introduction* (2nd edn). Routledge, London.

Heatley, J. (1995). *Antipredator conditioning in Mississippi Sandhill cranes (Grus canadensis pulla)*. Unpublished MSc Thesis, Texas A&M University.

Higginbottom, K. (ed.) (2004). *Wildlife Tourism: Impacts, Management and Planning*. Altona, Vic.: Common Ground Publishing.

Higham, J.E.S. (1998). Tourists and albatrosses: the dynamics of tourism at the Northern Royal Albatross Colony, Taiaroa Head, New Zealand. *Tourism Management* 19: 521–531.

Higham, J.E.S. and Lusseau, D. (2004). Ecological impacts and management of tourist engagements with Cetaceans. In Buckley, R. (ed.), *Environmental Impacts of Ecotourism*. CAB International, Wallingford, pp. 173–188.

Huber, L., Rechberger, S. and Taborsky, M. (2001). Social learning affects object exploration and manipulation in keas, *Nestor notabilis*. *Animal Behaviour* 62: 945–954.

Johns, B. (1996). Responses of chimpanzees to habituation and tourism in the Kibale Forest, Uganda. *Biological Conservation* 78: 257–262.

Lusseau, D. and Higham, J.E.S. (2004). Managing the impacts of dolphin-based tourism through the definition of critical habitats: the case of bottlenose dolphins (*Tursiops* spp.) in Doubtful Sound, New Zealand. *Tourism Management*, 25(5): 657–667.

Mazur, J. (2006). *Learing and Behaviour* (6th edn). Pearson Prentice Hall, Upper Saddle River, NJ.

McKercher, B. (1993a). The unrecognised threat to tourism: Can tourism survive 'sustainability'? *Tourism Management* 14(2): 131–136.

McKercher, B. (1993b). Some fundamental truths about tourism: understanding tourism's social and environmental impacts. *Journal of Sustainable Tourism* 1(1): 6–16.

McKercher, B. (1998). *The Business of Nature-Based Tourism*. Hospitality Press, Melbourne.

McKinlay, B., Houston, D. and Jones, J. (2004). Rehabilitation of injured or starving Yellow-eyed penguins (*Megadyptes antipodes*) at Katiki Point 1990–2000: a review of records. *New Zealand Journal of Zoology* 31: 119.

New Zealand Department of Conservation: Te Papa Atawhai (2005). *Conservation Action: Te Ngangahau ki te Taiao*. New Zealand Department of Conservation: Te Papa Atawhai, Wellington.

Newsome, D., Dowling, R. and Moore, S. (2005). *Wildlife Tourism*. Channel View, Clevedon.

O'Connor, C., Turner, J., Scobie, S. and Duckworth, J. (2006). *Stoat reproductive biology*. Retrieved August 4, 2006, from http://www.doc.govt.nz/publications/004%7escience-and-research/Science-for-Conservation/PDF/sfc268.pdf

Romero, L. and Wikelsi, M. (2002). Exposure to tourism reduces stress-induced corticosterone levels in Galapagos marine iguanas. *Biological Conservation* 108, 371–374.

Seddon, P., Smith, A., Dunlop, E. and Mathieu, R. (2004). Tourist visitor attitudes, activities and impacts at a Yellow-eyed penguin breeding site on the Otago Peninsula, Dunedin, New Zealand. *New Zealand Journal of Zoology* 31: 119–120.

Shelton, E.J., Higham, J.E.S. and Seddon, P. (2004). Habituation, penguin research and ecotourism: some thoughts from left field. *New Zealand Journal of Zoology*, 31(4): 119.

Shelton, E.J. and Lubcke, H. (2005). Penguins as sights, penguins as sites: the problematics of contestation. In Hall, C.M. and Boyd, S. (eds), *Nature-Based Tourism in Peripheral Areas: Development or Disaster?* Channelview Publications, Clevedon, pp. 218–230.

The National Park Service (2006). *Deer and people at Fire Island National Seashore*. Retrieved 22 June, 2006, from http://www.nps.gov/fiis/deerpeople/deer.html

van Polanen Petel, T. (2005). *Effects of human activity on Weddell seals (Leptonychotes weddellii) in Antarctica*. Retrieved 23 June, 2006, from http://www.crctourism.com.au/CRCServer/documents/education/TamaraCompletion_report.doc

Ecotourism and biodiversity conservation in Asia: institutional challenges and opportunities

Janet Cochrane

Introduction

An Indonesian on-line bulletin of tourism matters reported in 2005 that the head of the tourism office in East Java was seeking investment support for a cable-car at Mount Bromo (BisnisBali, 2005). For decades, people have trekked, ridden (or more recently driven) across a mile or so of flat, lava-ash plain known as the Sand Sea and climbed a steep flight of steps to stand on the narrow rim of the crater of Mount Bromo, peer into the glowing depths of the live volcano and watch the sun rise across the dramatic landscape. With the cable-car, the trip would be accomplished in a few minutes and with less effort, and would encourage the rapid tourism development of Bromo Tengger Semeru National Park, currently thwarted by lack of infrastructure.

Leaving aside the safety and technical challenges of installing a cable-car at an active volcano, the most interesting aspects of this proposal were its assumption of how the leisure needs of visitors might be satisfied and its failure to mention any aesthetic or environmental impacts of the scheme, despite its intended imposition on one of the most iconic protected landscapes in Indonesia. In the Asian context, however, the proposal was not as bizarre as it appears to Western observers, in that similar major infrastructural interventions have been proposed or created in protected areas elsewhere in Asia. For example, a road was proposed to link highland resorts in Malaysia in the 1990s, despite its potential impact on forests and wildlife (Mitton, 1997); the top of Mount Wudang, in China, is accessed by thousands of tourists each day via a cable-car, despite its religious and cultural significance (Sofield and Li, 2003); and the Bailong 'Sightseeing Elevator' is just one among several similar installations at the Zhangjiajie National Park, also in China (Chen *et al.*, 2006).

Such developments raise questions on the acceptable balance between satisfying the short-term physical and social needs of humans for economic welfare and leisure, and the longer-term need to protect the environment. These issues will be explored through examples from Asia, where ecotourism has become a significant form of economic use of protected areas, either as a strategically planned element of development or through spontaneous, market-led growth. The position of ecotourism in relation to Asian tourism generally will be examined and will include a discussion of domestic tourism, whose contribution to tourism flows and processes is often overlooked. The way ecotourism is developing is grounded in societal attitudes towards economic activity, biodiversity conservation and sustainability. It will be argued that indigenous attitudes towards biodiversity conservation and protected areas in Asia are often at variance with

Western norms, and that these differences are expressed through formal and informal institutional arrangements for ecotourism. The limitations to ecotourism's contribution to conservation will also be discussed, along with initiatives designed to overcome these.

Although much ecotourism takes place outside protected areas, in this chapter the discussion will focus mostly on activities taking place within them, since institutional constraints on stronger links between tourism and conservation are most prominent here. The meaning of 'ecotourism' used will be towards the weaker end of the spectrum, in other words 'tourism which takes place in natural areas'. In many cases, the examples given here would not qualify as ecotourism under the more rigorous definition used by The International Ecotourism Society and refined by authors such as Ceballos-Lascurain (1996) and Eagles *et al.* (2002), whose guidelines aim to confine ecotourism to a set of practices concerning conscious contribution to biodiversity and local socio-economic welfare. It is recognised that the term is often a form of communicative staging which masks the environmental damage caused by tourism: in Thailand, for example, criticism has been directed at the use of 'ecotourism' to subvert the purpose of protected areas from conservation to commercial ends (Pholpoke, 1998). But the reality is that 'ecotourism' has such popular appeal that commercial organisations are unlikely to relinquish it as a marketing tool, while government agencies and NGOs see it as a useful way of trying to combine the objectives of economic development and environmental conservation.

Ecotourism in Asia

The growth of tourism in Asia has been a major tourism industry phenomenon of the last quarter century. Over the decade 1980–1990 international tourism grew at an annual average rate of 4.7%, while Asia and the Pacific experienced double this rate, at 9.4%. In 1990–2000 average growth was slower internationally and regionally because of heightened fear of international insecurity and, in the last part of the decade, slower economic growth in Asia, but the relative figures were still 4.4% for global growth and 7.1% for the Asia–Pacific region (UNWTO, 2006). Since 2000 growth has been further stimulated by deregulation of aviation within Asia, with – despite initial protectionism – a vast expansion of regional low-cost carriers (Kua and Baum, 2004; Cambridge and Whitelegg, 2006). The figures reflect the region's increasing prosperity, shown in higher levels of travel for both business and leisure purposes.

Throughout much of Asia, nature-based tourism has so far been a low priority because tourism has been used as a key tool for economic development and diversification through export-oriented growth strategies, and governments have concentrated on industry segments which offer a quick economic return through increased investment, taxes, employment and direct expenditure by tourists. The principal draw for major international markets is the well-established 'beach-with-cultural-overtones' model, building on the attributes common to many Asian countries of a warm climate, extensive coastline, attractive scenery and hospitable local people offering a diversity of easily assimilated cultural manifestations. Nevertheless, an awareness of the need to diversify markets and create new products to satisfy changing demand has led many countries to look towards ecotourism as a niche market, which because of the frequently high spend of participants is a significant one. In 2000 Malaysia's Ministry of Culture, Arts and Tourism worked with WWF to produce a National Ecotourism Plan (Musa, 2002) and the state of Sabah has been particularly successful in developing a range of activities around Mount Kinabalu, its remaining 'jungle' environment of rainforests and rivers, and its offshore islands.

Land-locked countries such as Nepal and Laos have been forced, for obvious reasons, to complement their cultural attributes with activity tourism rather than a beach-resort model. In Nepal, the principal activity is trekking, while in Laos the government has deliberately chosen ecotourism as a strategy to meet the development needs of poorer, marginalised groups in outlying regions, and is targeting the high-value, longer-staying markets from Europe, North America and the Antipodes (Lao NTA, 2005). Manifestations of ecotourism vary enormously across Asia. On the one hand, there is a small scale, conscious appreciation of nature by people who focus on particular elements, such as bird-watchers, botanical hunters or sub-aqua divers, who require small-scale facilities and knowledgeable personnel to service their needs. At the other end of the spectrum, there are people who visit natural areas as a pleasant backdrop to standard recreational activities, such as picnicking with family and friends, without venturing far from the convenience of transport and shops. Recreational facilities are created to cater to these groups and in some places, such as the Chinese parks mentioned above, a substantial artificial infrastructure has been created to allow people access to key sites. In between these extremes, there are people keen to undertake adventure activities such as hiking up mountains and white-water rafting, or a gentler encounter with the outdoors such as camping or exploring canopy walkways.

The style of enjoyment of parks to a great extent depends on the origin of the visitor. Research into foreign and domestic users of national parks in Malaysia found that while Westerners sought an authentic wilderness experience, domestic tourists were looking for relatively they could enjoy more standard 'leisure' type amenities such as fishing or enjoying an outing with friends and family (Backhaus, 2001). A 1995 study in Thailand showed that the most popular activities for domestic visitors to Khao Yai National Park focussed on enjoyment of the natural environment but in a fairly passive way, such as visiting waterfalls, viewing the scenery and taking leisurely walks (TDRI, 1995). Hannam (2005) shows that Western and local tourists had different expectations of the Rajiv Gandhi National Park, in India, with the former seeking a contemplative experience while the latter had more hedonistic expectations. Such differences are partly due to development stages of the relevant markets, and partly to culturally determined perceptions of wilderness and acceptance of collective or individualistic behaviour. These characteristics have implications for the institutional organisation of tourism in national parks and are reflected in the structure and ethos of the institutions themselves.

First, the level of development of market segments has an important effect on consumer behaviour in relation to tourism, including ecotourism. Currently, East Asian markets are relatively unsophisticated, with a focus on heavily packaged tours with relatively unadventurous itineraries. This early stage of market evolution is most clearly seen in China, where the government is gradually awarding 'Approved Destination Status' to an increasing number of receiving countries (meaning that they are licensed to receive officially sanctioned tour groups from China). In the countries affected, this has not resulted in the expected sudden influx and dispersal of large numbers of Chinese visitors to a wide spread of attractions, but in a small trickle of groups briefly visiting a few prescribed locations. Similarly, East Asian groups (from South Korea, Taiwan and Hong Kong) visiting Bromo Tengger Semeru spend only two hours in the national park, which is precisely long enough to visit its principal attraction of Mount Bromo, as compared to an average of 1 or 2 days for domestic and Western tourists (Cochrane, 2006).

While international and intra-regional tourism are important for earning foreign exchange, domestic markets are even more significant in redistributing wealth from towns and cities to rural areas, and in satisfying the leisure needs of increasingly urbanised populations. Since the 1970s, no one visiting popular natural attractions in wealthy regions of Asia at weekends or public holidays can fail to have been struck by the large crowds of local holiday-makers. In China, the introduction of a 2-day weekend in the mid-1990s and of 3-week long annual holidays in 1999, combined with the gradual shift from a planned to a market economy, provided the conditions for growth in travel. The first 'wave' of holiday exploration has been within the country, and natural attractions are extremely popular: Wang and Qu (2004) found that being outdoors amidst natural scenery was the most popular leisure activity for Chinese domestic tourists, who also sought a nostalgic encounter with idealised landscapes through their leisure visits to parks (Kolås, 2004). The story is similar elsewhere in Asia. Hamzah *et al.* (2003) comment on the popularity of natural attractions for Malaysia, Kaosa-ard *et al.* (2001) remark that seaside and mountains are favourite destinations in Thailand for local visitors, and interviews by the author with domestic tourists in Indonesia have shown that many people, recently enfranchised by increasing prosperity and a more liberal socio-political climate, are keen to gaze on the natural beauty of their country outside their home regions.

The size of Asian populations – especially in China and India – and the growing class of mobile, higher-income people mean that numbers of visitors at protected areas can be considerable. For instance at Pangandaran, on the south coast of densely populated Java, sandy beaches on either side of a narrow isthmus are set off by scenery of sunsets and sunrises, and sea cliffs and coastal forest protected by a nature reserve. The resort is relatively small, but received nearly 2 million visitors in 2003 (Pikiran Rakyat, 2004). Similar patterns are reported elsewhere in Asia: Khao Yai National Park, in Thailand, received 4.8 million visitors in 2002 (Ross, 2003), and Sofield and Li (2003) comment on the very large numbers of visitors at natural sites in China.

Throughout Asia there is recognition that high-volume intra-regional and domestic markets will grow in importance, and these markets will undoubtedly diversify as the travelling public becomes more experienced. There will be opportunities for 'soft' nature-based products close to tourist hubs such as river rafting in Bali and trips to the canopy walkway at Poring, in Sabah – although it is likely that environmental compromises will result where economic imperatives achieve priority over conservation objectives, either through planned or spontaneous tourism processes. Cater (2000) reports on the conflict between small-scale ecotourism and resort-based tourism at the Jade Dragon Mountain Range in the Yunnan Great Rivers National Park, in China, and at many attractions it is clear that different market segments are consuming the same product in completely different ways, with general interest categories demanding a higher level of artificial infrastructure than special interest groups.

In fact, there are many signs that Asian markets are already becoming more diverse. In Indonesia there is a shift away from mass, low-budget day trips by chartered bus to beaches and other attractions capable of receiving large groups, to locations accessible mainly by private transport and with a supply of overnight accommodation. Diversification is facilitated not only by increasing wealth but by an attitudinal shift away from a collective and passive enjoyment of natural attractions towards a more individualistic and active engagement with nature. A series of research trips to Bromo Tengger Semeru by the author since the 1980s (most recently in 2005) has revealed more and more younger Indonesians visiting with small numbers of friends, family or work colleagues rather than with the very large groups which were formerly the only model, and White and Rosales (2003) remark on the increasing numbers of higher-income Filipinos who visit diving and snorkelling locations on holiday.

Having said this, the comment in the 1982 National Conservation Plan for Indonesia that 'we ... like to get away from the crowds and the dirt to sense the freedom of walking in wild unpeopled places' (FAO, 1982, p. 3) was a representation of the views of the Western biologists who wrote the plan rather than of Indonesian society, which values family or community togetherness rather than individualism. In fact, the desire to 'get away from the crowds' into 'wild unpeopled places' is considered by most Indonesians and other Asians a sign of a disturbed mind, and it is likely that the 'mass ecotourism' noted by Weaver (2002) in Asia will continue to be the dominant model for the foreseeable future. This is partly because of underlying attitudes to the environment and nature, which are reflected in attitudes to protected areas by park managers as well as by tourists.

Asian attitudes to the environment and park management

In the West, perceptions of ecotourism and national parks are influenced by historico-philosophical attitudes to wilderness and nature. National parks are regarded as places which provide opportunities for physical and spiritual refreshment and also preserve elements of a wilderness which, perhaps more in imagination than in reality, provides a contrast and counterbalance to the stable, ordered world of towns and managed countryside. A blend of ecocentrism and technocentrism underpins attitudes to parks and to nature, with the former centring on a romantic respect for nature in its own right, and the latter proposing that nature is separate from humans and can be understood and managed according to observable and mechanical processes (Nash, 1967; Pepper, 1996). These elements have resulted in a search for an inspirational encounter with a perceived wilderness and also in the urge to learn more about nature, while in general it is accepted that remaining wilderness areas should be managed for their intrinsic worth and for the wildlife within them rather than for the benefit of humans.

In most of Asia, however, the large-scale shift from rural to urban dwelling is still under way, and the pressure to exploit natural resources for economic gain is barely modified by residual unease about the spirits and 'dangers' of non-managed wild places. Some forests and mountains continue to be treated with circumspection, with particular places such as caves, pools and mountain peaks sometimes forming the focus of meditative prayers or pilgrimages, and some forest or mountain-dwelling peoples retain considerable spiritual significance. But the general story of relations with nature is one of domination and domestification, as reported by Raby (1995) from Croll and Parkin's (1992) comment on Malay attitudes to the environment, and the Javanese creation myth which describes how Java's primeval forests were cleared and settled (Geertz, 1960). Reports from all over Asia document the increasing consumerism and separation from traditional land ties of different peoples, for instance Vitebsky's longitudinal study of the Sora hill-people of India (Vitebsky, 1998). This background makes it easier to understand why in many parts of Asia wild landscapes are tidied up and managed for human benefit, as with the tourism installations in Chinese national parks mentioned at the beginning of this chapter.

The difference in attitudes is also significant for the way national parks have been established and managed in developing countries and how they are viewed by domestic populations. The poor local acceptance of national parks has been acknowledged since at least the early 1980s. By the time of the Third World Congress on National Parks, held in Bali in 1982, it was recognised by advisory agencies for protected areas that ways had to be sought to overcome local resentment towards national parks by incorporating human welfare needs into planning and policy-making in addition to conservation needs (McNeely and Miller, 1984).

Efforts towards this have been made by a number of means. Initially the approach of 'Integrated Conservation Development Projects' was applied. These tried to foster low-impact forms of economic activity in parks, such as small-scale ecotourism, with the intention of reducing pressure on the natural resources. In Nepal, once the environmental damage from trekking tourism in national parks such as Sagarmatha, Annapurna and Langtang was recognised, Western individuals and NGOs worked with local agencies to develop institutions which ensured better environmental controls and distributed income more fairly amongst local people and the agencies responsible for managing the parks. The best known of these schemes is the Annapurna Conservation Area Project. More often, though, such schemes have been ineffective: the number of people affected is tiny in comparison to the scale of the welfare needs of the local population; successful projects acted like a magnet in drawing in would-be beneficiaries from a wider area; the beneficiaries were generally so poor that they treated any income generated as additional to their normal livelihood activities rather than as an alternative; and the projects were too narrowly situated in villages or minor sectors, ignoring the wider societal and economic pressures which were often the cause of protected areas exploitation (Brandon and Wells, 1992; Wells *et al.*, 1999).

Becoming aware of such limitations, protected areas advisors sought more effective means of synthesising biodiversity conservation and human welfare needs. Advisors with purely biological concerns lost sway to more pragmatic strategists who, aware of a wider shift in development techniques, began to subscribe to the sustainable livelihoods approach. This uses participatory techniques to analyse people's needs and then places them in the context of government institutional structures and the wider economy. A protected areas management scheme which tried from the outset to encompass these wider sectors was at the Leuser Ecosystem, a huge region of northern Sumatra (Indonesia) which has the Gunung Leuser National Park at its core and includes a surrounding swathe of additional territory. Considerable effort has gone into involving all stakeholders, including – controversially – the military. Members of the armed forces in Indonesia are involved in many lucrative forms of resource exploitation – much of it illegal – and conservationists have traditionally considered them beyond the pale. However, they are such a powerful player both politically and economically in the local matrix of influences that a decision was taken early on to engage them in policy-making and implementation (Griffiths, 1998).

More commonly, two other stakeholder groups are involved in sustainable livelihoods approaches which are crucial to success and yet present considerable challenges. The first is government departments with responsibilities in the area concerned, which means – especially where tourism is chosen as the key development tool – those responsible for agriculture, education, health, water, forests, land use and infrastructural planning and coastal management, as well as tourism. The second group is formed by the indigenous peoples who, although often now recognised as driven by external influences in exploiting natural resources rather than as primary instigators, are still necessarily a key consideration in management strategies.

Hierarchies and institutional constraints

As far as government departments are concerned, the cross-sectoral approach of sustainable livelihoods conflicts with the usual pattern of projects being 'owned' by a particular government department. The problem is exacerbated in Asia because of the nature of social and bureaucratic structures, which are characterised by clientism, patronage, hierarchical linkages and respect for authority. Although this is changing under the influence of education and modern communications and economic systems, traditional structures remain strong in the rural areas where protected areas – and most ecotourism – are located. Thus, an account of development projects in Nepal found that villagers' acceptance of hierarchical structures and personal relations undermined the efforts of Western development planners, whose initiatives were based on cultural values which stressed individuality and equality (Carroll, 1992), while a study of water systems in southern India found that water management had always been based on political as well as natural principles, and attempts to graft modern participatory ideas onto a strongly hierarchical society resulted in patterns of power play within the communities affected which were as complex as the indigenous systems (Mosse, 1995).

Respect for traditional hierarchies was one reason for the political continuity experienced by post-independence Indonesia, with just two leaders from 1945 to 1998. The presidential, top-down system coincided with the traditional Javanese worldview, according to which the leader holds supreme power and makes wise decisions, and the needs and wishes of individuals are subordinate to the overall stability and prosperity of the nation (Mulder, 1996; Tsuchiya, 1988). Decisions are made by people at the apexes of different parts of the hierarchy, with the President at the summit, governors at the head of each province, and other government appointees as leaders of smaller administrative divisions (Rohdewohld, 1995). People in positions of power are reluctant to share decision-making powers, and decisions are invariably accepted without question by those lower down in the hierarchy, both because of the respect accorded to leaders and because of an emphasis on consensus and calmness. But these socio-political characteristics were also recognised as a barrier to sustainable practices by Timothy (1998) in a study of the lack of co-operative planning in the tourism sector in

Yogyakarta, Java, in that a reliance on a hierarchical model of power structures and a lack of cross-sectoral links resulted in a piecemeal and uncoordinated approach to tourism development. In Lao PDR, similarly, the vertical lines of communication within ministries and lack of horizontal communication between sectors and provinces resulted in inefficiency and overlap (Rigg and Jerndal, 1996).

In the case of tourism in protected areas, discrete sectoral responsibilities and jealousies over power sharing between different ministries can be especially acute. Throughout the region, 'appropriate and effective institutional arrangements for managing the relationship between tourism and the environment' (Hall, 2000, p. 96) are lacking. This is demonstrated in conservation areas such as the Malaysian offshore islands gazetted as Marine Parks, where management is nominally the responsibility of the Department of Fisheries, which is a federal body, but where the islands are administered by state governments, whose powers override those of federal agencies. This means that the Marine Park authorities are unable to prevent tourism development of the islands (Musa, 2000). Hannam (2004) discusses the conflict of interest affecting Indian parks, where the elite Indian Forest Service (which is part of the Ministry of Environment and Forests) stifles attempts at tourism initiatives generated by the Ministry of Tourism and Culture. In Indonesia the national parks are managed by the Directorate General of Forest Protection and Nature Conservation, which is part of the Ministry of Forestry and has no tourism expertise, while – as shown at the beginning of this chapter in the example of Mount Bromo – the tourism authorities feel free to propose interventions which override conservation interests. Overcoming the sectoral narrowness of the ministries in Indonesia by better communication between them is problematic, because of the entrenched hierarchical system, acceptance of the status quo, and unwillingness by each department to share administrative territory with others. A more practical constraint is that to travel from one government department to another for meetings, civil servants are paid a *per diem*, an allowance which augments their meagre salaries. If budgetary restrictions preclude the *per diem*, then civil servants do not move from their offices.

A further consequence of the poor salaries received by civil servants in Indonesia is their eagerness to become involved in what in the West would be considered ethically dubious ways of making money. Numerous reports testify to the involvement by civil servants in, for example, illegal logging, while the Directorate General of Forest Protection and Nature Conservation has for years been characterised by poor staff motivation (IIED, 1994).

There is a notable contrast between the general lassitude with which conservation duties are addressed and the enthusiasm devoted to money-making ventures. At Bromo Tengger Semeru, for instance, the head ranger responsible for the main touristic locus owns two hotels, one of which was built on national park land. Starting out modestly in 1996, this establishment had mushroomed by 2005 into an imposing 40-roomed hotel. Other forestry personnel were involved in other tourism-related business ventures, such as shops and Internet cafes. Research at Bromo has also shown systematic abuse of the entry-fee system, with entrance money diverted into the pockets of civil servants rather than accruing to government departments.

Corruption is accepted as an endemic part of the socio-political scene generally in Asia (Cameron, 1996). Although a democratic regime has been in place in Indonesia since 1998, established hierarchical systems with their networks of patronage do not appear to have shifted yet, despite the open discussion of corruption in the media and high-profile investigations initiated by the President (Jakarta Post, 2005). The transparent and accountable governance which would foster careful management of natural resources is largely missing, with private interests generally prevailing over the public good and poor control over market forces. The result for tourism in national parks is that economic opportunities are often over-exploited, to the detriment of the environment that the parks are supposed to protect. At the Bohorok Orangutan Centre in Sumatra, for example, spontaneous and uncontrolled tourism development since the mid-1980s resulted in an explosion of accommodation and catering infrastructure which caused pollution of water sources and destruction of forest resources (Cochrane, 1998; PanEco, various). It was in the interests of none of the stakeholders – except the environment, which did not have a voice – to change this situation, since in the short term all human parties benefited from the arrangements. In the event, Nature did take a hand in that a flash flood in November 2003 swept away most of the tourist village.

Moving on to the second category of local stakeholders in nature-based tourism – the indigenous people or other groups who live in and around the national parks – it is clear that hierarchical structures and poorly regulated market forces are also highly relevant.

Indigenous people and involvement in ecotourism

In the first place, there are difficulties in arranging a genuine level of participation in decision-making over natural resources by indigenous people and peasant farmers, since protected areas are often in economically marginal areas of the country and the people affected tend to have low educational levels and weak representation within the local polity. In the Malaysian park of Taman Negara the government promoted the job opportunities available to Malays in ecotourism but failed to include the indigenous Batek people in managerial processes (Raby, 1995): they were only involved as an attraction for tour groups to visit and try their hand at blow-darting, or were occasionally spotted going about their business in the national park and pointed out along the same lines as the wildlife. Malay tour guides or traders acted as middle-men in organising visits or trading handicrafts. Similarly, on the Indonesian island of Siberut, popular for trekking tours to visit the indigenous Mentawai people, only 9% of the price paid by tourists for ground arrangements reached the Mentawaians, with the rest accumulated by middle-men from the Sumatran mainland (Sproule and Suhandi, 1994).

A review of tourism amongst poorer communities in Asia concluded that local people gain most in the early stages of tourism development and when they retain control over the elements of service provision (Shah and Gupta, 2000), and numerous other case studies have shown that local involvement is a key factor in the acceptance of tourism by local communities or their alienation from it. Often, though, it is difficult to find mechanisms for genuine community involvement rather than as 'tourism objects', as in the case of the Batek of Malaysia. In Bromo Tengger Semeru, the local Tenggerese people were originally very much involved in tourism by providing accommodation and by transporting tourists to Mount Bromo on horseback. As the area has progressed through its life cycle, however, they have become increasingly marginalised, first by outside investment into better quality accommodation facilities, and then by changing patterns of tourism which shifted away from foreign tourists, for whom the horse-ride was an essential part of the experience, towards domestic tourists, who prefer to travel as far as possible towards the volcano by motor vehicle. The situation was exacerbated by institutional weakness and conflicts between different administrative regions responsible for different access points to the park: motor vehicles were permitted access from one side and not from another, while guards took bribes to turn a blind eye to vehicles entering even from the side which was nominally restricted.

In many places greater involvement in tourism is restricted by lack of capital resources, but at Bromo this was not the case: the Tenggerese were relatively wealthy because of their agriculture and strong entrepreneurial inclinations, shown in the alacrity with which they capitalised on tourism originally. However, the lack of social resources was a significant barrier to engagement: they tended to take advantage only of the opportunities which coincided with pre-existing skills or supply of facilities, such as with accommodation and the horse-rides and other forms of involvement such as portering, mountain guiding and cultural performances. As tourism evolved and they were sidelined, they turned back to their traditional livelihood strategy of peasant farming. But rather than becoming ever more alienated from the tourism in their midst, the Tenggerese have again shown the trait of reflexivity demonstrated several times during their history when outside forces threatened to remove a source of income from them. A new village headman appointed in the early 2000s recognised that a constraint to involvement in tourism was the lack of access to formal education. Employment in the hotels in a role involving interaction with customers necessitated a high-school certificate, which local people rarely had, meaning that almost all the hotel staff were Javanese from outside the immediate area. Previously, there was only a primary school in the village, with children having to travel long distances to high schools and board away from home. The new headman started up a second primary school and a high school, and announced that villagers would not be allowed to marry unless they graduated at least from primary school. While in Western societies this would be an unacceptable level of state interference in people's private lives, for the Tenggerese it was simply an example of good, forward-thinking leadership and an adaptation of traditional hierarchical powers.

This situation also illustrates the influence of individuals, which is undervalued by participatory approaches to development because the near-cosmic power of leaders in many parts of Asia conflicts with Western democratic ideals. In a study of conflicts and conflict-resolution surrounding a wildlife protection zone in northern Pakistan, Knudsen (1995) found that a respected local leader successfully negotiated a compromise agreement between villagers and government authorities, while a review of community-based wildlife management projects found that 'the role of an enlightened leader is critical' (Roe and Jack, 2001, p. 37). On the other hand, such influences are not always benign, and can result in unbalanced development: a review of small-scale tourism resorts in the Philippines showed that exercising local influence resulted in haphazard development rather than strategically planned, market-orientated enterprises (White and Rosales, 2003). Tensions and rivalries can also be exacerbated by individually driven developments, as in the case of a large hotel and diving enterprise owned by a local strongman on Banda, in the Indonesian Moluccan islands, which was resented by many islanders because they felt excluded from tourism (Cochrane, 1993). Nevertheless, development planning which takes account of socio-political realities is much more likely to succeed.

Seeking a solution: collaborative management initiatives

Just as it is said that people get the government they deserve, it can be argued that they also get the institutions they deserve, with the structure and operation of these reflecting the societal norms of the places where they are rooted. In Asia, a characteristic more and more frequently used in natural resource management is the desire for agreement by consensus and compromise which underlies social relations in many Asian societies. This has been captured in the emphasis on partnership and collaboration which has increasingly shaped protected areas policies since the turn of the millennium, as articulated in collaborative management, or co-management, initiatives (CMIs). Essentially, the co-management process establishes horizontal and vertical networks of social partners (or stakeholders) who agree to share access to and management of resources through negotiation, and to revise their practices through continuing learning processes (Borrini-Feyerabend *et al.*, 2000; Berkers, 2004). One of the many strengths of the CMI process is that it cuts across the institutional conflicts of interest which often afflict conservation management, particularly where tourism is concerned. By providing a forum for stakeholder groups to explore their spheres of influence in relation to others and establish negotiated institutional territories and responsibilities, CMIs can also help to rationalise the patchwork of overlapping (or missing) initiatives which affect protected areas.

Several CMIs have been set up in Indonesia, mostly involving management by a board of people representing local government institutions, communities, private sector entrepreneurs and NGOs. Many of the initiatives are funded by international NGOs, and they have been greeted with cautious optimism by conservationists (Purnomo and Lee, 2005). Bunaken Marine National Park, for example, is managed by an advisory board drawn from dive operators, environmental organisations, universities, government departments and resident communities. The structure was stimulated and facilitated by international NGOs and aid agencies to address resentment by local people that they were being excluded from the benefits generated by the diving tourism industry. The majority of the revenue from dive tags is distributed via conservation and community development programmes within the park, with the remainder split between different levels of government (Cochrane and Tapper, 2006).

CMIs also provide a way of overcoming another constraint to the poor linkages between ecotourism and biodiversity conservation in many parts of Asia, which is that revenues from tourism are rarely channelled back into conservation. Frequently, the only way that protected areas generate money from tourism is through entry fees, which under traditional institutional arrangements are remitted to national or regional treasuries for general development purposes. Globally, however, protected areas managers and regional governments are instigating a more diverse range of income-generating techniques, including user-fees, leasing and concessions, direct operation of tourism enterprises, taxes and use of volunteer help and donations (Font *et al.*, 2004), while development agencies are encouraging greater mutual learning between the tourism sector and the conservation sector (Tapper and Cochrane, 2005). CMIs are often the framework within which these learning and restructuring processes can be organised.

Conclusion

Whether CMIs can help engineer a change in the underlying ambivalent and predominantly anthropocentric attitudes to the environment in Asia remains to be seen. Given the huge diversity of Asian societies and politico-economic circumstances, of course, such ambivalence is not universal: the Indian Forest Service is fiercely protective of its parks and reserves, and the potential value of ecotourism to national and local economies has stimulated stronger governance in some countries, such as Nepal and Laos, and the emergence of community-based management schemes in Indonesia and the Philippines, amongst others. Environmental concerns are receiving greater emphasis at national and international levels, while at the level of individual personnel and sites, improved training, information exchange and more enlightened management techniques are resulting in some encouraging outcomes for protected areas. Regional markets for ecotourism are diversifying, for instance with more people joining bird-watching clubs and visiting diving resorts, and with increasing interest in protecting nature for its own sake.

While the early idealism which infused the idea of using ecotourism to dissolve the obstacles to biodiversity conservation in developing countries has rarely been justified, a greater understanding of the mechanisms and processes of tourism is resulting from more studies, and in particular from research into the interface between tourism, conservation and development. This understanding includes accepting that an ultra-conservationist stance on uses of protected areas and a prescriptive interpretation of 'ecotourism' will be stymied by reality. In the real world, different models of ecotourism prevail in different countries, and Asian manifestations reflect local values and local institutions. If ecotourism is to support biodiversity conservation under such circumstances, efforts to manage it must be made through planning and institutional frameworks which are firmly contextualised within the social and political environment where it takes place.

References

Backhaus, N. (2001). 'Non-place jungle' – the construction of authenticity in national parks of Malaysia. *Third EUROSEAS conference*, SOAS, London.

Berkers, F. (2004). Rethinking community-based conservation. *Conservation Biology* 18(3): 621–630.

BisnisBali (2005). Bromo needs investors for cable-cars. *Bisnis Bali Online*, January 30, 2005.

Borrini-Feyerabend, G., Farvar, M.T., Nguinguiri, J.C. and Ndangang, V.A. (2000). *Co-management of Natural Resources: Organising, Negotiating and Learning-By-Doing, GTZ and IUCN.* Kasparek Verlag, Heidelberg.

Brandon, K. and Wells, M. (1992). Planning for people and parks: design dilemmas. *World Development* 20(4): 557–570.

Cambridge, H. and Whitelegg, J. (2006). The environmental and social consequences of aviation growth in Asia. Paper presented at the *Conference on 'Tourism in Asia: New Trends, New Perspectives'*, Leeds Metropolitan University, June 10–12, 2006.

Cameron, O. (1996). Japan and South-East Asia's environment. In Parnwell, M.J.G. and Bryant, R.L. (eds), *Environmental Change in South-East Asia*. Routledge, London, pp. 67–93.

Carroll, T.F. (1992). *Intermediary NGOs: The Supporting Link in Grassroots Development*. Kumarian Press, Hartford, CT.

Cater, E. A. (2000). Tourism in the Yunnan Great Rivers National Parks System Project: prospects for sustainability. *Tourism Geographies* 2(4): 472–489.

Ceballos-Lascurain, H. (1996). Tourism, Ecotourism and Protected Areas: the state of nature-based tourism around the world and guidelines for its development. Based on papers presented at the tourism workshops held during the *IV World Congress of National Parks and Protected Areas*, Caracas, February 10–21, 1992. IUCN, Gland.

Chen, W., Wang, Y. and Xia, X. (2006). Sustainable tourism development and aesthetic values: a case study in Zhangjiajie National Park of Wuling Yuan, China. Paper presented at the *Conference on 'Tourism in Asia: new trends, new perspectives'*, Leeds Metropolitan University, June 10–12, 2006.

Cochrane, J. (1993). *Guidelines for Marine Tourism Development in Indonesia (Consultancy Report)*. WWF-Indonesia Program, Jakarta.

Cochrane, J. (1998). *Organisation of Ecotourism in the Leuser Ecosystem (Consultancy Report)*. Leuser Management Unit, Medan.

Cochrane, J. (2006). Indonesian National Parks: Understanding leisure users, *Annals of Tourism Research* 33(4): 979–997.

Cochrane, J. and Tapper, R. (2006). Tourism's contribution to World Heritage Site management. In Leask, A. (ed.). *Managing World Heritage Sites*. Elsevier Press, London, pp. 97–109.

Croll, E. and Parkin, D. (eds) (1992). *Bush Base, Forest Farm: Culture, Environment and Development*. Routledge, London.

Eagles, P.J., McCool, S.F., Haynes, C.D. (2002). *Sustainable Tourism in Protected Areas: Guidelines for Planning and Management*. Best Practice Protected Areas Guidelines Series No. 8. IUCN, Gland.

FAO (Food and Agriculture Organization of the United Nations) (1982). *National Conservation Plan for Indonesia*. UNDP/FAO National Park Development Project, Bogor, April 1982.

Font, X., Cochrane, J. and Tapper, R. (2004). *Pay Per Nature View: Understanding Tourism Revenues for Effective Management Plans*. Leeds Tourism Group, Leeds.

Geertz, C. (1960). *The Religion of Java*. The Free Press of Glencoe, USA.

Griffiths, M. (1998). Project Leader, Leuser Management Unit, Leuser Ecosystem, Medan, Sumatra, Personal Communication, March 3, 1998.

Hall, C.M. (2001). Tourism and the environment: problems, institutional arrangements and approaches. In Hall, C.M. and Page, S. (eds), *Tourism in South and Southeast Asia*, Butterworth-Heinemann, pp. 94–103.

Hamzah, A., Khalifah, Z., Dahlan, N.A. and Kechik, A.T. (2003). Planning for ecotourism in protected areas of Malaysia: some reflections on current approaches. *IMT-GT International Conference on Ecotourism: Issues and Challenges*, October, 12–14. Universiti Utara Malaysia.

Hannam, K. (2004). Tourism and forest management in India: the role of the state in limiting tourism development. *Tourism Geographies* 6(3): 331–351.

Hannam, K. (2005). Tourism management issues in India's National Parks: an analysis of the Rajiv Gandhi (Nagarahole) National Park. *Current Issues in Tourism* 8(2&3): 165–180.

IIED (The International Institute for Environment and Development) (1994). *Environmental Synopsis of Indonesia*. Prepared for the Overseas Development Administration, London.

Jakarta Post (2005). *President Summons Five High-Ranking Officials Over Illegal Logging*, February 22.

Kaosa-ard, M., Bezic, D. and White, S. (2001). Domestic tourism in Thailand: supply and demand, In Ghimire, K.B. (ed.), *The Native Tourist*. Earthscan Publications, London, pp. 109–141.

Kolås, Å. (2004). Tourism and the making of place in Shangri-La. *Tourism Geographies* 6(3): 262–278.

Knudsen, A. (1995). State intervention and community protest: Nature conservation in Hunza, North Pakistan, In Bruun, O. and Kalland, A. (eds), *Asian Perceptions of Nature: A Critical Approach*. Curzon Press, Richmond, pp. 103–126.

Kua, J. and Baum, T. (2004). Perspectives on the development of low-cost airlines in South-east Asia. *Current Issues in Tourism* 7(3): 262–276.

Lao NTA (2005). *National Ecotourism Strategy and Action Plan, 2005–2010*. Lao National Tourism Administration, Vientiane.

McNeely, J.A. and Miller, K.R. (1984). National parks, conservation and development: the role of protected areas in sustaining society, *Proceedings of the World Congress on National Parks and Protected Areas*, Bali, October 11–22, 1982, Smithsonian Institute Press, Washington, DC.

Mitton, R. (1997). Seeing red over a road. *Asiaweek*, June 20.

Mosse, D. (1995). Local Institutions and power: The history and practice of community management of tank irrigation systems in south India. In Nelson, N. and Wright, S. (eds), *Power and Participatory Development: Theory and Practice*. IT Publications, London, pp. 144–156.

Mulder, N. (1996). *Inside Indonesian Society: Cultural Change in Java*. The Pepin Press, Amsterdam.

Musa, G. (2000). Tourism in Malaysia. In Hall, C.M. and Page, S. (eds), *Tourism in South and Southeast Asia*. Butterworth-Heinemann, pp. 144–156.

Nash, R. (1967). *Wilderness and the American Mind*. Yale University Press, New Haven.

PanEco (various). Bulletins of NGO working for sustainable development at Bohorok.

Pepper, D. (1996). *Modern Environmentalism: An Introduction.* Routledge, London.

Pholpoke, C. (1998). *The Chiang Mai cable-car project: local controversy over cultural and ecotourism.* In Hirsch, P. and Warren, C. (eds), *The Politics of Environment in Southeast Asia.* Routledge, London/New York, pp. 262–277.

Pikiran Rakyat (2004). Pangandaran, Sekadar Kejar Target (Newspaper article: 30 August).

Purnomo, A. and Lee, R. (2005). The winds of change – recent progress towards conserving Indonesian biodiversity. *INCL,* Issue 8–3, January.

Raby, H. (1995). *The Batek in Modern Malaysia: The Identity of a Minority Hunting and Gathering Group in the Context of Rapid Economic Transition, Ethnic Politics and Ecological Tourism.* Undergraduate dissertation, University of Hull.

Rigg, J. and Jerndal, R. (1996). Plenty in the context of scarcity: forest management in Laos. In Parnwell, M.J.G. and Bryant, R.L. (eds), *Environmental Change in South-East Asia.* Routledge, London, pp. 145–162.

Roe, D. and Jack, M. (2001). *Stories from Eden: Case Studies of Community-Based Wildlife Management.* Evaluating Eden Series No. 9. IIED, London.

Rohdewohld, R. (1995). *Public Administration in Indonesia.* Montech Pty. Ltd, Melbourne.

Ross, W. (2003). Sustainable tourism in Thailand: can ecotourism protect the natural and cultural environments? *Second Meeting of the Academic Forum for Sustainable Development International Sustainability Conference,* September 17–19, 2003, Fremantle, Western Australia.

Shah, K. and Gupta, V. (2000). *Tourism, the Poor and Other Stakeholders.* Sustainable Livelihoods Working Paper Series. Overseas Development Institute-Fair Trade in Tourism, London.

Sofield, T.H.B. and Li, F.M.S. (2003). Processes in formulating an ecotourism policy for nature reserves in Yunnan Province, China. In Fennell, D. and Dowling, R. (eds), *Ecotourism: policy and strategy issues.* CABI Publishing, London, pp. 141–167.

Sproule, K.W. and Suhandi, A.S. (1994). Eco-cultural tourism development on Siberut, Ministry of Forestry, Directorate General of Forest Protection and Nature Conservation.

Tapper, R. and Cochrane, J. (2005). *Forging Links Between Protected Areas and the Tourism Sector,* UNEP, Paris.

TDRI (1995). *Green Finance: A Case Study of Khao Yai.* Thailand Development Research Institute and Harvard Institute, Bangkok.

Timothy, D.J. (1998). Cooperative tourism planning in a developing destination. *Journal of Sustainable Tourism* 6(1): 52–68.

Tsuchiya, K. (1988). *Democracy and Leadership: The rise of the Taman Siswa movement in Indonesia*(translated by Peter Hawkes). University of Hawaii Press, Honolulu.

UNWTO (2006). *Tourism Market Trends, Madrid: World Tourism Organization.* www.world-tourism.org.

Vitebsky, P. (1998). A farewell to ancestors? Deforestation and the changing spiritual environment of the Sora. In Grove, R.H., Damodaran, V. and Sangwan, S. (eds), *Nature and the Orient: The Environmental History of South East Asia.* Oxford University Press, pp. 967–982.

Wang, S. and Qu, H. (2004). A comparison study of Chinese domestic tourism: China vs the USA. *International Journal of Contemporary Hospitality Management* 16: 108–115.

Weaver, D. (2002). Asian ecotourism: patterns and themes. *Tourism Geographies* 4(2): 153–172.

Wells, M., Guggenheim, S., Khan, A., Wardojo, W. and Jepson, P. (1999). *Investing in Biodiversity: A Review of Indonesia's Integrated Conservation Development Projects.* World Bank, Washington.

White, A.T. and Rosales, R. (2003). Community-oriented marine tourism in the Philippines. In Gössling, S. (ed.), *Tourism and Development in Tropical Islands: Political Ecology Perspectives.* Edward Elgar Publishing, Cheltenham, pp. 237–262.

Indigenous ecotourism: conservation and resource rights

Heather Zeppel

Introduction

This chapter addresses critical issues for Indigenous-owned and operated ecotourism ventures that benefit Indigenous communities and conserve the natural and cultural environment. The spread of ecotourism into remote areas often coincides with regions of high biological and scenic value that are still the traditional homelands for surviving groups of Indigenous peoples. Ecotourism enterprises controlled by Indigenous people include cultural ecotours, ecolodges, wildlife safaris, hunting and fishing tours, cultural villages and other nature-based tourist facilities or services. Indigenous ecotourism is defined as 'nature-based attractions or tours owned by Indigenous people, and also Indigenous interpretation of the natural and cultural environment including wildlife' (Zeppel, 2003, p. 56). Indigenous ecotourism provides an alternative to extractive land uses such as hunting, farming, logging or mining, and it involves Indigenous people in managing tourism, culture and use of natural resources. Ecotourism supplements a subsistence lifestyle and aids the transition to a cash economy for many tribal groups. How various Indigenous communities develop and operate tribal ecotourism enterprises or joint ventures is a key focus of much recent research in this area. This chapter discusses key factors and constraints for sustainable development of Indigenous ecotourism and explores the growing links between biodiversity conservation, ecotourism and Indigenous land rights. Indigenous cultural perspectives about ecotourism, conflicts between hunting and ecotourism and key challenges for community-based ecotourism are discussed. The role of environmental non-government agencies (NGOs), ecotourism associations and government agencies in developing Indigenous ecotourism is also examined.

Indigenous groups and tourism

Worldwide, Indigenous peoples are becoming more involved in the tourism industry, and particularly with ecotourism (Sykes, 1995; Butler and Hinch 1996; Price, 1996; Ryan, 2000; Stronza, 2005; Mann, 2002; Smith, 2003; Christ, 2004; Hinch, 2004; Ryan and Aicken, 2005; Johnston, 2006; Notzke, 2006; McLaren, 2003). Tourism enterprises controlled by Indigenous people include nature-based tours, cultural attractions and other tourist facilities or services in tribal homelands or protected areas. These Indigenous ventures are largely a response to the spread of tourism into remote and marginal areas, including tribal territories, national parks and nature reserves that are traditional living areas for many Indigenous groups. Indigenous cultures and lands are frequently the main attraction for ecotours visiting wild and scenic natural regions such as the Amazon, Borneo, Yunnan (China), East Africa and Oceania. Indeed, 'Indigenous homelands rich in biodiversity are the prime target of most ecotourism' (Johnston, 2000, p. 90). Many of these ecoregions such as tropical rainforests, coral reefs, mountains, savannah and deserts are still inhabited by marginalised Indigenous groups (WWF, 2000; Weaver, 2001). Tourist encounters with tribal peoples during safaris, mountain trekking and village tours are growing areas of new tourism (SPREP, 2002; Harrison, 2003; Raffaele, 2003; Smith, 2003; Zeppel, 2006). Tourist experiences with Indigenous peoples now include trekking with Maasai guides in East Africa (Berger, 1996), visiting Indian villages in the rainforest of Ecuador (Wesche, 1996; Drumm, 1998), staying at Iban longhouses in Borneo (Zeppel, 1997) and Aboriginal rainforest tours in northeast Australia (Sofield, 2002; Zeppel, 2002). Native lands and reserves in developed countries such as Australia, New Zealand, Canada and the USA are also a growing focus for Indigenous ecotourism (Lew, 1996; Ryan and Aicken, 2005). The USA has 52 million acres of Indian reservation land, often near national parks, with many tribal governments involved in tourism ventures on these lands (Gerberich, 2005). Many Indigenous groups in North America are investing money from land claim settlements, mining or fishing royalties and gaming revenue from tribal casinos in tourism ventures on reserve lands (Ryan, 1997; Lew and van Otten, 1998). In these colonised countries, Indigenous ecotourism ventures are also found in or near protected areas that are co-managed with native people having traditional claims over this land (Hill, 2004; MacKay and Caruso, 2004). In developing countries, some Indigenous groups with communal or legal land titles now derive income from forest or wildlife resource use rights and from leasing land to tourism operators.

Indigenous ownership of tourism and the expansion from culture-based to service-based Indigenous tourism ventures, including ecotourism on traditional lands, has mainly occurred since the 1990s (Zeppel, 1998, 2001, 2003; Ryan and Aicken, 2005; Notzke, 2006). However, Indigenous tourism enterprises on tribal lands are often located in rural or remote regions, with limited infrastructure and access by tourist markets. High transport and tour costs, along with a lack of capital and business skills among Indigenous peoples also limit the development of Indigenous tourism ventures in tribal lands and territories. For Indigenous peoples, regaining control of Indigenous lands and territories are integral for self-determination and sustainable development of Indigenous tourism. Key issues for the development of ecotourism on Indigenous lands include the legal rights of Indigenous peoples on Indigenous territories; the com-modification of Indigenous cultural practices for tourism; the intellectual property rights of Indigenous peoples for the use of their designs and their traditional cultural or biological knowl-edge in tourism. Indigenous self-determination and control over tourism on Indigenous territories mainly relies on legal title to tra-ditional lands (Hinch, 2004). Hence, achieving sustainable tourism on Indigenous territories depends on several key factors such as 'land ownership, community control of tourism, government sup-port for tourism development, restricted access to indigenous homelands and reclaiming natural or cultural resources utilised for tourism' (Zeppel, 1998, p. 73). These crucial issues are reviewed for the growing area of Indigenous ecotourism.

Environmental, cultural and spiritual aspects of Indigenous heritage and traditions are featured in ecotourism, community-based tourism and alternative tourism. New ecotourism enter-prises managed by Indigenous groups are featured in travel guides and websites for community tourism and alternative travel (Franke, 1995; Mann, 2000, 2002; Tourism Concern, 2004; Redturs, n.d.). Globally, there is greater public awareness of both environmental impacts and Indigenous peoples. Ecotourism recognises the special cultural links between indigenous peoples and natural areas. A growing tourist demand for Indigenous cul-tural experiences also coincides with the Indigenous need for new economic ventures deriving income from sustainable use of land and natural resources. This global trend is reflected in increasing contact with Indigenous communities living in remote areas and also the opening up of Indigenous homelands for ecotourism (Honey, 1999; Christ, 2004). These Indigenous territories are usu-ally in peripheral areas, away from mainstream development, where Indigenous land practices have maintained biodiversity in 'wilderness' areas and key ecoregions (Hinch, 2004; Counsell, 2005). While Indigenous communities are vulnerable to increased accessibility and contact with outsiders, ecotourism is seen as one way to maintain ecosystems and provide an economic alter-native to logging or mining. Indigenous ecotourism involves native people negotiating access to tribal land, resources and cultural knowledge for tourists and tour operators.

Defining Indigenous ecotourism

Indigenous-owned and operated ecotourism ventures benefit Indigenous communities while conserving the natural and cultural environment. Key aspects of Indigenous ecotourism include a nature-based product, the presentation of Indigenous environmental and cultural knowledge and Indigenous owner-ship or control of ecotourism on tribal homelands. Ecotourism includes Aboriginal people and their traditions because of the strong bond between Indigenous cultures and natural environ-ment. This includes cultural, spiritual and physical links between Indigenous peoples and their traditional lands or nat-ural resources. Indigenous ecotourism then is 'tourism which cares for the environment and which involves (Indigenous) people in decision-making and management' (ANTA, 2001). It includes nature-based tourism products or accommodation owned by Indigenous groups, and Indigenous cultural tours or attractions in a natural setting. Much of this Indigenous tourism development focuses on community-based ecotourism that bene-fits local people (Liu, 1994; Drumm, 1998; Sproule and Suhandi, 1998; WWF, 2001; Fennell, 2003; Chen, 2004; Stronza, 2005; Notzke, 2006). According to Drumm (1998, p. 198), Indigenous community-based ecotourism involves 'ecotourism programs which take place under the control and active participation of the local people who inhabit a natural attraction'. These ecotourism enterprises involve Indigenous communities using their natural resources and traditional lands to gain income from tourism. Hence, Indigenous ecotourism ventures involve nature conser-vation, business enterprise (or partnerships) and tourism income for community development (Sproule, 1996, cited in Fennell, 2003). Hunting and fishing tours are also part of Indigenous ecotourism, with sustainable resource use, although consump-tive activities are not usually considered to be 'true' ecotourism (Hinch, 1998; Honey, 1999; Weaver, 2001).

The term Indigenous ecotourism has emerged since the mid-1990s to describe community ecotourism projects developed on Indigenous lands and territories in Latin America, Australia and Canada. Colvin (1994), Schaller (1996) and Wesche (1996) first used the term 'Indigenous ecotourism' to describe community-based ecotourism projects among Indian tribes in Ecuador. Wearing (1996) also presented a paper on training for Indige-nous ecotourism development at the Fourth World Leisure Congress. Karwacki (1999) used the term Indigenous eco-tourism in reviewing challenges for Indigenous groups seeking to develop ecotourism ventures on their lands, while Beck and Somerville (2002) and Sofield (2002) also referred to Aboriginal (cultural) ecotourism in Australia in this way. Fennell (2003) also refers to Indigenous ecotourism entrepreneurs, while the Mapajo Lodge in Bolivia describes their rainforest programme as Indigenous ecotourism. Furthermore, the Australian National Training Authority (2001) developed an Indigenous Ecotourism Toolbox, which includes case study examples and business plans for communities to set up their own ecotourism ventures. Nepal (2004, 2005) examined community capacity building for Indigenous ecotourism on the Tl'axt'en First Nation lands in British Columbia, Canada, while Hashimoto and Telfer (2004) reviewed Aboriginal ecotourism in northern Canada. Tsaur *et al.* (2006) evaluated sustainability indicators for Danayigu Ecological Park, an Indigenous ecotourism site in Taiwan. Finally, a new book by Zeppel (2006) reviews case studies of Indigenous ecotourism ventures in the Pacific Islands, Latin America, Africa and Southeast Asia that illustrate how Indigenous groups are conserving natural areas and educating visitors while developing and controlling ecotourism on Indigenous lands and territories. These case studies, therefore, challenge the common perception of 'minimal involvement in ecotourism by indigenous people in many countries' (Page and Dowling, 2002, p. 279). The published research in this area provides a non-Indigenous perspective of Indigenous ecotourism, since it is mostly non-Indigenous people who write the majority of case studies about tribal tourism ventures (Hinch, 2004; Ryan and Aicken, 2005; Johnston, 2006; Notzke, 2006; Zeppel, 2006). However, Indigenous views of tourism, culture, conservation and use of natural resources are reported.

With greater legal recognition and control over homeland areas, culture and resources, Indigenous groups in many areas are determining appropriate types of ecotourism development in traditional lands and protected areas. As well as being an exotic tourist attraction, Indigenous peoples are also increasingly the owners, managers, joint venture partners or staff of ecotourism ventures, cultural sites and other tourist facilities. Therefore, the roles of Indigenous people in ecotourism now include landowners, tribal governments or councils, traditional owners, land managers, park rangers, tourism operators and guides. This global expansion of tourism into remote natural areas and Indigenous lands, often in developing countries, has seen increasing concern for sustainable tourism development, particularly with Indigenous groups (Price, 1996; Honey, 1999; McIntosh, 1999; McLaren, 1999; Robinson, 1999; Duffy, 2002; Johnston, 2003; Mowforth and Munt, 2003; Smith, 2003; Sofield, 2003; Gerberich, 2005). For Indigenous peoples 'land rights are an absolute prerequisite for sustainable tourism' (Johnston, 2000, p. 92). Legal rights over tribal lands and resources allow Indigenous groups to benefit from ecotourism, through community-owned enterprises, joint ventures and other partnerships.

Zeppel (2006) evaluates the environmental, cultural and socioeconomic impacts of Indigenous ecotourism ventures in tribal areas of tropical developing countries. These case studies of

Indigenous ecotourism ventures are drawn from the Pacific region, South and Central America, Southeast Asia and Africa. Tropical rainforest areas are a main focus for these community-based Indigenous ecotourism projects (Wesche and Drumm, 1999; Mann, 2002; SPREP, 2002; *Tourism in Focus*, 2002a). Developing countries now attract 30% of all international tourists with a growth rate of 9.5% per annum since 1990. In addition, 19 of 25 biodiversity hotspots favoured by ecotourism, most with Indigenous populations, are in the Southern Hemisphere (Christ *et al.*, 2003). In developing countries, ecotourism ventures for Indigenous peoples are mainly implemented with the help of NGOs involved in conservation or community development projects. The nature or type of Indigenous ecotourism differs between developed and developing countries (see Table 16.1). This includes the legal status of Indigenous peoples, their lifestyle, type of Indigenous territories, extent of legal rights and land rights, and type of support from government agencies or NGOs for ecotourism on tribal lands. Indigenous groups in developing countries, threatened by land incursions, are still acquiring legal land titles and rely on support from NGOs to develop ecotourism. For many Indigenous peoples, controlled ecotourism is seen as one way of achieving cultural, environmental and economic sustainability for the community (Sofield, 1993; Butler and Hinch, 1996; Zeppel, 1998, 2000; Stronza, 2005; Notzke, 2006). Opening up Indigenous homelands to ecotourism, however, involves a balance between use of natural resources, meeting tourist needs and maintaining cultural integrity.

Indigenous involvement in ecotourism

Worldwide, Indigenous involvement and participation in ecotourism occurs with varied levels of ownership and input from Indigenous groups and organisations. Indigenous people may participate in ecotourism as individuals, families, a village or community, and through a tribal council or federation (Cater, 1996; Ashley and Roe, 1998; Wesche and Drumm, 1999; Mann, 2002; Notzke, 2006). Indigenous involvement in ecotourism can include full or part ownership, joint ventures, partnerships, services provision (e.g. lodge accommodation, boat transport, guiding and food) and employment by non-Indigenous tourism companies (see Table 16.2). Mann (2002) distinguishes between responsible tours that hire a local Indigenous guide, tribal partnerships with an external tour operator that markets the tours and community tours, with enterprises set up, owned and run by an Indigenous community though often with an

Table 16.1 Indigenous peoples and ecotourism in developed and developing countries

	Developed countries	Developing countries
Indigenous peoples	Minority cultures Officially recognised as Indigenous Traditional or modern lifestyles Colonised sovereign nations	Majority or minority cultures Varied status as Indigenous/tribal/minorities Traditional subsistence economies Colonised or independent nations
Indigenous territories	Mainly government reservations *Co-managed Aboriginal national parks* *Managed by tribal councils and government* Tax-free status on reserves (North America)	Ancestral lands and some Indigenous reserves *Live inside protected areas, share revenue* *Managed by Indigenous tribal councils* Threatened by resource extraction and settlers
Indigenous rights	*Traditional resource use rights* No direct wildlife ownership rights Intellectual and cultural property rights *Legal title to ancestral lands*	*Communal resource use rights (forest, reefs)* Limited wildlife ownership or use rights No intellectual and cultural property rights *Traditional or legal title to ancestral lands*
Indigenous ecotourism	*Supported by government agencies* *Funded by government grants* *Community, family or individual ventures* *Economic development of tribal areas*	*Supported by conservation and aid NGOs* *Funded by development agencies and NGOs* *Mainly community tourism ventures* *Economic alternative to extractive land uses*

Developed countries/regions: Canada, USA, Australia, New Zealand, Europe, and Japan.
Developing countries/regions: Pacific Islands (Oceania), Latin America, Africa, Southeast Asia, China, and India.

outside manager. Community-based ecotourism enterprises (e.g. lodges, tours) are owned and managed by communities, with tourism jobs rostered among members and profits allocated to community projects. Family or group initiatives in ecotourism may also employ or involve other community members. Joint

Table 16.2 Indigenous community involvement in ecotourism

Renting land to an operator to develop while simply monitoring impacts

Working as occasional, part- or full-time **staff for outside operators**

Providing **selected services** such as food preparation, guiding, transport or accommodations (or a combination of several or all of these) to operators

Forming **joint ventures** with outside operators with a division of labour, which allows the community to provide most services, while the operator takes care of marketing

Operating fully independent **community tourism** programmes

Enterprise run by **local entrepreneur**, supplying goods and services (e.g. guiding, campsites, homestays)

Sources: Drumm (1998, p. 201) and Ashley and Roe (1998, p. 8).

ventures involve formal business contracts or exclusive operating agreements between Indigenous communities or tribal councils with non-Indigenous tourism businesses. In joint venture arrangements, the outside operator is responsible for marketing, bringing tourists, a guide and most transport with the Indigenous group hosting and entertaining visitors. Alternatively, the outside company obtains a long-term lease on Indigenous land, builds tourist facilities and employs local people. The tour operator pays a lease rental fee and/or percentage of profits to the Indigenous group owning or claiming the land. Indigenous people also develop ecotourism ventures in partnership with conservation NGOs, national park agencies, government tourism bureaus, Indigenous organisations, development agencies, university researchers and other local communities (Fennell, 2003). Other related issues with these enterprises include limited community involvement and empowerment in ecotourism, especially by women (Scheyvens, 1999, 2000, 2002; Medina, 2005); business and social challenges for Indigenous groups in developing ecotourism ventures (Epler Wood, 1999a, 2002; Karwacki, 1999; Johnston, 2000, 2001); and potential conflicts between ecotourism and Indigenous hunting or land-use activities (Grekin and Milne, 1996; Hinch, 1998; Zeppel, 1998; Honey, 1999; Buckley, 2005). Zeppel (2006) assesses Indigenous involvement in a wide range of community and joint venture ecotourism ventures on tribal lands.

Indigenous peoples and resource rights

Tribal groups increasingly use the term 'Indigenous' and 'Indigenous peoples' due to growing national and international recognition of the existence and territorial claims of native groups. The category or status of being Indigenous is then linked to legally asserting cultural, political and economic claims, such as the ownership and use of land, river and sea areas, hunting and fishing rights, cultural or intellectual copyright of Indigenous knowledge and royalties from land use including tourism. Key issues for all Indigenous groups include human rights, use of land and resources (e.g. plants, wildlife, minerals and water), and intellectual and cultural property rights (e.g. traditional ecological knowledge and cultural copyright). The political and legal recognition of Indigenous status (i.e. people and territories) 'entails claim to certain rights over the use, management and flow of benefits from resource-based industries' (Howitt *et al.*, 1996, p. 3). Zografos and Kenrick (2005) describe how 'Indigenousness' is communicated through shamanic rituals in Ecuador, where ecotourism is used to reinforce Indian claims in decision-making over use of natural resources. Increasingly, Indigenous customary claims have been recognised as legal rights in national and international laws and conventions. These include both individual human rights and the collective property claims of Indigenous groups to land and resources (Wilmer, 1993; Hitchcock, 1994; McLaren, 1998; Pera and McLaren, 1999; Johnston, 2002, 2003; Mat Som and Baum, 2004; Walpole and Thouless, 2005). According to Honey (2003), Indigenous rights include fundamental, cultural, Indigenous knowledge and intellectual property, land, protected areas, economic, labour, local communities and a right to sustainable development of ancestral lands. In June 2006, the new UN Human Rights Council approved a Declaration on the Rights of Indigenous Peoples, after 25 years of discussion on the collective rights of Indigenous groups (Macdonald, 2006).

Indigenous territories include lands under the legal control of Indigenous groups, with this formal native title defined by nation states, and 'aboriginal', 'customary' or 'communal' title for lands long occupied and used by Indigenous peoples (Hinch, 2001). Most Indigenous groups are pursuing legal title to their traditional lands, reserves and national parks declared on Indigenous lands through treaties, native title claims, land-use agreements and other means (MacKay and Caruso, 2004; Weaver, 2006). These Indigenous territories are often in rural and remote areas; high in biodiversity, wildlife and scenic values; and a focus for traditional life ways and cultural practices such as art, music, ceremonies and handicrafts. For these reasons 'Indigenous territories are among the most significant of the cultural environments associated with ecotourism' (Weaver, 2001, p. 262). Indigenous peoples are developing ecotourism and other sustainable ventures based on natural resources to support the economic development of Indigenous lands. Ecotourism operators are also seeking new locations and products in tribal territories, often in joint ventures or exclusive agreements with Indigenous groups.

Indigenous resource rights are also being asserted in marine ecotourism. On the South Island of New Zealand, Whale Watch Kaikoura operates boat tours viewing resident sperm whales, along with humpback whales, orca and dolphins. It is 100% owned, operated and controlled by the Ngai Tahu Maori tribe as a community trust, in partnership with the local Ngati Kuri Maori people of Kaikoura. This venture began in 1987 after Maori people raised NZ$35,000 as equity for a loan and mortgaged four houses, then bought out a local competitor. In 1994, the Ngai Tahu Maori challenged government plans to issue other permits for whale watching at Kaikoura. A court case reaffirmed that the 1840 Treaty of Waitangi gave Maori rights over natural resources, including whales, ensuring a Maori monopoly on sperm whale watching. Whale Watch Kaikoura operates four boats, employs 50–80 mainly Maori people and has a turnover of NZ$3 million a year (Curtin, 2003). In 2003, Fiji granted control of coral lagoons and reefs to Indigenous people, with lease rentals for these marine areas paid to customary owners by island resorts and dive tour operators (Johnston, 2006).

Indigenous peoples and biodiversity

Indigenous land practices and cultural knowledge have ensured the conservation of global biodiversity. The UN Commission on Sustainable Development highlighted the key role of Indigenous peoples in the conservation of natural areas and species on their lands.

Indigenous peoples comprise 5% of the world's population but embody 80% of the world's cultural diversity. They are estimated to occupy 20% of the world's land surface but nurture 80% of the world's biodiversity on ancestral lands and territories. Rainforests of the Amazon, Central Africa, Asia and Melanesia are home to over half of the total global spectrum of indigenous peoples and at the same time contain some of the highest species biodiversity in the world (UN, 2002, pp. 2–3).

The Indigenous Peoples' Biodiversity Network was established in 1997 in Peru and has hosted workshops on Indigenous tourism and biodiversity conservation in Peru, Malaysia, Spain and Panama. Its position is that Indigenous peoples are the 'creators and conservers of biodiversity', with remaining forest areas or global 200 ecoregions with the highest biodiversity linked with surviving Indigenous groups in Asia, Africa, the Americas and Oceania (Nature Conservancy, 1996; Weber *et al.*, 2000; WWF, 2000; Colchester, 2003). The International Alliance of Indigenous and Tribal Peoples of the Tropical Forests, formed in 1992, and the Forest Peoples Programme (FPP) formed in 1990 also represent Indigenous views on conservation, parks and resource development. The UN *Convention on Biological Diversity* in 1992 recognised the environmental stewardship and traditional dependence of many Indigenous communities on biological resources. Article 8(j) requires governments to preserve Indigenous environmental knowledge to help conserve biodiversity and to share equitably any benefits arising from the use of traditional knowledge (Johnston, 2003). Since 1991, the UN's Global Environment Facility (GEF) has funded major projects on biodiversity conservation in developing countries with many including Indigenous lands. GEF funding from 2002 to 2006 was nearly US$3 billion (Griffiths, 2004). Funding for Indigenous projects on biodiversity conservation or ecotourism is mainly directed through key UN bodies (e.g. UN Environment Programme, UNEP; United Nations Development Programme, UNDP) to national governments, aid groups and environment NGOs. Increasing amounts of funding from international banks and development agencies are being directed towards ecotourism and the sustainable development of Indigenous communities (Halpenny, 1999; Griffiths, 2004; EBFP, 2005). In 2002, the UNEP invested over US$7 billion in 320 tourism-related projects with 21 development agencies (Selverston-Scher, 2003). Global funding for conservation projects in 2004, mainly World Bank and GEF, was US$8 billion (Counsell, 2005). Less than 1% of this global conservation funding goes directly to Indigenous communities and organisations (Arce-White, 2005).

Conservation NGOs such as WWF, The International Ecotourism Society (TIES), The Nature Conservancy (TNC) and Conservation International now play a major role in supporting Indigenous resource management and ecotourism projects (Epler Wood, 1999b; Sweeting and McConnel, 1999; Alcorn, 2001; WWF, 2001; Nature Conservancy, 2005; Cater, 2006). In fact, WWF adopted a policy on Indigenous peoples and conservation in 1996 that recognised the rights of Indigenous peoples to their traditional lands, territories and resources (Weber *et al.*, 2000; Alcorn, 2001; WWF, 2005) and published *Guidelines for Community-Based Ecotourism Development* (WWF, 2001). These major international conservation NGOs provide funding, staff and technical support for Indigenous ecotourism ventures that are located in global biodiversity hotspots such as rainforests. Conservation International supports the Chalalan Ecolodge in Bolivia, Gudigwa Camp in Botswana, and other Indigenous ecotourism and conservation projects (Sweeting and McConnel, 1999; Christ, 2004; Seligmann, n.d.). TNC works on protected area conservation projects and ecotourism business development with Indigenous peoples in Ecuador, Brazil, Colombia, Nicaragua and Papua New Guinea (TNC, n.d.). Increasingly, this funding for biodiversity conservation also involves alternative community development projects (e.g. ecotourism, organic agriculture, crafts).

Rare Conservation provides training and marketing support for Indigenous ecotourism businesses near world heritage areas in Mexico, Honduras and Guatemala. Most of these conservation NGOs are US-based organisations, with others from the UK, Europe and Africa (e.g. African Conservation Centre, Kenya). These environmental NGOs mainly aim to conserve key ecosystems and their wildlife.

Ecotourism is seen as one main way for Indigenous groups to conserve and benefit from biodiversity on their traditional lands (Butcher, 2003; Stronza, 2005). Ecotourism operators in Indigenous territories and protected areas with Indigenous claims also need to negotiate and be aware of the legal rights of Indigenous groups for ongoing use of natural resources. In 2002, new guidelines for tourism in Indigenous territories were drafted under the UN Convention on Biological Diversity. The World Summit on Sustainable Development (UN, 2002) and the World Parks Congress in 2003 also included resolutions on the rights of Indigenous peoples and conserving biodiversity (FPP, 2003). These are partly a response to the dominance of international agencies funding biodiversity conservation projects. In the mid-1990s, USAID had 105 ecotourism projects in 10 tropical developing countries and also Nepal. These had US$2 billion in funding directed through US conservation NGOs and the private sector (Honey, 1999). Since 2000, three international conservation NGOs (i.e. WWF, Conservation International and TNC) have together spent US$350 million a year on biodiversity conservation projects in developing countries, which is more than the UN's GEF programme. It is important to note, however, that the political efforts and funding of local NGOs fighting for Indigenous land rights are secondary to these major environmental NGOs funding conservation and ecotourism projects (Chatty and Colchester, 2002; Epler Wood, 2003; Arce-White, 2005). The World Conservation Union (IUCN) only recently devised guidelines to involve Indigenous communities in co-managing national parks, protected areas and community conservation areas (Beltran, 2000; Borrini-Feyerabend *et al.*, 2004; Igoe, 2004; Bushell and Eagles, 2006). Recent IUCN guidelines focus on securing Indigenous rights in legislation together with policies for co-managed protected areas and support for community conservation and resource management (Carino, 2004; Colchester, 2004; Hill, 2004).

Case studies of Indigenous ecotourism ventures highlight the key role of government policies on Indigenous lands and tourism, along with legal recognition of Indigenous land tenure and resource use rights (Zeppel, 2006). These national policies are shaped by international conventions on biodiversity conservation, cultural heritage and Indigenous rights, and the policies of the World Bank and the other donor agencies on Indigenous peoples. Globally, Indigenous peoples occupy 20% of land, in areas of high biodiversity, compared to 6% declared as protected areas (WWF, 2005). Hence, the growth of Indigenous ecotourism since the late 1980s reflects the strong links between global initiatives on biodiversity conservation; Indigenous rights and the development of ecotourism (Lash, 1998; Honey, 1999; Weber *et al.*, 2000; Alcorn, 2001; Johnston, 2006; Notzke, 2006; Zeppel, 2006) (see Table 16.3). International funding for the conservation of biodiversity hotspots, such as rainforests, and the spread of tourism into remote areas have involved more Indigenous groups in ecotourism.

Established in 1990, TIES also links conservation with sustainable tourism development. They began research on community-based ecotourism with Indigenous groups in Ecuador and the benefits of ecotourism for local communities near protected areas in Kenya (Epler Wood, 1999a,b, 2002). Their resource book, *Ecotourism: A Guide for Planners and Managers* included chapters about Indigenous ecotourism in Ecuador and in Southern Africa (Christ, 1998; Drumm, 1998). Tourism codes of conduct for Indigenous communities have also been compiled (Honey and Thullen, 2003). Allied research projects with the Center on Ecotourism and Sustainable Development reviewed community-based ecolodges run by Indigenous groups in Peru, Bolivia and Ecuador and, in 2006, the perspectives and roles of Indigenous peoples in Latin America on ecotourism certification programmes. Ecotourism Australia, established in 1991, supports partnerships with Indigenous groups and includes Indigenous cultural criteria in their Eco-certification programme (Ecotourism Australia, 2002). Aboriginal-owned business enterprises are a small part of Australia's ecotourism industry (*Ecotourism News*, 2000; Zeppel, 2003). The *2006 Ecotourism Australia Conference*

Table 16.3 Biodiversity conservation, Indigenous rights and ecotourism on tribal lands

Biodiversity conservation	Indigenous rights	Ecotourism
1980s		
Biosphere reserves	UN Working Group on Indigenous Populations (1982)	Ecotourism defined
World heritage areas	ILO Convention No. 169 on IP (1989)	
	UN Draft Declaration on the Rights of IP (1989/1990)	
1990s		
GEF established (1991)	World Bank Policy on IP (1991)	Ecotourism Associations (USA, Australia, Kenya)
UN Convention on Biological Diversity (1992)	UN International Year for the World's IP (1993)	
UN Earth Summit Rio (1992)	UN Decade of the World's IP (1995–2004)	Ecotourism: A Guide for Planners and Managers (TES, 1993/1998)
	Indigenous Tourism Rights International (1995)	
IP Biodiversity Network (1997)	WWF Policy on Rights of IP (1996)	
Ramsar Wetlands and IP (1999)	IP of Africa Coordinating Committee (1998)	
	Minority Rights Group International (1999)	
2000s		
World Summit on SD (2002)	UN Permanent Forum on Indigenous Issues (2000)	WTO SD of Ecotourism (2001/2003)
World Parks Congress (2003)	Dana Declaration on Mobile IP and Conservation (2002)	WWF Guidelines for CBE (2001)
World Conservation Congress (2004)	Business for Social Responsibility Rights of IP (2003)	Indigenous Ecotourism Toolbox
	International Forum on Indigenous Tourism (2002)	UN Year of Ecotourism (2002)
Protected Areas and IP (IUCN) (2000 and 2004)	World Social Forum includes IP (2005)	CBE Pacific Islands (SPREP, 2002)
	UN 2nd Decade of the World's IP (2005–2014)	Rights and Responsibilities (2003)[a]
	UN approves Declaration on the Rights of IP (2006)	Indigenous Ecotourism (2006)[b]

IP: Indigenous peoples; SD: Sustainable development; CBE: Community-based ecotourism; UN: United Nations; ILO: International Labour Organisation; GEF: Global Environment Facility; WTO: World Tourism Organization; WWF: World Wide Fund for Nature; TES: The Ecotourism Society; SPREP: South Pacific Region Environment Programme; IUCN: The World Conservation Union.
[a]Honey and Thullen, (2003), TIES.
[b]Zeppel, (2006), CABI.

included Aboriginal keynote speakers talking about opportunities for ecotourism within Native Title claims and the business potential for ecotourism on Indigenous land.

Indigenous views on ecotourism

Most tourism organisations consider Indigenous tourism, ecotourism and wildlife tourism as separate niche or special interest areas of nature-based tourism. *Ecotourism Australia* (2005), though, defines ecotourism as 'ecologically sustainable tourism with a primary focus on experiencing natural areas that fosters environmental and cultural understanding, appreciation and conservation'. In this definition, there is a primary focus on the natural environment with a secondary emphasis on cultural heritage, including Indigenous cultures. TIES (2004), based in the USA, defines ecotourism as 'responsible travel to natural areas that conserves the environment and improves the well-being of local people'. The focus, again, is on the natural environment, but with ecotourism providing benefits for local communities. For Honey (1999, p. 25), ecotourism 'directly benefits the economic development and political empowerment of local communities; and fosters respect for different cultures and for human rights' (see Table 16.4). Conservation International defined ecotourism as 'a form of tourism inspired primarily by the natural history of an area, including its Indigenous cultures' (Ziffer, 1989). Some Indigenous groups also refer to cultural ecotourism or ecocultural tourism, to emphasise the natural environment and resources are still managed as an Indigenous cultural landscape (Helu-Thaman, 1992; Beck and Somerville, 2002).

In addition to generating employment and income, there are often political motivations for Indigenous ecotourism. For many Indigenous groups, ecotourism is used to reinforce land claims, acknowledge cultural identity and land ownership, and regain their rights to access or use tribal land and resources. Ecotourism also shows that tribal land is being used productively to generate income and the ability of Indigenous groups to govern themselves or manage businesses (Hinch, 2001; Weaver, 2001, 2006). For Indigenous peoples, then, sustainable ecotourism development is based on 'conservation of resources and empowerment of local people through direct benefits and control over ecotourism activities' (Scheyvens, 2002, p. 80). However, government policies on community-based ecotourism and support from environmental NGOs (e.g. WWF, Conservation International, TNC) are essential for most Indigenous ecotourism and conservation projects to be implemented.

Table 16.4 Key features of general ecotourism and of Indigenous ecotourism

Ecotourism	Indigenous ecotourism
1. *Involves travel to natural destinations* Remote regions, protected areas and private reserves	Remote homelands, communal reserves, inhabited protected areas and tribal territories
2. *Minimises impact* Reduce ecological/cultural impacts of facilities and tourists Sustainable development of non-consumptive industry	Minimise environmental and cultural impacts Sustainable tribal use of natural resources
3. *Builds environmental and cultural awareness* Environmental education of tourists and residents by trained guides	Tribal guides share environmental knowledge Reinforces Indigenous cultural links with land
4. *Provides direct financial benefits for conservation* Tourism funds environmental protection, education and research Park entrance fees, tourist taxes and levies, conservation donations	Tourism funds conservation and community needs Tourist/lease fees, wildlife quotas, NGO funding
5. *Provides financial benefits and empowerment for local people* Park revenue sharing, community tourism concessions and partnerships	Park revenue sharing with local communities Legal land title to negotiate tourism contracts Lease land on reserves and sell wildlife quotas Business owned/co-owned by tribal community
6. *Respects local culture and sensitive to host countries* Culturally respectful of local customs, dress codes and social norms	Promotes ecocultural tourism and learning Tourism complements traditional lifestyle
7. *Supports human rights and democratic movements* Respect human rights; understand social and political situation	Tribal land rights and human rights recognised Indigenous political history acknowledged

Sources: Based on Honey (1999), Blake (2003), Scheyvens (2002) and TIES (2004).

According to Johnston (2000), there are some key differences between industry definitions of ecotourism and Indigenous views of ecotourism (see Table 16.5). Industry use of ecotourism includes commercialising Indigenous biological and cultural heritage; claims to be environmentally or socially responsible; and using criteria for sustainability derived without input from Indigenous peoples. Indigenous support for ecotourism, however, involves 'tourism that is based on indigenous knowledge systems and values, promoting customary practices and livelihoods'

Table 16.5 Industry and Indigenous perceptions of ecotourism

Industry ecotourism

Ecotourism as any form of industry monopolised tourism

Marketed as nature, cultural, ethnic or adventure travel

Commercialise Indigenous biocultural heritage, including collective property (knowledge) and/or homeland of 'host' peoples

Claim to be socially and environmentally responsible

Apply sustainability criteria determined without Indigenous input

Indigenous cultures commercialised (e.g. photographs on brochures)

Few companies obtain prior consent to promote Indigenous peoples

Few companies negotiate business partnerships or royalty payments

Indigenous ecotourism

Ecotourism based on Indigenous knowledge systems and values

Ecotourism based on promoting Indigenous customary practices and livelihoods

Ecotourism used to regain rights to access, manage and use traditional land and resources

Ecotourism used to manage cultural property such as historic and sacred sites

Takes place under the control and active participation of local Indigenous people

Includes Indigenous communities in ecotourism planning, development and operation

Managing Indigenous cultural property in terms of land, heritage and resources

Negotiating the terms of trade for the use of ecotourism resources, including people

---

Sources: Based on Drumm (1998), Johnston (2000) and Hinch (2001).

(Johnston, 2000, p. 91). Cultural aspects of Indigenous eco-tourism include the close bonds between Indigenous peoples and the environment based on subsistence activities along with spiritual relationships with the land, plants and animals. However, potential conflicts within Indigenous ecotourism include tourists objecting to traditional hunting activities and tribal people using modern items such as rifles and outboard motors (Hinch, 2001; Buckley, 2005). Hunting for subsistence and to preserve Indigenous cultural identity also clashes with new rules for conservation (Lai and Nepal, 2006). In Tanzania, East Africa, there are land-use conflicts between hunting companies killing wildlife and the walking or wildlife viewing safaris run as community ecotourism ventures by the Maasai people (*Tourism in Focus*, 2002b).

Cater (2006) highlights that ecotourism is based on western cultural views of conservation, sustainability and development. The dominant view of ecotourism as nature-based excludes the views of Indigenous people whereby nature is part of a living cultural landscape. The internationalisation of ecotourism, as a concept and as a form of nature-based tourism, further reinforces western views of conservation to maintain biodiversity and provide alternative livelihoods. Conservation NGOs such as WWF, TNC and Conservation International, with funding from USAID and the GEF, reinforce western views of ecotourism as preserving nature. Elite forms of up-market ecolodges, patronisation of local people with ecotourism as the only development option and devaluing other cultural views of nature all derive from this western view of ecotourism. Hence, aesthetic and scenic ideals of viewing nature and wildlife exclude Indigenous hunting and use of resources in ecotourism.

Indigenous groups argued that the UN *International Year of Ecotourism* in 2002 represented the commercial aspects of using 'ecotourism' to develop global mass tourism, further encroaching on Indigenous territories and the rights of Indigenous peoples. Organisations such as Tourism Concern, the Third World Network and the Rethinking Tourism Project raised key issues relating to the impacts of ecotourism on local communities. Indigenous groups held an alternative meeting in Oaxaca, Mexico in March 2002 to debate the issues around ecotourism development. Some 200 participants from 13 countries in the Americas reviewed case studies of Indigenous tourism projects in local communities. In a Zapotec Indian community in Oaxaca, ecotourism was seen as sharing Indigenous knowledge of sustainable land use with forest tours an economic alternative to other uses of forest resources (Vivanco, 2002). The International Forum on Indigenous Tourism at Oaxaca drafted a declaration reaffirming the rights of Indigenous groups to manage and control tourism on their lands.

Since 2003, Indigenous Tourism Rights International (formerly Rethinking Tourism Project) has focused on certification and standards for Indigenous ecotourism, in partnership with the International Indian Treaty Council based in Guatemala. An online rethinking certification conference in June 2004 discussed whether tourism certification was appropriate or not for Indigenous communities and alternative standards for eco-certification (Blake, 2003; Medina, 2005; Vivanco (in press)). Indigenous respondents expressed concern about the cost and market-driven nature of tourism certification whereby external standards replaced cultural concepts and customary practices. Hence, 'Aboriginal "accreditation" involves approval from elders' (Bissett *et al.*, 1998, p. 7). Non-Indigenous NGOs also dominated the online discussion about tourism certification programmes. Indigenous issues have a low priority compared to business and environmental matters in these certification schemes, one exception being the 'Respect our Culture' programme of Aboriginal Tourism Australia (ITRI, 2004).

Key issues in Indigenous ecotourism

Key issues in the published research and case studies about Indigenous ecotourism include community development (Russell, 2000; Fennell, 2003; Stronza, 2005; Lai and Nepal, 2006); empowerment (Scheyvens, 1999, 2000, 2002; Sofield, 2003; WTO, 2005) or self-determination (Johnston, 2003; Hinch, 2004); and sustainable tourism/ecotourism (Epler Wood, 1999b, 2002; Robinson, 1999; WWF, 2001; WTO, 2003; Mat Som and Baum, 2004; Mbaiwa, 2005; Tsaur *et al.*, 2006). Small-scale ecotourism promotes local conservation of natural and cultural resources, either individually or through tourism enterprises owned or managed by communities. Local participation, sharing economic benefits and control of tourism were essential for community-based ecotourism (Lash, 1998; Lash and Austin, 2003). Ecotourism, as a tool for community development, also involves new partnerships with tour operators, government agencies, conservation NGOs, researchers, other Indigenous communities and international groups (WTO, 2002; Butcher, 2003; Fennell, 2003; Suansri, 2003). According to Mann (2000), community tourism involves local people in decision-making and ownership of tourism; a fair share of profits from tourism ventures; and new tourism committees or organisations that represent the community while minimising environmental and cultural impacts.

For Indigenous people, the community is a tribe or village of related members, with shared decision-making and village ownership of forests or reserves held under traditional or legal land titles. For this reason, most Indigenous ecotourism projects are community-based tourism ventures. However, marginalised Indigenous groups require support from NGOs, aid groups and government agencies to control and benefit from community ecotourism or joint ventures on tribal lands.

Successful community-based ecotourism requires the empowerment of community members through local participation and control of tourism decision-making, employment and training opportunities, and increased entrepreneurial activities by local people. According to Fennell (2003, p. 159), the process of empowerment involves local people 'holding the will, resources, and opportunity to make decisions within the community'. This process needs to be supported by appropriate policies, education, training and partnerships. Moreover, 'if ecotourism is to be viewed as a tool for rural development, it must also help to shift economic and political control to the local community, village, cooperative, or entrepreneur' (Honey, 2003, p. 23). Scheyvens (1999, 2002) framework for community-based tourism included psychological, social, political and economic empowerment or disempowerment through tourism. Increased status and self-esteem, lasting economic benefits, community development and tourism decision-making are key aspects of empowerment through tourism. Sofield (2003) also proposed that tourism sustainability depends not only on empowering Indigenous communities, but also that traditional community mechanisms had to be supported by legal empowerment; along with environmental or institutional change to reallocate power and decision-making on resource use to local communities, supported and sanctioned by states.

Indigenous ecotourism ventures also required resource empowerment whereby local communities have ownership or use rights of land and resources. In the Okavango Delta of Botswana, land trusts for San Bushmen run community tourism ventures or leased their land and wildlife quotas to other hunting or tourism operators. This promotes wildlife conservation and local economic benefits, however to be successful, communities require further social and political empowerment through training in managerial skills and use of trust funds, direct resource ownership and more input in land use or wildlife quotas allocated to tourism (Mbaiwa, 2005). Empowering Indigenous communities in tourism depends on enhancing local control through traditional tribal or legal empowerment, and recognition of individual and collective rights to ancestral lands (WTO, 2005). Successful models of community-based ecotourism, such as Capirona in Ecuador (Colvin, 1994; Drumm, 1998) and ecolodges (Stronza, 2005) are based on community ownership and management of both natural resources and tourism (Lash, 1998; Sofield, 1991, 2002, 2003; Mat Som and Baum, 2004).

The sustainable development of ecotourism, then, is based on the integrated elements of ecological, economic and social–cultural sustainability (WTO, 2003). Ecotourism is based on the conservation of biodiversity, mainly in protected areas, and minimising the impacts of tourism in natural areas (Garen, 2000; Buckley, 2003). The economic benefits of ecotourism aim to assist nature conservation as well as provide returns to local communities through employment, the purchase of goods and services and other fees. Intrepid Travel (2002) reviewed the economic, socio-cultural and physical impacts of alternative tourism in five tribal villages they visited in Thailand and Borneo. While there were local economic and social benefits, most of the villages had little control over tourism. Ecotourism and pro-poor tourism projects focus on poverty alleviation and conservation to provide alternatives to traditional subsistence economies and resource use in rural areas (Butcher, 2003; Roe *et al.*, 2004; Epler Wood, 2005). Ecotourism also aims to foster local cultural practices, crafts and traditions. However, many conservation and community development projects in protected areas, including ecotourism, have had limited local participation through consultation, compensation or employment. Decisions about conservation and tourism still lie with NGOs and government agencies, with local communities limited or restricted in resource use (Honey, 1999; Counsell, 2005).

Ongoing Indigenous use of wildlife and natural resources, particularly in protected areas, conflicts with the environmental standards and sustainability criteria of developed nations, western tourists, national park agencies and conservation NGOs (Hinch, 1998; Robinson, 1999; Cohen, 2002; Duffy, 2006). Buckley (2005) describes kayaking tours near Baffin Island in the Canadian Arctic where local Inuit people also establish summer hunting and fishing camps in the area, using fast boats and rifles to shoot narwhal for their tusks and blubber. Kayakers heard rifle shots, met Inuit hunters with narwhal tusks and saw a drifting narwhal carcass. Inuit boat charters dropped of kayakers at a narwhal congregation area then left to hunt narwhal nearby. Some Inuit illegally sold narwhal tusks while the few narwhals seen by tourists dived to escape boats. Therefore, negotiating acceptable forms of resource use and conservation zones is a key part of many Indigenous ecotourism ventures. Community wildlife sanctuaries with no cattle grazing are established on

Maasai group ranches in Kenya and Tanzania while limited trophy hunting on communal lands is allowed in Southern Africa.

Indigenous cultural and environmental values influence and shape economic development strategies on tribal lands including ecotourism (Groenfeldt, 2003). In the Cuyabeno Wildlife Reserve of the Ecuadorian Amazon, Indian income from ecotourism depends more on the tourist attractiveness of the natural area, the type of tourism specialisation or services offered and the type of local tourism organisation or industry structure adopted (e.g. community run vs. joint ventures). Ecotourism had a positive impact on conservation only where tourism changed land-use decisions (e.g. no-take areas), and when tourism work reduced the local free time and need for hunting (Wunder, 2000). Wesche (1996) also suggested that as the ecotourism industry in Ecuador reached a consolidation stage, it became more concerned with sustainability and more willing to accommodate Indigenous interests. In developing countries, Doan (2000) found that ecotourism in private reserves, including Indigenous areas, was more sustainable and delivered better local benefits than ecotourism in public parks. In Peru, the Indigenous Uros people living on reed islands within Lake Titicaca National Reserve seek to establish a communal reserve to control tourism access and revenue in their territory (Kent, 2006).

Other studies highlight difficulties in the equitable sharing of ecotourism benefits among Indigenous communities. Social and political conflicts about the control of resources limit the capacity of local residents to negotiate ecotourism developments with private operators and government agencies. The dominant ethnic or clan groups, local elites and male landowners or committee members gain most economic benefits from community-based ecotourism or joint ventures with private operators. On Kimana Group Ranch in Kenya, Maasai people manage a wildlife sanctuary and lease three campsites generating Ksh2.4 million in annual revenue. Clan disputes over access to land have increased while younger Maasai control the management of land and resources for farming, cultivation and tourism.

Local Maasai elite received most economic benefits from an exclusive agreement with a safari operator approved by the Group Ranch Committee without wider consultation. However, on Eselenkei Group Ranch, there is broad community support for the more equitable contract with an ecotourism operator negotiated on behalf of the Maasai by the Kenya Wildlife Service (Southgate, 2006). Wholly community-initiated and managed ecotourism ventures, such as the Tumani Tenda Ecocamp in Gambia, West Africa, require a high degree of social cooperation to deliver benefits (Jones, 2005). The Escudo Jaguar ecotourism centre run by Chol Indians in the Lacandon rainforest, Chiapas, Mexico mainly benefits participating households, supported by NGOs (Cruz *et al.*, 2005).

Challenges for Indigenous ecotourism

The stages of Indigenous ecotourism development range from (1) tourism exploration of Indigenous peoples on tribal lands; (2) involvement of the local community in providing tourism facilities and (3) tribal tourism development based on secure land titles and partnerships with tour operators (see Table 16.6). Legal land tenure such as a Certificate of Ancestral Domain Title

Table 16.6 Stages of Indigenous ecotourism development

	Exploration	Involvement	Development
Land tenure	Traditional lands	Community reserves	Legal land title
Local system	Families, villages	Community organisations	Development organisations
Resource use	Subsistence only	Subsistence and for sale	Limits on subsistence use Regulated commercial use
Funding	Local funds	Indigenous agencies Conservation NGOs	External donor agencies (finance, aid, conservation)
Tourism	Independent visitors	Irregular tour groups Informal partnerships	Regular ongoing tour groups Formal joint ventures and contracts
Marketing	Word-of-mouth	Flyers, direct sales Ethnic brokers (volunteers)	Website – community/ tourism group Wholesaled by other tour operators
Certification	Tribal elders	Local tourism committees	Formal accreditation scheme
Cultural knowledge	Tribal elders	Local guides as 'cultural brokers'	Guides, brochures, books, and websites

Source: Based on the first three stages of Butler's (1980, 2005) resort life cycle model.

provides a secure basis for Indigenous groups to negotiate contracts and leases with private tourism operators. Small Indigenous ecotourism ventures in the Pacific Islands, Southeast Asia and West Africa are mainly in the tourism exploration or early involvement stage, while Indigenous groups with legal land titles in Eastern and Southern Africa and Latin America are developing joint ventures and their own community tourism (Zeppel, 2006). This stage often includes tourism training and support for Indigenous enterprise development from conservation NGOs. The development stage also includes formal marketing, partnerships with tour operators and regulation or local control of resource use.

Indigenous ecotourism occurs within a wider nature-based tourism industry dominated by non-Indigenous tour operators and travel agents. Ecotourism itself is one part of a global tourism industry. As such, Indigenous ecotourism is part of a broader environment that is influenced by non-Indigenous tourism, conservation and development activities (Cohen, 2002; Butcher, 2003; Mowforth and Munt, 2003). Therefore, issues associated with Indigenous control of ecotourism and factors that affect these enterprises need to be considered (see Tables 16.6 and 16.7). Indigenous ecotourism ventures face the same issues of product development, marketing, competition, quality control, training and profitability faced by other small ecotourism businesses (Weaver, 2001; Walpole and Thouless, 2005). However, Indigenous ecotourism businesses also have other objectives such as asserting territorial rights, maintaining cultural knowledge and practices and providing employment. For many Indigenous people, ecotourism is an alternative to other extractive land uses such as logging, mining (Weaver, 2001), oil drilling, ranching, fishing and sport hunting (*Tourism in Focus*, 2002a, b). The development of Indigenous ecotourism though is limited by poverty, the lack of infrastructure on reserves, community conflicts over tourism, gaining business knowledge and forming commercial links with the tourism industry. Guaranteed tourism revenue from lease fees and bed night or tourist levies may provide more stable income and employment than community-owned ventures with greater local control over tourism (Walpole and Thouless, 2005). Restrictions on use of natural resources may also drive involvement in ecotourism (King and Stewart, 1996). Small-scale Indigenous-owned ecotourism ventures, while conserving key natural areas, have local benefits but limited impacts or market linkages with mainstream tourism. Hence, a variety of government strategies, tourism and resource use policies and industry practices are needed to support Indigenous ecotourism on tribal lands.

Table 16.7 Sustainability and empowerment within Indigenous ecotourism

Environmental sustainability	Resource empowerment
Contribution to the conservation of natural areas	Tribal reserves and protected areas
Economic benefits for conservation	Maintain natural areas and wildlife
Educational and interpretation activities (host communities, tourists)	Environmental knowledge and training
Environmental practices (minimal impacts/ sustainable resource use)	Manage resource use and land practices
Social and cultural sustainability	**Social empowerment**
Community involvement and benefits	Facilitates stakeholder interest and income
Community participation and decision-making	Communities seen as key stakeholders
Community ownership and joint ventures	Supports traditional or local authority
Cultural activities and presentations	Supports and reinforces cultural identity
Economic sustainability	**Economic 'empowerment'**
Finance and funding (private, donor agencies)	Reliance on NGOs and foreign donors
Marketing and promotion	Market: Internet, NGOs, rural tourism groups
Profitability (private operators, community facilities)	Limited income, develop local infrastructure
Business cooperation and regulation	Joint venture partners, government agencies
Political sustainability	**Political empowerment**
Community organisation and decision-making bodies	Tribal councils and tourism committees
Community knowledge of legal rights (land, resources)	Legal titles to land and resource user rights
Negotiate with government agencies	Revenue sharing and community projects
Strategic alliances and networks	Tribal associations, NGOs, industry partners

Sources: Scheyvens (1999, 2002) and WTO (2001, 2003).

According to Epler Wood (2002, p. 45), Indigenous communities must have *'legal control over land* and full legal rights to protect any businesses that they establish' for ecotourism to be used for sustainable development of tribal areas. Since the 1990s, most new Indigenous ecotourism ventures have been established on communal lands, Indigenous reserves and wildlife conservancies under the legal control of Indigenous groups. This includes both land rights and also some resource use rights for wildlife on tribal lands, mainly with wildlife hunting quotas in Africa (Zeppel, 2006). With this legal control, Indigenous groups can sub-lease land to other operators, negotiate contracts with joint venture partners as well as establish and run their own tourism ventures on tribal lands. Hence, Indigenous peoples with legal land titles are now landlords, partners or ecotourism service providers. However, there is limited development or transfer of business skills to Indigenous peoples and organisations involved in ecotourism. In many areas, more Indigenous input in land use, wildlife quotas and tourism decision-making is needed in both government agencies and NGOs (Alcorn, 2001; Mbaiwa, 2005).

Indigenous ecotourism must also consider the environmental, cultural, economic and political factors that may limit or control tourism development on tribal lands (Zeppel, 1998, 2000, 2006). Indigenous ecotourism takes place within a global tourism industry, which dominates marketing, transport, accommodation and visitor services (Butler and Hinch, 1996). Socio-political factors that affect Indigenous groups developing ecotourism include land and property rights. Guiding principles for ecotourism on Indigenous territories include community involvement and benefit, small-scale ventures, land ownership, empowerment and cultural sensitivity (Scheyvens, 1999; Hinch, 2001). 'Real' ecotourism, then, has to empower local people and provide financial benefits used for community development rather than individual economic enhancement by local elites (Honey, 2003). NGOs and government agencies play a key role in channelling broader benefits of ecotourism into conservation and communities. Ecotourism and conservation, however, often limits other land-use options by Indigenous peoples (Cater, 2006; Duffy, 2006).

The 'successes' of Indigenous ecotourism ventures may also be measured in environmental, social or political outcomes (e.g. land rights) rather than in purely economic terms. Hence, economic and political criteria are often key motivators for Indigenous ecotourism, while environmental and cultural criteria are key outcomes for Indigenous groups involved in ecotourism. For example, Gerberich (2005) applied cultural, environmental, socio-economic and political factors to assess the sustainability of tourism on American Indian reservations. The political factors revolved around Indian sovereignty and tribal ownership of land and resources. Hence, tourism development on Indian reservations maintained tribal cultures and reinforced their autonomous powers. There are strong links between these four key criteria for sustainability and related aspects of community empowerment, especially use of resources, through Indigenous ecotourism ventures on tribal lands (see Table 16.7).

For many Indigenous groups, ecotourism is used to reinforce land claims, acknowledge cultural identity and land ownership and to regain rights to access or use tribal land and resources (Zografos and Kenrick, 2005). Ecotourism ventures thus demonstrate that tribal land is being used productively to generate income and the ability of Indigenous groups to govern their own affairs and to manage businesses (Hinch, 2001, 2004; Weaver, 2001, 2006; Zeppel, 2006). For Indigenous peoples, then, sustainable ecotourism development is based on 'conservation of resources and empowerment of local people through direct benefits and control over ecotourism activities' (Scheyvens, 2002, p. 80). The legal assertion of Indigenous land rights and government policies on community-based tourism and resource use rights, together with support from environmental NGOs, are essential for most Indigenous ecotourism and conservation projects on tribal lands to be successful.

In summary, key factors for the sustainable development of Indigenous ecotourism ventures on tribal lands and protected areas are (1) securing land tenure; (2) funding or technical support from NGOs, foreign donors and/or government agencies for community-based ecotourism and (3) links with the private tourism industry. A recent forum reviewed priorities for funding and investment in small ecotourism enterprises, including Indigenous projects, by development agencies, NGOs (Conservation International) and the private sector (Planeta, 2005). Another report reviewed the financial viability of ecolodges in developing countries, including joint ventures with Indigenous groups (EBFP, 2005).

Conservation values (i.e. biodiversity) rather than culture still drives Indigenous ecotourism projects.

Conclusion

This chapter has reviewed key issues for Indigenous ecotourism in tribal homelands and protected areas. Indigenous ecotourism is defined as nature-based attractions or tours owned by tribal groups, which feature Indigenous cultural knowledge and practices linked to the land. Tourist interest in visiting Indigenous peoples and their tribal lands around the world is growing. Areas of high biodiversity, such as tropical rainforests, are linked with surviving groups of Indigenous peoples. Key factors driving Indigenous involvement in ecotourism include gaining legal rights to land, preventing other extractive land uses and cultural revival. Many Indigenous groups now own or receive lease fees for ecotourism ventures located on traditional homelands and reserves. Indigenous control over ecotourism on tribal lands includes approval, ownership, partnerships and joint ventures. Ideally, Indigenous ecotourism will sustain and conserve natural areas, maintain Indigenous lifestyles and provide benefits for Indigenous communities. Key issues for Indigenous involvement in ecotourism include land and resource rights and the equitable sharing of tourism benefits. Indigenous ecotourism also operates within a broader framework of economic, political, cultural and environmental factors. Support from conservation NGOs, government agencies and Indigenous organisations are all crucial for developing Indigenous ecotourism ventures in tribal territories. Hence, Indigenous cultural perspectives and approaches to ecotourism, conservation and resource use need to be considered.

References

Alcorn, J.B. (2001). *Good Governance, Indigenous Peoples and Biodiversity Conservation: Recommendations for Enhancing Results Across Sectors*. Biodiversity Support Program, WWF. http://www.worldwildlife.org/bsp/publications/asia/120/Good_Governance_1.pdf (accessed October 17, 2006).

ANTA (Australian National Training Authority) (2001). *Indigenous Ecotourism Toolbox*. ANTA. http://www.dlsweb.rmit.edu.au/toolbox/Indigenous/ecotourismtoolbox/ (accessed October 17, 2006).

Arce-White, E. (2005). *Funding Indigenous Conservation*. International Funders for Indigenous Peoples. http://www.internationalfunders.org/pubs.html (accessed October 17, 2006).

Ashley, C. and Roe, D. (1998). *Enhancing Community Involvement in Wildlife Tourism: Issues and Challenges*. International Institute for Environment and Development, London.

Beck, W. and Somerville, M. (2002). Embodied places in indigenous ecotourism: the Yarrawarra research project. *Australian Aboriginal Studies* 2002/2: 4–13.

Beltran, J. (ed.) (2000). *Indigenous and Traditional Peoples and Protected Areas: Principles, Guidelines and Case Studies*. Best Practice Protected Area Guidelines Series No. 4. IUCN.

Berger, D.J. (1996). The challenge of integrating Maasai tradition with tourism. In Price, M.F. (ed.), *People and Tourism in Fragile Environments*. John Wiley & Sons, Chichester, UK, pp. 175–197.

Bissett, C., Perry, L. and Zeppel, H. (1998). Land and spirit: aboriginal tourism in New South Wales. In McArthur, S. and Weir, B. (eds), *Australia's Ecotourism Industry: A Snapshot in 1998*. Ecotourism Association of Australia, Brisbane, pp. 6–8.

Blake, B. (2003). The tourism industry's codes for indigenous peoples. In Honey, M. and Thullen, S. (eds), *Rights and Responsibilities: A Compilation of Codes of Conduct for Tourism and Indigenous and Local Communities*. Center on Ecotourism and Sustainable Development and The International Ecotourism Society. http://www.imacmexico.org/ev_es.php?ID=23341_201&ID2=DO_TOPIC (accessed October 17, 2006).

Borrini-Feyerabend, G., Kothari, A. and Oviedo, G. (2004). *Indigenous and Local Communities and Protected Areas: Towards Equity and Enhanced Conservation*. Best Practice Protected Area Guidelines Series No. 11. IUCN. http://www.iucn.org/dbtw-wpd/edocs/PAG-011.pdf (accessed October 17, 2006).

Buckley, R. (2003). *Case Studies in Ecotourism*. CABI, Wallingford, UK.

Buckley, R. (2005). In search of the narwhal: ethical dilemmas in ecotourism. *Journal of Ecotourism* 4(2): 129–134.

Bushell, R. and Eagles, P.F.J. (eds) (2006). *Tourism and Protected Areas: Benefits Beyond Boundaries*. CABI, Wallingford, UK.

Butcher, J. (2003). New moral tourism, the third world and development. *The Moralisation of Tourism: Sun, Sand … and Saving the World?* Routledge, London, pp. 113–136.

Butler, R. (1980). The concept of a tourist area cycle of evolution: Implications for management of resources. *Canadian Geographer* 24: 5–12.

Butler, R. (ed.) (2005). *The Tourism Area Life Cycle Model: Theoretical and Conceptual Implications*. Channel View Publications, Clevedon.

Butler, R. and Hinch, T. (eds) (1996). *Tourism and Indigenous Peoples*. International Thomson Business Press, London.

Carino, J. (2004). Indigenous voices at the table: restoring local decision-making on protected areas. *Cultural Survival Quarterly* 28(1). http://209.200.101.189/publications/csq/csq-article.cfm?id=1739 (accessed November 29, 2005).

Cater, E. (1996). *Community Involvement in Third World Ecotourism*. University of Reading, Reading, UK.

Cater, E. (2006). Ecotourism as a western construct. *Journal of Ecotourism* 5(1/2): 23–39.

Chatty, D. and Colchester, M. (eds) (2002). *Conservation and Mobile Indigenous Peoples: Displacement, Forced Settlement and Sustainable Development*. Berghahn Books, Oxford.

Chen, C.C. (2004). Indigenous community development through ecotourism: a case study. *Journal of Rural Development* 23(4): 491–512.

Christ, C. (1998). Taking ecotourism to the next level: a look at private sector involvement with local communities. In Lindberg, K., Epler Wood, M. and Engeldrum, D. (eds), *Ecotourism: A Guide for Planners and Managers*, Vol. 2. The Ecotourism Society, Vermont, pp. 183–195.

Christ, C. (2004). *A Road Less Travelled*. Conservation Frontlines online. Conservation International. http://www.conservation.org/xp/frontlines/people/focus32-1.xml (accessed October 17, 2006).

Christ, C., Hillel, O., Matus, S. and Sweeting, J. (2003). *Tourism and Biodiversity: Mapping Tourism's Global Footprint*. Conservation International and UNEP.

Cohen, E. (2002). Authenticity, equity and sustainability in tourism. *Journal of Sustainable Tourism* 10(4): 267–276.

Colchester, M. (2003). Salvaging nature: indigenous peoples, protected areas and biodiversity conservation. *World Rainforest Movement and Forest Peoples Programme*.

Colchester, M. (2004). Conservation policy and indigenous peoples. *Cultural Survival Quarterly* 28(1). http://209.200.101.189/publications/csq/csq-article.cfm?id=1738 (accessed November 29, 2005).

Colvin, J.G. (1994). Capirona: a model of indigenous ecotourism. *Journal of Sustainable Tourism* 2(3): 174–177.

Counsell, S. (2005). Greenbacks in the Garden of Eden. *Linking Circles IV: 2005 International Funders for Indigenous Peoples Conference Report*, New York, May 19–20, 2005. International Funders for Indigenous Peoples, pp. 94–104. http://www.internationalfunders.org/conference.html (accessed October 17, 2006).

Cruz, R.E.H., Baltazar, E.B., Gomez, G.M. and Lugo, E.I.J.E. (2005). Social adaptation: ecotourism in the Lacandon forest. *Annals of Tourism Research* 32(3): 610–627.

Curtin, S. (2003). Whale-watching in Kaikoura: sustainable destination development? *Journal of Ecotourism* 2(3): 173–195.

Doan, T.M. (2000). The effects of ecotourism in developing countries: an analysis of case studies. *Journal of Sustainable Tourism* 8(4): 288–304.

Drumm, A. (1998). New approaches to community-based ecotourism management: learning from Ecuador. In Lindberg, K., Epler Wood, M. and Engeldrum, D. (eds), *Ecotourism: A Guide for Planners and Managers*, Vol. 2. The Ecotourism Society, Vermont, pp. 197–213.

Duffy, R. (2002). Ecotourism and indigenous communities. *A Trip Too Far: Ecotourism, Politics and Exploitation*. Earthscan Publications, London, pp. 98–126.

Duffy, R. (2006). The politics of ecotourism and the developing world. *Journal of Ecotourism* 5(1/2): 1–6.

EBFP (Environmental Business Finance Program) (2005). *Ecolodges: Exploring Opportunities for Sustainable Business*. International Finance Corporation. http://www.ifc.org/ifcext/home.nsf/content/ecolodges (accessed October 20, 2006).

Ecotourism Australia (2002). *Cairns Charter on Partnerships for Ecotourism*. Ecotourism Australia. http://www.ecotourism.org.au/cairnscharter.asp (accessed October 17, 2006).

Ecotourism Australia (2005). *What is ecotourism?* Ecotourism Australia. http://www.ecotourism.org.au (accessed October 17, 2006).

Ecotourism News (2000). Aborigines offer ecotourism more than the didgeridoo. *Ecotourism News (Ecotourism Association of Australia)* Spring, 6.

Epler Wood, M. (1999a). Ecotourism, sustainable development, and cultural survival: protecting indigenous culture and land through ecotourism. *Cultural Survival Quarterly* 23(2). http://209.200.101.189/publications/csq/csqarticle.cfm?id=1431&highlight=ecotourism (accessed November 17, 2005).

Epler Wood, M. (1999b). The Ecotourism Society – an international NGO committed to sustainable development. *Tourism Recreation Research* 24(2): 119–123.

Epler Wood, M. (2002). Ecotourism and indigenous communities. *Ecotourism: Principles, Practices and Policies for Sustainability*. UNEP, Paris and The International Ecotourism Society, Vermont, pp. 44–45.

Epler Wood, M. (2003). *Community Conservation and Commerce*. EplerWood Reports, October 2003. EplerWood International. http://www.eplerwood.com/images/EplerWood_Report_Oct2003.pdf (accessed October 17, 2006).

Epler Wood, M. (2005). *Stepping Up: Creating a Sustainable Tourism Enterprise Strategy that Delivers in the Developing World*. EplerWood Reports, October 2005. EplerWood International. http://www.eplerwood.com/images/EplerWood_Report_Oct2005.pdf (accessed October 17, 2006).

Fennell, D.A. (2003). Ecotourism development: international, community, and site perspectives. *Ecotourism: An Introduction* (2nd edn). Routledge, London, pp. 150–170.

FPP (Forest Peoples Programme) (2003). WPC Recommendation 24: indigenous peoples and protected areas. *World Parks*

Congress 2003. http://www.forestpeoples.org/documents/ conservation/bases/wpc_base.shtml (accessed October 20, 2006).

Franke, J. (1995). *Walking the Village Path: A Worldwide Guide to Community-Generated Tourism Projects.* First Nations Health Project, Portland, OR.

Garen, E.J. (2000). Appraising ecotourism in conserving biodiversity. In Clark, T.W., Willard, A.R. and Cromley, C.M. (eds), *Foundations of Natural Resources Policy and Management.* Yale University Press, New Haven, CT, pp. 221–251.

Gerberich, V.L. (2005). An evaluation of sustainable Indian tourism. In Ryan, C. and Aicken, M. (eds), *Indigenous Tourism: The Commodification and Management of Culture.* Elsevier, Oxford, pp. 75–86.

Grekin, J. and Milne, S. (1996) Toward sustainable tourism development: the case of Pond Inlet, NWT. In Butler, R.W. and Hinch, T.D. (eds), *Tourism and Indigenous Peoples.* Thomson Business Press, UK, pp. 76–106.

Griffiths, T. (2004). Help or hindrance? The global environment facility, biodiversity conservation, and indigenous peoples. *Cultural Survival Quarterly* 28(1). http://209.200.101.189/ publications/csq/csq-article.cfm?id=1740 (accessed November 29, 2005).

Groenfeldt, D. (2003). The future of indigenous values: cultural relativism in the face of economic development. *Futures* 35(9): 917–929.

Halpenny, E. (1999). The state and critical issues relating to international ecotourism development policy. *Australia – The World's Natural Theme Park: Proceedings of the Ecotourism Association of Australia 1999 Conference,* Ecotourism Association of Australia, Brisbane, pp. 45–52.

Harrison, D. (ed.) (2003). *Pacific Island Tourism.* Cognizant Communication Corporation, New York.

Hashimoto, A. and Telfer, D.J. (2004). Canadian Aboriginal ecotourism in the north. In Diamantis, D. (ed.), *Ecotourism: Management and Assessment.* Thomson, London, pp. 204–225.

Helu-Thaman, K. (1992). Ecocultural tourism: a personal view for maintaining cultural integrity in ecotourism development. In Hay, J.E. (ed.), *Ecotourism Business in the Pacific: Promoting a Sustainable Experience.* Environmental Science, University of Auckland, Auckland, New Zealand, pp. 24–29.

Hill, R. (2004). *Global Trends in Protected Areas: A Report on the Fifth World Parks Congress.* Rainforest CRC, Cairns, Queensland. http://www.acfonline.org.au/uploads/res_protected_areas. pdf (accessed November 20, 2006).

Hinch, T. (1998). Ecotourists and indigenous hosts: diverging views on their relationship with nature. *Current Issues in Tourism* 1(1): 120–124.

Hinch, T. (2001). Indigenous territories. In Weaver, D.B. (ed.), *The Encyclopaedia of Ecotourism.* CABI, Wallingford, UK, pp. 345–357.

Hinch, T.D. (2004). Indigenous peoples and tourism. In Lew, A.L., Hall, C.M. and Williams, A.M. (eds), *A Companion to Tourism.* Blackwell Publishing, Malden, MA, pp. 246–257.

Hitchcock, R.K. (1994). Endangered peoples: indigenous rights and the environment. *Colorado Journal of International Environmental Law and Policy* 5(1): 11.

Honey, M. (1999). *Ecotourism and Sustainable Development: Who Owns Paradise?* Island Press, Washington, DC.

Honey, M. (2003). Summary of major principles regarding tourism and indigenous peoples and local communities. In Honey, M. and Thullen, S. (eds), *Rights and Responsibilities: A Compilation of Codes of Conduct for Tourism and Indigenous and Local Communities.* Center on Ecotourism and Sustainable Development and The International Ecotourism Society. http://www.imacmexico.org/ev_es.php?ID=23341_201& ID2=DO_TOPIC (accessed October 17, 2006).

Honey, M. and Thullen, S. (eds) (2003). *Rights and Responsibilities: A Compilation of Codes of Conduct for Tourism and Indigenous and Local Communities.* Center on Ecotourism and Sustainable Development and The International Ecotourism Society. http://www.imacmexico.org/ev_es.php?ID=23341_201& ID2 = DO_TOPIC (accessed October 17, 2006).

Howitt, R., Connell, J. and Hirsch, P. (eds) (1996). *Resources, Nations and Indigenous Peoples: Case Studies from Australasia, Melanesia and Southeast Asia.* Oxford University Press, Melbourne.

Igoe, J.J. (2004). *Conservation and Globalization: A Study of National Parks and Indigenous Communities from East Africa to South Dakota.* Thomson/Wadsworth, Belmont, CA.

Intrepid Travel (2002). *Literature Review: Impacts of Alternative Types of Tourism in Rural Village Communities in Less Developed Countries.* Responsible Travel Research. http://www.intrepidtravel. com/about/allabout/rt/research.php (accessed October 17, 2006).

ITRI (Indigenous Tourism Rights International) (2004). *Proceedings Report: ITRI 'Rethinking Tourism Certification': An Online Indigenous Conference*, June 14–July 2, 2004. ITRI. http:// www.imacmexico.org/ev_es.php?ID=16055_201&ID2=DO_ TOPIC (accessed October 17, 2006).

Johnston, A. (2000). Indigenous peoples and ecotourism: bringing indigenous knowledge and rights into the sustainability equation. *Tourism Recreation Research* 25(2): 89–96.

Johnston, A. (2001). Ecotourism and the challenges confronting indigenous peoples. *Native Americas* 18(2): 42–47.

Johnston, A. (2002). The meeting of peoples through ecotourism: Is the sacred for sale? *Submission of the International Support Centre for Sustainable Tourism to the World Summit on Ecotourism*, Quebec City.

Johnston, A. (2003). Self-determination: exercising indigenous rights in tourism. In Singh, S., Timothy, D.J. and Dowling, R.K. (eds), *Tourism in Destination Communities*. CABI, Wallingford, UK, pp. 115–134.

Johnston, A.M. (2006). *Is the Sacred for Sale? Tourism and Indigenous Peoples*. Earthscan, London.

Jones, S. (2005). Community-based ecotourism: the significance of social capital. *Annals of Tourism Research* 32(2): 303–324.

Karwacki, J. (1999). Indigenous ecotourism: overcoming the challenge. *The Ecotourism Society Newsletter*, First Quarter.

Kent, M. (2006). From reeds to tourism: the transformation of territorial conflicts in the Titicaca National Reserve. *Current Issues in Tourism* 9(1): 86–103.

King, D.A. and Stewart, W.P. (1996). Ecotourism and commodification: protecting people and places. *Biodiversity Conservation* 5: 293–305.

Lai, P.H. and Nepal, S.K. (2006). Local perspectives of ecotourism development in Tawushan Nature Reserve, Taiwan. *Tourism Management* 27: 1117–1129.

Lash, G. (1998). What is community-based ecotourism? In Bornemeier, J., Victor, M. and Durst, P.B. (eds), *Ecotourism for Forest Conservation and Community Development Seminar*. RECOFTC Report No. 15. RECOFTC, Bangkok, pp. 1–12. http://www.recoftc.org/site/index.php?id = 222 (accessed October 17, 2006).

Lash, G.Y.B. and Austin, A. (2003). *The Rural Ecotourism Assessment Program (REAP): A Guide to Community Assessment of Ecotourism as a Tool for Sustainable Development*. The International Ecotourism Society. EplerWood International. http://www.ursainternational.org/REAP_424k.pdf (accessed October 20, 2006).

Lew, A.A. (1996). Tourism management on American Indian lands in the USA. *Tourism Management* 17(5): 355–365.

Lew, A.A. and van Otten, G.A. (eds) (1998). *Tourism and Gaming on American Indian Lands*. Cognizant Communication Corporation, New York.

Liu, J. (1994). *Pacific Islands Ecotourism: A Public Policy and Planning Guide*. Pacific Business Centre Program, University of Hawaii, Hawaii.

Macdonald, T. (2006). New UN Human Rights Council approves Declaration of the Rights of Indigenous Peoples. *Cultural Survival Quarterly* 30(3). http://www.cs.org/publications/csq/csq-article.cfm?id=1916 (accessed October 20, 2006).

MacKay, F. and Caruso, E. (2004). Indigenous lands or national parks? *Cultural Survival Quarterly* 28(1). http://209.200.101.189/publications/csq/csq-article.cfm?id=1737 (accessed November 29, 2005).

Mann, M. (2000). *The Community Tourism Guide*. Earthscan and Tourism Concern, London.

Mann, M. (2002). *The Good Alternative Travel Guide* (2nd edn). Earthscan and Tourism Concern, London.

Mat Som, A.P. and Baum, T. (2004). Community involvement in ecotourism. In Weber, S. and Tomljenovic, R. (eds), *Reinventing a Tourism Destination: Facing the Challenge*. Institute for Tourism Zagreb, Zagreb, Croatia, pp. 251–260.

Mbaiwa, J.E. (2005). Community-based tourism and the marginalized communities in Botswana: the case of the Basarwa in the Okavango Delta. In Ryan, C. and Aicken, M. (eds), *Indigenous Tourism: The Commodification and Management of Culture*. Elsevier, Oxford, pp. 87–109.

McIntosh, I. (1999). Ecotourism: a boon for indigenous people? *Cultural Survival Quarterly* 23(2). http://209.200.101.189/publications/csq/csq-article.cfm?id=1418&highlight=ecotourism (accessed November 17, 2005).

McLaren, D. (1998). *Rethinking Tourism and Ecotravel: The Paving of Paradise and How You Can Stop It*. Kumarian Press, West Hartford, CT.

McLaren, D.R. (1999). The history of indigenous peoples and tourism. *Cultural Survival Quarterly* 23(2): 25–30.

McLaren, D.R. (2003). Indigenous peoples and ecotourism. In Honey, M. and Thullen, S. (eds), *Rights and Responsibilities: A Compilation of Codes of Conduct for Tourism and Indigenous and Local Communities*. Center on Ecotourism and Sustainable Development and The International Ecotourism Society. pp. 1–8. http://www.imacmexico.org/ev_es.php?ID=23341_201&ID2 = DO_TOPIC (accessed October 17, 2006).

Medina, L.K. (2005). Ecotourism and certification: confronting the principles and pragmatics of socially responsible tourism. *Journal of Sustainable Tourism* 13(3): 281–295.

Mowforth, M. and Munt, I. (2003). *Tourism and Sustainability: Development and New Tourism in the Third World*. Routledge, London.

Nature Conservancy (1996). *Traditional Peoples and Biodiversity Conservation in Large Tropical Landscapes*. The Nature Conservancy.

Nature Conservancy, (2005). The Nature Conservancy and Indigenous Peoples. How we work-our partners. http://nature.org/partners/partnership/art14301.html (accessed 17 November 2005).

Nepal, S.K. (2004). Indigenous ecotourism in central British Columbia: the potential for building capacity in the Tl'azt'en Nations territories. *Journal of Ecotourism* 3(3): 173–194.

Nepal, S.K. (2005). Limits to indigenous ecotourism: an exploratory analysis from the Tl'azt'en territories, Northern British Columbia. In Ryan, C. and Aicken, M. (eds), *Indigenous Tourism: The Commodification and Management of Culture*. Elsevier, Oxford, pp. 111–126.

Notzke, C. (2006). *The Stranger, the Native and the Land: Perspectives on Indigenous Tourism*. Captus University Press, North York, Ont.

Page, S. and Dowling, R.K. (2002). Community-based ecotourism: Management and development issues. *Ecotourism*. Pearson Education, Harlow, UK, pp. 244–247.

Pera, L. and McLaren, D. (1999). *Globalization, Tourism and Indigenous Peoples: What You Should Know About the World's Largest 'Industry.'* http://www.planeta.com/ecotravel/resources/rtp/globalization.html (accessed November 17, 2005).

Planeta (2005). *Ecotourism Emerging Industry Forum*, November 1–18, 2005. *Planeta.com*. http://www.planeta.com/ecotravel/tour/emerging.html (accessed October 17, 2006).

Price, M.F. (ed.) (1996). *People and Tourism in Fragile Environments*. John Wiley & Sons, Chichester, UK.

Raffaele, P. (2003). *The Last Tribes on Earth: Journeys Among the World's Most Threatened Cultures*. Pan Macmillan, Sydney.

Redturs (n.d.). *Network of Communitarian Tourism of Latin America*. Redturs. Sponsored by ILO. http://www.redturs.org/inicioen/inicio/index.php (accessed October 17, 2006).

Robinson, M. (1999). Collaboration and cultural consent: refocusing sustainable tourism. *Journal of Sustainable Tourism* 7(3/4): 379–397.

Roe, D., Goodwin, H. and Ashley, C. (2004). Pro-poor tourism: benefiting the poor. In Singh, T.V. (ed.), *New Horizons in Tourism: Strange Experiences and Stranger Practices*. CAB International, Wallingford, UK, pp. 147–161.

Russell, P. (2000). Community-based tourism. *Travel and Tourism Analyst* 5: 87–114.

Ryan, C. (1997). Book review: Tourism and Indigenous Peoples. *Tourism Management* 18: 479–480.

Ryan, C. (2000). Indigenous peoples and tourism. In Ryan, C. and Page, S. (eds), *Tourism Management: Towards the New Millennium*. Pergamon, Oxford.

Ryan, C. and Aicken, M. (eds) (2005). *Indigenous Tourism: The Commodification and Management of Culture*. Elsevier, Oxford.

Schaller, D.T. (1996). *Indigenous Ecotourism and Sustainable Development: The Case of Rio Blanco, Ecuador*, MA Thesis, University of Minnesota. Ecotourism Research. http://www.eduweb.com/schaller (accessed October 17, 2006).

Scheyvens, R. (1999). Ecotourism and the empowerment of local communities. *Tourism Management* 20(2): 245–249.

Scheyvens, R. (2000). Promoting women's empowerment through involvement in ecotourism: experiences from the Third World. *Journal of Sustainable Tourism* 8(3): 232–249.

Scheyvens, R. (2002). *Tourism for Development: Empowering Communities*. Prentice Hall, Harlow, Essex, UK.

Seligmann, P.A. (n.d.). *CI and Indigenous People*. Conservation International. Human Welfare. http://www.conservation.org/xp/CIWEB/strategies/humanwelfare/indigenous_people/ (accessed October 20, 2006).

Selverston-Scher, M. (2003). Indigenous peoples and international finance and development institutions. In Honey, M. and Thullen, S. (eds), *Rights and Responsibilities: A Compilation of Codes of Conduct for Tourism and Indigenous and Local Communities*. Center on Ecotourism and Sustainable Development and The International Ecotourism Society, pp. 148–151. http://www.imacmexico.org/ev_es.php?ID=23341_201&ID2=DO_TOPIC (accessed October 17, 2006).

Smith, M.K. (2003). Indigenous cultural tourism. *Issues in Cultural Tourism Studies*. Routledge, London, pp. 117–132.

Sofield, T. (1991). Sustainable ethnic tourism in the South Pacific: some principles. *Journal of Tourism Studies* 2(1): 56–72.

Sofield, T.H.B. (1993). Indigenous tourism development. *Annals of Tourism Research* 20(4): 729–750.

Sofield, T.H.B. (2002). Australian Aboriginal ecotourism in the Wet Tropics rainforest of Queensland, Australia. *Mountain Research and Development* 22(2): 118–122.

Sofield, T.H.B. (2003). *Empowerment for Sustainable Tourism Development*. Pergamon, New York.

Southgate, C.R.J. (2006). Ecotourism in Kenya: the vulnerability of local communities. *Journal of Ecotourism* 5(1/2): 80–96.

SPREP (South Pacific Regional Environment Programme) (2002). *Community-Based Ecotourism and Conservation in the Pacific Islands: A Tool Kit for Communities*. SPREP, Apia, Samoa.

Sproule, K.W. and Suhandi, A.S. (1998). Guidelines for community-based ecotourism programs: lessons from Indonesia. In Lindberg, K., Epler Wood, M. and Engeldrum, D.

(eds), *Ecotourism: A Guide for Planners and Managers*, Vol. 2. The Ecotourism Society, Vermont, pp. 215–236.

Stronza, A. (2005). Hosts and hosts: the anthropology of community-based ecotourism in the Peruvian rainforest. *National Association for the Practice of Anthropology Bulletin* 23: 170–190.

Suansri, P. (2003). *Community Based Tourism Handbook*. Responsible Ecological Social Tours, Bangkok. http://www.rest.or.th/training/handbook.asp (accessed October 17, 2006).

Sweeting, J. and McConnel, M.A. (1999). Tourism as a tool for biodiversity conservation. *Tourism Recreation Research* 24(2): 106–108.

Sykes, L. (1995). Welcome to our land. *The Geographical Magazine* 67(10): 22–25.

The International Ecotourism Society (2004). *Definition and Ecotourism Principles*. TIES. http://www.ecotourism.org/ (accessed November 17, 2005).

TNC (The Nature Conservancy) (n.d.). *The Nature Conservancy and Indigenous Peoples. How We Work.* http://nature.org/partners/partnership/art14301.html (accessed October 20, 2006).

Tourism Concern (2004). *What is Community Tourism?* Tourism Concern. http://www.tourismconcern.org.uk/resources/community_what_is.htm (accessed October 17, 2006).

Tourism in Focus (2002a). Communities choosing ecotourism. *Tourism in Focus* (Tourism Concern) 42: 10–11.

Tourism in Focus (2002b). The hunting ecotourism conflict in Tanzania. *Tourism in Focus* (Tourism Concern) 42: 12–13.

Tsaur, S.H., Lin, Y.C. and Lin, J.H. (2006). Evaluating ecotourism sustainability from the integrated perspective of resource, community and tourism. *Tourism Management* 27: 640–653.

UN (2002). *Dialogue Paper by Indigenous People*. Addendum No. 3. UN Economic and Social Council. http://www.redturs.org/inicioen/inicio/index.php?option=com_content&task=view&id=196&Itemid=166 (accessed October 20, 2006).

Vivanco, L.A. (2002). Ancestral homes. *Alternatives Journal* 28(4): 27–28.

Vivanco, L.A. (in press). The prospects and dilemmas of indigenous tourism standards and certifications. In Black, R. and Crabtree, A. (eds), *Quality Control and Certification in Ecotourism*. CABI, Wallingford, UK.

Walpole, M.J. and Thouless, C.R. (2005). Increasing the value of wildlife through non-consumptive use? Deconstructing the myths of ecotourism and community-based tourism in the tropics. In Woodroffe, R., Thirgood, S. and Rabinowitz, A. (eds), *People and Wildlife: Conflict or Coexistence? Cambridge University Press*, Cambridge, pp. 122–139.

Wearing, S. (1996). Training for indigenous ecotourism development. *Proceedings of the 4th World Leisure Congress*. http://www.worldleisure.org/events/congresses/previous_congresses/congress1996.html (accessed October 17, 2006).

Weaver, D.B. (2001). Indigenous territories. *Ecotourism*. John Wiley & Sons Australia, Milton, pp. 256–262.

Weaver, D.B. (2006). Indigenous territories. *Sustainable Tourism: Theory and Practice*. Elsevier, Oxford, pp. 143–146.

Weber, R., Butler, J. and Larson, P. (eds) (2000). *Indigenous Peoples and Conservation Organizations: Experiences in Collaboration*. WWF. http://www.worldwildlife.org/bsp/publications/africa/indigenous_conservation/indigenous_conservation.pdf (accessed October 17, 2006).

Wesche, R. (1996). Developed country environmentalism and indigenous community controlled ecotourism in the Ecuadorian Amazon. *Geographische Zeitschrift* 3/4: 157–198.

Wesche, R. and Drumm, A. (1999). *Defending Our Rainforest: A Guide to Community-Based Ecotourism in the Ecuadorian Amazon*. Accion Amazonia, Quito, Ecuador.

Wilmer, F. (1993). What indigenous peoples want and how they are getting it. In *The Indigenous Voice in World Politics*. Sage, Newbury Park, CA, pp. 127–161.

WTO (World Tourism Organization) (2001). Sustainable Development of Ecotourism: A Compilation of Good Practices. WTO, Madrid.

WTO (World Tourism Organization) (2002). *Enhancing the Economic Benefits of Tourism for Local Communities and Poverty Alleviation*. WTO, Madrid.

WTO (World Tourism Organisation) (2003). *Sustainable Development of Ecotourism: A Compilation of Good Practices in SMEs*. WTO, Madrid.

WTO (World Tourism Organization) (2005). Local control. In: Making Tourism More Sustainable: A Guide for Policy Makers, UNEP and WTO, Madrid, pp. 34–36.

Wunder, S. (2000). Ecotourism and economic incentives – an empirical approach. *Ecological Economics* 32: 465–479.

WWF (World Wildlife Fund) (2000). *Map of Indigenous and Traditional Peoples in Ecoregions*. World Wildlife Fund, Gland, Switzerland.

WWF (2001). *Guidelines for Community-Based Ecotourism Development*, July 2001. WWF International. http://assets.panda.org/downloads/guidelinesen.pdf (accessed October 17, 2006).

WWF (2005). *WWF Statement of Principles on Indigenous Peoples and Conservation*. WWF. Sustainability. http://www.panda.org/about_wwf/what_we_do/policy/people_environment/indigenous_people/index.cfm (accessed October 17, 2006).

Zeppel, H. (1997). Meeting 'Wild People': Iban culture and longhouse tourism in Sarawak. In Yamashita, S., Din, K.H. and Eades, J.S. (eds), *Tourism and Cultural Development in Asia and Oceania*. Universiti Kebangsaan Malaysia, Bangi, pp. 119–140.

Zeppel, H. (1998). Land and culture: sustainable tourism and indigenous peoples. In Hall, C.M. and Lew, A. (eds), *Sustainable Tourism: A Geographical Perspective*. Addison Wesley Longman, London, pp. 60–74.

Zeppel, H. (2000). Ecotourism and indigenous peoples. *Issues: All Australian Educational Magazine* July, 51.

Zeppel, H. (2001). Aboriginal cultures and indigenous tourism. In Douglas, N., Douglas, N. and Derrett, R. (eds), *Special Interest Tourism: Context and Cases*. John Wiley & Sons Australia, Brisbane, pp. 232–259.

Zeppel, H. (2002). Indigenous tourism in the Wet Tropics World Heritage Area, North Queensland. *Australian Aboriginal Studies* 2002/2: 65–68.

Zeppel, H. (2003). Sharing the country: ecotourism policy and indigenous peoples in Australia. In Fennell, D.A. and Dowling, R.K. (eds), *Ecotourism Policy and Planning*. CABI, Wallingford, UK pp. 55–76.

Zeppel, H. (2006). *Indigenous Ecotourism: Sustainable Development and Management*. CABI, Wallingford, UK.

Ziffer, K. (1989). *Ecotourism: The Uneasy Alliance*. Conservation International, Washington, DC.

Zografos, C. and Kenrick, J. (2005). Negotiating 'indigenousness' through ecotourism in the Amazonian Ecuador. *Tourism* 53(3): 205–215.

CHAPTER 17

Indigenous perspectives on ecotourism in Nepal: the Ghale Kharka-Sikles and Sirubari experience

Sanjay K. Nepal

Introduction

Declining economic activity, restructuring of the agriculture sector, dwindling rural industrialization, and out-migration of higher educated youth, has led to the adoption, in many countries, of tourism as an alternative development strategy for the economic and social regeneration of rural areas (Jenkins *et al.*, 1998; Briedenhann and Wickens, 2004). In the developing world, such as in Nepal, ecotourism and other forms of sustainable tourism have been used as a pro-poor strategy in rural regions lacking in other economic development potential (Nepal *et al.*, 2002; His Majesty's Government of Nepal (HMG), 2003).

Ecotourism development has become a priority for many national governments (World Tourism Organization (WTO), 2002; Buckley, 2003). Despite its many criticisms (Wall, 1997), there are several reasons why governments in these and other developing countries view the development of ecotourism favorably. First, are the economic reasons like growth, diversification, and stabilization through employment in both new (ecotourism related) and existing businesses, trades, and crafts (Page and Dowling, 2002). Second, it offers opportunities for socio-cultural development, revitalization of local crafts, customs and cultural identities, and increased opportunities for social interactions between hosts and the guests (Zeppel, 2002; Nepal, 2003). Third, ecotourism projects are often suitable, from the point of views of scope and scale of operations, for experimenting with community ownership and empowerment issues (Gurung and Coursey, 1994; Lama, 2000). Fourth, many non-governmental organizations (NGOs) have shown interests in conservation and have developed high-level expertise in implementing ecotourism projects (e.g. the World Wildlife Fund and Conservation International, both based in USA, and the King Mahendra Trust for Nature Conservation in Nepal (KMTNC)). Also, many multilateral agencies such as the World Bank and United Nations Development Programme (UNDP) have shown interests in funding ecotourism type projects in areas critical from a conservation standpoint (Lai and Nepal (in press)). Finally, ecotourism has also been considered a viable strategy for alleviating rural poverty (HMG, 2003).

One of the characteristics of ecotourism projects in countries like Nepal is the involvement of indigenous communities in the planning and decision-making processes. However, conflicting reports exist about whether the development of tourism and ecotourism in indigenous-controlled areas is an essential element of self-determination, or a process to assimilate indigenous societies into the mainstream culture (Smith and Ward, 2000). Those in favor of indigenous involvement in tourism argue that through the provision of economic stability and the reinstatement of traditional cultural practices, indigenous people can achieve self-determination and self-reliance. It is believed that 'showcasing' native culture and values, especially through the art of native storytelling and interpretation, in non-indigenous society will gain a fuller understanding and insight of their views, whilst providing indigenous peoples opportunities to assert their rights and autonomy through economic empowerment (Pfister, 2000; Smith and Ward, 2000). Development of indigenous-controlled tourism is expected to bring positive social and economic changes too (Butler and Hinch, 1996; Beltran, 2000; Nepal, 2002). In contrast, critics have argued that indigenous tourism is yet another form of cultural imperialism (Nash, 1989), and an example of Westernized attempts to assimilate indigenous peoples into mainstream societies (Francis, 1992; MacCannell, 1999). Tourism has often proved to be disastrous to the indigenous communities, resulting in their displacement, conflict, and violence within the community, and disruptions of social and cultural practices (Colchester, 2004). Nevertheless, given that indigenous peoples have lagged behind in economic development and face many social challenges, ecotourism appears to be a viable alternative. Ecotourism development is seen not just as an economic strategy, but also as a means to strengthening indigenous positions in regional and national development policies. The development of ecotourism is seen as an integral aspect of this process toward indigenous control, self-reliance, and improvement of social and economic conditions.

This chapter examines the involvement of indigenous people in two ecotourism projects implemented in rural Nepal and provides their perspectives on the opportunities and uncertainties associated with ecotourism development. The two project sites, or villages, are the Ghale Kharka–Sikles (GKS) trekking corridor and Sirubari (SBR), both located in the central hills of Nepal. Both villages are inhabited mainly by the *Gurung*, an ethnic group that resides mainly in the central hills of Nepal. The primary focus of ecotourism is village festivities and culture, and some trekking. Diversifying the local economy and making village-level economic activities sustainable are the main long-term goals. The two case studies are examined to determine local responses and key processes that determine the success of ecotourism in rural areas.

Indigenous ecotourism in Nepal

The Himalayan kingdom of Nepal has experienced rapid growth and development of tourism over the last three decades (Nepal, 2000). Much of this development has occurred in its rural and remote, 'marginal' regions. Beyond some well-known tourism destinations such as the Mt. Everest and Annapurna regions (Nepal *et al.*, 2002), rural areas in Nepal are characterized by high levels of poverty, strong reliance on subsistence farming, low income and employment opportunities, and outward migration of young people (Karan *et al.*, 1994). In order to bring some balance between the 'tourist regions' and the 'non-tourist regions,' several international development agencies and NGOs have assisted the Nepalese government in developing ecotourism destinations in areas rich in natural and cultural diversity (HMG, 2003). Village tourism, which focuses on the cultural heritage of an area, has emerged as a subset of ecotourism. The idea of village tourism is to market the rural areas and their farming traditions as unique attractions to overseas visitors. Visitors are enticed to explore and experience what it feels like to be a farmer in the hills of Nepal. Combined with this experience is a cultural exposition, that is, village rituals, festivals and dances, performed by village folks for the entertainment of visitors. Included in these activities are also short hiking and trekking excursions to mountain summits to enjoy the scenery and landscape. For a lack of a better term, given the characteristics of nature and culture-focused activities, low-scale operations, low volume of visitors, and intensive community involvement, the two villages examined here are considered ecotourism destinations.

Methodology

The study was conducted during the months of March and April 2005. First, two micro-level case studies on ecotourism were completed. The case study was developed using existing published and unpublished documents. Based on this preliminary information, household surveys were conducted with participants of the ecotourism projects. Preliminary discussions with field-level officials were helpful in compiling a tentative list of participants involved in each project. Once the first participant was identified, a snowball sampling method was applied to identify all participants, based on which participants were approached for questionnaire interviews. A total of 45 interviews in GKS areas and 40 interviews in SBR were completed.

The overall purpose of the interview questionnaire (in Nepali vernacular) was to elicit local perspectives on ecotourism on three main issues – ecotourism as an economic diversification option, local-level ecotourism-related training issues, and long-term viability of ecotourism. The questionnaire was primarily based on a 19- item, five-point Likert scale questions (ranging from strongly agree to strongly disagree), which addressed three attitudinal themes linked to the challenges of local-level ecotourism enterprises. The five-point scale was reduced to a three-point scale (agree, disagree, don't know) for data analysis. Other questions were asked to elicit background information on socio-economic characteristics of households; one open- ended question elicited respondents' general comments about opportunities and challenges for developing ecotourism. Analysis is mainly descriptive, due to the small sample size. Ninety percent of the respondents were male and between the ages of 25–64.

SBR and Ghale Kharka villages are located in the central hills of Nepal (Figure 17.1). Both villages were selected as pilot projects on ecotourism that is built upon the rural characteristics of the region and its farming culture. Both projects exemplify Nepal's effort toward creating a demand for ecotourism activities, managed by a community and not by individual entrepreneurs. The two projects were initiated as a demand-driven strategy instead of the conventional supply-driven approach to tourism

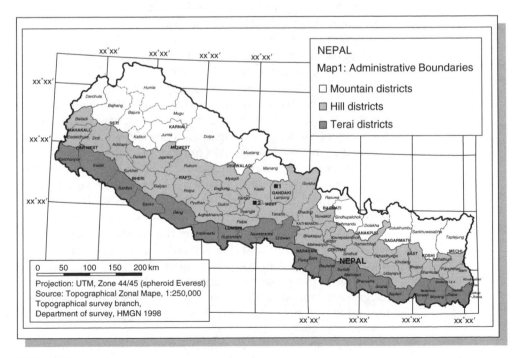

Figure 17.1
Location of (1) GKS and (2) SBR in Nepal

development. The demand-driven approach assumes that if a truly environment-friendly tourism product is developed and marketed accordingly, it would be popular among environmentally conscious visitors. In this case, products and activities are planned, developed and then marketed to specific group of clients resulting in a demand for such products. Tourism development under the supply-driven approach is responsive to visitors needs; products and activities are not planned but sprout automatically to fulfill the growing needs and desires of the visitors. The development of tourism services and facilities is spontaneous, mainly as a result of the increasing number of visitors.

The GKS Ecotourism Project

In 1992, based on its experience in integrated conservation and development project in Annapurna, the KMTNC launched the ecotourism development project in the GKS area, with financial support from the Asian Development Bank (ADB). The GKS area is off the main tourist trail but is within the jurisdiction of ACAP. Because of the negative impacts of tourism along the main trekking corridors in the Annapurna region, an alternative ecotourism project was implemented to provide income and employment opportunities to local people.

Tourism in the GKS area was planned and developed with local participation. Local residents organized themselves into various management committees, which included a lodge management committee, mothers' group, kerosene management committee, electricity management committee, conservation management committee, and campsite management committee. Members of the lodge management committee were active participants in the determination of number of lodges and campsites and selection of locations. Similarly, under the kerosene management committee several kerosene depots were established along the main trekking trail, and energy saving devices were introduced to households. Fuelwood use in lodges and campsites was prohibited. Learning from the Annapurna experience where social friction and disharmony due to differential earnings from lodges had been a problem (Nepal et al., 2002), the emphasis in this project was on small-scale, community-owned lodges and campsites. Once basic facilities such as a visitor center, trekking trails, and campsites were in place, the area was opened for potential trekkers.

Since its opening, the annual number of visitors to this area has not exceeded 1,000. Of the total income generated from tourism, 50% is spent on local community development activities,

35% on tourism infrastructure, and 15% on conservation (Ghurmi, 1997). Since the launching of the project, two forest nurseries have been established and some 12 ha of land have been planted at community and household levels. Three micro-hydro stations are managed by the electricity management committee. The stations generate a total of 73 kW of electricity, which is supplied to approximately 500 households. As for tourism infrastructure, eight campsites were developed, some 12 km of trail, two community lodges, 12 rubbish dump sites, and 14 toilets for tourists were constructed. Similarly, a natural and cultural history museum and two visitor information centers were also built. Training on various aspects of tourism was provided to local people.

This project is different from other ACAP projects in that it encourages community as opposed to individual benefits. Though this initiative is greatly appreciated by local communities, the sustainability of such a project has been seriously questioned. For example, the fate of the project is uncertain if KMTNC withdraws its support. Without funding from ADB and the involvement of KMTNC, local people can hardly initiate and manage such a project. Tourism is less likely to generate the amount that was invested for this project, mainly because of low visitor traffic in that area. Negative environmental impacts have been minimal, but so is the impact on the local economy. Should there be an increased number of trekkers in this region, which probably what the local people hope for, negative impacts of tourism are bound to occur.

Recently, the viability of this project has been an issue, primarily due to declining tourist activity in the region. Infrastructure built to support the project has now become a liability due to maintenance costs. Because the revenue generated has not been substantial, it has been reported that local communities are apprehensive about the success of this project as an economic diversification strategy (see below).

Village tourism in SBR

Unlike the Annapurna Conservation Area Project, which is a regional exercise in relating tourism to conservation and development (Nepal *et al.*, 2002), the village tourism initiative in SBR, a hill village south of the Annapurna region, may be considered a micro-exercise in making tourism relevant to local economic and environmental development.

The concept of village tourism is one of 'home stay' or 'paying guest' with an emphasis on interacting and living with the host community. It offers the visitor an opportunity to experience first hand the culture, customs, and daily life of the host household and the community. The guests stay in groups of two to five in assigned households where arrangements for accommodation, meals, snacks, etc. are made. It is a complete family atmosphere. The management of the supply component through a participatory institution, broad-based sharing of benefits, and a new approach to visitor satisfaction are other unique features of SBR.

The initiative began in 1998 in SBR, a predominantly Gurung village on a ridge about 4-h trek from the nearest road-head along the Pokhara–Sunauli road. The village is located at an altitude of about 1,700 m. From the highest point one can see great Himalayan peaks such as Annapurna, Machhapuchhare, and Dhaulagiri. Most of the Gurung households rely on remittances and pensions, mostly from army service.

The idea was initiated by a retired army captain who approached the government for support to develop village tourism in SBR. Contacts with an Australian expatriate tour operator proved fruitful. After the identification of SBR as the site for promoting village tourism, a Tourism Development and Management Committee (TDMC) was established in the village with the Village Development Committee (VDC) chair as its head. The expatriate and his associates formed a company – Nepal Village Resorts (NVR) – to take over the sole responsibility of promoting and marketing village tourism in SBR. Detailed contractual arrangements were made specifying the obligations and responsibilities including operating procedures and fees of the two parties. The TDMC represents the Mothers' Group, Fathers' Group, the Youth Club, and other members chosen through consensus among villagers; the tenure is 2 years. The TDMC has developed its own rules and procedures and decides about the upkeep of guestrooms, sanitation and hygiene, assignment of guestroom accommodation on a rotational basis, type and quality of meals and snacks, as well as arrangements for welcoming the guests, sight-seeing, and cultural programs. Even before the TDMC, the village had an active Mothers' Group and Youth Club. The Mothers' Group raised funds by organizing cultural programs to welcome or bid farewell to army men who came on home leave. The Mothers' Group has provided money for quite a few local development projects.

With the signing of the agreement with NVR, interested and willing families from the central village began establishing guestroom accommodation in consultation with the TDMC. The TDMC set minimum standards for guestrooms. The conditions for participation in guestroom accommodation include the construction of permanent structures for toilets and bathrooms, cleanliness, specified minimum provisions in rooms, and security guarantees for visitors. The TDMC carries out monitoring of accommodation and other facilities regularly. The NVR has the responsibility of ensuring that the guests abide by the code of conduct; and this basically seeks to respect local traditions in clothing and behavior. NVR promotes and markets village tourism through a network of international travel agents. They also have a site on the worldwide web. All visitor groups are booked through the NVR Kathmandu office. The guests are provided with a full round-trip package from Pokhara to SBR with no extra liabilities. This avoids the need for payment of bills by visitors in the village. It also gives a sense of being part of the host family. The TDMC is given prior notice by telephone for arrangement of porters, guides, a welcome ceremony, and cultural programs.

The visitors' arrival in the village is a memorable affair. A procession welcomes the guests with much fanfare and traditional music and dance. The guests are assigned to host families with whom they stay for the next 2 days. The guests have Nepali meals with the host family but an afternoon snack is organized jointly in a traditional roundhouse in the center of the village. The 2 days are spent visiting the natural and scenic sites around the village. The main natural attractions are the hill top about 2-h walk uphill to view the Himalayan peaks, the prize-winning, approximately 500 ha of community forest, and the serene higher pastures. Among other attractions is the village itself with about 146 households, the Buddhist Monastery, and the Shiva temple. In the evening a cultural program is organized in the 'Tourist Building' (constructed with support from the government and funds raised by the Mothers' Group, the Youth Group, and from tourism fees).

International tariff rates vary according to the number of tourists per package. A rate of US$ 230 (for three nights, 4 days) is charged for a single person. For a group of between 10–20 guests, the charge is $145 per guest. Following the agreement between TDMC and NVR, a lump sum of NRs 1,700 ($25) per guest (for a two-night stay) is provided to TDMC. Of this amount NRs 1,000 goes to the guestroom owner. The remaining amount goes to the TDMC and part of it is used to meet the cost of the welcome ceremony, porters, and gifts for the guests. So far, 50 families in the village have opened up their homes to accommodate visitors, but only 18 have entertained guests so far. Village tourism in SBR started in April 1997. By November 1999, a total of 278 international tourists had visited SBR, mostly from Europe. Most of the visitors are above 40 years of age. Meanwhile SBR has also been attracting quite a few domestic tourists. Thus far, 421 domestic visitors have visited the area mainly from surrounding districts to observe its model nursery and community forest. The TDMC is planning to introduce set tariff rates for domestic visitors also.

Apparently, the TDMC has been able to build on the community's social capital (rich heritage, homogenous community, developed social infrastructure, active local organization, and TDMC itself). The degree of participation and leadership and the decision-making process have been the key elements in initiating village tourism (Banskota and Sharma, 1999). The need for training in housekeeping and food preparation is already felt. There is enough scope for expanding household participation in village tourism as tourist volumes increase. Economically, tourism has to increase incomes and employment to be viable and has to develop linkages with the local production system. It is reported that about 68% of the total food expenses for tourists go to imports from outside and 28% are reported to come from their own production (Banskota and Sharma, 1999). It was found that, on an average, an amount of NRs 22,400 per bed was invested in SBR. Over half of the investment was incurred in constructing toilets and bathrooms. SBR is an exceptional village by Nepalese standards of income. But the study also shows that the present level of investment for developing guestrooms is within the reach of an average rural household if comfortable lending terms are offered. From an environmental perspective, village tourism has made the community aware of cleanliness and good sanitation, even among those who do not have guest accommodation. However, as tourist numbers rise, the demand for fuelwood will increase and so will the urgency to introduce affordable, renewable energy options and efficient technologies.

Community perspectives of ecotourism as a viable option

The household interview revealed that ecotourism was considered a diversification option mainly for the purpose of obtaining additional income to support farm-based activities (Table 17.1). An overwhelming majority (>89%) of the respondents indicated that long-term economic viability of their rural livelihood was their major reason for supporting and engaging in ecotourism. Ecotourism provided the best opportunity for economic diversification (GKS >74%; SBR >82%). More than two-thirds of the respondents felt that ecotourism was the only choice for diversification, and only a small proportion of residents felt that the community should not have pursued it as a diversification strategy. One-third of the respondents felt that there were other economic

Table 17.1 Local perspectives of ecotourism as an economic diversification option (percentage of respondents)

Statements	GKS (n = 45)			SBR (n = 40)		
	Agree	Disagree	Don't know	Agree	Disagree	Don't know
It is important for our community to diversify our economy for longer-term viability	89.1	4.2	6.7	92.0	2.8	5.2
Ecotourism provides the best opportunity for diversification	74.2	9.8	16.0	82.4	7.5	10.1
Ecotourism is the only choice we have for diversification	68.6	22.3	9.1	72.6	18.4	9.0
The community should not have pursued ecotourism as a diversification strategy	21.3	67.7	11.0	20.5	64.5	15.0
There are other economic opportunities than ecotourism	24.2	66.6	9.2	21.0	70.2	8.8
The community was told that diversification with ecotourism is a good strategy	82.0	14.5	3.5	89.6	7.0	3.4
I am personally in favor of ecotourism as a diversification strategy	75.2	20.2	4.6	82.7	11.2	6.1
In my opinion, the community too is in favor of ecotourism	78.3	12.0	9.7	78.2	16.2	5.6

diversification opportunities in the village. When prompted by the question what these opportunities were, references were made mostly to retail commerce (e.g. grocery stores, cloth shops, etc.) and commercial agriculture. In response to the question about whether ecotourism was suggested by people from outside the community, an overwhelming majority indicated that was indeed the case (GKS = 82%; SBR = 89.6%). When asked if they had personally favored ecotourism as a diversification strategy, 75% in the GKS and 83% in the SBR indicated that to be the case. Also, 78% felt that the community too was in favor of ecotourism.

Follow up questions related to training needs for ecotourism revealed that adoption to tourism was relatively easier for more SBR (72%) than GKS (56%) residents. Over 70% respondents felt that there were many training needs in ecotourism; references were made mainly to trainings in meal preparation, hygiene, customer service, and language. Many thought formal training in offering their services to tourists is necessary; however, only 42% in GKS and 54% in SBR stated that they did not have any trouble getting the necessary trainings. Interestingly, nearly 50% in GKS and 42% in SBR thought training in ecotourism is not necessary. The implication is that experience was considered a substitute for formal training. Indeed, the Gurung community elsewhere in Nepal (mainly Pokhara and Kathmandu and along the Annapurna circuit trekking) has been actively involved in the tourism industry. Awareness of this phenomenon could have influenced local perceptions about tourism training in SBR. More than 80% stated that trainers are available locally; however, many also indicated that there is a need to bring trainers from outside the community (Table 17.2).

Responses to questions about the long-term viability of community-based tourism as a diversification option were somewhat mixed. In the current circumstances, tourism as a revenue generating enterprise was not seen viable in the future; however, more in SBR (23%) than GKS (12%) were optimistic about the viability of tourism. Generally, respondents were optimistic about the future of tourism in both areas. Respondents from both areas stated that fewer tourists are visiting their communities compared to the previous years. Forty-two percent in GKS and 36% in SBR thought that it might be wise to pursue other economic opportunities than tourism (Table 17.3).

Discussion, summary, and conclusions

For both entrepreneurs and policy makers, the SBR and Ghale Kharka success has inspired that ecotourism can be very useful

Table 17.2 Perspectives on training needs for ecotourism

Statements	GKS (n = 45)			SBR (n = 40)		
	Agree	Disagree	Don't know	Agree	Disagree	Don't know
I found it easy to adopt to ecotourism	56.2	35.2	8.6	72.0	24.1	3.9
There are many training needs in ecotourism	70.1	18.3	11.6	74.2	23.8	2.0
It is important to be formally trained in offering services to tourists	82.0	12.0	6.0	86.4	9.6	4.0
I have had no troubles getting the necessary training	42.1	56.9	1.0	53.8	34.0	12.2
Training in ecotourism is not necessary	49.2	48.8	2.0	42.6	53.4	4.0
We have locally available trainers	80.0	18.9	1.9	84.2	13.6	2.2
We need to bring trainers from outside our village	58.3	31.7	10.0	52.0	36.1	11.9

Table 17.3 Perspectives on long-term viability of ecotourism (%)

Statements	GKS (n = 45)			SBR (n = 40)		
	Agree	Disagree	Don't know	Agree	Disagree	Don't know
Considering the present situation, ecotourism is not viable in the future	85.0	12.1	2.9	58.0	22.9	19.1
Ecotourism in our community will remain viable in the future	74.2	22.8	3.0	76.1	18.3	5.6l
Compared to the previous years, fewer tourists are visiting our community	72.9	22.1	5.0	68.0	26.4	5.6
In the future, it is better to pursue other economic opportunities than ecotourism	42.1	34.9	23.0	36.1	43.3	20.7

in bringing about improved local social, economic, and environmental conditions. It has helped implant ideas among rural communities to adapt to changing economic realities and modern ways of thinking.

The successful initiation and implementation of these two projects have depended on some key drivers. These include:

1. overwhelming local support for community-oriented projects,
2. proactive marketing and publicity at the national level,
3. strong social and economic standing of the participants,
4. community support for ecotourism and willingness to adapt to economic opportunities,
5. projects built upon principles of partnership and collaboration,
6. external support to the project from the government and NGOs.

In both villages, local community support for ecotourism was very strong from the outset of the project initiation. While the confidence in ecotourism seems to have waned a little bit, as indicated by the results of the survey reported above, the two communities are hopeful that things will improve in the near future. Because the projects emphasize small scale, local control, community involvement, which are the hall marks of ecotourism, the projects have received national-level attention from the government and donor agencies who view these programs as part of the micro-level pro-poor rural development efforts (Nepal Tourism Board (NTB), 2001; HMG, 2003). Indeed, the National Tourism Board has promoted the two projects as part of a pro-poor tourism strategy. One characteristic common to both case studies is that a few key individuals have provided the necessary leadership and vision to make the project a reality. In the GKS area, the KMTNC provided facilitation and leadership in organizing the community and holding meetings and resolving differences among the community. In the SBR, an influential person of high social standing brought the community together and facilitated networking with outside agencies. In both cases, local representatives willingly assumed responsibilities, provided directions, planned and organized community meetings, and established committees to oversee and implement various activities. Most important of all, local communities saw that ecotourism could be a viable opportunity and were willing to invest their capital for creating necessary infrastructure for visitor services and facilities.

The projects were built upon the principles of partnership and collaboration between various stakeholders like tour agents, NGO representatives, local communities, and foreign guides. At the outset, project objectives and community expectations were clarified – it was clear that the projects were experimental in nature, and that everyone had to be fully committed to make them work. External support from local government and NGOs in the areas of policy, planning, and financing local-level projects was also a critical factor.

Both projects have suffered due to the downward trend in tourism in recent years. Nepal's political problems and lack of a sense of security outside the capital have been the major hurdles in attracting visitors to the countryside. The GKS project is in a critical state due to growing Maoist activities in the region. As a result, maintenance of tourism infrastructure in both villages has become problematic due to increasing costs but diminishing returns.

It appears that tourism is not necessarily a 'magic wand that will speed up economic progress' in rural areas (Hoggart et al., 1995, p. 36). Adopting an ecotourism policy that seeks to attract both foreign and domestic tourists is sensible, but to do this communities need to get over the mentality that tourists are mainly foreign, and need to embrace a culture of providing hospitality services to domestic visitors as well. Indeed, the long-term viability of these projects will depend also on how much domestic tourists these areas can attract. There is a sizable middle class in Kathmandu with adequate disposable income to visit places like GKS and SBR; however, whether or not these areas represent the idyllic landscapes that domestic tourists would desire remains a critical issue. SBR was marketed to the domestic tourists too; however, the initial euphoria among the middle class about visits to rural areas like SBR has waned due to on-going political strife in the country.

In conclusion, the GKS and the SBR ecotourism projects share similar characteristics in basic principles, objectives, structure, and implementation mechanisms. The projects represent national-level pro-poor rural development initiatives. Small-scale tourism development programs have been launched in various rural regions of the country as a move toward diversifying the local economy to include more off-farm employment opportunities. Initial implantation of the program has been successful; however, the anticipated integration of ecotourism with other village-based economy has yet to materialize in a concrete way. Moreover, questions have been raised with regard to the market viability of the concept and the potential to solve problems of local unemployment and poverty.

The drivers for the success of ecotourism include strong local support for community-managed ecotourism, community willingness to adapt to new opportunities, local-level leadership and facilitation skills, social and economic capacity of involved entrepreneurs, strength in partnership with local and outside agents, and external support from the government and donor agencies. The success of ecotourism and similar other forms of tourism in Nepal will ultimately depend on the resolution of on-going political violence in Nepal, which has affected small and lesser-known destinations like Ghale Kharka and SBR.

Acknowledgment

Funding for this research was provided by the Foreign Agricultural Services, US Department of Agriculture (Award No. 58-3148-5-149).

References

Banskota, K. and Sharma, B. (1999). *Village Tourism: Implications for Sustainability*. ICIMOD, Kathmandu.

Beltran, J. (ed.) (2000). *Indigenous and Traditional Peoples and Protected Areas. Principles, Guidelines and Case Studies*. Gland and Cambridge, IUCN/WWF.

Briedenhann, J. and Wickens, E. (2004). Tourism routes as a tool for the economic development of rural areas – vibrant hope or impossible dream? *Tourism Management* 25: 71–79.

Buckley, R. (2003.) Case studies in ecotourism. CABI Publishing, Oxon.

Butler, R. and Hinch, T. (eds) (1996). *Tourism and Indigenous Peoples*. London, Routledge.

Colchester, M. (2004). Conservation policy and indigenous peoples. *Cultural Survival Quarterly* 28: 17–22.

Francis, D. (1992). *The Imaginary Indian: The Image of the Indian in Canadian Culture*. Arsenal Pulp Press, Vancouver.

Gurung, C.P. and Coursey, M. (1994). The Annapurna Conservation Area project: A pioneering example of sustainable tourism? In Cater, E. and Lowman, G. (eds), *Ecotourism: A sustainable option*? John Wiley, Chichester, pp. 177–194.

Ghurmi, G. (1997). Developing a tourist destination: the experience of the King Mahendra Trust for Nature Conservation with ecotourism. In Bornemeier, J. Victor, M. and Durst, P.B. (eds), *Ecotourism for Forest Conservation and Community Development*. In *Proceedings of an International Seminar*, 28–31 January 1997, Bangkok, RECOFTC and FAO, pp. 176–186.

His Majesty's Government of Nepal (HMG), United Nations Development Programme (UNDP), Department for International Development (DFID), and Netherlands Development Organization (SNV). (2003). *Tourism for Rural*

Poverty Alleviation Programme (TRPAP) – Annual Report 2003. TRPAP, Kathmandu.

Hoggart, K., Buller, H. and Black, R. (1995). *Rural Europe: Identity and Change.* Arnold, London.

Jenkins, J.M., Hall, C.M. and Troughton, M. (1998). The restructuring of rural economies: rural tourism and recreation as a government response. In Butler, R.W., Hall, C.M. and Jenkins, J. (eds), *Tourism and Recreation in Rural Areas.* John Wiley, Chichester.

Karan, P.P., Ishii, H., Kobayashi, M., Shrestha, M., Vajracharya, C., Zurick, D. and Pauer, G. (1994). *Nepal: Development and Change in a Landlocked Himalayan Kingdom.* Tokyo University of Foreign Studies, Tokyo.

Lama, W.B. (2000). Community-based tourism for conservation and women's development. In Godde, P.M., Price, M.F. and Zimmermann, F.M. (eds), *Tourism and Development in Mountain Regions.* CAB International, Oxon, pp. 221–238.

Lai, P. and Nepal, S.K. Local perspectives of ecotourism development in Tawushan Nature reserve, Taiwan. *Tourism Management* 27: 1117–1129.

MacCannell, D. (1999). *The Tourist – A New Theory of the Leisure Class* (3rd edn). University of California Press, Berkeley.

Nash, D. (1989). Tourism as a form of imperialism. In V.L. Smith (ed.), *Hosts and Guests: The Anthropology of Tourism* (2nd edn). University of Pennsylvania Press, Philadelphia, pp. 37–52.

Nepal, S.K. (2000). National parks, conservation areas, tourism, and local communities in the Nepalese Himalaya. In Butler, R.W. and Boyds, S.W. (eds), *Tourism and National Parks: Issues and Implications.* John Wiley, London, pp. 73–94.

Nepal, S.K. (2002). Involving indigenous peoples in protected area management: comparative perspective from Nepal, Thailand, and China: *Environmental Management* 30: 748–763.

Nepal, S.K., Kohler, T. and Banzhaf, B. (2002). *Great Himalaya: Tourism and the Dynamics of Change in Nepal.* Swiss Foundation for Alpine Research, Berne.

Nepal, S.K. (2003). Indigenous ecotourism in Central British Columbia: The potential for building capacity in the Tl'azt'en Nations Territories. *Journal of Ecotourism* 3: 173–194.

Nepal Tourism Board (NTB) (2001). National ecotourism strategy and marketing programme of Nepal. Nepal Tourism Board, Kathmandu.

Page, S.J. and Dowling, R.K. (2002). *Ecotourism.* Prentice Hall, Essex.

Pfister, R.E. (2000). Mountain culture as a tourism resource: Aboriginal views of the privileges of storytelling. In Godde, P., Price, M.F. and Zimmermann, M.F. (eds), *Tourism and*

Development in Mountain Regions. CABI Publishing, Oxon, pp. 115–136.

Smith, C. and Ward, G.K. (2000). *Indigenous Cultures in an Interconnected World*. UBC Press, Vancouver.

Wall, G. (1997). Is ecotourism sustainable? *Environmental Management* 21.

Williams, A.M. and Shaw, G. (1991). *Tourism and Economic Development: Western European Experiences* (2nd edn). Bellhaven Press, London.

World Tourism Organization (WTO) (2002). The World Ecotourism Summit, Quebec City, Canada, 19 to 22 May 2002. *Portfolio of Statement and Presentations*. CD version. WTO, Madrid.

Zeppel, H. (2002). Cultural tourism at the Cowichan Native Village, British Columbia. *Journal of Travel Research* 41: 92–100.

CHAPTER 18

China: ecotourism and cultural tourism, harmony or dissonance?

Trevor Sofield and
Fung Mei Sarah Li

Introduction

The forms that ecotourism and cultural tourism take in China are often at variance with approaches adopted by western nations. The differences, and they are substantial, have their genesis in five major endogenous factors that result in a China-specific environment for contemporary tourism policy planning and development. These five (in no particular order of priority) are: a transition economy in which the ideology of a centrally controlled economy is giving way to a western style market economy to develop 'capitalism with a Chinese face'. Many 'private sector' for-profit companies including resorts and hotels are in fact owned by state ministries, including the Peoples Liberation Army. Second, and allied to this is the way in which communist doctrines in many ways still set the parameters or boundaries of what can be done because they determine the political system and therefore what is acceptable or unacceptable in many situations. A third factor is modernization, at a pace that is far swifter than most and which in China invariably translates into constructing something: if a project does not result in a lot of building it is not seen as achieving very much. Ecotourism for example is more about investment-driven supply side construction than environmental conservation. A fourth factor is the demographics of China, the most populous nation on earth. Over the centuries, Chinese have directly or indirectly impacted on almost every corner of their nation, and 'natural' or pristine ecosystems have largely disappeared, so that human-dominated or -influenced ecosystems are inevitably the focus of ecotourism, in contrast to much western ideal ecotourism that is centred in and around 'wilderness'. And finally, traditional values, deeply rooted, have withstood political changes over centuries and remain as culturally determined foundational elements underpinning a Chinese approach to ecotourism development and cultural tourism in contemporary China, so much so that in effect virtually all natural landscapes in China are equally cultural landscapes (Li, 2005).

These endogenous factors, already vigorous, already creating tension and dissonance because of internal inconsistencies and contradictions, must contend with the exogenous forces of globalization that impinge upon China. Part of the globalization process is the acceptance at a certain level of western paradigms of development, but often it is an imperfect adoption and/or adaptation that produces a significant 'implementation gap' (Dunsire, 1978) between policy and praxis. In addition, with its accession to the World Trade Organization (WTO) in 2002, China must now abide by the General Agreement on Trade in

Services (GATS) administered by WTO. From 1978 to 2002, China largely controlled all matters pertaining to tourism including foreign investment, employment, exchange rates, and product, scale and structural effects according to its own systems, but it must now contend with the exogenous pressures of WTO membership. All of these factors, both endogenous and exogenous, combine to produce an even more dynamic mix of forces that contribute to the current directions of ecotourism and cultural tourism and the forms that they take in China.

This chapter examines contemporary eco- and cultural tourism policy, planning and development in China in the context of these competing, conflicting – but at times, paradoxically, mutually reinforcing forces.

Transition economy, communist doctrine and globalization

As an economy in transition, increasingly participating in multifarious aspects of globalization despite attempts for many years to isolate itself from such influences, China must now deal with the tensions and dissonance that arise on the one hand from its communist-oriented political system and its traditional value system, embedded in several thousand years of continuous cultural continuity, with many of the newly penetrating influences of westernization on the other hand. Tourism is at the cusp of many of these diverging and divergent forces.

The OECD definition of a transition economy is of a country in the process of change from a centrally planned economy towards a market economy, a process that involves enormous changes at every level of society (OECD, 2003). It may also distinguish any economy that attempts to replace bureaucratic mechanisms with greater reliance on free market forces. Such countries include those of the former Soviet Union and eastern and central European members of the communist bloc, as well as more recently countries in Asia and Africa undergoing market transformations of various degrees, such as China, Cambodia and Vietnam.

Entrepreneurship is central to the functioning of market economies, and China, in common with other transition economies, faces several obstacles such as an opaque tax system, heavy administrative burdens (and sometimes related corruption), an inadequate legal system that does not always protect and support the private sector, and a slow uptake of private sector/public sector partnerships in which the public sector invariably dominates (OECD, 2002). However, one area where China differs significantly from other transition economies is that there is ample access to credit because its booming economy has created substantial reserves. Indeed the World Bank in a recent report suggests that 'abundant liquidity will re-fuel bank credit and investment' (World Bank, 2006, p. 1) and tourism development is a beneficiary of this situation.

Tourism development requires an environment favourable to entrepreneurship, particularly for small and medium enterprises (SMEs), given the fact that in most countries with mature tourism industries the majority of operators (up to 80%) are SMEs. The building blocks of a successful tourism strategy include integrating the private sector and fostering collaboration among SMEs. In a transition economy such as China's, however, there are a number of weaknesses that tend to inhibit these factors from progressing smoothly:

(i) Privatization is not always easy or effective.
(ii) Key opportunities may be seized by the governing elite and favoured partners so that free market entry is curtailed.
(iii) Often only the 'crumbs' are available for private entrepreneurs.
(iv) The viability of some tourism SMEs will be doubtful because of weak business acumen and experience arising from the fact that tourism is a new sector (only legitimated after 1978 as an appropriate form of economic development) so there is no corporate history or prior family involvement to guide new entrants.
(v) Standards of SMEs can vary considerably often because of the use of sub-standard construction of facilities.
(vi) There is a lack of appropriate HRD inputs and insufficient training facilities to keep up with the massive expansion in tourism activity (of all kinds) in the past decade (Sofield and McTaggart, 2005). This is particularly acute given that in 1988 an estimated 7 million international arrivals were recorded and by 1998 that had grown to more than 30 million. The estimate for international arrivals for 2006 is in excess of 40 million. In 1978 tourism, both domestic and international, was virtually at 'ground zero', but domestic tourism in China has grown from less than 150 million visitations in 1995 to more than 1.2 billion visitations in 2005 (CNTA, 2006). The result is a huge shortfall in qualified and adequately trained staff for the tourism industry. While China has introduced national qualifications standards, this rapid growth has simply outstripped the capacity of training and education institutions to meet the demand. As a result service quality in tourism is uneven at best.

Another point is that in approaching the issues of a move to a market economy and entrepreneurship, it is important to pursue a steady, staged strategy that avoids jumping from one extreme to the other. It needs to be understood that competition is not about the law of the jungle and that some regulatory mechanisms are necessary. As Denman (2005) states, it is vital to create favourable conditions for doing business, in order to encourage both local enterprise formulation and FDI (Foreign Direct Investment). In China there is still an imbalance evident in determining an appropriate level of regulatory activity so that at times there is over-protection of business interests allied to state ownership and/or the governing elite, and at times a hands-off approach that results in 'the law of the jungle' driving enterprises out of business because of questionable practices by larger concerns. At other times there is an unwillingness to enforce regulations. For example, in a study of 83 nature reserves in China, Ren Zhuge (2000) found that 68 (82%) had at least 1 of 10 activities specifically prohibited by legislation (*Regulations of the Peoples Republic of China on Nature Reserves 1994*) occurring inside their boundaries, 54 of them had 3 or 4 activities, and 14 of them had 5–8 activities. The banned activities ranged from hunting and logging, to quarrying and mining. In this context, two major problem areas identified by the World Bank (1999) were (i) weak corporate governance and accounting practices in financial institutions and (ii) inadequate environmental protection. In the past 3 years, however, following China's membership of the WTO, there have been significant improvements in the first area although there is still a substantial implementation gap between legislation and practice with reference to the latter.

In considering environmental resources (which form the backbone of ecotourism) there is a legacy of local environmental pollution and poor waste management such that uncontrolled development may put natural heritage resources at risk. While China has enacted comprehensive environmental protection legislation, much of it based on global best practice (China National Environmental Protection Agency, 1994), its implementation is not always effective and the regulatory machinery for conservation and protection is weak. This situation is sometimes exacerbated by a degree of unwillingness by both the state and the private sector combined to adopt voluntary measures and self-regulation to protect the environment. Opposition to strict rules for environmental protection and natural resource management is the norm, not the exception (Gale, 2005).

Fifth, top-down planning is invariably the rule. In western paradigms of development for ecotourism and cultural tourism, community consultations, stakeholder involvement in meaningful dialogue and acceptance of non-governmental organization (NGO) inputs are widely accepted and practiced. However in China the culture of a centrally controlled economy is still deeply embedded in many senior officials and trying to move to a more inclusive approach to tourism planning is simply not present. Much tourism planning takes place in government offices removed from communities and sites, and stakeholders are simply presented with government fiat. Attempts to involve communities in meaningful dialogue for tourism development that has a capacity to maximize benefits for them are often unwelcome, brushed aside or simply met with puzzlement by government officials since communities, especially rural ethnic minority communities by definition in Chinese Communist Party (CP) ideology, are 'backward', uneducated and require 'uplifting' (Sofield and Li, 1998).

One of the strengths of a transition economy is that, despite these limitations, there is often a political willingness to prioritize tourism in the national development agenda. This is particularly the case with China, which has recognized that tourism is a key sector that can make a major contribution to its national economy and it was identified as a 'pillar' sector 10 years ago (Sofield and Li, 1996). The Chinese Government is active in support of tourism development as a key driver of development and is currently embarking on tourism planning on a scale unmatched anywhere else in the world. This takes the form of formulating 5 or 10 year Tourism Master Plans for each of its 26 provinces (more than 12 have now been completed), supported by several hundred detailed regional plans at the prefecture-, county- and site-specific levels. The drive to develop its poorer western provinces is spearheaded by tourism, e.g. the Greater Shangri-la Regional Tourism Master Plan, which covers northern Yunnan Province, southwestern Sichuan Province and the Tibet Autonomous Region (Sofield, 2003, Sofield and Li, 2003).

Modernization and globalization

For the first 5,000 years China developed its civilization independently from the rest of the world. Isolated from its neighbours by the vast deserts of central Asia and the Tibetan plateau to the west, by tropical forests to the south, and the Pacific Ocean to the east, it evolved with minimal contact with the other great civilizations of the Asian continent. Indeed, it called itself *Zhongguo*, the 'Central Kingdom', superior to all other civilizations and therefore needing no interaction in any substantial way with others (Sofield and Li, 1996). A strong xenophobic thread runs consistently through China's history from the ancient kingdoms to the CP rule of Mao Zedong. Only in the last 200 years has China, however unwillingly, become part of the global community (Ogden, 1992). In the latter half of the 20th century, influenced by the anti-western bias of the Maoist years from 1949 to 1976, the outsider's vision of China was obscured by the Bamboo Curtain which was drawn across its landscapes for those three decades. However, while Mao's fortress mentality denied globalization, he embarked on a process of modernization built entirely on internal resources and endeavour, embodied in his infamous 'Great Leap Forward' in 1955 when he attempted to industrialize China overnight.

The failure of modernization without globalization impelled China to reverse many of Mao's policies after his death in 1976. Two years later China voluntarily embraced some aspects of globalization in a new approach to modernization, with structural change originating from the December 1978 'Open Door' policies announced by then Premier, Deng Xiaoping, who 'embarked on a unique modernization process involving the gradual transformation of a centrally planned economic system into an open socialist market economy' (Gale, 2005). Deng's multi-faceted modernization programme combined agriculture, industry, national defence and science and technology (the 'four modernizations') in the context of opening China up to the world and beginning the process of dismantling the centralized command economy. In justifying the move towards a capitalist economy two of Deng's comments were elevated to national prominence and are still repeated by Chinese citizens today: 'It is honourable to get rich' and 'No matter whether the cat is black or white, it is a good cat if it catches rats' (Sofield and Li, 1998).

Deng's 'Open Door' policies unleashed pent-up energy that has manifested itself in one of the most sustained periods of construction activity and national economic growth of any country, with gross domestic product (GDP) increasing at more than 20% per annum for a decade. While it has slowed to about 8–9% per annum it shows little signs of abating, and is far in advance of most western 'developed' nations (World Bank, 2005). Massive infrastructure projects funded by the government culminated in the decision in 2001 to embark on the world' single largest infrastructure project, the Three Gorges Dam across the Yangtze River, a project which has involved technological transfer and expertise from more than 20 foreign countries and constitutes an expression of the duality of modernization and globalization in contemporary China. With a lake more than 620 km long that transformed much of the landscape, the Chinese authorities used the Dam to revision the tourism master plan for Hubei Province, where it is located (Sofield and Li, 2001; Sofield and Li, 2002).

Twenty years after Deng's 1978 reforms began, the structure of the Chinese economy was fundamentally different, as indicated by changes in employment and GDP. Gale (2005) has detailed these changes: in 1980, 69% of employment was in primary industries, 18% in manufacturing and 13% in services (Table 18.1). By 2000 this had changed to 49%, 23% and 28%, respectively.

In 2001, agriculture represented 15% of GDP, industry 53% and services 33%, indicating even further structural change (Gale, 2005). Tourism is of course a key component of the services industry.

Tourism in China

The communist regimes in China from 1949 until 1978 were dismissive of tourism as an appropriate form of economic activity. Both domestic and international tourism were almost non-existent (Chow, 1988; Hudman and Hawkins, 1989). Entry for overseas visitors was strictly controlled and tourism activity was held tightly in the hands of the state machinery. The little foreign tourism that existed was sanctioned on the grounds that the successes of communism could be paraded before a selected international audience (Sofield and Li, 1998). From 1954 to 1978 the China International Travel Service (set up to arrange visits by 'foreign friends') played host to only 125,000 visitors (Richter, 1989). Internal travel was suppressed even more rigidly with a permit system required for any travel outside one's local district. 'Tourism' was not an approved reason for travel.

Table 18.1 Employment by sector – China, 1980, 1990 and 1995–2000

Year	Primary	Secondary	Tertiary	Distribution (%)
1980	69	18	13	100
1990	60	21	19	100
1995	52	23	25	100
1996	50	24	26	100
1997	50	24	26	100
1998	50	24	27	100
1999	50	23	27	100
2000	49	23	28	100

Source: China Statistical Year Book, Tables 4.2 and 5.5.

The tourism industry gained a new acceptance as part of Deng's reform programme, its foreign exchange earnings recognized as being able to make a significant contribution to financing the four modernizations. The Bamboo Curtain was pulled aside and the Chinese door opened to world tourism in a comprehensive way. The first national conference on tourism in China was held in 1979 to formulate guidelines and organizational structures for its development (Gao and Zhang, 1982). Politically, tourism as an acceptable industry was justified in socialist terms because it would advance economic reforms and the policy of opening to the outside world, it would further friendship and mutual understanding between the Chinese proletariat and other peoples of the world, and it would contribute to world peace (Li and Sofield, 1994). In three different speeches in 1979 Deng Xiaoping stated the need for the swift growth and development of tourism (*Tourism Tribune*, 1992). Over the next two decades China began to focus on developing clearly identified tourism sectors, and two sectors which have been given prominence are ecotourism and cultural tourism.

Ecotourism and cultural tourism

The coupling of these two sectors in this heading is quite deliberate. This is because the Chinese paradigm is one which, contrary to the western paradigm, does not separate them into distinct and distinctive fields, but views them as a single entity, based on the two millennia-old Daoist tenet of 'man* and nature in harmony'. A Chinese worldview sees cultural and natural heritage as a single unitary construct in contrast to the differentiation espoused by a western, positivist, scientific approach. This Chinese worldview is both anthropocentric (humans first) and anthropomorphic (attributing human characteristics to non-human features, natural formations, animals, plants, etc.). The Chinese word for 'nature' – *da-jiran* may be translated literally as 'everything coming into being' and expresses the entirety of mountains, rivers, plants, animals, humans, all bound up in their five elements – metals, wood, water, fire and earth (Tellenbach and Bin, 1989). 'Man is based on earth, earth is based on heaven, heaven is based on the Way (*Tao*) and the Way is based on *da-jiran* (nature): all modalities of being are organically connected' (Tu, 1989, p. 67). Under Confucian values scholars and

---

* The use of the masculine noun here is a faithful translation of the Mandarin phrase.

mandarins were exhorted 'to seek ultimate wisdom in Nature' (Overmyer, 1986). Confucian thought and Daoist philosophy encompassed the need for man and nature to bring opposing forces into a symbiotic relationship where 'harmony' rather than 'difference' or 'opposites' was dominant (Rawson and Legeza, 1973). This is an anthropocentric perspective with an active sociological determinant which prescribes that because nature is imperfect, 'man' has a responsibility to improve on nature (Chan, 1969; Elvin, 1973). It is thus distinct from a western perspective that separates nature and civilization (humans), that views nature ('wilderness') ideally as free from artificiality and human intervention.

These differences are starkly portrayed in tourism development all over China. Thus, when the Chinese construct a pagoda on a round hilltop in a forest (e.g. Huangshan) it is 'man improving on nature' because the perfect shape is a spire; but westerners may see human domination over nature. When that pagoda provides shelter and a facility for rest and meditation it is anthropocentric because it is providing a service for people that nature alone cannot provide; but westerners may see it as intruding on and destroying the 'wilderness' values of that place. When the pagoda is approached through a flight of 500 vertical stairs constructed recently out of reinforced concrete, Chinese see a 'stairway to heaven' (as was cut into the living rock for their emperors to undertake pilgrimage visits to sacred mountains), and thus a symbolic link that brings past and present into a unitary 'now'; but westerners may see only a geometric concrete 'scar' that degrades the environment and spoils its aesthetic appeal. When the hill is described as 'benevolent' it is ascribed a human characteristic (anthropomorphism) that may jar with western sensibilities of pristine wilderness untrammelled by humans. When 20-m-high Chinese characters are cut into the cliff next to a hanging pine tree below the pagoda the Chinese see the high art of calligraphy reflecting the intrinsic Chinese values of the site, for example the Ouyang Xun style, one of three famous calligrapers whose style is infused with sentiments such as strength of personality, as steadfast as the lone pine tree clinging to a high mountain cliff buffeted by winds and storms (Fan, 1996). The content of the characters may be a poem by Li Bai (701–762 A.D.) perhaps the most renowned Tang dynasty poet, that has made the site famous for centuries. But the lack of any translation or interpretation will leave westerners bemused.

When such calligraphy is highlighted in red, yellow and green paint, the profound significance of the sight/site will be further enriched for Chinese because the colours themselves have deep symbolism for their Chinese viewers – red for happiness, green for longevity, yellow for prosperity. Western archaeologists from ICOMOS (International Council for Monuments and Sites) who have responsibility for assessing world heritage site cultural values for UNESCO may recognize the ancient inscription as significant because they place a very high value on antiquity, but they will frown on the addition of the modern paint on grounds of destroying the integrity of the historico-cultural fabric of the site. For the Chinese, however, a newly engraved inscription may have similar authenticity as a much older inscription because they 'see' the continuity in an age-old process that should not be museumized according to some western notion of separating out the past from the present. Authenticity is culturally defined, not a concept that can be scientifically and objectively measured and universally applied (Li and Sofield, 2006). In short, for Chinese tourists, the calligraphy will enhance their appreciation of the site as they make the association between the calligrapher and the pine tree in a fusion of history, psychology, botany and literary art; whereas westerners may see only graffiti that further degrades the site.

This unitary approach to nature and culture is embedded in *shan shui* (literally, *mountain water*), a major Chinese literary and artistic movement that was firmly established between the 8th and 11th centuries and continues to the present day. By incorporating values that imbue nature/natural scenery with a range of human social and cultural values, such as likening mountains to benevolence and waters to wisdom ('The Analects of Confucius', 5th century B.C.) *shan shui* philosophy has had a profound influence on the aesthetics of natural landscapes. Because the Chinese worldview privileges literary and cultural heritage before the sciences, Chinese tourists to World Heritage Site national parks like Huangshan will interpret their experience through the culture of *shan shui* rather than through western paradigms of biological and geological sciences, or 'wilderness' which in the ideal western construct has no visible presence of humans. Ecotourism in China is therefore as much about culture, including built culture, as it is about natural heritage, and because of this fusion much of what is identified by the Chinese themselves as ecotourism draws disbelieving comment from western visitors. The crux of the matter is that a definition of ecotourism is culturally derived and the values which surround 'western' ecotourism and 'Chinese' ecotourism are equally valid in the context of their different national locations and socio-cultural environments. They are, simply, different.

Thus when China sought World Heritage Site (WHS) listing for Huangshan (Yellow Mountains) UNESCO insisted that it disconnect its natural heritage values from its cultural heritage, and it withheld approval for cultural world heritage listing for a number of years because its science-based experts from ICOMOS considered that its cultural integrity and authenticity had been compromised (Li and Sofield, 2006). In the Chinese value system however, such severance of the connections between the two is artificial and simply non-Chinese. In preparing their WHS application for UNESCO, the Chinese were forced to produce two documents, one focusing on the biological and geological attributes of this 135 km^2 mountain range, and one on its cultural heritage. But when listing the 1,450 native plant species, 28 significant endemic plants and 300 vertebrates (PRC, 1989) the Chinese interspersed the necessary scientific terminology with aspects of cultural heritage and anthropomorphic descriptors. For example, in describing the vegetation of Huangshan and its endemic conifer species, *Pinus huangshanensis*, the submission by the Chinese authorities to IUCN (International Union for the Conservation of Nature) noted that: 'A number of legendary trees are celebrated on account of their age, grotesque shape, or precipitously perched position, and more than 100 bear special names' (PRC, 1989), such as 'Two Lovers Embracing' (two pines with intertwined trunks) and 'Welcoming Guests Pine' (so named because its branches open out like the arms of a host gesturing to visitors to enter his/her house). Such anthropomorphizing is regarded as inappropriate in western scientific texts but is the norm in a Chinese context. While the Huangshan pine is of intrinsic botanical interest to western science its significance for Chinese visitors to Huangshan lies in cultural attributes, many of the trees so well known from literary references over the centuries that they form 'must-see' sights (Li and Sofield, 2006).

Similarly when describing the geological attributes of Huangshan, folk legends and other cultural referents were integrated. For example, the signage prepared for one particular vista of a group of peaks within the range makes references in its first two sentences to 'medium-to-fine-grained porphyritic granite bodies, ... densely distributed vertical and horizontal joints ... and the NW–SE-trending fault zone', but then quickly goes on at much greater length about how 'the peaks and interesting and odd stones' have resulted in 'countless fairy stories and sayings being handed down.' The signage continues with reference to the names of famous peaks and rocks such as Paiyunting (Clouds Overwhelming Temple), An Immortal Airing His Boots, Wu Song's Fighting Tiger, Heaven Dog's Watching Moon [Rock] and King Wen Pulling a Wagon.

As with most other signage in Huangshan, the information relies upon Chinese common knowledge to deliver understanding and Chinese visitors will automatically draw upon their knowledge of ancient poets, Confucian and Daoist philosophy and religion, imperial history, and Chinese classical literature to recognize the significance and symbolism that is captured in the scenery before them. But this information requires very lengthy interpretation if it is to be comprehensible to non-Chinese visitors. For example, 'Immortals' in Chinese culture are integral to Daoist belief. They are not gods in the western sense of that word although they may be worshipped and shrines built for them. Nor are they angels although they are celestial beings; they are mischievous, fun-loving, carousing creatures with superhuman strengths and skills, constantly playing tricks on each other. They dwell in mountains, and caves (the Daoist 'passage-way to Heaven') are often their abode. Evidence of the presence of immortals in mountains thus abounds and Huangshan is no exception as this example demonstrates. The reference to Emperor Wen also links Immortals to Confucian philosophy. In the famous 'Analects', Confucius discussed the meaning of an ancient story in which Wen pulled the cart of an Immortal for 800 steps before stopping, exhausted. As a result the Immortal blessed his descendents with 800 years of unbroken rule. The reference to Wu Song fighting a tiger is taken from two of China's most famous classics, '*Outlaws of the Marsh*' (Shi Nai'an and Luo Guanzhong, *ca.* 1350 A.D.) and '*The Plum in the Golden Vase*' (anonymous, *ca.* 1618 A.D.). Every educated 10-year old Chinese knows that the character Wu Song personifies manly strength because he killed an attacking tiger with his bare hands (Li and Sofield, 2006).

The Chinese cultural heritage submission for Huangshan did not record such aspects of its cultural heritage but focused on detailing 2,000 years of active pilgrimage to the 72 peaks of the range. By the time of the Yuan Dynasty (1271–1368 A.D.), for example, 64 temples and many pavilions had been constructed. More were subsequently built, for example Fahai Meditation Temple and Wonshu Temple in the 17th century, connected by steps cut into the mountains (PRC, 1989). Although only 20 temples now survive they form a focal point for many contemporary Chinese visitors to Huangshan. In its original assessment of the Chinese Government's nomination, the IUCN (1990, p. 11) declared that Huangshan's natural values were 'predominant over its cultural heritage'; and ICOMOS (1990) deferred its recommendation for cultural heritage listing. The IUCN (1990, p. 12) also recommended that the Chinese authorities 'should be encouraged to reduce the human influence on the mountain', a startling comment given that the mountain has for more than 2,000 years been a very rich cultural site. UNESCO's response to these two submissions encapsulated the difference between the two value systems (Li and Sofield, 2006).

In examining how Chinese values about landscape and wilderness are translated into tourism attractions, the anthropocentric position encourages and facilitates programmes to alter the physical and biological environment in order to produce desired 'improvements' (Sofield and Li, 1998). These may include landscaped gardens, artificial lakes and waterfalls, facilities for recreation and tourism, roads for ease of access, observation towers and so on. Increasing direct human use is the objective of management and the character of the 'wilderness' will be changed to reflect the desires of humans and contemporary standards of 'comfort in nature'. Styles of recreation and tourism will be tuned to the convenience of humans, so trails will be concreted, resorts and restaurants permitted inside reserves, cable cars approved and so forth. Huangshan exhibits all of these examples of 'man improving on nature' (Li and Sofield, 2006).

The biocentric approach that underlies the IUCN's approach to WHS assessment by contrast emphasizes the maintenance or enhancement of natural systems, if necessary at the expense of recreational and other human uses (Hendee and Stankey, 1973, cited in Hendee et al., 1990). 'The goal of the biocentric philosophy is to permit natural ecological processes to operate as freely as possible, because wilderness for society ultimately depends on the retention of naturalness' (Hendee et al., 1990, p. 18). But this definition of wilderness is a western perception and one that is alien to Chinese values. This western approach requires controlling the flow of external, especially human-made, pressures on ecosystems by restricting excessive recreational or touristic use of the biogeophysical resources. The recreational use of wilderness is tolerated with this position only to the degree that it does not change the energy balance inordinately. A biocentric philosophy requires recreational users to take wilderness on its own terms rather than manipulate it to serve human needs. Like the anthropocentric approach the biocentric approach also focuses on human benefits, but the important distinction between them is that, according to Hendee et al. (1990, p. 19) 'biocentrically the benefits are viewed over a longer term and as being dependent upon retaining the naturalness of the wilderness ecosystems.'

Caves as tourist sites in China are probably the best example of the stark differences between east and west (Li, 2005). In China they are imbued with immense cultural significance that relates to Daoism, Buddhism and literary classics such as 'Journey to the West' (probably the most famous of all Chinese classics). Many caves have entered Chinese common knowledge because of the writings of poets, essayists and philosophers, and most are adorned with calligraphy often more than a thousand years old. Caves are 'dong', the Immortals' pathway to 'tian' or heaven. Visitation involves light, sound, laughter and games. Photographic opportunities will be found around every corner and floodlights switched on for visitors to dress up in imperial robes and sit on throne-shaped flow stones or on the backs of dragon-like formations. Guides will encourage visitors to touch formations for good luck, good fortune, good health or longevity. There is no natural lighting, no concern for these sites as fragile environments for a range of equally fragile organisms: conservation and ecology play no part in the presentation of caves for tourism in China. By contrast, in most parts of the western world the environmental and conservation paradigm determines how caves will be managed for tourism, interpretation will invariably be based on scientific geological and biological elucidation; and once underground it may be difficult for a visitor to identify what country they are in. But in China ALL caves are cultural sites and every visitor will know that they are in China (Li, 2005).

Conclusions

In examining ecotourism and cultural tourism in China the internal imperatives are much stronger than external forces although those external demands have been harnessed for, and in turn have influenced to a degree, the shape and form of cultural tourist product inside China. However, the 'Chineseness' (Ogden, 1992) that determines the socio-cultural environment of the Middle Kingdom sets the processes of modernization through tourism apart from those global forces which are considered by some to impose significant homogenization and standardization of tourism products on societies – the so-called 'global village' concept (Bonniface and Fowler, 1993). The relative unity of China as a single entity over a 4,000 year period and its accompanying 'Chineseness' have resulted in a cultural resilience which has defied this wide range of both endogenous and exogenous forces for change. The result is that one cannot draw the same distinctions between ecotourism and cultural tourism that can be drawn in western countries. 'Man in harmony with nature' predominates and while it is slowly changing as western influences continue to penetrate, virtually all ecotourism in China is cultural tourism even if the forms are not instantly recognizable to most western visitors. The result is that when one visits a natural landscape site in China, cultural elements abound and every visitor unmistakably knows that they are in China.

References

Bonniface, P. and Fowler, P. (1993). *Heritage and Tourism in the 'Global Village'*. Routledge, London.

Chan, W.-T. (1969). *A Source Book of Chinese Philosophy*. Colombia University Press, New York.

China National Environmental Protection Agency (1994). *China: Biodiversity Conservation Action Plan*. National Environmental Protection Agency, Beijing.

China National Tourism Administration (CNTA) (2006). *China Tourism Statistics 2005*. CNTA, Beijing.

Chow, W.S. (1988). Open policy and tourism between Guangdong and Hong Kong. *Annals of Tourism Research* 15: 205–218.

Denman, R. (2005). Policies and tools for sustainable tourism and their application to transitional economies. *WTO European Meeting on 'Tourism: A Tool for Sustainable Development in Transition Economies'*. WTO, Belgrade.

Dunsire, A. (1978). *Implementation in a Bureaucracy*. Martin Robertson, Oxford.

Elvin, M. (1973). *The Pattern of the Chinese Past*. Stamford University Press, Stamford.

Fan, Y. (ed.) (1996). *Commentary on the Best Ancient Landscape Poems*. Guanxi Normal University Press, Guanxi.

Gale, R. (2005). Sustainable tourism: the environmental dimensions of trade liberalization in China. In Shrubsole, D. and Watson, N. (eds), *Sustaining Our Futures: Perspectives on Environment, Economy and Society*. University of Waterloo, Waterloo, Ontario.

Gao, D.-C. and Zhang, G. (1982). China's tourism: policy and practice. *International Journal of Tourism Management* 4(2): 75–84.

Hendee, J.C. and Stankey, G.H. (1973). Biocentrity in Wilderness Management. *BioScience* 23(9): 535–538.

Hendee, J.C., Stankey, G.H. and Lucas, R. (1990). *Wilderness Management* (2nd edn). North America Press, Golden.

Hudman, L.E. and Hawkins, D.E. (1989). *Tourism in Contemporary Society*. Prentice Hall, Englewood Cliffs.

International Council on Monuments and Sites (1990). *World Heritage Nomination – ICOMOS Summary 547 Mount Huangshan Scenic Beauty and Historic Site (China)*. http://whc.unesco.org/archive/advisory_body_evaluation/547 (accessed February 2, 2005).

IUCN (1990). *World Heritage Nomination – IUCN Summary 547 Mount Huangshan Scenic Beauty and Historic Site (China)*. Summary prepared by IUCN (April 1990) based on the original nomination submitted by the Peoples Republic of China.

http://whc.unesco.org/archive/advisory_body_evaluation/ 547 (accessed February 2, 2005).

Li, F.M.S. (2005). *Chinese Common Knowledge, Tourism, and Natural Landscapes: Gazing on 'Bie you tian di'– 'An Altogether Different World.'* PhD Thesis, Murdoch University, Perth, Western Australia.

Li, F.M.S. and Sofield, T.H.B. (1994). Tourism development and socio-cultural change in rural China. In Seaton, A. (ed.), *Tourism. The State of the Art*. John Wiley and Sons, Chichester.

Li, F.M.S. and Sofield, T.H.B. (2006). World heritage management: the case of Huangshan (Yellow Mountain), China. In Leask, A. and Fyall, A. (eds), *Managing World Heritage Sites*. Elsevier, London.

OECD (2002). China in the World Economy: The Domestic Policy Challenges. OECD, Brussels.

OECD (2003). *Governance in China*. OECD, Brussels.

Ogden, S. (1992). *China's Unresolved Issues. Politics, Development and Culture*. Prentice Hall, Englewood Cliffs.

Overmyer, D.L. (1986). *Religions of China: The World as a Living System*. Harper and Row, San Francisco.

PRC *Regulations of the Peoples Republic of China on Nature Reserves 1994*.

PRC (1989). Chinese Communist Party Central Documents Study Centre. *Thirteenth National Congress of the Communist Party of China*, 1987 (Documents). Foreign Languages Press, Beijing.

Rawson, P. and Legeza, L. (1973). *Tao. The Chinese Philosophy of Time and Change*. Thames and Hudson, London.

Ren Zhuge (2000). Questionnaire survey on participation of local communities in nature reserve management. In Chinese National Committee for MAB, *Study on Sustainable Management Policy for China's Nature Reserves Chinese National Committee for Man and the Biosphere Programme*, Beijing, pp. 76–85.

Richter, L.K. (1989). *The Politics of Tourism in Asia*. University of Hawaii Press, Honolulu.

Shi Nai'an and Luo Guanzhong (*ca.* 1350). *Outlaws of the Marsh* (Compilation attributed to Shi Nai'an (*ca.* 1290–*ca.* 1365); revision attributed to Luo Guanzhong (*ca.* 1330–*ca.* 1400).

Sofield, T.H.B. (2002). Master plan for tourism development for Hubei Province: windows of discovery! *A Report for the Chinese Government Panel of Experts on Tourism Development for Hubei Province*, Wuhan, May 2002, 144 pp.

Sofield, T.H.B. (2003). Tibet – The Myth of Shangri-la. Presented at the *Ninth Annual APTA Conference*, University of Technology Sydney, July 2003.

Sofield, T.H.B. and Li, F.M.S. (1996). Rural tourism in China. In Page, S. and Getz, D. (eds), *The Business of Rural Tourism*. Routledge, London, pp. 57–84.

Sofield, T.H.B. and Li, F.M.S. (1998). China: tourism development and cultural policies. *Annals of Tourism Research* 25(2): 323–353.

Sofield, T.H.B. and Li, F.M.S. (with Bao, Jigang and Xu, Hong Gang) (2001). *Master Plan for Tourism Development for Hubei Province: Ecotourism Strategy*. A Report for Hubei Provincial Government.

Sofield, T.H.B. and Li, F.M.S. (2002). Tourism policy and planning in China: the case of the Three Gorges Dam. *CAUTHE Annual Conference*, Perth, February 2002.

Sofield, T.H.B. and Li, F.M.S. (2003). Processes in formulating an ecotourism policy for nature reserves in Yunnan Province, China. In Fennell, D. and Dowling, R. (eds), *Ecotourism: Policy and Strategy Issues*. CAB International Academic, Oxon, pp. 141–168.

Sofield, T.H.B. and McTaggart, R. (2005). Tourism as a tool for sustainable development in transition economies. *DFID/GRM Conference on Development Learning in Transition Environments*, London, October 18, 2005.

Tellenbach, H. and Bin, K. (1989). The Japanese concept of 'Nature'. In Callicott, J.B. and Ames, R.T. (eds), *Nature in Asian Traditions of Thought: Essays in Environmental Philosophy*. State University of New York Press, New York, pp. 153–162.

Tourism Tribune (1992). China must speed up tourism development: Deng Xiaoping. *Tourism Tribune* 7(6): 1–2 [Title in English, text in Chinese].

Tu Wei-Ming (1989). The continuity of being: Chinese visions of nature. In Callicott, J.B. and Ames, R.T. (eds), *Nature in Asian Traditions of Thought: Essays in Environmental Philosophy*. State University of New York Press, New York, pp. 67–78.

World Bank (1999). Country brief. *China: The Political Economy of Uneven Development*. World Bank, Washington, DC.

World Bank (2005). *Transition to a Market Economy*. http://www1.worldbank.org/sp/Transition (accessed February 1, 2006).

World Bank (2006). *East Asia Update: China, March 2006*. World Bank, Washington, DC.

CHAPTER 19

Ecotourism certification: potential and challenges

Xavier Font

the applicant firms. For example, it is not known whether a firm that applies many of the standards proposed will be financially better off or not, although we know that for some of the criteria such as water/waste/energy management there are eco-savings (particularly for resorts), but there are few examples of quantifying added costs from meeting other criteria, particularly labour and social standards, particularly for ecotourism small firms. A market-led standard would take this into account, and ensure that it can be accurately claimed that overall the firm does not increase its operational costs. The standards are set by benchmarking best practice, usually aiming very high, but there is no assessment of the commitment, cost, and time that a company is required to invest in order to meet such standards.

The demand for certification needs to be created (Rainforest Alliance, 2002). Market studies might say that the demand is not there, but it remains unclear as to whether this is because certification is not known, understood, or wanted. Demand will take time in tourism, just as it did in other sectors. Because critical mass is required (World Bank, 2005), programmes targeting key vulnerable areas (e.g. SmartVoyager with Galapagos) or the most vulnerable groups (ROC with indigenous people) is essential. Achieving pockets of critical mass and managing those pockets as learning networks both for sustainability and quality are necessary.

Monitoring market demand and particularly market satisfaction will give the data to prove some of the benefits of certification. Raising awareness of the tourism industry alone will not be sufficient incentive to increase applications. Certification programmes will need to collect evidence to prove what percentage of firms are making improvements to become certified, and when certification is of interest to those firms that already had high standards. It is likely that the applicants in the first years are of the latter group, and only when certification programmes have been operating for some time they will become attractive propositions to improve performance. Large firms do not want to be certified as a method to attract business, but to protect their brand for public relations reasons against possible negative publicity (Kahlenborn and Dominé, 2001; Fairweather et al., 2005). At present multinational hotels might not perceive the need for ecolabels and a Costa Rican study found that when they did, they scored low in sustainability criteria (Rivera, 2002). It is important to understand what increasing the trade/marketing benefits, and subsequently broadening the type of applicants, does to the credibility of the certification programmes.

Equity and small firms

Equity refers to the fairness of an instrument, which is here considered as the ability of tourism firms to access certification. Certification in Ecuador, Belize, Costa Rica, and Guatemala, has shown how useful certification standards are for capacity building and levelling the playing field (Ronald Sanabria, personal comment, October 2005). Programmes that encourage small firm participation usually receive financial support from their governments, in the form of access to capacity building, marketing, or less often physical investments, and these funders will need to assess the ability of certification to change practice in comparison with other policy tools such as taxing negative behaviour or rewarding positive behaviour through tax breaks, providing market-based incentives such as additional marketing, amongst others, although no study has been conducted to make comparisons of policy tools. Clearly all voluntary tools require an effort to ensure small firms benefit, certification is not an exception, and the analysis below needs to be understood in this context.

Small and medium firms, and particularly disadvantaged segments of society particularly in poverty, need equitable access to information, training, and technology, before being able to promote certified firms. Certification as a tool tries to promote equitable market access, by providing opportunities to promote good practice; the same can be said for accreditation. Even after acknowledging the benefits to sustainable or ecotourism certification, many questions remain on how to ensure these benefits reach a wide variety of businesses, as there is evidence that firms most interested in certification in the early days already have high standards (UNEP, 2006) which can inflate the value of the project in the short term and set unrealistic targets for future interventions. It is logical that these are the first companies targeted, to showcase models of good practice. The challenge comes when there is inequitable access to certification, as explained below, because inequitable access means that certification can be a trade barrier. This is still an issue for voluntary programmes if we find that tour operators request certification as a requirement to trade.

The first years of each certification programme are characterised by working with best practice firms to showcase the application of the standards. However there is little consideration of whether beyond the period of standard setting, other firms will be able to meet those standards based on the advice that can be provided through the training materials available via the certification programme, or whether meeting the standards will increase costs to the firm (other than for those programmes focusing on environmental issues alone that emphasise eco-savings).

The point debated here is the extent of the benefits that firms should receive from certification, because tourism companies do not start from a level playing field that allows them access to be certified (Medina, 2005). The International Ecotourism Society (TIES) own survey 'of the US experts that had an opinion on whether the programmes either advantaged or disadvantaged small and medium sized enterprises (SMEs), the sense was that the programmes were much more likely to be used by larger and foreign-owned firms. This is primarily because of the direct costs and management burdens of participating in these schemes' (TIES, 2005, p. 9). A different study conducted for TIES concludes that:

The same structural problems of high costs, complexity, and lack of flexibility to reflect local conditions apply with special force to smaller enterprises. The SMEs can't afford expensive programs, need simpler designs, and require latitude to adjust to management and physical limitations. The respondents were unanimous in their view that SMEs need comprehensive support if they are not to be disadvantaged by certification programs. Accordingly, governments, NGOs, industry associations and other potential donors should be prepared to provide integrated packages of financial, technical and marketing assistance to SMEs. The primary focus of this assistance should be to enable disadvantaged small enterprises to improve the overall quality of their offerings. A side benefit of this assistance would be to position them for higher sustainable travel certification rankings, but this should not be the primary objective of the assistance

(TIES, 2004, p. 19).

In developing proposals for Western Europe, the issue of whether developed countries could have a certification programme has not been questioned and not seen as a hurdle, but this is a key concern when thinking of a global reach. The 2005 report from TIES notes that in fact European programmes do target small applicants, but 'while this may cover the primary concerns of equity in Europe, it is likely that most people in the five target countries (Belize, Brazil, Costa Rica, Ecuador, and Guatemala) will remain concerned about equal access to certification opportunities in the region, especially for micro and community-based tourism firms' (TIES, 2005, p. 10). The only data collected to back up this point are a survey from 2000 where participation in the Costa Rican programme correlated highly with the Chief Executive Officer's level of education and environmental expertise – but no difference for Costa Rican nationals/expatriates as initially expected (Rivera and de Leon, 2005).

While scaled fees are suggested as one way to address this inequity (World Bank, 2005) there is no evidence to suggest that is more than an acknowledgement of the problem, rather than providing a credible solution. Increasing the number of companies that meet these standards allows in the medium term to reach the economies of scale to produce better training for applicants and marketing of their products. The key challenge is the potential impact this can have on those firms that are not suited to it, if it becomes a powerful tool for increased trade, or if governments and industry associations aim to enforce compulsory standards.

Effectiveness

Effectiveness is a measure of how well an instrument achieves its objectives. 'Certification schemes, although increasing in their number and scope over the past 10 years, have not enabled SMEs greater access to market opportunities, nor have they moved the tourism industry significantly forward towards sustainability' (World Bank, 2005, p. 4). Certification was also found to be unsuccessful in allowing greater access to new market segments (World Bank, 2005, p. 31). Certification in other sectors such as forestry has focused on closing the gap between 'very best' and 'good' practice, while poor forest management is little affected (Bass *et al.*, 2001). The claims that certified firms perform better have been used in promoting certification by TIES (i.e. Green Tourism Business Scheme having higher occupancy rates, or Costa Rica's Certificate for Sustainable Tourism certified companies having higher room prices) are politicised: it is unlikely this is the result of certification, and instead it is more possible that better managed firms in the first place happen to have the resources and knowledge to get involved in certification. As put by the World Bank (2005, p. 5):

certification programmes have enabled companies to reduce costs, mainly related to the environment (water, waste, and energy savings). This cost saving advantage or training aid has helped improve management practices and processes, however there is little incentive to continue being part of a certification label as there is no proven marketing benefit. Certification programmes are costly to run and most are subsidised by governments or international funding agencies. They are also costly to join for the individual operations, and so far have not delivered on promised marketing benefits and consumer awareness. Overall, industry awareness of such schemes is negligible.

Measuring and further improving effectiveness will be paramount. While 'guidelines within the industry are becoming more common, however, implementation and evaluation is still weak' (World Bank, 2005, p. 4). Most ecolabel schemes are not adequately resourced to undertake a scientifically valid monitoring of their effectiveness, but they seem to recognise its importance (UNEP, 2006). UNEP suggests that this is 'integrated into the conformity assessment process, as long as means can be found to limit the impact of conflicts of interest' (UNEP, 2005, p. 39). All that exists at present are excellent rich stories, usually collected by the certification programmes themselves, and with little evidence of the added value that was provided by the process of certification. Anecdotally we know that many of those firms already performed well before considering certification, but we also have many examples of firms that have learned through the process of becoming certified. However we cannot quantify the added benefit of certification in itself. The challenge is to collect data independently from the actual certification programmes, which will have a vested interest in always showcasing exemplary practices. The methodology needs to be standardised so comparisons can be made across different certification programmes. Because market access is a key benefit (although maybe only in the future) for certified firms, the author would suggest including an indicator on additional trade that can be directly attributed to being a certified firm.

Certification programmes must be publicly accountable whenever they use public or donor funds. More robust data are needed to report to donors or other funding bodies as well as stakeholders in general, beyond numbers of certified firms. Without any further evidence, the ratio of number of certified firms divided by the investment on the certification programme is the only indicator of success of the project. During the 2005 World Tourism Forum (WTF) in Rio de Janeiro, a workshop with over 30 certification specialists was conducted which brought up that this is not a good measure of the achievements of these programmes (UNEP, 2006). This issue is being addressed by the introduction of performance-related indicators to measure and communicate the achievements of certified firms through the process of certification.

Efficiency and financing

Efficiency is a measure of how well an instrument uses the resources available. Just as for other sectors (UNEP, 2005), at present there is limited scientifically reliable evidence of the value for money of standard certification as a policy instrument (Rivera, 2002) as costs are not clear and effectiveness cannot be measured. Case studies of good practice usually report on experiences of companies that were already good before applying because these were the first target in setting up the certification programmes, and these programmes have not been operating for long enough to measure their cumulative impact on change in behaviour. In the next few years it is necessary to measure efficiency to allow comparisons with other sustainability tools.

To understand efficiency it is necessary to look at the financing mechanisms. There are hardly any certification programmes that can claim to be self-financing, here understood as the certification programmes' ability to pay all of its fixed and variable costs through the revenues they generate from certification applicants. In some cases being self-financing was mistaken by having secured donor funds for the long term. Most rely on short-term start-up funds from governments and NGOs. Few have industry buy in from the outset, and they do not have clear funding strategies that in the next 5 years can make them self-sufficient. In many cases a firm's application fee only covers part of the costs of the service they receive (training and verification), but the services received are not sufficient to reduce their operating costs (through eco-savings) or to increase turnover (through marketing) to offset the price paid and time invested, particularly for small firms. This is only possible because certification programmes are government (or NGO) subsidised (for the period of developing the certification programmes only), the main challenge being how to run certification programmes in the long term. Being self-financing might not necessarily have to be the goal, if funders (particularly governments) find that the improvements in sustainability performance are higher through certification than through other tools. There are however no data to compare the cost efficiency of certification against other tools.

Business to consumer

Companies adopting a sustainability label for tourism, just as when adopting the Forest Stewardship Council label, are co-branding their product. This is most important for small firms with no international market recognition, where they can use this label as a sign of quality and reliability. A label is a means to communicate and overcome lack of trust. In industries where the consumer does not have the capacity to undertake tests, a label ensures that a product is what it promises (e.g. organic). In tourism, the consumer can experience first hand many of the aspects of the production of their holiday, but only when they have already paid for the product, and often cross-cultural borders means they cannot tell whether what they are experiencing is environmentally friendly or fair trade, according to local customs. Tourists are unable to tell either whether their enjoyment of the destination is contributing to the long-term deterioration of the site, although market research shows that this is a concern (Gordon, 2001).

A key challenge for tourism certification is that having a label does not necessarily equate to a higher-quality product than a competitor. Many high-performing tourism firms are not certified. The brand therefore loses meaning as tourists can find the same sustainability elsewhere. Certified products are not meaningful to the consumer because they do not have significantly different attributes. Consumers cannot tell from the available information whether a certified product is better than others in terms that matter to the tourist.

'Case after case has demonstrated that consumer demand develops long after a certification programme is well established' (Bien, 2005, p. 16), with consumer demand taking between 8 and 15 years (sometimes as long as 20) to develop. Certification programmes need further understanding of why companies apply, and why distribution channels might use certification as part of their supply chain. UNEP (2005, p. 35) concludes that the main drivers for sustainability are not linked to consumption, but to 'employee concerns, access to capital and reputational risk management, or protecting the "license to operate"'. Tour operator experiences prove this point too, as put by Chris Thompson from the Federation of Tour Operators, 'we want to sell holidays that happen to be sustainable, not sell sustainable tourism' (personal comment, July 2005). This relates back to the issue of what is certification meant to achieve. Is it always keeping standards high to only certify the top-performing companies? Or is it to increase standards across all tourism firms?

The message of being certified is unlikely to make it to the final consumer either, just the benefits of a better holiday experience. UNEP (2005, p. 37) states that 'what is important is not that consumers are willing to pay more for ecolabelled products, but simply that one of the market actors in the value chain has a financial incentive to promote ecolabelling'. The market incentive is easier in other sectors, such as organic products, where the retail price of the product is considerably higher than the cost of production. In tourism, where profit margins are low, it will be very difficult to market certified products at a price premium, and also the margins do not allow for absorbing increased production costs.

Business to business

There is agreement amongst experts consulted in preparation for this chapter, the World Bank (2005) study, TIES research (2004), and the outcomes from an increasing number of projects (Rainforest Alliance, 2003; Bien, 2005) that, business-to-business marketing, particularly through sustainable supply chain management, is the key avenue for marketing certified products. A recent study for UNEP shows that most distribution and communication channels are willing to give preference to sustainable tourism products, and for most this can be done without unmanageable additional costs (Font and Carey, 2005). Those reviewed were destination management organisations and tourist boards, tour operators, guidebooks, media, travel fairs, Internet retailers, and consumer associations. They all stated that they would need to develop guidelines of what sustainability meant for their suppliers, and then find ways to encourage those suppliers to meet these standards.

While this provides an opportunity, it does not mean that certification is necessarily the answer. For certified forest products for example, retailers did not need an ecolabel to green their supply chain, and 'they are often content with a supplier's declaration of conformity, a second-party audit or a third-party audit that does not lead to the application of an ecolabel' (UNEP, 2005, p. 34). While the Federation of Tour Operators (UK) and ANVR (The Netherlands) are developing preferred codes of practice on sustainability for accommodation, wildlife tourism, animal attractions, marine recreation ... they are seeking more cost-efficient forms of verification than those provided by the current certification programmes, and more tailored to their product and geographical needs (Chris Thompson, personal comment, July 2005, see also http://www.fto.co.uk/responsible-tourism/best-practice/). Their aim is to slowly mainstream sustainability by raising the bar for the majority of suppliers, while certification showcases best practice. Certification programmes need to capitalise on tour operators' need for corporate social reporting but understand how the product they are after differs from what certification offers today.

If certification does prove to become a powerful tool, it is necessary to consider again whether certification can only deliver for best practice firms, or whether it is a transferable model for the industry as a whole. 'While certification schemes may be described as ways for SMEs in lower income countries to obtain access to market, interviews with both major and specialist tour operators, travel providers and certification programmes do not support this view' (World Bank, 2005, p. 30).

Particularly in the case that certification could become a requirement to trade, the challenge is to ensure that tour operators mainly, but also other distribution channels, provide help to suppliers to meet the required standards, ensuring equity, and no barriers to market access. It will be the way in which tour operators work with their suppliers, and whether standards are simply imposed or they are facilitated, that will determine the success of standard setting. These standards can be however introduced in ways other than certification as we understand it today (UNEP, 2005, pp. 35–36).

Standards and the message to the market

Certification relies on having a credible message that is remembered by the market and is meaningful in purchasing decisions. Most of the (tourism and otherwise) certification programmes have spent a large proportion of their start-up funds developing standards, and this increased understanding of what sustainability might mean and how it can be measured is already a key benefit from certification. The most frequent reason given for companies' support of the Forest Stewardship Council (pioneer in timber certification and years ahead of the tourism experience) is not the environmental effectiveness of the standard, but the fact that it has been developed in a multi-stakeholder forum (UNEP, 2005, p. 35). Therefore only consensus-based standards can lead to a successful certification programme.

Global standards make sense in the marketplace. Transnational corporations can benefit from certification (Conroy, 2002) but they want to work to one standard that makes sense at corporate level regardless of operational location (Kahlenborn and Dominé, 2001). International trade rules favour international standards as these are believed to create an equal playing field that benefits competition (Bendell and Font, 2004). Markets want to be communicated one single meaningful message, and both small ecotourism firms, and the many current certification programmes trying to represent them, are fighting for a voice with their small budgets.

However, the politics of engaging different partners that are doing good work on the ground is leading to compromises that are different from rational market-based solutions. This is, the more politically palatable proposal of not having one international standard but many local standards and a process of mutual recognition, based on the common ground that has been found so far. Any international brand would be the result of an accreditation process to confirm compliance of transparency in the way certification is conducted, but each label would keep their identity.

The author thinks that the need for local differences in standards will need to be well communicated to stakeholders that would instinctively prefer one standard. For example, when the Federation of Tour Operators has asked to compare their preferred suppliers code of practice against the VISIT standard, complex explanations about what VISIT is and the fact that there are as many standards as certification programmes had to be given, which slowed down the process of mutual recognition. On the other hand, within the Network of the Americas, members have successfully developed a baseline standard and they are now marketing jointly based on the criteria they have in common. Comparisons of this baseline standard have been made with the sustainability criteria of associations like ANVR and with individual tour operator's requirements (like TUI Nederland) to help companies reach a better understanding on how to use certification programs in the Americas as a business-to-business tool.

It is easier to send one message with only one standard. A challenge from the author's point of view is that even if only one logo exists, the products that will be under this umbrella will not be sufficiently homogeneous in quality and type of product. The small number of certified companies, and the fact that the basic-quality attributes are very different (a five star hotel and a guest house can have the same environmental label) makes the author think that choosing providers based on an ecolabel is not likely, but clearly this opinion could be disputed.

Government support

Certification programmes rely generally on government support. Font and Bendell (2002) analysed the data collected for the World Tourism Organization (2002) to find that 20 of the 59 standard certification schemes at the time were led by government agencies, and a further 18 had government involvement either through direct financial support, marketing support, expert know-how in standard setting, verification procedures, or surveillance of procedures being followed by the certification body. Government agencies involved generally include environment ministries or equivalent, tourist boards, and in fewer cases standards institutes. Government financial support is crucial to half the schemes from which data are available. Grants or loans are available through a variety of schemes for consultants and assessment process.

There are other costs that currently the applicant does not pay for and are generally subsidised by governments, donors, and NGOs, and it is expected that this will continue in the future (WTO, 2003). Examples are standard setting, consultation and maintenance, verifier training, marketing, administrative costs, and quality assurance of the certification programme. These costs make certification not equitable for those governments that do not have the funds to set up their own national certification programmes or to operate low-interest loans for efficiency improvements. In a survey conducted for the World Tourism Organization in 2001, 26 national tourist boards responded with many having an interest in running certification programmes, but reporting at the time that this was not their priority (Maccarrone-Eaglen and Font, 2002), while in other countries circumstances do not allow (there are examples from Fiji, Kenya, South Africa, Dominican Republic, Venezuela where early attempts of setting up a certification programme have failed).

Font and Bendell (2002) also found that 38 out of the 59 schemes had government involvement in highlighting and advising on best practice. Marketing is a key benefit promoted to applicants of most schemes, and government support can be the single most important incentive to apply. There is no evidence of changes in the legal regime from the data available, and it seems more probable that the opposite occurs; governments introduce voluntary measures to incentive industry to adopt higher standards as a method to test the feasibility of further legislation, or to encourage the adoption of recent legislation, as was the case of the Blue Flag in Europe, instrumental in the implementation of Bathing Water Quality legislation.

In this sense, certification would be more appealing to governments if it was integrated with other instruments for sustainability, several of which were recently outlined if not compared (UNEP and WTO, 2005). Its origin stems from the formalisation of industry awards and showcasing best practice, and in this sense is more representative of industry practice than from externally set agendas. Yet generally certification is only integrated with other instruments for sustainability only in as far as they are generally linked to voluntary initiatives and incentives to encourage a more sustainable approach to management. Certification does currently provide a mechanism to operationalise international treaties and agreements. The fact that half of the ecolabels receive government support suggests it is feasible to further integrate them with government sustainability targets and to be used as methods to implement international agreements, as recommended by the WTO (2003), notwithstanding the challenge of funding. There are limited data available on the link between national sustainable tourism policies and certification programmes to comment on progress on this matter.

Accreditation

Many of the challenges faced by certification programmes have been explained because they are small, often regional or national programmes, that do not have sufficient visibility. As such, most of the current discussions are about setting up regional networks, peer recognition and quality assurance, and marketing. The accreditation function of a stewardship council has a very specific purpose: ensure transparency and due diligence, aimed at helping solve the problem of fragmentation, lack of credibility, and support marketing. The challenge is whether these functions from accreditation can turn around the inability of certification programmes individually to provide the benefits that applicants expect. The report from the World Bank (2005, p. 5) suggests that 'if certification is to continue and be successful ... there is a need for one global body to set and monitor the adoption of industry wide criteria'. This does not mean that accreditation is the solution, or that accreditation will be the answer to the many problems faced by certification programmes. 'One brand would help certification to be internationally recognised and also comply with generally accepted international criteria, and thus have a stronger chance of brand recognition in the industry. However, no single approach has so far been put forward successfully due to the varying degrees of infrastructure in countries and the lack of sufficient markets to attract certifiable product' (World Bank, 2005, p. 31).

The feasibility proposal for a Sustainable Tourism Stewardship Council (STSC) suggested there are a variety of governance structures widely accepted and potentially transferable to new accreditation bodies; however financial benchmarking has shown great weaknesses in the sector, over-relying on seed funding from donors and the general inability of the sector to be self-financing, which cast a shadow over the long-term survival of accreditation in its present form (Rainforest Alliance, 2003). The feasibility proposal explains that few, if any, environmental or social accreditation agencies were in 2002 financially sustainable through accreditation fees alone. These agencies are seeking alternate models such as segmenting accreditation functions from standard setting, education, and marketing, as well as new ways to capture revenues. These agencies are finding that accreditation fees are not sufficient to cover expenses associated with providing the comprehensive services that an accreditation body must provide. Even in the long run, accreditation agencies may need to rely on significant outside commitments from governmental agencies and private foundations. In those proposals, the annual cost of accreditation was estimated at around $US900,000 but most of it would have to come from subsidies (Rainforest Alliance, 2003; Skinner *et al.*, 2004). There is wide consensus that only a streamlined, cost-effective STSC can be supported, and the business plan should explain what this can mean in practice. Tourism certification, and accreditation in other industries, is however improving fast. This information is well documented in the STSC feasibility study and it will be used in the next phase of this initiative. The networks created have been successful in strengthening national programmes, the newly created programmes are showing they have learned from the weaknesses of past programmes and operate more efficiently from the outset, and there are transferable lessons from accreditation that should be fed into the STSC business plan.

Conclusions

Sustainable tourism and ecotourism certification programmes are voluntary instruments to improve the environmental, social, and economic performance of tourism companies; they offer trade and marketing advantages to certified firms, provide credible information to suppliers and consumers, and encourage more sustainable consumption. Over 60 schemes have been operating mainly in Western Europe since the 1990s, with more developing in the Americas, Eastern Europe, Asia, Africa, and Oceania (the figures depend on actual definitions of what is a certification programme). These programmes have many good examples of how their actions have contributed to improvements in the field, in a variety of geographical contexts and for many types of tourism firms. However for these programmes to expand, they will need to address amongst others the issues of equity, effectiveness, and efficiency. Further data are needed to conduct a cost-benefit analysis of certification in comparison to other instruments and fully appreciate the potential of certification. Areas that need further development in order to make sustainable tourism certification more robust and effective include establishing performance indicators to measure the benefits of certification, developing market demand, and an adequate supply of certified products to enable the demand to develop; harmonising standards among different programmes; assuring compliance with normalisation procedures; and reinforcing credibility and consumer recognition through standardised baseline criteria and accreditation.

Although there is scattered evidence of the effectiveness of some programmes, as well as the weaknesses of others, there is no systematic set of data that can demonstrate just how effective and cost-effective certification is for improving environmental, social, and economic performance. Many certification programmes do not publish articles or produce documents on how their actions contribute to their aims; hence there are little quantifiable or independent and scientifically reliable data available on their ability to promote sustainable change. Anecdotal reports from many programmes indicate that most businesses, after the first few already sustainable pioneers, show substantial improvement in their performance benchmarks as a direct result of the certification process. However, most programmes cannot demonstrate what part of the sustainable behaviour of the certified firms can be attributed to the process of being a certified firm, as opposed to sustainability actions that these companies were already taking before considering certification.

Experience from many other industries has shown that, in its early years, certification is not led by consumer demand, but rather by other forces. This applies to the present stage of sustainable tourism and ecotourism certification, with a few marked exceptions. At present consumer recognition is very low, and industry intermediaries are just beginning to consider certification as a tool for due-diligence and preliminary selection of suppliers. This is mainly for large tour operators speaking mainly to accommodation suppliers, and to a lesser extent areas where sustainability overlaps with health and safety, such as wildlife tourism. Without an effective strategy for increasing demand from businesses that wish to be certified, there will not be enough certified products to educate the consumer or enable tour operators to fill their catalogues with sustainable products. At present it would be misleading to promote certification as a way of directly increasing occupancy and sales, other marketing strategies should be used to encourage businesses to be certified and suppliers to use those businesses.

There are many instruments that can be used to promote more sustainable performance and that can contribute to ecotourism, but not necessarily providing marketing advantages. However, a closer inspection of certification shows that at present these trade and marketing advantages are not there. Direct consumer marketing is expensive and ineffective. Marketing to communication and distribution channels, and below the line marketing in general, has not been sufficiently exploited, but has proven successful in several instances when tour operators have collaborated. Excess of logos, no consumer recognition, and no collaboration from tour operators were the main bottlenecks perceived. The need for differentiation, repositioning sustainability as more than quality, and designing simpler and well-communicated messages was stressed. In reflecting on these many challenges in this chapter, the author has aimed to provide an element of realism to the often overly enthusiastic claims of what certification can achieve. An element of differentiation for ecotourism providers in the marketplace is desirable and necessary, and promoting market-based systems to encourage more honest ecotourism claims and more responsible performance is preferable to alternative policy tools such as subsidies and legislation.

References

Bass, S. Font, X. *et al.* (2001). Standards and certification: a leap forward or a step back for sustainable development? *The future Is Now: Equity for a Small Planet*, Vol. 2. IIED, International Institute for Environment and Development, London, pp. 21–31.

Bendell, J. and Font, X. (2004). Which tourism rules? Green standards and GATS. *Annals of Tourism Research* 31(1): 139–156.

Bien, A. (2005). *Marketing Strategy for Sustainable & Ecotourism Certification Ecocurrents First Quarter 2005*. The International Ecotourism Society, Washington, DC.

Black, R. and Crabtree, A. (eds) (2006). *Quality Control and Certification in Ecotourism*. CABI, Wallingford, Oxon.

Buckley, R. (2002). Tourism ecolabels. *Annals of Tourism Research* 29(1): 183–208.

Conroy, M. (2002). Certification systems for sustainable tourism and ecotourism: can they transform social and environmental practices? In Honey, M. (ed.), *Ecotourism & Certification: Setting Standards in Practice*. Island Press, Washington, DC, pp. 103–132.

Fairweather, J., Maslin, C., *et al.* (2005). Environmental values and response to ecolabels among international visitors to New Zealand. *Journal of Sustainable Tourism* 13(1): 82–98.

Font, X. (2001). Regulating the green message: the players in eco-labelling. In Font, X. and Buckley, R. (eds), *Tourism Ecolabelling: Certification and Promotion of Sustainable Management*. CABI, Wallingford, Oxon, pp. 1–18.

Font, X. (2002). Environmental certification in tourism and hospitality: progress, process and prospects. *Tourism Management* 23(3): 197–205.

Font, X. (2005). Sustainable tourism standards in the global economy. In Theobald, W. (ed.), *Global Tourism*. Butterworth-Heinemann, Oxford, pp. 213–229.

Font, X. and Bendell, J. (2002). Standards for sustainable tourism for the purpose of multilateral trade negotiations. World Tourism Organization, Madrid.

Font, X. and Buckley, R. (eds) (2001). *Tourism Ecolabelling: Certification and Promotion of Sustainable Management*. CABI, Wallingford, Oxon.

Font, X. and Carey, B. (2005). Marketing sustainable tourism products. Florence, Regione Toscana and United Nations Environment Programme.

Font, X. and Tribe, J. (2001). Promoting green tourism: the future of environmental awards. *International Journal of Tourism Research* 3(1): 9–22.

Gordon, G. (ed.) (2001). *Tourism: Putting Ethics into Practice*. Tearfund, London.

Honey, M. (ed.) (2002). *Ecotourism & Certification: Setting Standards in Practice*. Island Press, Washington, DC.

Honey, M. and Rome, A. (2001). *Protecting Paradise: Certification Programs for Sustainable Tourism and Ecotourism*. Institute for Policy Studies, Washington, DC.

Kahlenborn, W. and Dominé, A. (2001). The future belongs to international ecolabelling schemes. In Font, X. and Buckley, R. (eds), *Tourism Ecolabelling: Certification and Promotion of Sustainable Management*. CABI, Wallingford, pp. 247–258.

Maccarrone-Eaglen, A. and Font, X. (2002). *Sustainable Tourism Stewardship Council Feasibility*. Report for the World Tourism Organization on Consultation of Member States. Leeds Metropolitan University, Leeds.

Medina, L.K. (2005). Ecotourism and certification: confronting the principles and pragmatics of socially responsible tourism. *Journal of Sustainable Tourism* 13(3): 281–295.

OECD (2003). Voluntary approaches for environmental policy: effectiveness, efficiency, and usage in policy mixes. OECD, Paris.

Rainforest Alliance (2002). Sustainable Tourism Stewardship Council homepage, http://www.rainforest-alliance.org/programs/sv/stsc.html.

Rainforest Alliance (2003). *Sustainable Tourism Stewardship Council: Raising the Standards and Benefits of Sustainable Tourism and Ecotourism Certification*. Rainforest Alliance, New York.

Rivera, J. (2002). Assessing a voluntary environmental initiative in the developing world: The Costa Rican Certification for Sustainable Tourism. *Policy Sciences* 35(4): 333–360.

Rivera, J. and de Leon, P. (2005). Chief Executive Officers and voluntary environmental performance: Costa Rica's Certification for Sustainable Tourism. *Policy Sciences* 38(2–3): 107–127.

Skinner, E., Font, X., *et al.* (2004). Does stewardship travel well? Benchmarking accreditation and certification. *Corporate Social Responsibility and Environmental Management* 11(3): 121–132.

TIES (2004). *What Businesses Seek from Certification and the Range of Incentives that Governments, NGOs, Trade Associations, and Others Could Offer.* The International Ecotourism Society, Washington, DC.

TIES (2005). *Demand for Certification According to Consumer Demand Experts and Consumer Advocacy Organizations.* The International Ecotourism Society, Washington, DC.

Toth, R. (2002). Exploring the concepts underlying certification. In Honey, M. (ed.), *Ecotourism & Certification: Setting Standards in Practice.* Island Press, Washington, DC, pp. 73–102.

UNEP (2005). *The Trade and Environmental Effects of Ecolabels: Assessment and Response.* United Nations Environment Programme, Paris, p. 44.

UNEP (2006). *Tourism Certification as a Sustainability Tool: Assessment and Prospects.* United Nations Environment Programme, Paris, p. 71.

UNEP and WTO (2005). *Making Tourism More Sustainable: A Guide for Policy Makers.* United Nations Environment Programme, Paris, p. 209.

World Bank (2005). *CSR in the Tourism Industry? The Status of and Potential for Certification, Codes of Conduct and Guidelines.* World Bank, Washington, DC. http://www.ifc.org/ifcext/economics.nsf/Content/CSR-Research.

WTO (2002). *Voluntary Initiatives for Sustainable Tourism.* World Tourism Organization, Madrid.

WTO (2003). *Recommendations to Governments for Supporting and/or Establishing National Certification Systems for Sustainable Tourism.* World Tourism Organization, Madrid, p. 11.

Negotiating the obstacles: owner/operator perspectives on 'nature' tourism in New Zealand

Anna Carr

Introduction

This chapter discusses the business characteristics of, and relevant issues encountered by, owner/operators providing nature tourism and ecotourism in New Zealand. The first stage of the research involved interviews with individual tourism owner/operators at three established or emerging nature tourism destinations – the Otago Peninsula, Banks Peninsula (Canterbury) and Northland. The interviews informed the design of a nationwide survey of nature tourism owner/operators who hosted visitors' experiences of protected species and/or habitats. For the preparation of this chapter, business and owner/operator characteristics were determined from the quantitative survey. Operators' perspectives regarding both the obstacles and the opportunities encountered during daily operations were determined through both the in-depth interviews and the survey responses to identify, through the participating sample, key issues concerning the providers of ecotourism and nature-based tourism experiences in New Zealand. Furthermore, the chapter will examine the commitment to conservation and provision of interpretation-based experiences.

The nature tourism sector

New Zealand's commercial tourism industry is predominantly characterised by micro and small/medium tourism enterprises (SMTEs), many managed by owner/operators and their immediate families (Warren and Taylor, 1994, 2001; Tourism New Zealand, 2003; Ministry of Economic Development, 2004a, b). International visitors are motivated to visit by scenic landscapes, natural attractions, access to recreational activities and the 'clean, green' image emphasised by Tourism New Zealand's successful 100% PURE campaign (Higham *et al.*, 2001; Van Aalst and Daly, 2002). According to the Ministry of Tourism *'the natural environment is fundamental to the New Zealand brand. ...'* (2003). The government's commitment to environmental sustainability has resulted in initiatives such as the Green Globe 21 certification scheme for tourism operations and more generic schemes for wider industry such as the Zero Waste Initiative. Efforts are being made by the Ministry of Tourism and the Tourism Industry Association of New Zealand (TIANZ) to collaborate with the Department of Conservation (DoC) in such areas as visitor research; clarification of compliance with DoC regulations for operations and the improvement of general visitor experiences (Tourism Strategy Group, 2001; Ministry of Tourism, 2003).

Higham *et al.* (2001) used defining criteria based on accepted ecotourism definitions (e.g. provision of interpretation and conservation advocacy) to identify a total of 247 ecotourism operations within a sector of 479 New Zealand nature tourism operations. Opportunities for visitors to experience environmentally beneficial activities extend from commercial nature tourism attractions to non-commercial schemes such as DoC volunteer programmes and WWOOFING (Willing Workers on Organic Farms). The nature-based tourism sector is regarded as diverse and broad in scope, including consumptive and non-consumptive activities, for example small scale bird watching, wilderness adventure experiences (e.g. mountaineering, rafting), wildlife viewing, hunting or large-scale mass tourism ventures receiving more than 100,000 visitors per annum (Higham *et al.*, 2001; Warren and Taylor, 2001; Van Aalst and Daly, 2002).

In the past three decades the diversity of nature tourism businesses offering activities related to wildlife has increased especially bird watching; viewing of and interactions with marine mammals (seals, dolphins and whales); and single species focussed activities, for example the Yellow-eyed Penguin colonies or the Royal Albatross colony located on the Otago Peninsula (Juric *et al.*, 1996; Higham *et al.*, 2001; Van Aalst and Daly, 2002). The increase in interactions with endangered species is not without its critics, with concerns being expressed that the natural behaviour of wildlife populations may be negatively impacted upon by the additional human attention resulting from tourism. This concern is countered by observations that tourism operators perform useful functions, for example assisting with collecting research data or monitoring inappropriate behaviour by people in sensitive habitats (e.g. Higham *et al.*, 2003a, c; Department of Conservation, 2005).

Another distinguishing feature of the New Zealand nature tourism industry is that numerous sites are managed by trusts or government agencies, primarily DoC. The role and experiences of such organisations as participants in the New Zealand tourism industry has been neglected in previous research with the exception of the 1999–2001 ecotourism study by Higham *et al.* (2001) which included Mount Bruce National Wildlife Centre (DoC), the Miranda Shorebird Centre (Miranda Shorebird Trust) and Taiaroa Royal Albatross Centre (Otago Peninsula Trust) in the selection of case study operations. In the international setting, the research of non-commercial tourism ventures is similarly limited but there are exceptions, for instance Campbell and Salus (2003) study of conservation land trusts in Wisconsin.

According to past studies, business performance in New Zealand depends on a combination of internal factors such as lifestyle and personal values or external business factors such as compliance with government regulations and legislation (Ateljevic and Doorne, 2000b; Hall and Rusher, 2004). New Zealand's tourism sector is dominated by family owned businesses where (a) lifestyle motivations amongst owners could contribute to financial underperformance or mismanagement, (b) there is limited business expertise and (c) limited resources (Deloitte Touche Tohmatsu, 1995; TIANZ, 2001; Silva and McDill, 2004).

In terms of financial investment, it has been suggested that larger (10+ employees) operations, many of which are long-established nature tourism businesses, are more likely to succeed in terms of economic business performance (e.g. Deloitte Touche Tohmatsu, 1995; Page *et al.*, 1999; TIANZ, 2001). Yet the personal characteristics and behaviours of SMTE tourism operators are also considered to affect the performance, including environmental performance, of businesses (Thomlinson and Donald, 1996; Sirakaya, 1997; McKercher and Robbins, 1998; Page and Lawton, 1999; Culkin and Smith, 2000; Ateljevic and Doorne, 2000a; Lerner and Haber, 2001; Hall and Rusher, 2004; Silva and McDill, 2004; Ministry of Economic Development, 2004a, b;). There are continual reports indicating the need for quality interpretation delivery and commitment to conservation projects at ecotourism businesses in New Zealand and overseas; researchers noting operators' personal values or interests in wildlife or conservation may affect such participation (Warren and Taylor, 2001; Higham and Carr, 2002, 2003a, b; Curtin and Wilkes, 2005; Department of Conservation, 2005). Owner/operator nature tourism operations in New Zealand have been noted to embrace environmental initiatives or interpretation training and planning, often undertaken by employing specialists, as they realise the potential for quality interpretation and tour guiding to enhance their business performance (Higham *et al.*, 2001; Curtin and Wilkes, 2005; Interpretation New Zealand, 2005). Indeed the DoC has acknowledged the contribution to conservation from concessionaires operating in protected areas in providing an advocacy service for the Department and assisting with the day to day management of visitors' behaviour through guided experiences, environmental education or interpretation of various habitats (DoC, 2005).

Despite the nature tourism industry producing notable ecotourism ventures attracting an international visitor market there has been limited examination of the characteristics of, and issues facing, nature or ecotourism operations and managers or owner/ operators. The research findings reported in the following pages seek to profile New Zealand's nature/ecotourism owner/operators in an attempt to understand owner/operator characteristics and the diverse issues that affect the economic and environmental performance of their businesses.

Methodology

The research was undertaken in four distinct stages. Firstly, an in-depth literature review was then followed by the collation of a database of nature tourism operators developed from website and/or brochure analysis. Thirdly, site visits and semi-structured interviews were conducted at selected case study areas. Finally, the interviews were utilised to design a nationwide postal survey.

During the qualitative phase of the research the researcher was assisted by her past participation in a nationwide ecotourism study and her 8 years as a tourism operator attending industry workshops, conferences and participating in joint marketing. Thus the researcher had a personal knowledge of the operational aspects of such businesses within the New Zealand context, including compliance, safety, legislative and taxation requirements. This was a vital element in the research process as it contributed to gaining the trust and cooperation of other operators.

Two established South Island destinations, Otago (10 interviews) and Banks Peninsula (4 interviews), and one emerging destination, the Hokianga/Kaitaia districts of Northland (11 interviews), were selected as case study areas. All three areas have experienced Maori and European settlement and tourism is significant to the local economies. These areas are frequented by domestic (including second home owners) and international visitors seeking experiences related to local culture, recreation and wildlife. Whilst the Otago and Banks Peninsula have an array of small- to large-scale nature and ecotourism ventures, the Hokianga/Kaitaia operations are small scale in terms of annual visitor numbers, with larger scale nature-based experiences are available in the Bay of Islands area, the major visitor hub in Northland. The Hokianga/Kaitaia regions of Northland provide an interesting contrast to the other sites because of access issues. The Hokianga lacks a regional airport while services into nearby Kaitaia are limited to small commuter planes. The Hokianga, with its wealth of indigenous cultural history, *kauri* forests and scenic coastline, depends on harbour ferry crossings, gravel and sealed roads to link the Northern and Southern shores of the Hokianga harbour.

The involvement of trusts in the management of wildlife species/habitat at the Otago Peninsula and Banks Peninsula sites are another feature lacking in the Kaitaia/Hokianga area.

The Otago Peninsula Trust manages the commercial visitor centre and tours of the Royal Albatross Colony, staff assisting DoC with daily management of the albatross breeding area. This assistance includes such tasks as monitoring the general wellbeing of birds in the colony, predator control and informing visitors of various DoC environmental initiatives during the tours of the colony. Another Otago Peninsula operation, Elm Wildlife Tours, recently formed the New Zealand Sea Lion Trust to encourage visitor awareness, protection and research of this rare marine mammal. At the Otago and Banks Peninsulas, DoC and another trust, the Yellow-eyed Penguin Trust (YEPT), are active in habitat restoration, track and hide maintenance at penguin viewing areas that can be visited by independent travellers and small guided groups. On the Banks Peninsula the 1,050 hectare Hinewai Reserve, established by the Maurice White Trust, occupies the Otanerito Valley and upper bluffs of Stony Bay Peak overlooking Akaroa. Hinewai features a 12 kilometre track network linking the outer peninsula to the inner harbour via Purple Peak Saddle; the track system primarily facilitating reserve management and secondly, contributing to the Banks Peninsula Track (walked by approximately 2,700 people per year).

The site visits and interviews were conducted between August 2004 and March 2005 to provide the researcher with an understanding of the daily realities facing operators, whilst examining the conservation and visitor education activities at the operations. The interviews were conducted at the work sites at a time selected by the participants to allow interviewees to describe their experiences in detail. The questions were open-ended and developed to allow operators to describe the historical development of their operations and their personal philosophies about conservation or the natural environment. Other questions focused on business characteristics (e.g. activity types; areas visited; numbers of visitors/employees); reasons for establishing the business; environmental issues; choice of interpretation themes and identification of obstacles or opportunities that affected businesses performance. All interviews (n = 14) were tape recorded, transcribed and analysed using a thematic guideline based on the question topics, the findings informing subsequent survey design. During site visits, detailed written records and participant observations provided valuable insights into the operations. The majority of interview participants (n = 17) were owner/operators of family owned businesses and three interviews involved spouses. Seven interview participants were the employees or CEOs of trusts and a further five participants were employees of local or central government agencies directly involved with nature tourism management including DoC and Te Puni Kokiri (Ministry of Maori Development).

The site visits and interviews informed the key component of the research – a nationwide postal survey consisting of 20 open-ended and Likert scale questions and including the collection of motivational and demographic data. The survey was distributed nationwide between May and July 2005 to SMTEs operated by nature tourism owner/operators who had both financial and personal involvement in the hosting of visitors' experiences of protected species and/or habitats. Commercial operations, where the owner/operator was not involved with the day to day management and operations of the business, were excluded from the survey. The operations were compiled in a database developed after an intensive search of relevant Internet websites, including the New Zealand Birding Network, Maori Tourism Council of New Zealand and Tourism New Zealand's 100% PURE sites. Written contact with the nationwide network of I-Sites (formerly VIN, the Visitor Information centres) yielded further operations. The database resulted in the identification of 316 nature-based owner/operator tourism businesses throughout New Zealand. The businesses were first sent a letter or email requesting their participation in the survey; 187 owner/operators responded that they would be willingly to complete a postal questionnaire. The questionnaires were mailed with a post-paid return address envelope and responses requested within 14 days. The final survey yielded 115 valid responses (61.5% response rate), 36% of the SMTEs identified in the owner/operator database.

Nature tourism owner/operator profile

The majority of nature tourism owner/operators (61%) reported owning small-scale businesses providing personalised experiences in the form of guided adventure activities, nature walks, wildlife viewing and accommodation provision within the respondents' homes (Table 20.1).

Forty per cent of the respondents were sole owner/operators with only 24 businesses employing one other full-time staff member, usually a spouse. Twenty-one per cent employed other staff with eight per cent employing more than 10 people. Five businesses, all of which had been in existence for more than 15 years, employed between 25 and 32 additional full-time staff. Forty-one per cent reported having operated for more than 10 years and nine per cent of respondents had operated for more than 20 years. One business had been in operation for 33 years.

Table 20.1   Profile of nature tourism respondents (n = 115*)

Sector	%
Adventure guiding	36.2
Wildlife viewing	33.6
Guided nature walks	30.0
Accommodation	9.7
Gender	
Male	68.0
Female	32.0
Age	
20–34 years	10.5
35–44	19.0
45–54	39.0
55–64	23.5
65 years+	5.0
No response	3.0
Educational qualifications*	
Secondary	32.5
Polytechnic	15.0
Trade qualification	15.0
Tertiary degree	32.5
Postgraduate degree	9.0

*Several respondents reported more than one qualification so total exceeds 100%

Forty-nine per cent of respondents had been operating for less than 8 years whilst 23 per cent had operated for fewer than 5 years. On average, the businesses hosted fewer than 1,000 visitors per annum (47.8% of responses), whilst 13% of respondents hosted more than 10,000 visitors per annum. These larger-scale operations had been established for between 15 and 33 years, apart from two operations that had commenced business 4 and 8 years previously. Two of these well-established operations hosted more than 50,000+ visitors per annum. Fifty per cent were registered companies; thirty-nine per cent were family ventures; whilst six per cent were registered as 'not for profit' organisations and four per cent were legal partnerships.

When asked to identify their motivations or goals for entering business (using a list in Getz and Carlsen, 2000), the participants reported similar rankings to previous studies of small business operators from other tourism sectors (e.g. Getz and Carlsen,

2000; Ateljevic and Doorne, 2000a; Hall and Rusher, 2004). This suggests the nature tourism owner/operators share common desires, such as being in control of one's own lifestyle through self-employment, facilitated by the ease of entering the New Zealand tourism industry. Owner/operators' reasons for establishing their businesses tended to be weighted towards intrinsic, personal factors with self-control and lifestyle factors being of more importance than financial independence. There were no significant differences between operators based on age, gender, business scale, date of establishment or those marketing themselves as 'ecotourism' operators. Nor were differences found between Maori and non-Maori operators. Respondents with seasonal businesses were, however, more likely to have entered business to support leisure interests, perhaps suggesting a strong link with lifestyle motivations ($\chi^2 = 14.559$, df $= 7$, p $= 0.042$). The main business goals, ranked in order of importance, were 'To be one's own boss' followed by 'to enjoy a good lifestyle', 'to be in control of one's own future' and 'to live in the right environment' (Table 20.2). Other important goals were 'to be financially independent' and 'to contribute positively to nature' whilst the least important was 'to gain prestige from operating a business'. When the organisational aspects of the businesses were examined it

Table 20.2 Owner/operators' business goals

Goals	Important/very important (%)	Mean* (average)	Standard deviation
To be my own boss	93	5.82	1.63
To enjoy a good lifestyle	81	5.77	1.64
To be in control of own future	80	5.73	1.57
To live in the right environment	82	5.44	1.94
To be financially independent	74	5.40	1.69
To contribute positively to nature	70	5.37	1.55
To have a challenge	73.5	5.35	1.59
To meet interesting people	72	5.16	1.64
To increase personal income	61.5	4.86	1.71
To support leisure interests	54	4.61	1.88
To provide a retirement income	55	4.53	1.98
Provide employment for family	36	3.71	2.23
To keep property in the family	34	3.45	2.41
To gain prestige from operating a business	18	2.75	1.81

*Scale: 1 = Not at all important; 4 = neutral; 7 = Very important

was notable that 76 participants (66%) reported having a business plan whilst 75 (65.5%) had a marketing plan, yet several respondents noted they did not always consult the plans on a regular basis. Similarly the majority of respondents were neutral towards having a formalised written business plan yet generally they were conscious of the need to reinvest in and manage profitable businesses (Table 20.3).

Table 20.3 Attitudes to aspects of business management

Statement	Totally agree/ agree (%)	Mean	Standard deviation
It is essential to continually improve facilities	63.2	3.11	2.0
My business is proactive with environmental issues	63.2	3.15	2.22
It is crucial to keep the business financially profitable	57.9	3.16	2.42
I want to present a good public/corporate image	60.2	3.17	2.33
The business is highly seasonal	57.9	3.29	2.37
There are more risks owning a business than another occupation	54.1	3.40	2.44
I want to keep the business growing	47.8	3.48	1.86
It is hard to separate work and family life in the business	53.1	3.5	2.06
Government assistance is essential for industry growth	46.0	3.54	2.03
Enjoying the job is more important than making money	52.6	3.58	2.03
The business responsibility is worth the gains in lifestyle	47.7	3.62	1.75
I come into daily contact with customers	50.9	3.69	2.50
My personal/family interests take priority over the business	38.1	3.79	1.78
I would rather keep the business small than it grow too big	45.6	3.82	2.15
One day the business will be sold for the best possible price	42.0	3.89	2.17
The business meets my performance targets	42.3	3.93	1.75
It is not necessary to have a formal business plan	41.6	4.08	2.19
Decisions are made purely on business principles	30.1	4.28	1.61

*Scale: 1 = totally agree; 4 = neutral; 7 = totally disagree

Conservation initiatives

A slim majority (56%) of respondents were involved in conservation projects with habitat conservation, recycling and composting being the most regular activities reported (Table 20.4). Relevant to this was the response to a Likert scale question exploring general business attitudes where being 'proactive with environmental issues' was the second highest scoring aspect of business management after investing in facilities (refer Table 20.3).

Composting and recycling, whilst time consuming, were generally low cost and easy to incorporate within business routines, even for remotely located operators. Habitat restoration could be undertaken in collaboration with other organisations or, as reported by 17 respondents, through considerable investment of personal finances and time. Four operators were research scientists in previous careers and used their academic knowledge frequently by becoming involved with conservation projects. Operators reported a variety of projects such as assisting with the transportation of DoC and other research scientists, the gathering of research data and the translocation and release of endangered bird species. One charter boat operator had 'completed scoping projects for a Fiji marine reserve and wetland restoration'. Twenty-one per cent of respondents reported that making contributions to the conservation of New Zealand flora and fauna was most feasible when involved with existing initiatives managed by DoC or trusts. Several operators made sizable

Table 20.4 Regular participation in conservation activities*

Activity	%
Habitat conservation	77.5
Recycling/composting	73.0
Writing submissions/advocates for protected areas	62.0
Predator management	62.0
Financial contributions	62.0
Volunteer participation	61.0
Research/monitoring species/habitat	57.5
Revegetation projects	54.0
Eco-friendly cleaning products; chemicals	44.0
Attended environmental seminars/workshops	37.0
Energy (solar; wind; biodiesel; hybrid)	30.0

*Owner/operators regularly reported multiple activities, total exceeds 115

contributions of sponsorship money or land to external groups; for instance, 'we give regular financial support for the Kaikoura Dusky Dolphin project and Southern Seabird Solutions'. Eight operators who were interviewed specifically felt they had a moral obligation to 'set an example' in terms of business environmental performance. Five interview participants considered the setting of environmental benchmarks by their businesses as another important contribution.

Whilst visitor education and conservation projects were commercially driven (attracting visitors to operations) 11 respondents specifically alluded to being motivated by non-financial rewards such as enhancement of the local community's environmental resources and regular hosting of school (or other educational) groups at no charge. Writing submissions for or against proposals affecting the environment were another activity reported by eight participants, for example '… we opposed the construction of mussel farms in the bay that would be a serious threat to the environment and endanger all marine species through, for example, rope entanglement and drowning.' Several operators participated in the production of educational kits for schools and DoC. The Otago Peninsula was one area where individual operators, trusts and a government department (DoC) collaborated to improve wildlife habitat with the Taiaroa Head 'buffer zone' – an area of intensive predator control and fencing around the Royal Albatross Colony. Despite this localised initiative the same operators and other stakeholders shared a common concern that the wider area lacked an overall tourism development plan or strategy in the face of increasing visitor numbers to the area.

Commitment to visitor interpretation

Fifty-eight per cent of respondents reported that they were committed to offering some form of interpretation/visitor educational programmes, 50% reporting that interpretation was a priority for the business. By emphasising the need for conservation, or interpreting the protected habitats visited, businesses operators mentioned they considered themselves to be strong advocates for DoC. Whilst there appears to be a significant commitment to interpretation, it was impossible to gain a complete indication of the quality of interpretation through the survey. Several respondents admitted a 'loose', 'informal' or 'unplanned' approach to interpretation and that visitor education was a skill 'learnt on the job' developed without external advice. 'Looking and learning' and gathering ideas for improving businesses from contact with other attractions was reported by 14% of respondents. With interview participants the narrative or communication of significant conservation themes often reflected individuals' passions for particular species. At the same time such localisation of conservation messages through interpretation was viewed by several interview participants as a way of providing visitors with a unique local experience. This 'localisation' of experience is strategic in a business sense as personalised interpretation becomes a unique selling point, but one which is very dependent on staff having the skills to develop and present such interpretation.

Issues affecting nature tourism operations

Apart from the increasing cost of fuel/energy, which was the primary concern for respondents (74%), the main issues were very specific to the New Zealand context (Table 20.5). International concerns related to climate change, global warming, rising aviation fuels and the competitive global market were of less importance than issues affecting the day to day running of the businesses. Prices for transportation and aviation fuels have continued to increase since the survey and fuel costs undoubtedly remain a pertinent consideration yet only one operator used biofuels and wind energy in an attempt to reduce such costs and improve environmental performance. The prohibitive cost of alternative energy sources or availability of eco-friendly building supplies and general products were mentioned by four interview

Table 20.5 Critical issues identified by businesses (n = 115)

Issue	%
Increased cost of fuel/energy	74.0
Government regulations/compliance	69.5
Competition from other businesses	59.0
Inflation	50.0
Impacts from environmental mismanagement	47.0
Lack of skilled employees/labour costs	43.0
Lack of customer demand	40.0
Bank interest rates	35.0
Poor cash flow	35.0
Lack of ecommerce access	35.0
Impacts of climate change	30.0

participants as hampering their attempts to improve environmental performance.

Compliance costs and the complexities of government regulations, even for trusts with multiple volunteers assisting with staffing, were a common concern for 69.5% of respondents and regarded as major obstacles to business performance. This is not an issue confined to the tourism sector. Alexander *et al.* (2004) interviewed and then analysed the recorded diaries of 25 New Zealand businesses over a 13-week period to gain an understanding of issues surrounding compliance. The businesses included tourism operations and the compliance issues studies apply to the majority of small and medium sized enterprises (SMEs) in New Zealand (e.g. taxation; employer relations, health and safety, accident compensation and Resource Management Act regulations). One of the main conclusions was that '*Simply reducing the amount of time spent on each individual compliance task will not seem like an improvement to some firms. What is needed to satisfy them is a reduction in the number of tasks, and a reduction in the external, or monetary costs of compliance*' (Alexander *et al.*, 2004, p. 27).

At the same time that government agencies support SMTE development, respondents identified other external organisations and government agencies, such as the Inland Revenue Department, as increasing office time and costs associated with compliance or regulation. Environmentally sustainable initiatives (e.g. the use of alternative fuels or sustainable energy sources) that operators were interested in participating in, often lacked coordination or similar assistance from a central or local government agency, deterring involvement from smaller businesses. The DoC (unsurprising given DoC's significant role in managing the majority of New Zealand's natural areas) was the organisation operators most often networked with (88.5%) followed by Tourism New Zealand (70%) and TIANZ (68%) (Table 20.6). The low level of regular communication with regional tourism organisations (RTOs) reported by survey respondents (8%) was of concern considering the need for marketing initiatives in the national and international marketplace. Nevertheless, interview participants reported regularly accessing their local tourism promotion organisations. Whilst specific tourism organisations had significant impacts on the businesses' marketing performance, for instance TIANZ and TNZ providing vital marketing information and opportunities to market aboard, such external organisations also contributed to concerns (such as the costs of membership).

Recent national initiatives backed by government funded departments and agencies to introduce certification programmes such as Qualmark and Green Globe 21 were met with mixed enthusiasm by most of the interview participants who

Table 20.6 Memberships/networks with external organisations (n = 113)

Name of organisation	%
Department of Conservation	88.5
Tourism New Zealand	70.0
Tourism Industry Association New Zealand	68.0
Ministry of Tourism	54.0
Qualmark	51.0
BIZinfo	51.0
Maritime Safety Authority	47.0
Green Globe 21	34.0
Forest and Bird	32.0
Local Chamber of Commerce/Business Association	26.5
Aviation Travel Tourism Training Organisations (ATTTO)	11.0
Outdoors New Zealand	9.0
Sea Kayaking Operators' Association (SKOANZ)	8.0
Local RTO	8.0

*Note: Respondents could indicate multiple networks/memberships

regarded such processes as requiring a softer form of compliance. Such schemes were mentioned by survey and interview participants as being (a) time consuming, (b) expensive, (c) not necessarily delivering on the 'promise' and (d) out of reach of small owner/operator businesses, particularly if they are seasonal. Font's conclusion, *'there are too many ecolabels, with different meanings, criteria, geographical scope, confusing messages, limited expertise and expensive systems, only partly meeting the requirements of the process of compliance assessment'* (2002, p. 203), may well apply within the New Zealand context. Such schemes, whilst not prolific, have been viewed by tourism agencies as fulfilling criteria to be considered during the granting of concessions to undertake activities in areas under DoC's management. A common fear expressed in this study was that operators felt pressure from government agencies or tourism organisations to participate in the schemes in order to be included in future marketing or other operationally advantageous initiatives managed by the latter groups.

Operators reporting frustrations at having to interact with local and central government departments that were under-resourced or inadequately staffed. For instance one operator suggested a government agency 'needs to be more engaging and responsive to small-scale biodiversity tourism on their estate'. Other respondents (26%) were concerned about the lack of independent monitoring of visitor behaviour (both commercial and non-commercial) around wildlife or significant habitats.

Common themes emerging from the interviews included the difficulties of operating in New Zealand due to being geographically isolated from the main international visitor markets (United States, United Kingdom and Australia). At another level, Hokianga and Kaitaia operators were concerned by limitations on their businesses as a result of poor road access that could deter FIT travellers. Several operators, ironically, saw poor access as a bonus as it could limit visitors accessing sensitive habitats. The need for improved local or regional signage to direct visitors to operations was a common local concern at all three areas, as was the need for improved regional marketing to increase the customer base.

Social isolation at all three areas was reported as limiting owner/operators regularly accessing financial advisers (for instance bankers or accountants) or attending formal workshops organised by RTOs or TIANZ. Often operators experienced difficulties networking with local operators let alone networking on a regional or national level, possibly hampered by the fact that competition from other local or larger businesses was a concern to 59% of respondents. Surprisingly, few operators mentioned global competition of the international nature tourism market or how management of visitors' experiences could direct their future development. It appears that the visitors' experiences of the operation (the rationale for the businesses' existence to begin with), is often neglected when operators review their businesses performance. The current research indicates concern with the lack of training available for operators wishing to develop and deliver visitor interpretation. The provision of interpretation experiences that augment the nature tourism experience can be time-consuming and beyond the skill levels of many operators. Of minor importance were the stresses and social strains of working in isolation or with family members where work and personal life often merged.

Otago Peninsula, Banks Peninsula and Northland interviews all included one or two participants who were affected by Treaty of Waitangi claims that bear upon access to various natural resources or areas, a situation unique to New Zealand. The Treaty of Waitangi was New Zealand's founding constitutional document signed between Maori and the British Crown. Various *iwi* (Maori tribes) have claims to land and resources confiscated or removed from their ancestors during the 19th and 20th centuries which staff at the Treaty Office (a government agency) are processing through a formal procedure. As a result of settlement many commercial operations applying for resource consents or concessions may have a procedural obligation to consult with local Maori or *hapu* (family) groups. Whilst this was seen as having both positive and negative effects on businesses the Treaty was only mentioned as an issue by one survey respondent.

Finally, whilst the research focused on owner/operators within the New Zealand nature tourism industry it was found that the industry is also host to dedicated social 'ecopreneurs' working within trusts or non-profit organisations that enabled visitors to experience natural areas without necessarily expecting financial gain from nature tourism. The role of environmental trusts within the industry should not be ignored by other operators or government agencies with respect to trusts' dedication to habitat restoration and the provision of interpretation. Trust participants were found to utilise business strategies (i.e. they developed marketing plans) to achieve environmental goals and reported similar issues affecting their performances to that of other small businesses in the study. Several trusts examined in this research were managed by individuals who display entrepreneurial traits similar to owner/operators of nature tourism businesses. The need for a sound financial basis from which to successfully undertake daily activities has led to trust managers adapting business tactics to meet government requirements for compliance and financial purposes. Thus the initial environmental reasons behind the establishment and management of trusts develop to include administrative and operational procedures bearing similarities to those found within the work places of owner/operators of commercial businesses.

Conclusions

This research has found that nature tourism operators, through economic necessity, may offer a range of complimentary but diverse experiences in what has been termed the New Zealand 'eco-nature tourism' industry (Van Aalst and Daly, 2002, p. 3). For example, a charter boat operator whose dominant business venture was guided fishing also offered historic harbour cruises and specific wildlife watching tours to ensure year-round employment. Similarly, a back country guiding operation offered guided walks, trekking and climbing alongside shorter duration, personalised, ecotourism activities in an effort to succeed in business. Thus whilst the dominant function of the business was general nature or adventure tourism each business also engaged in traditional ecotourism activities. Participants ranged from sole individual operations to large-scale multi-employee operations; non-profit organisations to large-scale commercial ventures. The majority of respondents reported participating in conservation initiatives, reflecting findings from previous studies which found ecotourism and nature tourism operators to be more ethical or genuinely interested in contributing to wildlife conservation than operators from other tourism sectors (e.g. Fennell and Malloy, 1999; Higham *et al.*, 2001, 2002b, 2003a, c). Other research and anecdotal evidence exists of nature tourism operators with strong environmental values who deliberately shun the 'ecotourism' label, disillusioned about the term's misuse in the past resulting from a lack of commitment to environmental performance or visitor education by so-called 'ecotourism' operators (e.g. Wight, 1993; Lawrence *et al.*, 1997; Burton, 1998; McKercher, 1998). Observations during site visits and analysis of survey responses and marketing material indicated that seven interview participants and nineteen survey respondents were not associating their businesses with the term 'ecotourism', with specific mention of 'green-washing'. Countering this finding was the observation of several operators who adopt the term yet lacked any obvious commitment to conservation, visitor education or contribution to local communities beyond that which directly benefited the businesses in question – undoubtedly one of the complex characteristics of the wider industry that is difficult to control.

This chapter has revealed that many New Zealand eco-nature tourism owner/operators are challenged by numerous issues in the pursuit of social, environmental and economic sustainability. Central and local government agencies have requirements of businesses resulting from regulatory controls and administrative procedures that can be stressful for owner/operators. Issues related to economic and social concerns (e.g. family commitments, compliance costs and administration tasks) often affected the time and resources respondents felt they had to devote to improving business performance. Other issues that concerned respondents were increased fuel prices and competition from other businesses which are external to the business and thus difficult to manage. Operators' individual business goals appeared to affect involvement in conservation projects and themes chosen for visitor interpretation – any such participation often indicating the long-term commitment owner/operators have to the local environment and community.

Finally, the nature tourism industry is one where owner/operators often act independently of, or in competition with, each other. Common ground for collaboration could be established through habitat conservation or similar environmental management projects. Local councils were reported to lack resources and leadership in the strategic planning of regional tourism development and initiatives, as noted previously by Warren and Taylor (1994). This remains a significant concern at a regional level. The New Zealand nature tourism industry has the potential to develop localised or regional conservation projects where operators could voluntarily work alongside agencies such as DoC with identified projects that benefited the environmental and local economies. DoC is strategically influential on the environmental and economic success of many tourism operations but, from the perspective of participants' in this research, it is apparent that the department requires additional resources to improve management, communication and collaboration with the nature-based tourism industry, culminating in the enhancement of the New Zealand environment. Similarly, there have been sporadic attempts in the past to unite nature tourism or ecotourism operators under joint marketing networks (e.g. the New Zealand Birding Network) however a national interpretation or ecotourism association is yet to be formed. Apart from involvement with local RTOs or TIANZ, owner/operators or other individuals managing nature tourism attractions have limited access to a dedicated nature tourism association that can provide guiding or interpretation training; act as a forum to discuss issues; and contribute to the development and management of the industry at a national level. Any initiatives to form a specific nature tourism industry organisation are currently *ad hoc* and informal thus limiting the potential for action which could benefit the viability, environmental performance and market appeal of the ecotourism sector at an international level.

References

Alexander, W.R.J., Bell, J.D. and Knowles, S. (2004). *Quantifying Compliance Costs of Small Businesses in New Zealand*, University of Otago, Economics Discussion Papers No. 0406, July 2004.

Ateljevic, I. and Doorne, S. (2000a). 'Staying within the fence' lifestyle entrepreneurship. *Journal of Sustainable Tourism* 8(5): 378–392.

Ateljevic, I. and Doorne, S. (2000b). Local government and tourism development: issues and constraints of public sector entrepreneurship. *New Zealand Geographer* 56: 25–31.

Burton, R. (1998). Maintaining the quality of ecotourism: ecotour operators' responses to tourism growth. *Journal of Sustainable Tourism* 6(2): 117–143.

Campbell, M.C. and Salus D.A. (2003) Community and conservation land trusts as unlikely partners? The case of Troy Gardens, Madison, Wisconsin. *Land Use Policy* 20: 169–180.

Culkin, N. and Smith, D. (2000). An emotional business: a guide to understanding the motivations of small urines decision makers. *Qualitative Market Research* 3: 145.

Curtin, S. and Wilkes, K. (2005). British wildlife tourism operators: current issues and typologies. *Current Issues in Tourism* 8(6): 455–478.

Deloitte Touche Tohmatsu (1995). *Small Business Survey: New Zealand Tourism Industry*, Deloitte Touche Tohmatsu, (NZ) Christchurch.

Department of Conservation (2005). *Tourism Operators Contributing to Conservation*. Department of Conservation, Canterbury.

Fennell, D.A. and Malloy, D.C. (1999). Measuring the ethical nature of tourism operators. *Annals of Tourism Research* 26(4): 928–943.

Font, X. (2002). Environmental certification in tourism and hospitality: progress, process and prospects. *Tourism Management* 23: 197–205.

Getz, D. and Carlsen, J. (2000). Characteristics and goals of family owner-operated businesses in the rural tourism and hospitality sectors. *Tourism Management* 21(6): 547–560.

Hall, C. and Rusher, K. (2004). Risky lifestyles? Entrepreneurial characteristics of the New Zealand bed and breakfast sector. In Thomas, R. (ed.), *Small Firms in Tourism: International Perspectives*. Elsevier Ltd, Oxford, UK, pp. 83–98.

Higham, J.E.S., Carr, A.M. and Gale, S. (2001). *Profiling Visitors to New Zealand Ecotourism Operations*. He tauhokohoko ngä whakaaturanga a ngä manuhiri ki rawa whenua o Aotearoa. Research Paper No. 10. Department of Tourism, University of Otago.

Higham, J.E.S. and Carr, A.M. (2002). Ecotourism visitor experiences in Aotearoa/New Zealand: challenging the environmental values of visitors in pursuit of pro-environmental behaviour. *Journal of Sustainable Tourism* 10(4): 277–294.

Higham, J.E.S. and Carr, A.M. (2003a). The scope and scale of ecotourism in New Zealand: a review and consideration of current policy initiatives. In Fennell, D.A. and Dowling, R.K. (eds), *Ecotourism: Policy and Planning*. CABI Publishing, Oxon, UK, pp. 235–255.

Higham, J.E.S. and Carr, A.M. (2003b). Defining Ecotourism in New Zealand: differentiating between the defining parameters Negotiating obstacles: owner/operator perspectives on 'nature' tourism within a national/regional context. *Journal of Ecotourism* 2(1): 17–32.

Interpretation New Zealand (2005). *Newsletter*. http://www. interpretationnz.co.nz/projects.htm (accessed on 10 November 2005).

Juric, B., Cossens, J. and Barton, R. (1996). Ecotourism: an examination of the motivations of ecotourism visitors to New Zealand. *Proceedings of Towards a More Sustainable Tourism Conference Centre for Tourism*, University of Otago, Dunedin, pp. 207–222.

Lawrence, T.B., Wickens, D. and Phillips, N. (1997). Managing legitimacy in ecotourism. *Tourism Management* 18(5): 307–316.

Lerner, M. and Haber, S. (2001). Performance factors of small tourism ventures: the interface of tourism, entrepreneurship and the environment. *Journal of Business Venturing* 16: 77–100.

McKercher, B. (1998). *The Business of Nature-Based Tourism.* Hospitality Press, Elsternwick, Australia.

McKercher, B. and Robbins, B. (1998). Business development issues affecting nature-based tourism operators in Australia. *Journal of Sustainable Tourism* 6(2): 173–188.

Ministry of Economic Development (2004a). *SMEs in New Zealand: Structures and Dynamics.* Ministry of Economic Development, Wellington, New Zealand.

Ministry of Economic Development (2004b). *Small and Medium Businesses in New Zealand: Report of the Small Business Advisory Group 2004.* Ministry of Economic Development, Wellington, New Zealand.

Ministry of Tourism (2003). *Towards 2010: Implementing the New Zealand Tourism Strategy.* Ministry of Tourism, Wellington, New Zealand.

Page, S., Forer, P. and Lawton, G. (1999). Small business development and tourism: terra incognita? *Tourism Management* 20: 435–459.

Silva, G. and McDill, M.E. (2004). Barriers to ecotourism supplier success: a comparison of agency and business perspectives. *Journal of Sustainable Tourism* 12(4): 289–305.

Sirakaya, E. (1997). Attitudinal compliance with ecotourism guidelines. *Annals of Tourism Research* 24(4): 919–950.

Thomlinson, E. and Donald, G. (1996). The question of scale in ecotourism: case study of two small ecotour operators in the Mundo Maya region of Central America. *Journal of Sustainable Tourism* 4(4): 183–200.

Tourism Industry Association New Zealand (2001). *New Zealand Tourism Strategy 2010.* Tourism Industry Association New Zealand, Wellington.

Tourism New Zealand (2003). *Tourism New Zealand 3 Year Strategic Plan 2003–2006.* Tourism New Zealand, Wellington.

Tourism Strategy Group (2001). *New Zealand Tourism Strategy 2010.* Tourism Strategy Group, Wellington.

Van Aalst, I. and Daly, C. (2002). *International Visitor Satisfaction with their New Zealand Experience: The Nature Tourism Product*

Market – A Summary of Studies 1990–2001. Tourism New Zealand, Wellington.

Warren, J.A.N. and Taylor, C.N. (1994). *Developing Eco-Tourism in New Zealand.* NZ Institute for Social Research and Development, Wellington.

Warren, J.A.N. and Taylor, C.N. (2001). *Developing Nature Tourism in New Zealand.* Centre for Research, Evaluation and Social Assessment, Wellington.

Wight, P. (1993). Ecotourism: ethics or eco-sell? *Journal of Travel Research,* Winter 3–9.

Ecotourism: which school of thought should prevail?

James Higham

'Ecotourism is often advocated as being a sustainable form of tourism but inprecision in terminology clouds basic issues and there are strong economic, ecological and cultural reasons for believing that, even in its purist forms, ecotourism is likely to present substantial challenges to destination areas, particularly if it competes for scarce resources and displaces existing uses and users

(Wall, 1997, p. 483).

The concept of ecotourism, and our understanding of it, has evolved and developed significantly in a relatively short period of time. Since Hetzer (1965) began to speculate on the emergence of a form of tourism based principally on natural and cultural resources in the 1960s, ecotourism has developed into a global travel phenomenon. Initially endorsed by the United Nations and World Tourism Organization as the harbinger of sustainable tourism development, the attention of the academic community has instead clearly demonstrated that ecotourism is a unique form of tourism development that is inevitably developed in association with its own unique impacts and considerable management challenges (Wheeller, 1991).

Yet remarkably, blind adherence to the principles of ecotourism development as a universal template and panacea for community, indigenous, regional development and employment issues (among many others) persists in many quarters. Because of this many critics found the United National declaration of the International Year of Ecotourism in 2002 both premature and problematic given the groundswell of feeling that the myriad of challenges associated with ecotourism are far from being adequately understood (Cater, 2006). Such sentiments have been clearly articulated particularly by scholars (Wheeller, 1991, 1993; Hall, 1994; Cater, 2006) and non-government organisations (NGOs) such as *Tourism Concern* and Third World Network (TWN). It would seem that the overly simplistic viewpoints of the past, epitomised by the UN statement that tourism is a benign 'smokeless' industry, must be discarded in favour of a more critical and analytical understanding of ecotourism.

The rhetoric associated with ecotourism has hitherto rung with promises of economic opportunities, employment creation, the empowerment of communities, the renaissance of indigenous cultures and genuine contributions to environmental management and conservation. Yet increasingly questions have been raised as to the failure of delivery on the promises so widely associated with ecotourism development (Cater, 2006). In multiple instances, in a diverse range of contexts, it has been demonstrated that few of the promised benefits of ecotourism accrue to local people (Wells and Brandon, 1992), and the conservation benefits of ecotourism are commonly overshadowed by concerns for environmental impacts (Buckley, 2004; Higham and Lusseau, 2004). Furthermore, Cater (2006) argues that where employment opportunities do accrue to local people, it is most commonly restricted to low-skilled, low-paid, usually seasonal and short-term employment.

Cater (2006) argues that many of these failings exist because the 'advocacy of ecotourism as a universal template arises from western hegemony' (Cater, 2006, p. 24). She explains that, given that the origin of ecotourism and the principles underpinning this form of tourism lie in western ideology, the domination of western interests, regardless of the national context within which it is developed, poses a critical challenge to the future development of ecotourism. The development of ecotourism as a diverse rather than prescribed phenomenon in respect to the social and cultural values of those who live with ecotourism is a challenge for the future of significant proportions.

If one accepts this broad ecotourism context then a range of complex and challenging issues associated with ecotourism development then emerge. A range of such issues have been addressed in the preceding chapters. They include such things as energy use, climate change, biosecurity and biodiversity, the ethics of ecotourism, gender issues in destination communities, poverty alleviation and corporate social responsibility. Many of these issues have been raised and addressed by a number of scholars serving the study of ecotourism. Yet remarkably, most are largely disregarded by those who advocate for ecotourism, and ecotourism development initiatives have, as a rule, been poorly served by government agencies responsible for sustainable development.

Visitor management, widely viewed in the late 1980s and early 1990s as a solution to the growing impacts of tourism, is a case in point. Three decades have passed since Budowski (1976) wrote that tourism and conservation may exit in a relationship of conflict, coexistence or symbiosis, and that most commonly the relationship is one of conflict, or coexistence moving towards conflict. Since that time many words have been written to the effect that tourism may contribute in meaningful ways to conservation. Some have critically explored the relationship between tourism and conservation and offered valuable insights into the potential for symbiosis to be achieved (Beaumont, 2001; Orams, 1997; Tarrant and Cordell, 1997), but three decades later examples of genuine symbiosis remain the exception rather than the rule. In many parts of the world the evidence for symbiosis between tourism and conservation interests is either nonexistent or, at best, worryingly obscure (Higham and Lusseau, 2004).

One could be forgiven for thinking that at present coexistence is the best that can be realistically expected. In 1992 Wheeller stated that 'visitor management... is currently being bandied about by all and sundry as the latest in a series of answers to tourism's negative effects. Unfortunately, the concept remains just that – a vague, nebulous notion of glib generalisation, all things to all people, a ready answer to every problematic situation' (Wheeller, 1992, p. 105). These words still ring true today.

Within the broad field of ecotourism, the failure of visitor management applies with particular concern to tourist interactions with wildlife (Newsome *et al.*, 2005). The interactions of tourists with populations of wild animals have, rather belatedly, become acknowledged for their complexity (Buckley, 2004; Newsome *et al.*, 2005). The research literature on the potential impacts of tourist engagements with cetaceans, for example, has been well established in the last 5 years or more (see Beale and Monahan 2004; Bejder *et al.*, 1999; Bejder *et al.*, 2006; Constantine, 2001; Corkeron, 2004; Gill *et al.*, 2001; Lusseau, 2004; Williams *et al.*, 2002). All evidence points towards the sustainable management of tourists engagements with wildlife populations as a critical test for tourism sustainability. While sustainable wildlife-based tourism poses a considerable challenge, it need not be seen as an insurmountable challenge.

Thus, questions have also been raised as to the failure of policy and planning initiatives associated with ecotourism management. The sustainable management of interactions of tourists with marine mammals, a form of ecotourism that has experienced a phenomenal increase in popularity over the last 10–15 years (Hoyt, 2001), is interesting. Duffus and Dearden's (1990) conceptualisation of wildlife–tourist interactions provides extremely valuable insights into the dynamics of change that typically unfold at wildlife tourism sites. Their conceptualisation clearly indicates the need to carefully manage the sites at which wildlife tourism experiences are achieved within clearly stated limits of acceptable change (LAC). While the LAC management planning framework was developed in order to assist in the management of environmental impacts, in the case of wildlife-based tourism the LAC model must clearly be applied to oversee limits to physiological, biological and ecological change as it relates to local wildlife populations.

It is most unfortunate, then, that a comprehensive understanding of precisely what this entails has barely been advanced since the publication of Duffus and Dearden's (1990) conceptual framework. Clearly baseline data should be collected in advance of commercial tourism being established, and comparative data should continue to be generated from control sites following the initiation of tourist activities. LAC criteria should state carefully identified and clearly stated monitoring criteria which may include population numbers, animal fatalities, reproductive rates and critical behaviours. Key indicators of these criteria, in the case of tourist interactions with cetaceans, may include population structure, displacement of individual members of a local animal population, behaviour budget and mortality/morbidity rates (Higham, Bejder and Lusseau, personal communication). It does not seem unreasonable to suggest that biological studies at both operational (tourism) and control (non-tourism) sites should be a fundamental component of the management regime for ecotourism operations that bring tourists into interactions with marine mammals.

However, for wildlife tourism sites to be managed within LAC, as conceptualised by Duffus and Dearden (1990), it is also necessary for management agencies to be empowered by both effective legislation and political will. In terms of the management of tourist interactions with marine mammals, legislation that is effective, legally enforceable and enforced remains notable only by its absence. In terms of the licensing of commercial tourism operators it is necessary that any licensing system limits the number and conditions of issued permits based on sound logic, that permits are effective over a clearly stated timeframe, and that permits can be revoked if necessary. It is also patently obvious that numbers of permits and/or permit conditions (e.g. spatial range of operations, temporal conditions, operator capacities, boat speed/noise and aspects of visitor management) should be subject to immediate change if the outcomes of biological science deem it necessary (Higham, Bejder and Lusseau, personal communication). At present no such comprehensive management systems exist anywhere in the world, and few (if any) sites where tourists are able to interact with populations of cetaceans exist under management regimes with anything akin to this. Where any aspects of such a system are absent the sustainability of tourist interactions with wildlife will remain dubious at best. Clearly, once again, these are issues that are outstanding in terms of adequate understanding and satisfactory management action.

From the outset this book has been built upon two competing schools of thought that reflect Butler's (1990) original conceptualisation of ecotourism as 'pious hope' or 'Trojan horse'. So which school of thought should prevail? In Chapter 1 it was suggested that the reader should ultimately decide, and that suggestion still holds. The preceding chapters would indicate that the answer almost certainly varies with context. They also demonstrate the absurdity of suggesting that ecotourism is the guiding light for sustainable tourism development. Ecotourism is a unique and complex tourism phenomenon. At present a full appreciation and adequate understanding of the manifold complex issues associated with ecotourism remains a work in progress.

References

Beaumont, N. (2001). Ecotourism and the conservation ethic: recruiting the uninitiated or preaching to the Converted? *Journal of Sustainable Tourism* 9(4): 317–341.

Beale, C.M. and Monaghan, P. (2004). Behavioural responses to human disturbance: a matter of choice. *Animal Behaviour* 68: 1065–1069.

Bejder, L., Dawson, S.M. and Harraway, J.A. (1999). Responses by Hector's dolphins to boats and swimmers in Porpoise Bay, New Zealand. *Marine Mammal Science* 15(3): 738–750.

Bejder, L., Samuels, A., Whitehead, H., Gales, N., Mann, J., Connor, R., Heithaus, M., Watson-Capps, J., Flaherty, C. and Kruetzen, M. (2006). Decline in relative abundance of bottlenose dolphins (*Tursiops* sp.) exposed to long-term disturbance. *Conservation Biology* 20(6): 1791–1798.

Buckley, R. (ed.) (2004). *Environmental Impacts of Ecotourism.* CAB International, Wallingford.

Budowski, G. (1976). Tourism and environmental conservation: conflict, coexistence, or symbiosis? *Environmental Conservation* 3(1): 27–31.

Butler, R.W. (1990). Alternative tourism: Pious Hope or Trojan horse? *Journal of Travel Research* 28(3): 40–45.

Cater, E. (2006). Ecotourism as a western construct. *Journal of Ecotourism* 5(1&2): 23–39.

Constantine, R. (2001). Increased avoidance of swimmers by wild bottlenose dolphins (*Tursiops truncatus*) due to long-term exposure to swim-with-dolphin tourism. *Marine Mammal Science* 17(4): 689–702.

Corkeron, P. (2004). Whale watching, iconography, and marine conservation. *Conservation Biology* 18: 847–849.

Duffus, D.A. and Dearden, P. (1990). Non-consumptive wildlife-oriented recreation: a conceptual framework. *Biological Conservation* 53: 213–231.

Gill, J.A., Norris, K. and Sutherland, W.J. (2001). Why behavioural responses may not reflect the population consequences of human disturbance. *Biological Conservation* 97: 265–268.

Hall, C.M. (1994). Ecotourism in Australia, New Zealand and the South Pacific: Appropriate tourism or a new form of ecological imperialism? In Cater, E. and Lowman, G.L. (eds), *Ecotourism: a sustainable option?* John Wiley and Sons, Chichester, UK, pp. 137–158.

Hetzer, D. (1965). *Environment, tourism, culture. Links* 1: np.

Higham, J.E.S. and Lusseau, D. (2004). Ecological impacts and management of tourist engagements with Cetaceans. In R. Buckley (ed.), *Environmental Impacts of Ecotourism.* CAB International, Wallingford, pp. 173–188.

Hoyt, E. (2001). *Whale Watching 2001.* Unpublished report to IFAW and UNEP, London.

Lusseau, D. (2004). The hidden cost of tourism: detecting the long-terms effects of tourism using behaviour information. *Ecology and Society* 9(1): 2.

Newsome, D., Dowling, R. and Moore, S. (2005). *Wildlife Tourism.* Channel View, Clevedon.

Orams, M.B. (1997). The effectiveness of environmental education: can we turn tourists into 'greenies'? *Progress in Tourism and Hospitality Research* 3: 295–306.

Tarrant, M.A. and Cordell, H.K. (1997). The effect of respondent characteristics on general environmental attitude-behaviour correspondence. *Environment and Behaviour* 29(5): 618–637.

Wall, G. (1997). Is ecotourism sustainable? *Environmental Management* 21(4): 483–491.

Wells, M. and Brandon, K. (1992). *People and Parks: Linking protected area management with local communities.* World Bank, WWF and USAID, Washington, DC.

Wheeller, B. (1991). Tourism's troubled times: responsible tourism is not the answer. *Tourism Management* 12(2): 91–96.

Wheeller, B. (1992). Is progressive tourism appropriate? *Tourism Management* 13(1): 104–105.

Wheeller, B. (1993). Sustaining the ego. *Journal of Sustainable Tourism* 3(1): 29–44.

Williams, R., Trites, A.W. and Bain, D. (2002). Behavioural responses of killer whales (*Orcinus orca*) to whale-watching boats: opportunistic observations and experimental approaches. *Journal of Zoology* 256: 255–270.

Index